In the Name of Lykourgos

To Marion

In the Name of Lykourgos

The Rise and Fall of the Spartan Revolutionary Movement (243–146 BC)

Miltiadis Michalopoulos

Translated by Marion Kavallieros and Maria Anna Niforos

Pen & Sword
MILITARY

First published in Great Britain in 2016 by
Pen & Sword Military
an imprint of
Pen & Sword Books Ltd
47 Church Street
Barnsley
South Yorkshire
S70 2AS

ISBN 978 1 78303 023 1

A CIP catalogue record for this book is available from the British
Library

Typeset in Ehrhardt by
Mac Style Ltd, Bridlington, East Yorkshire
Printed and bound in the UK by CPI Group (UK) Ltd,
Croydon, CRO 4YY

Pen & Sword Books Ltd incorporates the imprints of Pen & Sword
Archaeology, Atlas, Aviation, Battleground, Discovery, Family
History, History, Maritime, Military, Naval, Politics, Railways, Select,
Transport, True Crime, and Fiction, Frontline Books, Leo Cooper,
Praetorian Press, Seaforth Publishing and Wharncliffe.

For a complete list of Pen & Sword titles please contact
PEN & SWORD BOOKS LIMITED
47 Church Street, Barnsley, South Yorkshire, S70 2AS, England
E-mail: enquiries@pen-and-sword.co.uk
Website: www.pen-and-sword.co.uk

Contents

List of Plates

List of Maps

Preface

This book examines the rise and fall of a revolutionary movement that was associated with the last revival of Sparta, after a long period of decline and obscurity. It was the final attempt of a city-state to recover its former splendour and claim the supremacy in the Peloponnese in the end of the third century BC.

One of the most essential principles of the movement was the return to the true Spartan traditions and 'Lykourgan' law that had declined by the third century BC. In order to restore them, the leaders of the movement undertook a series of radical, political and social reforms that greatly affected the Spartan society. Ironically, the leaders of the movement were forced to infringe on the very values that they were trying to preserve. And so, in the name of Lykourgos, almost every Lykourgan characteristic of Sparta was destroyed. This study records all the phases of the so called Spartan Revolution from its early feeble steps to its victorious domination (and henceforth) to its crushing defeat and its final demise.

An essential problem in the research of this period is that the sources are relatively scanty and controversial resulting in divergent opinions and confusion among scholars. A prominent example is the case of the Stoic philosopher Sphairos and his influence on the Spartan revolutionary movement. A spectrum of contradicting theories has emerged ranging from those which reject any influence of Sphairos on Kleomenes III to those which consider him to be Agis' and Kleomenes' mentor and the inventor of the Spartan *agoge*(!) Equally confusing are the issues of Kleomenes' and Nabis' social policy, even the concept of the Spartan 'movement', the degree of its revolutionary nature and especially its relation to the Spartan tradition.

Historians have particularly enjoyed re-examining such 'popular' matters as the above but have disregarded other important problems or have only superficially dealt with them. Such is the case of Kleomenes' seizure of the fort of Athenaion, an action that sparked the beginning of the so called 'Kleomenic War'. Research is limited to analysing the political significance of this act neglecting the strategic planning that played a crucial role in Kleomenes' decision. Other important issues that have been overlooked so far are the strategic importance of the town of Sellasia, the reason why Kleomenes chose it for his final battle against Antigonos, as well as the topography of the Sellasia battlefield about which prevalent theories were put forward more than four decades ago without having been re-examined since. All this will be addressed exhaustively and answered in detail in this study.

Compared with the extensive bibliography on Classical Sparta, there has been little research about the period 243–146, whereas in most of it, this period is examined as part of a broader historic period, such as Hellenistic Sparta or as part of Spartan history in general. One bright exception is Benjamin Shimron's formidable study *The Spartan Revolution*. Shimron does a thorough research on the nature and the development of the Spartan revolutionary movement. However, he refers only briefly to its historical background, considering it either beyond the scope of his work or known to the reader. Particularly enlightening also is Pavel Oliva's *Sparta and her Social Problems*, especially its last five chapters where the author examines extensively the period 243–146, and provides detailed bibliography.

Linda Piper's *Spartan Twilight* is a rather general study of Hellenistic and Roman Sparta that has nothing of note to contribute on the subject. Finally, Paul Cartledge's *Hellenistic Sparta* covers the period 371–146. Three chapters of his essay are dedicated to the period in question which is examined thoroughly. However, he systematically keeps safe distances from many controversial issues that may cause friction among scholars.

The study *In the Name of Lykourgos* is divided into three sections. The Introduction includes a brief review of the creation and the evolution of the Spartan polity with emphasis on the internal problems of Sparta. The section ends with a historical outline of the Hellenistic age, particularly of third century BC. Greece.

The second section is composed of five chapters and describes the Spartan movement that started with the radical reforms of King Agis IV and culminated with Kleomenes III and of Nabis' revolutions. It also describes the tragic events after the fall of Nabis and the last small glimmers of the revolutionary movement up to its final demise.

The third section of the book reviews and evaluates the Spartan movement. It examines its nature, its revolutionary character, its relation to the Spartan traditions it attempted to revive and its role in portraying an idealized image of Sparta, the so called 'Spartan Mirage'. Pivotal in this study is the role of the Spartan Revolution in creating the 'Mirage'.

A special appendix will deal with an interesting issue, the military roads of Lakonia. Stoic philosopher Sphairos and his relation with Agis and Kleomenes are dealt separately in the second appendix of this book. A third appendix deals with the problems regarding the topography of the battlefield of Sellasia and the deployment of the opposing forces on it. Finally, a fourth appendix is devoted to Arnold Toynbee and presents his bold theory about the two prominent figures of the Spartan movement, Agis and Kleomenes. If one applies the strict criteria of scholarship, this theory would never have a place in this book. The reader may approach it as an intellectual game, a twentieth century genius by-product. It is included here to accentuate the fact that some historical figures of the Spartan revolution have an everlasting value.

I would like to express my sincere gratitude to Mr Marios Bletas, Historian and Librarian at Athens College for his invaluable help in the completion of this study. Special thanks to Mr Kriton Psiakis for motivating me to start this research and for accompanying me to Sellasia, to Mr Christos Baloglou, to Mrs Maria Anna Niforos for translating the book, to my wife Marion Meropi Kavallieros for editing the English translation and last but not least, to Dr Aris Kosionidis for his support and final touch.

In this study most of the Greek proper names are transcribed phonetically, not in their Latinized form (i.e. Kleomenes versus Cleomenes), with the exception of some broadly accepted names of persons and places like Aristotle, Alexander, Achaea, Corinth etc. Present-date citations and official translations of the ancient sources are cited in their original Latinized spelling, except for the rare instances where an alternative translation is used or a modification has been made, in which case this is always indicated.

Introduction

Oliganthropia

'The state did not succeed in enduring a single blow,
But was destroyed through dearth of manpower'
Aristotle, Politics II 1270a.34

On 6 July 371 horrific news convulsed Sparta like an earthquake. The Spartan army was crushed by the Thebans at Leuktra in Boeotia.[1] 1,000 Lakedaimonians had fallen on the battlefield including the cream of the Spartan army and King Kleombrotos.

The news arrived at the most inopportune moment. It was the last day of Gymnopaidiai, the biggest and brightest Spartan celebration. A chorus of men was on stage while in the audience there were many foreigners attending the feast.[2] In true Spartan reaction, the *ephors* decided to continue the celebration and urged the women and relatives of the victims not to publicly express their feelings. Yet, despite their fervent efforts to save the prestige of the city, nothing could undo what had occurred at Leuktra. For the first time in her history and before the eyes of friend and foe, the Spartan army had fled.[3]

The cause of Sparta's defeat, however, could not have been attributed to her army's lack of courage for her soldiers had fought with bravery worthy of their reputation. Yet, Epameinondas' strategic genius and the revolutionary innovation of the 'oblique phalanx', a new tactic that he had invented and implemented on the battlefield for the first time, were unrivalled. The Theban general managed to gather substantially superior forces in one place and plunged into the right flank of the Spartan army exactly where king Kleombrotos commanded. At the point of collision, the Spartans, who were arrayed twelve men deep, sustained the terrible pressure of a powerful phalanx fifty men deep. For a while they were able to hold off the enemy fighting with self-sacrifice. Kleombrotos was killed almost instantaneously and the 'best of the Spartans'[4] that surrounded him claiming his body from the enemy also perished. Nevertheless, the fact that sealed that day was not the rescue of Kleombrotos' body by the defeated Spartans but the trophy that was erected on the battlefield by the victorious Thebans.

No sooner than later, the impact of this disaster became apparent. One after the other the entire fabric of the Peloponnesian cities, which had been interwoven ever since the sixth century with Sparta through the Peloponnesian League, began to unravel and seek autonomy. Mantineians and Tegeans along with the inhabitants of towns in south-western Arcadia united in an independent confederacy and founded the Arcadian *Koinon*. Soon, Thebans, Argives, Arcadians and Eleians would be invading Lakonia panicking the women of the non-walled city which had never before seen enemies tread on her soil. Sparta managed to survive at the cost of losing most of her territories. To the dismay of the Spartans, the fertile region of Messenia which had for centuries been dominated by Sparta became independent and – even worse – Messene was re-established as the capital city of the new state. Finally, the coalition of the Arcadian communities created a new city, Megalopolis, that was destined to become Sparta's nemesis and remained hostile to her thereafter. For a period of time, Sparta turned a deaf ear to the new reality and refused to recognize the independence of the two cities. Yet, she could no longer turn volition into action because she did not have the power to impose her will. After Leuktra, the strongest city of Greece was now deprived of her power and had the reputation of being second-rate. But what caused her sudden and abrupt collapse?

First and foremost, the defeat at Leuktra was a heavy blow for Sparta. The myth of the invincible Spartan army instantaneously dissolved and, as her strength and reputation was based on her invulnerability, her defeat triggered friction within the fragile Peloponnesian League. Those of Sparta's allies who had been discontent with her arrogant policy did not hide their satisfaction at the defeat and easily sided with her enemies. Second, the cost in casualties was heavy. Of the approximately 1,000 Lakedaimonians who fell on the battlefield, four hundred were Spartans most of whom belonged to the elite corps of the 300 *hippeis* who were annihilated while fighting alongside King Kleombrotos. But what made the destruction of Leuktra irrecoverable was that Sparta was unable to make up her losses. The four hundred hoplites who perished there comprised one third of Sparta's combat forces.[5] Despite the mobilization and the utilization of every available Spartan hoplite, after the battle at Leuktra the defenders of the non-walled city 'were and seemed very few'.[6] Scarce and defeated, the Spartans did not inspire further awe to their opponents and seemed hopelessly inadequate to protect their territory. What followed was a direct consequence of this fateful revelation.

The Spartan Polity

Historians agree that the dearth of manpower (*oliganthropia*) in Sparta was not a random result of one particular event. On the contrary, the reduction in the number of Spartans was the result of a long process that had begun much earlier and had its roots in the socio-political system of Sparta, known as 'Lykourgan' regime.[7] The Spartan constitution was created in the seventh century[8] through a series of reforms aimed at perpetuating the domination of a handful of Spartans over the populous masses of an area that covered forty per cent of the Peloponnese. These inhabitants were divided into two major categories: the *perioikoi*, namely the free inhabitants of the cities in the vicinity of Sparta and the *helots*, the enslaved inhabitants of the areas that Sparta had conquered in the Lakonian plain[9] and later in Messenia by the end of the eighth century. The conquest of Messenia was not accomplished peacefully but after a twenty-year war, the First Messenian War. Sparta's victory was absolute. The fertile land of Messenia passed over completely to Spartan jurisdiction while the Messenians were turned into helots and were forced to cultivate the land on behalf of the Spartans. Thus, Sparta emerged as the wealthiest and most powerful city in Greece. Nevertheless, her domination came at a price: the constant threat of revolt by the oppressed helots, especially the helots of Messenia, who never ceased to seek an opportunity to rebel whenever Sparta had difficulties. In 669, when the Spartans were defeated by the Argives at the battle of Hysiai, the Messenian helots revolted and a long, destructive war broke out. It was the Second Messenian War that shook Sparta and was about to play a key role in shaping her socio-political system.

Despite the victorious outcome of yet one more war that sealed Sparta's supremacy throughout the southern Peloponnese, the prospect of a revolt by the helots was a permanent threat that forced the city to maintain constant vigilance. In order to maintain her dominance, Sparta relied on every one of her citizens, irrespective of origin or social status. Furthermore, the unity and harmony of all Spartans was necessary for the survival of the city. The kings' and nobles' power that had never been supervised until then could not remain so any longer and it was high time that all of Sparta's defenders be entitled to voice an opinion on the fate of their city.[10] This change in the Spartan attitude is deeply connected with the new battle tactics of the hoplite phalanx, which began to be implemented on a wide scale in Sparta and Greece from the mid-seventh century. Unlike the previous battle tactics which involved fighting in loose formations, personal duels between the nobles (*promachoi*) and the throwing of javelins to the enemy from a distance, now the hoplites of the phalanx fought one alongside the other in tight formations and aimed at a massive clash with their opponents.[11]

Under the Lykourgan reforms, the land was re-allotted among all Spartans,[12] the old aristocracy was weakened and the political power devolved to *damos*, i.e. the citizens, or the *homoioi*.[13] Naturally, these changes did not occur peacefully. Both after the First and after the Second Messenian War, Sparta was agitated by internal turmoil triggered by the re-allotment of the conquered land. Everyone who participated in the conquest demanded a share. Through these intense internal crises, the city became acutely aware of the need for bold reforms. There was no radical break with the past. Many archaic elements survived but their character changed. Such was the institution of the *diarchy*, or dual kingship,[14] which was upheld. The two kings kept their position as army commanders but their role in the governance of the city was reduced to being mere members of equal power to the other members of the *Gerousia*. Similarly curtailed were the powers of the aristocracy. Their seats as representatives were now strictly established at twenty-eight and along with the kings they created the thirty-member *Gerousia* (Senate). The *gerontes* (the elders) had life-long tenure[15] but were elected directly by the *ekklesia*, the Assembly of Damos.[16] More importantly, the *Gerousia* was not able to make decisions on political issues but could only submit proposals (*provoulevseis)* which needed to be voted by the Assembly of Damos before they were implemented. The role of the latter in the governing of the city was considerably strengthened[17] and Sparta became the first city in history where power was transferred from the kings and the aristocracy to the people.[18] The rights of the people were protected by the five elected representatives, the *ephors*. The latter were an age-old institution[19] that from the mid-sixth century played a significant role in strengthening the position of the people. Any Spartan could be elected as an *ephor* if he were voted for by the popular assembly. The *ephors*' term was annual and their role was to oversee the proper functioning of government and control the power of the kings. In essence, therefore, the Spartan constitution was formed as a social compromise between the people on one hand and the nobles and the kings on the other.[20] The result was that in the early sixth century, when most Greek cities suffered from political instability and internal turmoil often ending with the imposition of the arbitrary power of a tyrant, Sparta had ensured her internal stability and possessed the mightiest military machine of her time.[21]

Sparta: A Camp-City

The essential problem of Sparta was not eliminated, nor could it be eliminated, as it was interwoven with her very structure. Spartans remained a small minority surrounded by the oppressed helots[22] and thus 'lived on top of a volcano which could erupt at any time'.[23] To prevent this eruption, Sparta became a military camp. The *homoioi* constituted a closed society of warrior-landowners and their income came almost exclusively from the occupation and exploitation of the land. Everyone had a share of land, the *klaros* or *kleros*,[24] which ensured him a relatively comfortable income in order to meet his needs. The *kleroi* were cultivated by the helots[25] while the Spartans did not tend the land nor did they do any kind of job. In fact, it was forbidden to pursue anything but the art of war which required continuous military training and readiness. Everyone shared an equally austere life starting from infancy with the harsh *agoge* and continuing to their death. Simplicity in appearance, common life in barracks and *syssitia* aimed at creating team spirit and at forging military discipline.[26]

This does not mean that social differences among *homoioi* had totally disappeared. Social differences existed and never ceased to exist[27] but were largely mitigated to a great extent by the fact that each one of the *homoioi*, without exception, had the same rights and shared the same obligations towards the state. The Spartans obeyed and showed deference to all these institutions.

Transforming Sparta to a military camp was not enough. The danger of her enemy within, the helots, demanded constant vigilance. Therefore, it had to be ensured that the operation of this camp would be undisturbed by external influences. After the mid-sixth century,[28] Sparta withdrew within herself and tried to limit the effects of the outside world: when all the other cities had already adopted silver coinage, she refused to abandon her unwieldy iron currency[29] and deliberately remained closed to trade with other cities. Sparta discouraged her citizens from travelling abroad occasionally imposing the *xenelasia*, (the expulsion of foreigners from the city) in order to preserve her character.

Finally, to ensure the Spartan polity perspective for some time, people had to be guided by public morals. At this point, the role of the *agoge*, the compulsory education which every youth was subject to before he was admitted to the citizen body, was decisive. A series of tests and initiations from hard physical exercise to competitive games instilled obedience to strict authority and so the personality of the young Spartan was shaped in a way that guaranteed two aspects: that he would be an excellent fighter and that he would never challenge the status quo. As aptly noted, the *agoge* was at the heart of the Spartan polity integrating all its elements into a unified whole.[30] Thus, Sparta ensured internal stability and served as a 'law-abiding' model city, free from violent internal conflicts (*staseis*) and those personal dictatorships (tyrannies) that plagued most other Hellenic cities.

Behind Sparta's good order, the so called *eunomia*, hid the need for Sparta to maintain order and stability. The city had no room for internal wavering. Even the slightest deviation from the established socio-political system would have had much worse consequences than the imposition of a tyranny: it would jeopardize its very existence.

Sparta's persistence in adhering to the constitution had a dark side: it deprived it of development, flexibility and ability to meet future challenges. Sparta remained locked in a rigid socio-political system designed to meet the challenges of a specific time period. Considering sixth-century politics, it was a pioneering system; two centuries later, though, it was completely outdated and yet it was still in effect in its initial form. The consequences of this socio-political ossification were to prove fatal.

The Causes of Decline

One could remain in the privileged class of the *homoioi* (peers) as long as he fulfilled two qualifications: his military obligations and participation in the public masses, the *syssitia* (or *phiditia*). The latter was an ancient Doric institution of special importance for the city's military organization. The upkeep of the *syssitia* was managed by its members, who were bound to make regular monthly contributions and if one was unable to meet his obligations, he would lose his Spartan citizenship.[31] The *syssitias'* compulsory levy was closely connected with the military character and the identity of Spartan society. By paying their monthly dues to the *syssitia*, the citizen-hoplites proved emphatically that they belonged to the upper class of the *homoioi* since their income was above a certain threshold. In fact, the wealthy Spartans contributed a great amount of goods to the *syssitia* because there was no upper limit to their monthly contribution.[32] Yet, the established minimum amount was mandatory for all members and indicated their social standing. This institution was not exclusively Spartan, it was also applied in Crete but with a key difference. In Crete,[33] the cost of running the *syssitia* was assumed by the state. In Sparta, though, this was impossible. The city-state could not afford the *syssitia* because after the Lykourgan reforms and the distribution of the conquered land among the *homoioi*, the state had no regular income and relied on private contributions.[34]

Thus, Sparta, which more than any other Greek city needed her citizens, was also the only city-state that undermined their position. What made her different

Lykourgos (Mary Joseph Blondel 1781–1853) is a characteristic example of the effect of Spartan Mirage on art. Legislator Lykourgos is depicted contemplating in a god-like fashion. The laws (clause) in his right hand and the typical symbols of military power, the shield (hoplon), sword and spear behind him compose this romantic painting.

from the other Greek cities, and especially Athens after the development of democracy, was that those who could not afford their dues to the *syssitia* were expelled from the elite class of the *homoioi*, while in Athens even the most impoverished citizens were entitled to an opinion on the matters of their city.

This discrepancy did not go unnoticed by Aristotle who was the first to severely criticize the Spartan polity:

'Also the regulations for the public mess-tables called *Phiditia* have been badly laid down by their originator. The revenue for these ought to come rather from public funds, as in Crete; but among the Spartans everybody has to contribute, although some of them are very poor and unable to find money for this charge, so that the result is the opposite of what the lawgiver purposed. For he intends the organization of the common tables to be democratic, but when regulated by the law in this manner it works out as by no means democratic; for it is not easy for the very poor to participate, yet their ancestral regulation of the citizenship is that it is not to belong to one who is unable to pay this tax.'[35]

A Spartan was incapable of increasing his income since he was prohibited from having a job and, therefore, his remaining in the privileged class of the *homoioi* depended exclusively on the production of his land.[36] As long as his *kleros* was profitable, his social position was secure. Yet, what if a disaster destroyed the harvest? How could he avert, in this case, the grim prospect of losing his political rights?

Consequently, it was imperative for the Spartan to preserve and further accrue his assets. In meeting this need, not everyone had equal opportunities. The wealthy always had an advantage over the others as they had the means to influence their social environment. Through endowments, adoptions and marriages of convenience they increased their property at the expense of the other *homoioi*.[37] As Arnold Toynbee notes, 'wealth has a tendency to marry wealth, and this leads to the concentration of property in the hands of a minority.'[38] In order to preserve the family fortune, the practice of intermarriage became common in Sparta. Endogamy was not an unknown practice in Greece, but in Sparta it took great dimensions among wealthy Spartans and especially among the Royal Houses.[39]

Beyond the rise of social inequalities, the fear of expulsion from the class of *homoioi* had another much worse consequence: low birth rates. Giving birth to many children would mean the division of paternal land property and the decrease of income for the heirs. For the wealthy Spartans this was certainly an unpleasant prospect but for the poor it was disastrous. It meant that in the long term some of their descendants would certainly lose their civil rights and would necessarily be reduced to an inferior status referred to as *hypomeiones*. Thus, the restriction of procreation, which for the wealthy Spartan was a desirable option, for the poor one was an imperative need.

In effect, this was an irreversible phenomenon due to the exclusive nature of the Spartan society that did not embrace foreign membership thus depriving her of every opportunity to replenish her human resources.[40] In fact, the state was concerned about the problem of population decline and took measures to amend it. It imposed penalties on the unwed and gave benefits to those who bore many children.[41] However, no measure was taken to eliminate the causes that created the problem. The state didn't make an effort, as correctly pointed out by Aristotle, to smooth out the property imbalances[42] and to change the institution of mandatory contribution to the *syssitia*. Yet, change in any institution, and especially in the fundamental institution of the *syssitia*, was unthinkable in Sparta. It came into conflict with the very essence of government and jeopardized its *eunomia*. Besides, the change in institutions was an extremely revolutionary practice and in the consciousness of the Spartans, the revolution had been achieved since the seventh century. Thus, neither was the contribution to the *syssitia* abolished nor was there any restriction implemented in the management of landowners. This resulted in the accumulation of land to fewer owners and in the steady dwindling of the number of *homoioi*.

This phenomenon evolved slowly so for a long period the results were not obvious. However, during the fifth century various external factors contributed to its aggravation. In 464 Sparta suffered the consequences of a terrible earthquake which devastated her and decimated a large part of her population.[43] The worst was yet to come. Sparta was confronted with her living nightmare: the uprising of the helots. To suppress this rebellion another even bloodier and more destructive war was required, the Third Messenian War.[44]

Both the earthquake and the Third Messenian War simply accentuated an already existing problem. Human casualties, great as they were, could be replenished within a few generations by a society with a sound demographic development.[45] But that was not the case with Sparta and so her population was unable to recover from such a disaster.

The fact is that all possibilities of population recovery vanished in the next generation. In 431 Sparta played a leading role in the 'greatest commotion that ever happened among the Grecians'[46] which further weakened her precious human resources. The Peloponnesian War proved as disastrous to the winner, Sparta, as to her defeated rival, Athens. While this twenty-seven year war sealed the supremacy of Sparta in Greece, this era was far from peaceful. From 404 until 369 Sparta was almost permanently embroiled in combat operations resulting in a continuous attrition of her warriors.[47]

The victory over Athens came at a high price for Sparta. Firstly, the Spartan society experienced a sudden influx of money which she did not have the infrastructure to absorb.[48] The wealth of the rich class accrued gradually at first but then it accelerated to an uncontrollable degree.[49] Secondly, in order to limit the influx of money, the *ephors* passed a law that sentenced to death those who possessed gold and silver coins.[50] It appears that the law was finally repealed or fell into disuse[51] and the phenomenon of sudden affluence continued, leading to the prevailing reputation at the time that the Spartans were the wealthiest in all Greece.[52]

Sparta's dominance over Greece required that she send an increasing number of Spartan commanders to her newly expanded realm. Thus, the protective shield that the city-state had erected between her citizens and the outside world abruptly fell. Spartans came into contact with extrinsic lifestyles, unknown to most of them. Away from the pressures and commitments of their homeland, they completely changed their behaviour. Spartan officials and high commissioners showed an unprecedented tendency to be bribed and indulged in corruption, behaviour that made them notorious in Greece.[53] At the beginning of the fourth century, the abandonment of the 'Lykourgan Laws' by the Spartans was so obvious that even the 'most Spartan of Spartans',[54] Xenophon, bitterly confesses:

'Should anyone ask me whether I think that the laws of Lycurgus still remain unchanged at this day, I certainly could not say that with any confidence whatever. For I know that formerly the Lacedaemonians preferred to live together at home with moderate fortunes rather than expose themselves to the corrupting influences of flattery as governors of dependent states. And I know too that in former days they were afraid to be found in possession of gold; whereas nowadays there are some who even boast of their possessions. There were alien acts in former days, and to live abroad was illegal; and I have no doubt that the purpose of these regulations was to keep the citizens from being demoralized by contact with foreigners; and now I have no doubt that the fixed ambition of those who are thought to be first among them is to live to their dying day as governors in a foreign land.'[55]

Internal tensions and deep rift in the social fabric of Sparta are explicitly revealed in the following incident described by Xenophon. In early 397, when Sparta was at the height of her power, a conspiracy to overthrow the regime was uncovered to the *ephors*. It was led by a man called Kinadon.[56] Kinadon belonged to the *hypomeiones* and plotted to seize power relying on the support of all those who resented the regime in Sparta. It was a very well organized conspiracy which was fortunately averted at the last minute. The informer claimed that Kinadon led him to the *agora* and asked him to give him an account of all the actual Spartans present. When the informer responded that including the king, the *ephors* and the elders who were present, the true Spartans at that time were not more than forty, Kinadon said 'believe that these men are your enemies, and that all the others who are in the market-place are your allies.'[57] Kinadon even claimed that the conspirators knew well the feelings of all the helots, *neodamodeis*,[58] *hypomeiones* and the *perioikoi*; 'for whenever among these classes any mention was made of Spartiatae, no one was able to conceal the fact that he would be glad to eat them raw'.[59] In fact, the conspiracy was smothered at its inception and Sparta, despite her subsequent challenges, was never again seriously threatened 'from within', which means that the ruling class had good control of the situation.[60] But repression alone can never address the major social problems, as history has bitterly proved and, of course, Sparta was no exception to this rule.

The contamination of the Spartan life of virtue by the influx of money is also noted by Plutarch, who believes the dissolution of the Athenian supremacy to be the beginning of the decline for Sparta.[61] According to Plutarch, the free trading of property that was institutionalized by the *ephor* Epitadeus' famous *rhetra* (clause) played a crucial role in the corruption of the Spartan society.

Until then, the Spartan *kleroi* were bequeathed only after the death of their owner. Selling land was considered a shameful act, while trading the 'ancient portion' was completely prohibited.[62] But Epitadeaus' law now allowed a Spartan 'during his lifetime to give his estate and allotment to anyone he wished, or in his will and testament so to leave it'.[63] This covert release of the sale of property resulted in the accumulation of land in the hands of a few landowners, many of whom were women. In the fourth century, it became common practice to give large dowries to daughters[64] either in order to pass the paternal property to the grandchildren through the daughter or simply in return for political and social benefits by the in-laws. This phenomenon, combined with the steady decline in the number of Spartans, led to the concentration of a large part of land to women. According to Aristotle, two-fifths of the land belonged to women in the late fourth century.[65] This resulted in an increase of their indirect influence on the Spartan system. This influence, in fact, strengthened the system since the Spartan women shared the same motives as the Spartans: to ensure that they and their descendants would remain in the class of the economically powerful. In a society that was evolving into plutocracy, great wealth offered special prestige to the Spartan woman and its loss would be as painful for her as it would be for a Spartan to be degraded to *hypomeion*.[66]

It's true that, despite her enormous internal problems, Sparta succeeded for three decades to dominate the political life of Greece and exert her supremacy on all other Greek cities. This supremacy was based on a powerful but small army which was constantly dwindling as Sparta did not have the manpower to sustain it. The impressive edifice of Sparta stood on shaky foundations and, as aptly stated by Aristotle, required only a strike to collapse. The verdict of Leuktra was irrevocable.

Except the Lakedaimonians

> '*So, except the Lakedaimonians at Granicos*
> *And then at Issos; and in the final*
> *Battle where the awesome army was swept away,*
> *Which the Persians had amassed at Arbela,*
> *Which set out from Arbela for victory, and was swept*
> *away...*'
>
> K. P. Kavafy, *In the Year 200 BC*

After the battle of Leuktra, a new political order emerged that displaced Sparta to the margin of politics of her time. Following the loss of Messenia, the city was deprived of half her territory and returned abruptly to the state she was in more than three centuries before. The sudden loss of Messenian *kleroi* had fatal consequences for their owners and accentuated social tensions.[67] Sparta, as expected, refused to compromise with the new status quo. Considering that the area belonged to her, Sparta refused to recognize the independence of Messenia in 368 at the peace meeting in Delphi and also three years later in 365.[68] In 362 at Mantineia, she attempted to avenge the defeat at Leuktra but was defeated for the second time by the allied Arcadians, Argives, Greeks from central Greece and Boiotians under the hegemony of Thebes. Despite the defeat, she continued to administer intransigent policies. Sparta refused to participate in the Pan-Hellenic convention of common peace that followed the end of the battle of Mantineia because in this case she would have to officially recognize the independence of Messenia.

Twenty-five years later, although Messenia remained an independent territory and Messene had evolved into a prosperous city Sparta would continue her long-standing arrogance. In 338 she defied Philip II of Macedonia, who after the battle of Chaironeia had become the undisputed leader of all the Greeks. She refused to participate in the Congress of Corinth because that would put her – even indirectly – under the Macedonian rule. The consequence of this policy was another invasion of Lakonia by the strongest army of its time. As a result of this invasion, Sparta lost a significant part of her territory which Philip divided among Sparta's hostile or rival cities. Thus, the northern border area of Belminatis along with parts of Maleatis and Aigytis were granted to Megalopolis; Skiritis and Karyatis were awarded to Tegea, while Argos received Thyreatis and a large part of the coastal *perioikic* cities of eastern Lakonia up to Zarax[69]. Finally, Sparta lost Dentheliatis (an area between modern city Kalamata and Langada stream), Pharai, the area on the western side of Taygetos and all *perioikic* cities of the northeast coast of the Messenian gulf up to Thalamai, which Philip gave to Messene. Sparta was left with the Valley of Eurotas River between Mount Parnon and Mount Taygetos. However, Philip withdrew from Lakonia without attempting to conquer the non-walled city.[70] Sparta maintained her independence with the additional satisfaction that she was the only Greek city that had refused to comply with Philip's commands in his Pan-Hellenic campaign against the Persians. Yet in 336, two years after the battle of Chaironeia, Philip was assassinated and thus his ambitious dream was realized without him and of course without the Spartans. For the latter, the campaign in Asia of Philip's son and successor, Alexander, was nothing but an ideal opportunity to regain their lost territory. Therefore, shortly after Alexander's departure for Asia, King Agis III formed an anti-Macedonian uprising in Greece with the help of the Persians. But this attempt ended ingloriously as all the previous ones. In 331 the Spartans and their allies were annihilated at Megalopolis by the Macedonian regent Antipater and Agis III fell at the battlefield. When Alexander, who had crushed the Persians in Gaugamela the same year, heard of it he sarcastically stated: 'It would seem, my men, that while we were conquering Dareius here, there has been a battle of mice there in Arcadia.'[71] Certainly, for the conqueror of the largest empire in the world, the suppression of a rebellion in Greece seemed nothing more than 'a battle of mice'. Yet, for the defeated Spartans and their allies, it was a massacre. More than 5,000 soldiers among whom many Spartans and their king was the tragic account of this 'battle of mice', which 'didn't have any other purpose in history but to untimely remind that Sparta once called all the shots in world history'.[72]

After the battle of Megalopolis, any prospect of recovering the Spartan supremacy disappeared. Sparta was no longer a power to be reckoned with. Her citizens, however, continued to maintain their reputation as excellent warriors. Therefore, they were in great demand since the Hellenistic age was the golden age for being a mercenary.[73] There was a reciprocal relationship between the Spartans and the mercenaries. Ever since the Peloponnesian War, the Spartans hired mercenaries, mostly light infantry, in order to replenish their shortage in human resources.[74]

At the end of the fourth century, the wall-less city was confronted twice with the nightmarish prospect of invasion. She began to hastily fortify herself to face the impending invasion of Kassander (318/7) and Demetrios Poliorketes (294). Sparta was fortunate enough that these invasions were not realized.[75] What Philip, Kassander and Demetrios did not achieve was attempted a few decades later by King Pyrrhos of Epeiros. In 272 he led a powerful force which included 25,000 infantry, 2,000 cavalry and twenty-four elephants, invaded Lakonia and camped in front of un-walled Sparta. The Spartans tried strengthening the inadequate fortifications of their city, which was in fact defenceless, while King Areus I was in Crete with the bulk of the army fighting on the side of the allied city of Gortys. The situation looked so grim that initially the *ephors* thought about negotiating Sparta's surrender to Pyrrhos. The event was averted thanks to the intervention of the Spartan women, and specifically Archidamia, the widow of King Eudamidas I. For two days, the defenders managed to repel the successive assaults of Pyrrhos while reaching the limits of their physical endurance.[76] The city was saved only at the last minute, thanks to the timely arrival of King Areus I with 2,000 men from Crete and with a Macedonian force rushing to his aid.[77] Repulsing Pyrrhos was a strong lift to the prestige of Sparta. Areus I tried to exploit the achievement diplomatically and expand the influence of the city not only in Peloponnese but also beyond it.[78] His ambitious plans, though, collapsed in the first military challenge that Sparta faced. In 265, during the Chremonidean war, the Spartan army was defeated by the Macedonian garrison in Corinth and Areus was killed. A few years later, when his son and successor Akrotatos attacked Megalopolis, he was defeated by the Megalopolitans and also lost his life (262). Sparta's defeat by Megalopolis, a newly established city with no military tradition, indicated the degree of decline of the once 'most powerful and most celebrated city in Greece'.[79]

The decline of Sparta was not a unique phenomenon. In her own way, the city followed the general economic, social and moral crisis of the Classical world during the third century. This crisis had started much earlier but reached its peak because of the enormous changes that occurred in metropolitan Greece after Alexander's conquest of the East.

The Crisis of the Old World

> *The old things have passed away.*
> *Behold, all things have become new.*
> Second Letter to the Corinthians 5.17

Undoubtedly, Alexander left his mark on the ancient world forever. For metropolitan Greece his conquests meant the opening of new horizons and the expansion of its borders to the ends of the world. The world now took new dimensions; it became immense, attractive and promising. The East had been known to the Greeks for centuries but for the first time now they could travel freely and relatively safely from Athens to India and from Pella to the depths of Egypt. The implications of this prospect for the Greek cities were comparable to those of the discovery of the New World by the Europeans many centuries later. The Greek cities experienced a period of economic prosperity owed to the influx of money in the form of loot and precious metals and to the development of trade with the markets of the East.[80] Simultaneously, the prospects of easy wealth and the quest for a better life were created through massive migratory waves to Egypt and Asia similar to the great European emigration to America in the nineteenth century.[81]

These changes had a profound effect on the Greek society. The Hellenistic kingdoms of Egypt and Asia grew rapidly and thus the centre of economic life shifted from the Aegean to the East. Competition was disproportionate as the city-states of Greece, which had limited natural resources and sparse population, could not compete with the new Hellenistic populous cities whose

rate of growth was tremendous. Gradually, the traditional trading centres of
the Aegean, such as Athens, gave their place to new ones, such as Alexandria
and Antioch. These prevailed in the Mediterranean in a similar way as did the
countries (i.e. Portugal and England) which turned to the New World after the
discovery of America, slowly pushing aside the old leading trading empires.[82]
The economic crisis of the Classical world burdened mostly the middle class.
Small traders, small farmers and craftsmen were forced to liquidate or mortgage
their property, a fact which led to their economic destruction and the widening
of the gap between rich and poor.[83]

The inadequacy of the city-states in human and natural resources became
more evident in the field of military warfare. The small armies which the city-
states managed to recruit seemed insignificant compared to the huge professional
armies of the Hellenistic monarchies which had inexhaustible reserves of
money, supplies, weapons and great numbers of human resources. The city-
states became victims of the ambition and the opportunism of powerful leaders
who seized them and then lost them one after the other in their devastating wars.
In order to ensure a proper treatment, people would not hesitate to resort to
flattering their occasional leaders sometimes reaching the point of proclaiming
them as gods and worshipping them with sacrifices and feasts in their honour.[84]
Although these were, of course, diplomatic tactics, they indicate the extent of
decline of the Classical world at that time.

This sense of vulnerability and insecurity contributed to resenting the
institutions, traditions and even the religion of the city state. Once the old
gods of the city proved unable to protect it, they were demolished from their
pedestals and replaced by a new deity, Fortune, who expressed the prevailing
feeling of uncertainty at the time. Similar changes occurred within the
intellectuals. Insecurity and wavering of traditional values led to the search for
new ones. Philosophers strived to achieve perfect bliss through calmness and
spiritual tranquillity. The new philosophical schools idolized complacency and
self-sufficiency and in order to acquire them, the individual had to withdraw
from political life. The Epicureans together with the Cynics were indifferent
toward public affairs and chose to live in obscurity away from anything that
might disturb their peace. More indirectly, by preaching the elimination of
discrimination between origin, race and class, the Stoics also undermined the
values of the *polis*.[85]

Despite their wide appeal, the new philosophical theories addressed a limited
circle of educated elite who were only a small minority of the population.
Traditional values may have faded but were not completely lost and so ordinary
people followed more or less the old way of life.[86] The decadence of the classical

world occurred at a very slow pace and in the third century despite its deep crisis this world was still vibrant. The city-states still existed and many of them were prospering[87] – yet, their character had changed. They were no longer safe from the threat of the mighty Hellenistic empires and their walls no longer guaranteed their independence. The awareness of the cities' inability to meet on their own the challenges of their era led to a major civic innovation: their union in federations and the creation of the *Leagues*.

The union of individual cities into larger formations was not a new phenomenon because there had already been communities (*koina*) in previous centuries and, in a sense, the federations were the evolution of these communities into a more sophisticated form. The Leagues' special feature lay in the complete equality among the participating cities. This was an important innovation compared with previous federations of the Classical era. For example, in the Delian League or in the Peloponnesian League, Athens and Sparta respectively, determined the policy of the allies, while in the new Leagues all cities participated equally in the formulation of a common policy without raising any hegemonic claims against others. At the same time each citizen was a citizen of the League and his political rights extended to all other cities. The League united its city-members without limiting their autonomy. Instead, it constituted a strong federation able to guarantee the security and independence of its members. It became 'the answer of the Greeks who wanted to defend their autonomy and political rights against the challenge of Hellenistic absolutism'.[88]

Two Leagues, the Aitolian in central Greece and the Achaean League in the Peloponnese stood out and became important regulators of the developments of their time. The latter outshone the former and affixed its fate with the significant moments of Greece. It was founded in 281–280 as a union of four Achaean cities: Dyme, Patrai, Tritaia and Pharai. Aigion and many other cities of the northern Peloponnese joined later.

In 251 Aratos, a youth from Sikyon, expelled the tyrant of the city and managed to integrate it to the Achaean League. Sikyon became the first non-Achaean city that was incorporated in the League. Thanks to Aratos, it wouldn't be the last. Aratos was a charismatic and controversial personality who soon became such a leading figure in the Achaean League that six years after the entry of his city he was elected in the highest office of *strategos* (general). Since then he was continually elected general every other year[89] and even when he was not elected, he still wielded power. In 243 only two years after his election, he succeeded with courageous agility to drive out the Macedonian garrison from Corinth and to incorporate the city in the Achaean League. This was a major success which enhanced the League and Aratos with special prestige setting the stage for Megara and other cities of Argolid to willingly join this union later. Thus the Achaean League went beyond its narrow geographical notion; thereafter, the concept 'Achaean' did not have just a local character but would suggest a greater citizenry similar to that of the Roman citizen a few centuries later.[90]

The cities of the Achaean League retained their own laws and elected their own leaders to govern their internal affairs. The Assembly of the League held four meetings a year called *synodoi*. The meetings were open to all men of military age and were attended by the federal counsel and magistrates.[91] In urgent cases, such as when a war was declared or an alliance was forged, a special meeting, the *synkletos*, was called. By rule, all meetings of the League took place in the city of Aigion. To prevent abuse of power by the general, there was the body of the ten *damiourgoi*. Their tenure lasted for one year and it was banned for them to be re-elected before the expiry of at least one year of their previous term.

The constitution of the Achaean League was, at least officially, democratic. Every citizen could participate in the administration of the federation by attending regular and special meetings and was able to take administrative office regardless of his social position. In practice, however, the magistrates came from the upper classes and had the time and the resources to campaign for their election while the poorer citizens did not have the time or the money required for a journey to Aigion four times a year in order to participate in the meetings.[92] Furthermore, the *damiourgoi* were not paid for their services and therefore only the wealthy citizens could afford to pursue this position.[93]

Despite its shortcomings, the Achaean League was the best way to save the character of the city-state and in the mid-third century it emerged dynamically by combining 'the distinctive quality of each city with a wider vision'.[94] In contrast, Sparta was a typical example of the old world that was fading. Having traced her idiosyncratic route in history, she seemed to walk steadily and irreversibly towards its end.

Nevertheless, against all odds, the impossible happened. Mobilizing all her forces, Sparta revived. With unexpected vitality she launched out into an unequal struggle against superior opponents and managed to be on the forefront of the political developments of her times for nearly half a century. Yet before her final and inevitable collapse, she came close to realizing her big dream: the restoration of her hegemony. This last glimmer of Sparta, as well as the movement that created it, will be discussed in the following chapters.

Chapter One

Dawn

'*Economic and social reasons cannot be ignored, but men fight and die for ideals,
be they good and just ones or the contrary. They are ready to give their lives
only for something that touches their imagination and is of value for themselves
and for others in a similar condition of life. They need, as has been said, a flag.
Only for a flag, a symbol of an ideal, will they give everything. The possession
of land, desirable as it is in itself, is not such a flag, but equality is. The power
and glory of the polis is another. Spartan tradition stood for all these and more,
and Spartans still knew of the times when Sparta had equality and power, and
was rich, too, both she and her citizens.*'

B Shimron[1]

Sparta in the mid-third Century: A Plutocratic Society

In the middle of the third century, Sparta displayed acute symptoms of deep internal crisis. All the elements of the Lykourgan polity that had until then ensured the unity and cohesion of Spartan society were now largely degraded to mere formalities. The Spartans' external appearance was no longer simple, the *syssitia* became sites of pageantry of the rich to demonstrate their social standing[2] and the *agoge*, the cornerstone of the Spartan constitution, was practically abandoned.[3]

Moreover, Sparta had begun for some time to incur the negative consequences of the monetization of her economy. The wide circulation of money,[4] which had been official from the beginning of the third century, favoured the concentration of wealth by a few. Lending and debt were common phenomena in cities with developed economies. Yet the special social economic conditions in Sparta gave rise to these phenomena forcing many Spartans to mortgage their *kleroi*. Sparta turned into a plutocratic society of several hundred privileged citizens. As their numbers dwindled, so did the widening of the social and economic gap between them and the other social groups in the city.

According to Plutarch, by the middle of the third century, 'there were left of the old Spartan families not more than seven hundred, and of these there were perhaps a hundred who possessed land and allotment.'[5] All the others were the 'destitute and disfranchised mob sitting idly in the city showing no zeal or energy in warding off foreign wars, but ever watching for some opportunity to subvert and change affairs at home'.[6]

In fact, the crisis of the Spartan society was not confined only to Spartans and to the 'destitute and disfranchised mob sitting idly in the city' but affected all the social groups of the Spartan society, each in a different way. The way each social group was affected and its response to the problem was directly connected to its special characteristics and motives.[7]

The *helots* constituted the base of the social pyramid and remained the most populous while also the most impoverished and oppressed social group in Lakonia. The living conditions were aggravated for most of them because of the destruction of the countryside by the frequent raids of Lakonia during the fourth century and afterwards. However, this did not apply to all helots. For many of them, the decline of the Spartan socio–economic system had also its positive side and it appears that they were able to take advantage of its weaknesses in order to improve their own living conditions.[8] When a system is ailing, it ceases to be effective. The reduction of the number of *homoioi* and the influx of money must have had disastrous consequences for Sparta. For the helots, however, this meant less oppression by the Spartans and the opportunity, forbidden to the Spartans, to partake in commercial transactions. Since the *apophora* (the commodity tax paid by the helots to their masters) was fixed, some helots could save a surplus of the production for themselves and profit from it.[9]

The *perioikoi* experienced a dramatic deterioration of their standards of living. Those who were farmers saw their land being destroyed because of the frequent invasions in Lakonia, culminating with that of Pyrrhos in 272,[10] while those among them who were merchants and craftsmen could not compete with the major commercial cities. In other words, the *perioikic* cities also suffered the disastrous consequences of the crisis of the city-state. The deterioration of the *perioikic* cities contributed even more to the decline of Sparta since she was closely associated with and to some degree depended on them economically, politically and militarily.[11]

Of all social groups that lived in Sparta, the '*hypomeiones*' embodied in the most distinctive way the Achilles' heel of the Spartan socio–political system. Although Plutarch does not mention their numbers, modern historians estimate them to have been between 1,800 and 2,300 around the middle of the third century.[12] Little is known about how these deposed *homoioi* survived. Historians assume that some of them 'still served in the army in some capacity or another, supported by state funds or by rich citizens'.[13] Yet most, in order to survive, were forced to undergo an extremely denigrating process for a Spartan; that of practising a skill, as the *perioikoi* and the foreigners did. The only alternative for those who refused to undergo this humiliation was to become mercenaries which however was not an outlet exclusively reserved for the *hypomeiones*. After Leuktra, mercenary work constituted the main source of employment for most Spartans in order to secure money and livelihood. Some wealthy Spartans even became mercenaries in order to increase their wealth and secure political power when they would return to their homeland.[14]

The body of the *homoioi* was divided into subgroups with conflicting interests so it could literally be said that it was a 'class struggle within a class'.[15] Plutarch distinguishes two categories: the 600 Spartans who only possessed the ancestral *kleros* and the 100 privileged rich who owned both 'land and *kleros*'. Of the 600 Spartans, only a few managed to keep their ancestral *kleros* intact. Most were poor and in order to remain in the social body of *homoioi* resorted to mortgaging their *kleroi*.

At the top of the social pyramid were the approximately 100 privileged Spartans who owned land beyond their original *kleros* and constituted 'an oligarchy within an oligarchy'.[16] They had come gradually into the possession of most of the land through those processes that had converted the majority of citizens to *hypomeiones*. Their landholdings consisted of accumulated *kleroi* which had been lost by their original owners. Besides large tracts of farmland some of them also possessed movable property in the form of monetary wealth or in the form of registered mortgages, the renowned *klaria*.[17] These were the wealthiest citizens of Sparta, who found a good way to further increase their wealth by lending money in exchange mainly for land. The Spartan economy was rural and the concept of the Spartan *homoios* presupposed the possession of land and not of money. Land retained enormous importance in Spartan society, making it the best investment for those who had money and at the same time the only security for those in need. The poor were not the only borrowers, so were the great landowners as well. There were thus two categories of wealthy Spartans: those who were exclusively big landowners (*ktematikoi*), and those who possessed both land and capital which they could lend to others (*plousioi kai daneistikoi*).[18] Some of the former were indebted to the latter.

Besides the 100 wealthy Spartans, there were also female landowners. Women had owned forty per cent of the full extent of the land since Aristotle's times.[19] A result of the widespread practices of dowry and marriages between the wealthy, the phenomenon of female ownership of land intensified in the years after Aristotle. Thus in the mid-third century affluent women held the majority of wealth in Lakonia.[20]

Considering all the above, the conditions in Sparta at the time were ripe for revolution. One would expect that it may as well have been initiated by the base of the social pyramid but it did not happen this way. In the first of a series of paradoxes associated with the Spartan movement, it seems extraordinary that the person who would manage to deal the plutocratic minority a hard blow was its authentic offspring and perhaps its most typical representative, Agis IV of the House of Eurypontidai.

Agis IV: From Reform to Subversion

When Agis IV[21] ascended the throne in 244, he was not yet twenty years old. It is not known whether he received the *agoge,* which had become substandard anyway, since as crown prince he had no such obligation.[22] His father, Eudamidas II, had died when Agis was still a minor and until he came of age Agis remained under the guardianship of his uncle Agesilaos. According to Plutarch, he was brought up in comfort and luxury by his mother Agesistrata and grandmother Archidamia 'who were the richest people in Sparta'.[23] However, young Agis' ambition was not limited to being exceptional in the exclusive community of his homeland. He wanted to 'win the name and fame of a truly great king'.[24] His ambition clashed with the harsh reality: a poor and weak city of seven hundred citizens could never meet his expectations. Yet everyone knew that at one time things were different and Sparta was the strongest city in Greece. Apparently, neither Agis nor any of his contemporaries had lived in that distant Sparta. All they knew about her came from the narrations of elders who had also learned of them from previous narrations. However, Agis had formed a clear view why his homeland had declined and attributed it to the alienation of the Spartans from their ancestral laws which had been established by the great legislator, Lykourgos. As long as the Spartans were on equal footing, shared an austere military lifestyle and were dedicated to the service of their homeland, Sparta's supremacy shone over Greece. Therefore, prerequisite for the recovery of his homeland was the return to her ancient traditions.

This naïve theory that was formed during the third century resonated with a new concept for Sparta. It was closely linked to the dominant philosophical pursuits of this turbulent era,[25] an era that was marked by profound social crisis, major economic contradictions and questioning of traditional values. Most thinkers of the time were deeply disappointed by the insecurity and political instability of their time. Many tried to 'escape' and sought refuge in utopias envisaged, as Euhemeros and Iamboulos did, imaginary and idealized states.[26] Others chose to idealize existing states and gave them imaginary traits coated with wishful thinking. Such was the case of Sparta as she was in her most glorious times. Everyone who envisioned a better world saw her as a bastion of non-corruption and as a well-governed society where her members, without personal property and without social differences, shared a common austere life and were devoted to the service of the state. Such a perception of Sparta was certainly 'a retreat into a past that never was'[27] which, however, did not cease to attract like a mirage all those who needed to hold on to an ideal, especially the Spartans who were haunted by their past. Their legacy contained not only the concept of equality (since Spartans continued to remain *homoioi* despite their glaring socio-economic differences), but also the restoration of her lost supremacy. The latter was a vision that Sparta did not mean to abandon despite her marginalization. For the sake of this vision she did not hesitate to defy Philip and then confront Alexander and the Epigonoi. She remained rigid in her claims despite her successive defeats on the battlefield. One could say that every time a new generation of Spartans came of age to bear arms, Sparta campaigned for the fulfilment of that vision.

Knowing this, it would be easy to understand the attitude of the young king who envisaged the restoration of the lost splendour of his homeland. Obviously, he was not alone. There were many Spartans who associated the marginalization of their city with her social problems and dreamt of the moment when, after healing her wounds, she would regain her former power and glory.

More important than the theoretical interpretation that the young Agis gave for the decline of his homeland was the fact that he was a man of action. He was determined to radically change the situation and had a clear plan. To restore Sparta back to her former grandeur, he had to recruit a powerful and large army. Two things were necessary: firstly, the Spartans had to be relieved from the stress of mortgaging their *kleroi* and secondly, they had to increase their numbers by adding new blood in the city. The former meant abolition of debts and the latter entailed the division of land so that new *kleroi* would be secured for the newly integrated Spartans. Agis sought to solve the problems of his city by tackling the two main demands of his era, 'debt cancellation' and 'land redistribution'.[28]

Agis began his campaign cautiously by seeking supporters not only among the Spartans but also among all the freemen of Sparta.[29] He set the scene with symbolic gestures and made himself a living example of the return to the traditional way of life. His behaviour elicited memories of the '*lakonomania*' which Aristophanes had satirized two centuries before. Disparaging any kind of pretence and luxury, he walked around proudly in the simple Spartan *chiton*, the *trivonion*, ate scantily and declared that he would renounce his throne if he were not 'able to restore the law and the traditional *agoge*'.[30]

Among his close friends and supporters were distinguished personalities such as Lysandros, son of Liby and descendant of the namesake winner of the Athenians at Aigos Potamoi;[31] Mandrokleidas, son of Ekfanes, whose 'sagacity and craft were mingled with daring'; Kleombrotos, the son-in-law of the Agiad King, Leonidas; his cousin Hippomedon, who had previously excelled in many wars and was popular among the youth.[32]

Therefore, the movement for Sparta's renaissance began 'from above' with the king as its leader and prominent Spartans and young men from the best families of the city as members. Plutarch's accounts give the impression that the youth of the city as a whole had responded positively and enthusiastically while the older generation appeared to be mostly hostile to new ideas.[33] However, Agis had supporters even among the more mature Spartans. One of them was his uncle Agesilaos, a man of great wealth and powerful connections in Sparta who was persuaded by his son Hippomedon to join the movement. According to Plutarch, Agesilaos did not share the ideas of the reformers but had selfish motives; in fact, he anticipated to have his debt written off as promised by Agis because he owed large amounts of money and had mortgaged his property. However, at least at the start of his struggle, the accession of Agesilaos to the reformers' party was beneficial for Agis. With the intervention of his uncle, Agis managed to gain the support of his mother who also had her reservations in the beginning, like most wealthy women of Sparta, and was opposed to any change in the existing status quo.

Thanks to the endorsement of his uncle and his mother, Agis managed to increase his influence in Sparta and have his friend and supporter Lysandros elected in the body of the *ephors* as an *eponymous ephor*.[34] The reform movement began with a formal action by Lysandros. Lysandros filed a clause as part of a list of all the proposed reforms. He specifically asked for the following: firstly, the cancellation of all debts and secondly, the redistribution of the land 'from the ravine of Pellene to Taygetos, Malea and Sellasia'[35] to 4,500 equal *kleroi*, equivalent to the number of Spartans. This meant the opening of the exclusive Spartan society for the first time in her history. The number of 700 citizens would be increased by the addition of approximately 2,000 *hypomeiones* as well as 1,800 selected *perioikoi* and foreigners (*xenoi)* provided that they had received 'the rearing of free men and were, besides, of vigorous bodies and in the prime of life.'[36] Thirdly, the land of the *perioikic* cities would be divided into 15,000 *kleroi* shared among the *perioikoi* 'who were capable of bearing arms.'[37] Finally, the *agoge* would be re-established in its traditional form and the *syssitia* would regain their austere and military character. These 'renewed' *syssitia*, however, were to be significantly different from the former ones. The 4,500 'new' Spartans would participate there in groups not of fifteen, as was the case until then, but of 200 and often 400 men.[38]

Agis justified his reforms by stating that his goal was to restore order in the city which had strayed from Lykourgos' laws. Obviously, this was not entirely true. If the restoration of the *syssitia* and the full restoration of the *agoge* confirm his allegations, the same did not occur with the other reforms. Thus, the equality among the Spartan citizens and the increase in their number by integrating local *perioikoi*, especially foreigners, was a sharp contrast to the laws and traditions of *Lykourgan* Sparta. What was happening with Agis? Did he truly believe that he was acting in the spirit of Lykourgos or did he use the name of the great legislator to pass his reforms more easily? The truth is that the latter possibility does not exclude the former. The nineteen-year-old Agis, who dreamt of reviving Sparta's former glory, must have believed he was acting in the spirit of Lykourgos. For every Spartan, the notion of Sparta was inextricably connected with the reverent legislator regardless of how he interpreted the law.

Despite the radical nature of his reforms, Agis wanted to operate within the framework of legitimacy. Yet from the first moment it was obvious that this would not be so simple. According to the normal procedure, in order to establish a law it first had to be proposed by at least one *ephor,* then be approved by the *Gerousia* and finally be submitted to the Assembly for validation.[39] Nevertheless, the majority of the *Gerousia*, whose members apparently belonged to the most affluent Spartans, were opposed to the reforms. The reformers considered going directly to the people in the hope that if their proposals to the Assembly were well received, the Assembly would use its influence with the *Gerousia* so that it would be pressed to vote in favour of reforms. When the Assembly convened, Lysandros along with Agesilaos and Mandrokleidas asked the Spartans to support the proposed reforms inviting them 'not to suffer the insolent opposition of a few to blind them to the prostration of Sparta's dignity'.[40]

The reformers succeeded first in securing divine validation for their proposals. This had special significance for the conservative and religious Spartan society. Lykourgos had once requested validation of his own reforms from the oracle of Delphi. For Agis, though, the favourable prophecy did not come from Delphi but from the oracle of Ino-Pasiphae in Thalamai, a region in the eastern coast of the Messenian Gulf.[41] According to the oracle, the Spartans had to be all *equal*, as required by the law that was originally established by Lykourgos. Having prepared the groundwork, Agis presented himself to his fellow citizens and spoke openly about the reforms that he intended to apply. In a dramatic gesture, he was the first to donate his property to the city along with 600 talents in cash. His friends followed along with their mothers and relatives 'who were the wealthiest among the Spartans'.[42]

The opposing camp couldn't possibly ignore such provocation. Their representative was the Agiad King Leonidas II, who publicly confronted Agis. Leonidas' life and principles were, at least according to what Agis' biographer presents, a typical example of the anti-Lykourgan culture which the young king sought to eradicate. Following in the footsteps of his father Kleonymos, Leonidas had abandoned Sparta and had lived abroad for some time in the court of the King of Asia, Seleucus, where he had married and had children with a foreign woman. In Sparta he was married to Kratesikleia and had a daughter, Chilonis and two sons, Kleomenes and Eukleidas. Leonidas was opposed to Agis' radical ideas from the beginning. Observing, however, the growing popularity of the latter he did not choose to confront him openly and was limited to slandering him. He propagated that supposedly Agis' reforms were not intended to increase the number of Spartans but to redeem mercenaries so that he would be able to impose his personal tyranny on Sparta.[43] According to Plutarch, Leonidas' opposition to Agis was not only politically motivated. The Agiad king knew that if he approved of Agis' programme, he would degrade himself to the awkward position of having to accept someone else's measures. Thus, the glory and honour for the reforms would be accredited to Agis alone.[44]

Speaking before the Assembly, Leonidas questioned the legitimacy of the proposed reforms and argued that they were contrary to Lykourgos' laws. Lykourgos never established relief from debts and, especially, he never included foreigners in the political body. On the contrary, he periodically imposed *xenelasia*, the expulsion of foreigners from the city.

Leonidas' arguments were correct[45] yet Agis found a way to refute them. Initially, he taunted Leonidas and said that since he had lived in the Seleucids' court for such a long time, it was natural for him to ignore the Lykourgan laws.[46] He then observed that debt cancellation and borrowing were self-explanatory conditions since Lykourgos had abolished monetary transactions. As for the expulsion of foreigners from Sparta, this was limited only to those whose habits and lifestyles were at odds with the strict Spartan lifestyle and endangered the polity. To support his arguments, Agis reported cases of distinguished foreigners, such as the poet Terpandros of Lesvos, the wise mathematician Thales of Miletos and the philosopher Pherecydes of Syros who, although foreigners, were extremely honoured by Sparta. He concluded by stressing that not only Lykourgos but also he aimed at attacking the extravagance, luxury and ostentation that 'made the city dissonant and out of tune with itself'.[47] In reality, Agis' sarcasm, insinuations and use of examples rather than evidence indicate that he had no compelling arguments against Leonidas.[48] One wonders why he did not openly claim that he intended to follow the spirit and not the letter of the Lykourgan law. In other words, in order to restore the principles of the Lykourgan law, he would have to sacrifice some formalities.[49]

Agis unequivocally succeeded to impress his fellow citizens in his favour but was unable to do so with the *Gerousia*. When the clause was finally brought up in the *Gerousia*, it was rejected 'by a single vote'.[50] It was undoubtedly a defeat but it was one that Agis was unwilling to accept. Having the *ephors'* backing and at least the majority of the Spartan Assembly, he decided to move dynamically keeping up pretences as much as possible. The movement thus passed into a new phase that could be described under the oxymoron term of 'legitimate' infringement.

The reformers targeted exclusively at the leader of the opposing faction, King Leonidas. Lysandros accused Leonidas of leaving Sparta and having children with a foreign spouse. There was an antiquated law that prohibited a Spartan king from doing so and if found guilty, he would have to be put to death.[51] The accusation was further reinforced by a divine sign, such as in the case of the Ino–Pasiphae oracle. It appeared at the right moment during a nightly observation of the starry sky by Lysandros and the other *ephors*. This was within the jurisdiction of the *ephors* and typically involved the practice of an ancient rite. However, since the *ephors* were on the side of the reformers right from the start, it is more than certain that the only sign which Lysandros saw in the sky 'was the star of Agis in ascendancy'.[52]

Lysandros asked that Leonidas be summoned to appear in court on charges that he had lived for a long time at Seleucus' court and that upon returning to Sparta he had usurped the legitimate authority.[53] Frankly speaking, despite Leonidas' 'reprehensible' past, nobody in Sparta had ever challenged the legitimacy of his royal authority until then. Lysandros even presented witnesses attesting to the accusations and persuaded Kleombrotos to lay claim to the throne. When Leonidas realized the gravity of his position, he worried for his life and sought refuge in the temple of Athena Chalkioikos. Under the pretext of his refusal to appear in court, the reformers deposed him, and Kleombrotos was made king in his place.[54]

Agis and his supporters gained full control of the situation. The next step would be to proceed with the immediate implementation of their reforms. At this point, however, Plutarch's narrative ends abruptly. Suddenly and without the slightest reference to the events that occurred in the meantime, Agis' biographer refers to the expiration of the term of Lysandros and of the other *ephors*. New *ephors* were elected who were opposed to the reforms. But if the majority of the Spartans supported the young king, as repeatedly stressed by Plutarch,[55] then such a development is rather inexplicable. Moreover, this development shows that the reformers did not have a serious foothold in power. How much time elapsed between Leonidas' deposition and the election of the new *ephors*? What occurred during this period? Were there any reactions from Agis' opponents or not?[56] Leaving these questions unanswered, Plutarch continues his narration saying that the new *ephors* revoked Leonidas from the temple of Athena Chalkioikos where he had sought refuge. They also brought an indictment against Lysandros and Mandrokleidas 'for violating the law in proposing an abolition of debts and a distribution of land'.[57] It appears that Agis and his followers pressed to legalize their reforms in retrospect but did not have time to implement them. However, Plutarch's fragmented narrative is not suitable for reliable deductions.

After the election of the new *ephors* and Leonidas' return, it became apparent that Agis and his supporters no longer could afford to ostensibly follow the law. If they did not want to find themselves at the mercy of their political opponents, they had to overthrow them by force. The movement thus passed to the phase of revolutionary violence.

Pretending to a free interpretation of the law, according to which unanimity gave the kings supreme power over any other constitutional authority,[58] reformers moved against the *ephors* who had dared challenge them:

'Persuaded by these arguments, both the kings went with their friends into the market place, removed the *ephors* from their seats, and appointed others in their stead, one of whom was Agesilaus. Then they armed a large body of young men and set free all who were in prison, thus striking fear to their opponents, who thought they would put many of them to death.'[59]

Those who were freed from prison were obviously political prisoners, such as *ephors* who belonged to Agis' party and possibly other supporters.[60] This is to say that there was sharp political competition and that Agis' opponents were sovereigns of Sparta for a short time. In fact, Plutarch carefully avoided mentioning any bloodshed and violence by the reformers. However, the previous citation leaves no doubt as to the exercise of psychological violence on their behalf and the climate of terror imposed against their opponents. Agis violently overturned the legal regime of Sparta with the help of his followers and without the participation of the people.[61] Bloodless though as it may have been, it was clearly a coup.

Reformers proceeded to depose the elected *ephors* and replaced them with people they trusted. Among the new *ephors* was also Agis' uncle, Agesilaos. Leonidas fled to Tegea[62] leaving Agis in full control.

The first act of the triumphant king was the abolition of debts. This measure was applied in a spectacular fashion at the market place where under the cheers of the crowd all mortgages of land, the *klaria*,[63] were gathered and thrown into the fire. Then began the rigorous application of the neglected *agoge* and along with it the reopening of the *syssitia* in order to serve the purpose for which they were initially created: the revitalization of the Spartan army.

However, Agis' most important declaration remained unfulfilled. It was land redistribution, the most desired reform not only for the poor Spartans and the *hypomeiones* but also for a large number of *perioikoi*. According to Plutarch, the person most responsible for not implementing it was Agesilaos, Agis' uncle. Agesilaos' main argument was that if land reform and abolition of debts were implemented simultaneously, there would be great unrest in the city. So the abolition of debts had to be prioritized so as to satisfy those in debt at the expense of land re-allotment that had to be postponed. According to Plutarch, Agesilaos, who had gained a vast fortune with the abolition of debts and did not want to lose it, sought to avert land re-allotment.

This view is not entirely acceptable. It is possible that Agesilaos had selfish and cheap motives, such as his 'insatiability' as Plutarch remarks. However, his arguments were inherently correct. The redistribution of land was a difficult task. It included complex and time-consuming processes such as the selection of new citizens from *perioikoi* and foreigners, the reintegration of '*hypomeiones*' in the citizen body and, of course, the measurement of the land and its division to the new owners. Instead, the abolition of debts was an immediate measure which, apart from indebted landowners such as Agesilaos, also satisfied all the Spartans who were at risk of losing their mortgaged farms and along with them their civil rights.[64] Moreover, Agesilaos must not have been the only one who resisted the implementation of land re-allotment. After the abolition of debts, many Spartans – not only wealthy landowners like Agesilaos but also ordinary owners as well – no longer wanted the implementation of this measure since it meant that they would lose a portion of their property and social status in favour of the *hypomeiones*, the *perioikoi*, and especially the foreigners.[65] These Spartans were a minority compared to Agis' potential supporters that he was planning to recruit; nevertheless, they were not numerically negligible.

Apart from his young nephew, Agesilaos managed to convince other leaders also, such as Lysandros, about the need to postpone land redistribution. He utilized various excuses to continue postponing the immediate implementation of this measure despite the subsequent pressures of the two kings, Agis and Kleombrotos.

The failure to implement land redistribution disappointed a large part of the population and created an unpleasant atmosphere in the city which was compounded by Agesilaos' behaviour. After securing his own property and consolidating his nephew to power, he began to behave in an arrogant and defiant manner towards his fellow citizens. The turning point for the movement came in 241, when the *ephors* among whom was Agesilaos, asked the young king to come to the aid of their ally, the Achaean League[66] which was facing invasion by the Aitolians. Agis gathered his army, largely composed of his most ardent supporters, and departed. Most were young descendants of poor families who knew they were allowed only a small share of the already meagre paternal property and faced the prospect of losing their rights. They had followed Agis in the hope that upon returning, land would be redistributed and that they would gain extra land in order to remain in the class of *homoioi*. In fact, Agis' decision to depart from Sparta along with his supporters conveniently facilitated the plans of his political opponents, who were more than just a few. Either because he hesitated or because he failed to take action against them, Agis let them free to orchestrate a conspiracy to overthrow him.

Although the reorganization of the Spartan army might not have been completed, its morale was extremely high. All the soldiers shared their king's enthusiasm, showing exemplary discipline and inspiring admiration in the cities through which they passed.[67] In contrast, the rich were concerned about the young reformer and the sensation he created in his path because they feared lest his example be imitated in their own cities.[68] Evidently, among those who watched Agis with scepticism was Aratos who, as a true exponent of the upper class, opposed every social reform.

When Agis arrived in Corinth, he surprisingly heard that the leader of the Achaeans sought in every way to avoid open conflict with the Aitolians and that he preferred to let them pass unhindered. The excuse put forward by Aratos was that farmers had already collected their harvest from the fields and, therefore, the Aitolian raid would not cause major damage.[69] Such a decision made the presence of the Spartan army at Corinth superfluous. After this, Agis was forced to comply with the wishes of his allies and take the road back to Sparta.[70] Aratos knew that by doing so, he had alienated the Spartan king and that he had effectively put an end to the alliance between Sparta and the Achaean League. But what interested him most was the withdrawal of the Spartan army from his dominion. For Aratos, the danger of an enthusiastic army from a city that had established 'debt cancellation' and proclaimed 'land redistribution' was far greater than the danger of the Aitolians. A hostile raid, predatory in nature as were usually the raids of the Aitolians,[71] could be tackled one way or another but the uprising of the poor was something completely different, which Aratos did not want to risk.

The consequences of this futile campaign were devastating for Agis and the movement. Agis was drawn into pointlessly mobilizing his army away from Sparta during a very critical period. Some historians believe that this might have been deliberately initiated by his enemies in order to stifle the movement, as they eventually did.[72] The popular king of Sparta and most of the supporters who had followed him on the campaign were absent from the city while Agesilaos, who was an *eponymous ephor*, did his best to escalate the crisis claiming the payment of taxes and maintaining a personal guard of mercenaries like a tyrant. According to Plutarch, Agesilaos spread the rumour that he was going to be an *ephor* again, causing the people's indignation.[73] It was not difficult for his opponents to exploit the spreading discontent to their advantage. Soon they succeeded in deposing Agesilaos and Kleombrotos. They called King Leonidas from Tegea and restored him to power. Upon his return, Agis came across an unexpected situation that had gone completely out of control. It is interesting that none of his soldiers, who just shortly before had followed him with enthusiasm, moved in his defence. One possible explanation for their stance might be the deep respect of the Spartans to legal authority which was now represented by King Leonidas.[74] According to Plutarch, it was Agis who chose to be sacrificed rather than turn his weapons against his fellow citizens.[75] Others, however, argue that the movement gradually collapsed *after* Agis' return to Sparta.[76] Most likely, the enthusiasm of most followers faded away along with their hopes of acquiring property.[77] Beyond this, a clear reason for the collapse of the movement was the personality of its leader: the twenty-year-old young man proved simply inferior to the circumstances.

Isolated and without support, the leaders of the movement were hunted down one after another by their opponents. The despised Agesilaos was saved only through the intervention of his son Hippomedon and left Sparta to settle in Egypt.[78] Agis' brother Archidamos fled to Messenia.[79] Damokrates, whom Plutarch had not mentioned before, fled to Achaea.[80] Lysandros was exiled.[81] Kleombrotos and Agis sought asylum in Sparta: the former in the temple of Poseidon at Tainaron[82] and the latter in the temple of Athena Chalkioikos. Leonidas was infuriated with his son-in-law, Kleombrotos, because he did not hesitate to persecute him and usurp his throne. Kleombrotos was saved thanks to the intervention of his wife and Leonidas' daughter Chilonis, who pleaded that her husband not be sentenced to death but sent to exile. She then followed him to exile.[83] Leonidas appointed new *ephors* and began to organize the physical elimination of his most dangerous political opponent, Agis.

Three *ephors*, all from Leonidas' circle, Arcesilaos, Amfares and Damochares, succeeded in gaining the confidence of the young king,[84] then arrested him and finally imprisoned him. Immediately, Leonidas rushed there with a strong force of mercenaries and surrounded the building. Later, the newly appointed *ephors* arrived and invited their allies from the *Gerousia*.[85] Agis was asked to apologize before this audience. When, despite the urgings of his accusers, he refused to recant his ideas and put the blame on the other members of the movement, they sentenced him to death.

The arrest and imminent execution of a Spartan king could not pass without a reaction. More so Agis who, despite the mistakes and the offences he had committed, had never dyed his hands with blood. Although overdue, his followers began to mobilize and towards the end of the day a noisy crowd with lighted torches began to gather outside the prison. Among the assembled were

Kleombrotos is banished by his father in law, King Leonidas II (Benjamin West 1770). Inspired by Plutarch's biography of King Agis, the artist portrays infuriated King Leonidas II expelling Kleombrotos. By her devasted husband stands Chilonis with her two children consoling him affectionately..

Agesistrata and Archidamia who demanded 'that the king of Sparta should have a hearing and a trial before the citizens.'[86]

Risking having the crowd free Agis, Amfares and the other *ephors* decided to quickly do away with him. They precipitated the process and immediately hanged the young king. Plutarch's respective narrative is driven by Phylarchos' strong emotive and melodramatic style which he had completely copied at this point. The events led to a climax like the last act of a tragedy. Agis, with a calmness and courage reminiscent of Socrates,[87] took responsibility for his actions and defended once again his actions in the name of Lykourgos. Marching to the gallows, he turned to comfort a crying servant while at the end without displaying any sign of cowardice he did not hesitate to put his own head in the noose. Believing the assurances of Amfares that Agis was still alive, Agisistrata and Archidamia were dragged into the prison to suffer for themselves the same fate as Agis. The dramatic narrative culminates with the words that Agisistrata exclaimed before the gallows, 'my only prayer is that this may bring good to Sparta.' The curtain falls with the display of the three corpses and the disclosure of *hybris* to a bewildered and aggrieved audience: 'it was thought that nothing more dreadful or heinous had been done in Sparta since the Dorians had dwelt in Peloponnese.'[88] It is, however, noteworthy that apart from their expression of sorrow and silent disapproval of the event, the assembled took no other action. No one tried to avenge the dead king and the two women who, as one would expect, were highly respected in the city, especially the elderly Archidamia. Thirty years earlier, she had saved the honour of Sparta by leading the defence against Pyrrhos' invasion. It appears that the loss of the revolution leaders and the fear of retaliation by their opponents who had in the meantime established their position in power, made the followers of the reformers stifle their objections and comply blindly with the new situation.

So this was the tragic end of Agis' attempt to restore his homeland's lost glory. According to Plutarch, his failure is owed to his gullibility toward his collaborators and his tolerance towards his enemies.[89] Certainly, his confidence in Agesilaos, the non-implementation of land redistribution and especially the fact that he did not do away with his political opponents were instrumental to his downfall. But the exalted image of a young idealist who fell victim to his virtues, as presented in his biography by Plutarch, is somewhat exaggerated. Agis initially tried to impose his reforms through legal procedures but then he did not hesitate to violate them and to attempt a coup in order to achieve his purpose. One must come to the conclusion to wonder, like Shimron, how idealized the picture of Agis would have been, had he not been murdered at the age of twenty and had he instead lived many more years to complete his reforms, as Kleomenes did later.[90]

Theoretically, Agis' murder marked the end of the attempted overthrow of the old regime wherein after two turbulent years of challenges and reversals, Sparta returned to the state she had been before with the old oligarchy recovering full control of power. This occurred only ostensibly, though. In fact, despite the restoration of the old order, nothing was the same anymore. Agis had shaken the waters forever. Until the time he attempted his coup, Sparta's constitution had never been openly challenged and no institution had ever been nullified. In the aftermath of the movement, the governing body of the *ephors* had been violently overthrown twice, a king had been dethroned, another had been killed by the *ephors* and a not so negligible number of people were exiled or had voluntarily fled en masse from the city for the first but not the last time in her history.

Finally, the standard of revolution raised by Agis had only temporarily been lowered. The revolution had just begun and would soon enter a new phase more violent and more subversive than the previous one.

Herein lies a second paradox associated with the Spartan movement: the person who would continue and would complete Agis' abortive reforms would be none other than Kleomenes III, the son of King Leonidas, the biggest enemy of the reformers and leader of the restoration.

Chapter Two

Zenith

Never did the eye see the sun
Unless it had first become sun like

Plotinos[1]

The Restoration Years

For the next six years King Leonidas II reigned essentially without a regent. Little is known about the duration of his reign. It appears that at least in the first years of the restoration, he imposed in Sparta a regime of terror and intense censorship of anything that had to do with Agis and his reforms.[2] It is uncertain whether the reforms that Agis had managed to implement were repealed, in particular the abolition of debts. After the public burning of *klaria,* it would not have been easy for lenders to re-claim payments from borrowers. Despite this, new debts might have been created after the restoration of the old order for the same reasons that they were created in the first place.[3]

It would have been impossible for King Leonidas II to formally repeal the *syssitia* and the *agoge* which had been restored by Agis since these institutions were fundamental to the polity of Sparta. Yet, the state's indifference toward their proper implementation must have led them to degenerate to mere formalities, as they had in the past.[4]

According to Plutarch, after the restoration Sparta appeared as a city in a state of internal dissolution. Her king lived a life of luxury, her rich citizens were interested only in increasing their wealth, and her people were indifferent to public affairs and lacked the desire to fight for their country.[5] Although not far from reality, the above description carries Phylarchos' stamp and reflects his own biases. King Leonidas is clearly a victim of these prejudices. Phylarchos depicts him in the gloomiest manner possible by making him seem monstrous compared to the noble figures of his wife, Kratisikleia, his daughter Chilonis, and of course his son Kleomenes.[6] This should not be interpreted to mean that the Agiad king had a charismatic personality. The only event associated with his reign, apart from Agis' assassination, is an extensive attack on and pillage of Lakonia by the Aitolians which Leonidas did not even care to confront.

The Aitolians invaded Lakonia sometime between 240–239 and plundered the *perioikic* cities.[7] According to Polybios' testimony, their intention was to restore Agis' exiled followers in Sparta.[8] Most possibly, it was more of a predatory raid, a display of force to the Achaeans and at the same time a challenge to their aspirations for supremacy in the Peloponnese.[9] During their invasion, the Aitolians did not engage with Sparta at all. Instead, they bypassed the city and headed into southern Lakonia where they continued their raids, culminating with the destruction of the ancient Temple of Poseidon at Tainaron, an inviolable asylum for the helots. The Aitolians withdrew undisturbed reaping rich booty. Plutarch speaks of 50,000 slaves, certainly an excessive number but indicative of the turmoil they created.

After Agis' assassination, the House of the Eurypontidai was temporarily left without a representative as his son, Eudamidas III was a newborn and his brother Archidamos had escaped to Messene. Leonidas foresaw in this a wonderful opportunity to strengthen his power. He rushed to arrange a marriage between Agis' young and beautiful widow Agiatis and his young son Kleomenes, so that the latter could gain guardianship of Eudamidas III. There was not only political motive in this marriage. Leonidas had his sights set on Agiatis' great fortune which she had inherited from her father Gylippos.[10]

Plutarch states that Kleomenes immediately fell in love with his charming wife and that she played a key role in shaping his political ideology. Kleomenes often asked her to recount details about Agis' life and aspirations and the recent events that had shaken Sparta. Besides Agiatis, Kleomenes would also ask his tutor Xenares for information about Agis' movement and the way in which he had seized power.[11]

This is Plutarch's version of the events.[12] However, it is certain that Kleomenes did not learn about Agis' movement and ideology through Agiatis' and Xenares' narrations. In fact, Agis' movement and the riots that followed in Sparta marked the end of Kleomenes' puberty and so he must have had direct experience of these events.[13] Fanatical enemies and supporters of the reformers existed even within his own family. What was Kleomenes' stance when his sister's husband sent his father into exile in order to usurp his throne? Was he on the side of the reformers or did he stand by his father, like his sister Chilonis? It is quite impressive that while Phylarchos describes the behaviour of Chilonis in vivid colours, in this event, he does not mention Kleomenes at all. Essentially, there is no reference to Kleomenes until 235 when he took the throne after the death of his father Leonidas. Despite the silence of the sources, Kleomenes, like all his compatriots, would have experienced not only the tragic events connected with the rise and fall of Agis but also the humiliation of Sparta by the Aitolian invasion which appears to have convinced him of the need for radical changes in order to restore his homeland.

Another factor that has allegedly contributed to the shaping of Kleomenes' ideology was the Stoic philosophy, especially the teachings of the Stoic philosopher Sphairos of Borysthenes.[14] An admirer of Sparta like many other Stoics, Sphairos wrote a doctrine, *Polity of the Lakedaimonians*, and a treatise about Lykourgos and Socrates.[15] Plutarch mentions that Sphairos was interested in studying the *agoge* of the Spartan youth, that he remained in Sparta for some time, and that the young Kleomenes attended his lectures.[16] However, this information has not been confirmed.

The question of Sphairos' presence in Sparta is complicated by the fact that Plutarch (*Kleom.* 11.2) makes a second reference to him, claiming that the Stoic philosopher was assigned to restore the Spartan youth's *agoge* after Kleomenes' full consolidation in power.

It would, therefore, appear that Sphairos visited Sparta twice: the first during Kleomenes' youth and the second after the Spartan king had been fully established in power. But this is more of a conjecture since there is no other evidence to confirm it apart from Plutarch's brief references. As Rostovtseff observes, 'the extant evidence is slight and the role of Sphaerus in the reform, if any, is obscure.'[17] The issue of the number of Sphairos' visits to Sparta and their effect on Kleomenes remain highly controversial and has divided historians.[18]

However, Sphairos' visit to Sparta as Kleomenes' tutor does not constitute proof that Kleomenes was influenced by the Stoic philosophy. This is something that needs further investigation to be proven. Based on the available evidence, even if Sphairos was Kleomenes' teacher, which cannot be proven beyond doubt, it is unlikely that he influenced him in any way. None of Kleomenes' actions reflected in the least the tenets of stoicism and as it has been pointed out, his violent overthrow of power was fundamentally contrary to the teachings of the Stoa.[19] Therefore, Sphairos most likely came to Sparta after the triumph of Kleomenes to offer his services to the new regime. He may have been 'a tool of Kleomenes' and a propagandist of the revolution'[20] or he may have even influenced the Spartan youth through his teachings contributing significantly to the reconstruction of the *agoge*.[21] Yet, his effect on Kleomenes was probably insignificant.

Kleomenes proved above all to be a man of action. Regardless of the extent to which he was affected by Agiatis, Xenares and Sphairos he was determined to solve the socio-political gridlock in the city in the same way that Agis IV had attempted before him. He had learned the lessons from Agis' futile efforts and was not going to make the same mistakes. In the climate of terror that prevailed in Sparta after the restoration of the regime, there was no room for Agis' flamboyant '*lakonomania*', so Kleomenes proceeded cautiously without revealing his intentions. It appears that he slowly formed a circle of supporters among prominent Spartans, such as the rich and powerful Megistonous. Kleomenes persuaded his mother Kratesikleia to marry Megistonous in order to unite his property with that of his new stepfather and so increase his influence.[22] Furthermore, he sought other ways to increase his power. As a Spartan king and head of the army, he knew well that it would be easier to carry out his plans by increasing his glamour as a general. Therefore, he sought opportunities to gain distinction through war.[23] Apart from polishing his personal prestige, his leadership of the military in times of war would supply him with devoted mercenaries which would be essential for his ultimate goals.

This wouldn't be easy, though. The Spartan king was no longer entitled to declare war since the king's power had been significantly reduced in favour of the *ephors*. But these were reluctant to take such a decision under the circumstances. The city of Sparta had fallen in a quagmire of indecision and passivity that allowed the Aitolians to raid Lakonia with impunity. Kleomenes had to wait six full years until 229, the year when the *ephors* assigned him his first mission: to occupy with military forces and fortify Athenaion, a strategic position on the border of Sparta and Megalopolis.

The Struggle for the Arcadian Corridor

This sudden shift in Sparta's policy was the climax of a series of events that were evolving for more than a decade in the Peloponnese.

In the years that followed the assassination of Agis, Sparta's already weakened position became even more precarious due to the strengthening of her neighbours, in particular of the Achaean League. It should be noted that in 235, the same year that Kleomenes became king, the fervently anti-Spartan city of Megalopolis joined the Achaean League. Its ruling tyrant Lydiadas, who until then followed a pro-Macedonian policy, was persuaded to change sides and ally his city to the new rising power of the Peloponnese.[24] Lydiadas' action marked a turning point for the Achaean League since by including this great Arcadian city it also adopted its traditional hostility towards Sparta.[25] Six years later the power of the Achaean League was destined to grow even more thanks to a favourable situation which Aratos managed to exploit to the fullest.

In 229 the Macedonian dynasty experienced a crisis. King Demetrios died and as his son and successor Philip (the future Philip V) was a minor, Antigonos (also referred to as Doson) was appointed his guardian. Almost immediately the new leader was faced with serious problems throughout his domain. In the north he had to face the invasion of the Dardanians and almost simultaneously suppress the rebellion of the Thessalians.[26] The difficulties that the Macedonians were facing at the time enhanced the tendencies of secession from the Macedonian sphere of influence in many cities of southern Greece. For the Achaean League, it was a wonderful opportunity to significantly increase its political power and influence both in and out of the Peloponnese. In the late spring of 229, six years after the entry of Megalopolis to the Achaean League, the tyrant of Argos Aristomachos followed Lydiadas' example and abandoning his pro-Macedonian policy, he agreed to join the Achaean League. The territory of the Achaean League increased dramatically. The event also affected the smaller and weaker cities of the Peloponnese which had remained independent. The cities of Hermione and Phleious could no longer resist the pressures around them and neither could Aegina. One after the other, they all joined the Achaean League.

In the summer of 229 Athens asked for Aratos' help in order to overthrow the Macedonian occupation. With his mediation, the Athenians came to an agreement with the commander of the Macedonian garrison and for the sum of 120 talents, twenty of which was donated by Aratos himself, they managed the withdrawal of the Macedonian troops from all strategic points in their city. Despite the expectations of Aratos, who had assisted in the hope to add Athens to the Achaean League, the Athenians did not accept to join in the end. That notwithstanding, it was obvious that he had achieved a reversal in the political arena with the strengthening of the Achaean League and the simultaneous weakening of the Macedonian domination. The territory of the Achaeans stretched from the Gulf of Patrai to the Saronic Gulf including the greater part of Arcadia and all of Argolis. Its territorial continuity was interrupted by four Arcadian cities which extended on the Arcadian plateau between Mount Mainalon and Mount Artemision on an axis from south to north extending to the foot of the mountains of Achaea. These cities were Tegea, Mantineia, Orchomenos and Kaphyai which from 233 had forged an alliance with the Aitolian League.[27] The accession of Argos in the League was not a good sign for the cities which suddenly found their lands surrounded by the Achaeans. The Aitolians were not able to help, given the geography. The Arcadian cities sought another patron and this role was undertaken by Sparta. The same year that Argos joined the Achaean League (229), these four cities allied with Sparta with the consent, and possibly at the instigation of the Aitolians who, despite their alliance with the Achaeans[28] since 239, were concerned about the rise of the Achaean League. Sparta found herself in control of four cities which penetrated like a wedge into the heart of the Arcadian plateau forming a narrow corridor

Map 1. The Peloponese 229.

among the cities of the Achaean League. Her problem was to ensure unhindered access to them in order to exploit the newly acquired Arcadian Corridor.

In order to exert such influence on the area, Sparta would need to impose her military presence in the territory of the Arcadian cities. In other words, she would have to transfer troops into this territory without the threat of interference by the two hostile neighbouring cities it shared borders with: Megalopolis from the west and Argos from the east.

The transport of military forces would necessarily follow the routes imposed by the topography of the area, axes established for centuries and used consistently either by the Spartan army when it left the boundaries of Lakonia or by enemy forces when they invaded the Spartan territory.

There were two such major axes and their branches which served Sparta's road of communication with the cities in the north. These were, in order, from west to east as follows:

a. The road from Sparta to Megalopolis, most of which followed the Eurotas valley in a general north–western direction.
b. The stretch of 'straight' road from Sparta to Tegea which joined the Arcadian plateau with the Lakonia plain crossing the dry and sparsely populated region of Skiritis.

These two main axes and their branches were used by the Spartan army during the Classical era when Sparta was at the height of her power.

At the time of decline and with the reduction of her territory, Sparta lost the border regions of Skiritis in the north and Belminatis, Aigytis and Maleatis in the northwest. The immediate strategic impact for the city was that she was deprived of control of these routes. As long as she controlled them, she constantly threatened the basins of Tegea, Megalopolis and Asea with her ability to invade before the opponents had time to react. After the loss of these territories, the situation was reversed. Sparta was now under the threat of invasion from her neighbours without having the advantage of early response.

Between the two main axes of communication in the north, the 'diagonal' and the 'straight', historical evidence suggests that the Spartans consistently preferred to use the former and more convenient route, despite its greater length. The latter appears to have been utilized only by hostile forces invading Lakonia via the Arcadian plateau.

From the description of the 'long diagonal avenue', it was already evident that a major node of the road network was the area of Belminatis from which various branches departed. This area already belonged to Megalopolis from the time of Philip II (337). If Sparta wanted a resurgence of her extrovert politics, this is where she was required to begin her expansion knowing that this would reopen the long drawn-out conflict with Megalopolis.

The small plain of Belminatis, with its centre in what today is Agia Eirene, is dominated by the Hill of Chelmos (altitude 769m or 2,523 feet), which today bears the traces of fortifications from different historical periods. It is

Map 2. Accesses to Lakonia.

beyond any doubt that this location is Athenaion at Belbina,[29] a prominent and strategically important fort commanding the access to Megalopolis and Asea.[30]

When in 228 the *ephors* assigned Kleomenes to occupy and fortify the Athenaion with a military detachment of 300 men and a few cavalry, they were essentially asking him to hold the entrance to Arcadia open and from there the access to the Arcadian Corridor.

Thus, at least formally, this action by Kleomenes was an indirect confrontation with the Achaean League. But this was not the real issue. Certainly, the Achaeans would have preferred to keep their control of the four Arcadian cities. To maintain good neighbour relations with the Aitolians, they were willing to allow Aitolian control of these four cities as a price for extending their alliance even formally. By contrast, under no circumstances would they tolerate Spartan control of these cities thereby allowing their opponent access into the heartland of the Achaean League. The crisis escalated with a series of incidents that led to war between Sparta and the Achaean League, a war which Polybios refers to as 'Kleomenic' since he held Kleomenes responsible for starting it.

The Kleomenic War

In its early stages the war was limited to a series of border skirmishes and it was not an extensive conflict. Kleomenes, with courage and determination, captured the Athenaion and fortified it hastily.[31] After the occupation of Athenaion by Kleomenes, Aratos attempted to seize Tegea and Orchomenos by a surprise night attack. But for some unknown reason, his allies within these cities did not venture to help him and his plan failed. Kleomenes did not resist the temptation to deride Aratos and sent him a mocking message in which he criticized him about his failure, perhaps provoking an open confrontation. But it appears that neither the Achaean nor the Spartan leaders wanted this. One possible explanation is that both the Spartan and the Achaean League were King Ptolemy III's allies, consequently a war between them would jeopardize his favour and support which neither force wanted to lose.[32] In fact, Aratos did not react to Kleomenes' insults while the *ephors* called Kleomenes back to Sparta. In May 228 after the departure of the Spartan army, Aratos succeeded in seizing Kaphyai, thus severing the chain of the Arcadian Corridor. This angered the Spartan leaders. The belligerent section of the city reacted and this resulted in the *ephors'* sending Kleomenes with a force of about 5,000 men[33] on a second campaign. He moved north and after a daring manoeuvre with which he bypassed Megalopolis to the west, he launched an attack in Arcadia and occupied Methydrion, a town in the heart of central Arcadia.[34] From there, with another impressive manoeuvre, he invaded Argolis and began plundering it.[35] General of the Achaeans at the time was the former tyrant of Argos, Aristomachos. Seeing his country under threat, he rushed against Kleomenes with 20,000 infantry and 1,000 cavalry.[36] Despite the numerical superiority of his enemy, Kleomenes did not hesitate to confront him. When the two armies met at Palladion,[37] the Achaeans avoided battle. According to Plutarch, this occurred because Aratos intervened and managed to convince Aristomachos to avoid battle with Kleomenes. But why did Aratos react in this manner? Plutarch attributes it to his personal cowardice for it was not the first time this occurred. When he had attempted to seize Argos for the first time some years earlier, he had reacted in the same manner preferring to leave than to confront the enemy. Yet, during his turbulent career and on more than one occasion, Aratos carried out daring tasks and did not hesitate to put his life in danger. The overthrow of the tyrant Avantidas of Sikyon in 251 after a surprise attack as well as the expulsion of the Macedonian garrison from Corinth in 243 were remarkable operations that display no lack of courage on the part of the organizer. However, the accusations of his enemies 'who would recount how the general of the Achaeans always had cramps in the bowels when a battle was imminent, and how torpor and dizziness would seize him as soon as the trumpeter stood by to give the signal', regardless of the degree of exaggeration, suggest that Aratos was seized by a kind of nervous breakdown before battle.[38] Beyond this, at a tactical level, he could not be compared to Kleomenes' genius.

Apart from his phobia of combat, Aratos had other reasons to avoid a pitched battle. Whatever the outcome, it would lead to a major conflict with unknown and possibly unpleasant complications, such as a rapprochement between Sparta and the Aitolian League,[39] or the annoyance of King Ptolemy who, depending on his interests, financed both warring parties.[40] The result was that

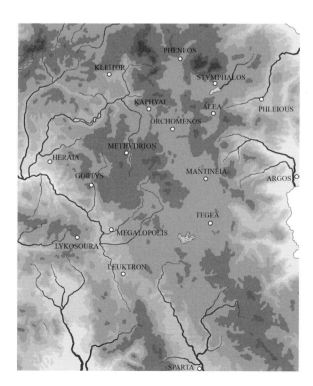

Map 3. The first phase of the Kleomenic War. The operations in central Arcadia.

Aratos made a fool of himself not only in the eyes of Kleomenes' men but also in the eyes of his fellow citizens. The more Aratos was humiliated, the more the Spartan king's prestige rose. His boldness reminded one of the ancient kings who had stated that the Lakedaimonians did not ask how many the enemies were but rather where the enemies were.[41]

In the spring of 227 Aratos attempted to invade Elis. The area was strategically important since it was the base of the Aitolians' raids on the Peloponnese. Therefore, whereas Aratos aimed at severing these ties,[42] Kleomenes moved against him from Arcadia. Aratos who did not want to confront him, attempted to retreat to Megalopolis. Kleomenes caught up with him and the two armies finally clashed at the foot of Mount Lykaion near modern Karytaina. The Achaeans were defeated and fled having suffered heavy losses.[43] It was Kleomenes' first major victory. The crowning touch to the victory was the news that Aratos, the leader and soul of the Achaean League, had fallen on the battlefield.

Unfortunately for Kleomenes, this was just a rumour which Aratos managed to exploit in the best way. He gathered his scattered forces and with a quick manoeuvre entered Arcadia and reached Mantineia. There he surprise attacked the city with the help of supporters from within,[44] managed to seize it and established a garrison of 300 Achaeans and 200 mercenaries. He then proceeded to Orchomenos and blockaded it.[45]

The occupation of Mantineia by Aratos was of supreme strategic importance. It gave the Achaeans the control of the passage in Arcadia and interrupted the continuity of the Arcadian Corridor. It was a powerful blow to Kleomenes' prestige which not only deprived him of the glory of his victory at Lykaion but also caused the *ephors* to recall him to Sparta.

During his stay there, a gloomy and controversial incident occurred which has divided historians from antiquity until today. It is the murder of Agis' brother, Archidamos who after Agis' overthrow had fled to Messenia.[46] Kleomenes had requested that he return to Sparta with the intention of elevating him to the vacant throne of the Royal House of the Eurypontidai.[47]

According to Plutarch, Kleomenes intended to weaken the power of the *ephors* by restoring the institution of the *diarchy* to its full strength.[48] His decision was in line with his political objectives. Kleomenes sought a powerful ally in the brother of the assassinated reformer king.

Instead, Polybios suggests that there was rivalry and competition between the Eurypontide Archidamos and the Agiade Kleomenes. The latter wanted to get rid of a potential challenger to his rule. According to Polybios, Archidamos had departed Sparta because he feared Kleomenes' greed for power.[49] Kleomenes invited Archidamos back to Sparta after guaranteeing his safety through a

Messenian friend of Archidamos, named Nikagoras. But on their return from Messene, Kleomenes 'assassinated Archidamus, sparing however Nicagoras and his companions'.[50] This view is inconsistent and leaves open questions. If we assume that Archidamos left Sparta because of his rivalry to and his fear of Kleomenes, then his agreeing to return to Sparta, even after assurances for his safety, seems impossible to explain. Moreover, if Kleomenes were behind Archidamos' assassination, why would he let Nikagoras and the other witnesses leave? Finally, if Kleomenes wanted to get rid of Archidamos, there was no reason to do so in Sparta. He could have had his men kill him in Messenia.[51]

Plutarch reports that Archidamos was murdered, soon after his return to Sparta by those who had killed Agis earlier and feared the consequences of his brother's return and the strengthening of the kingdom. In connection with Kleomenes' role in the murder, Plutarch cites two versions: that of Phylarchos which states that Archidamos was murdered without Kleomenes' consent and another according to which Kleomenes was persuaded by his friends to turn Archidamos over to those who wanted to assassinate him. The greater part of the blame, Plutarch concludes, was put on Kleomenes' friends since they were thought to have coerced him into murdering Archidamos.[52] However, Plutarch does not consider Kleomenes completely innocent: '... he [Kleomenes] persuaded Archidamos, who belonged to the other [royal] house and should have been his colleague on the throne, to come back to Sparta from Messene, and upon his death, by not following up the murder, he fixed upon himself the blame for his taking off.'[53]

All that is of course 'massively controversial'.[54] One thing, however, is certain: Kleomenes had nothing to gain from Archidamos' assassination. Instead, the return of the latter to Sparta would have helped Kleomenes to win over all those who tacitly supported Agis IV. At the same time, it showed clearly that Kleomenes' policy was differentiated from that of his father Leonidas II.[55] Archidamos' murder would serve only Kleomenes' political opponents and specifically the *ephors*.[56] Therefore, according to all indications, Kleomenes was not responsible for the murder of Archidamos. And yet, Plutarch's reproach that Kleomenes was indifferent to it cannot be ignored. Kleomenes had not yet consolidated his position and knew well that an open confrontation with the *ephors* would eventually turn against him. Agis' tragic end may have been highly instructive for Kleomenes. It should not be surprising that he avoided prematurely revealing his true intentions and preferred to 'look the other way' regarding the murder of Archidamos.

The failure to strengthen his political position limited Kleomenes to the only domain where he had proven successful and could increase his influence in

Sparta: military operations. Thanks to his strong connections – and possibly by bribing the *ephors* – Kleomenes succeeded in being assigned a new campaign.[57] Thus, in the summer of 227, he once more led his army into Arcadia choosing again the 'diagonal avenue' to invade the valley of Megalopolis. Having been elected general of the Achaean League for the tenth time, Aratos was waiting for him in front of Megalopolis but despite the appeals of the Megalopolitans, he refrained from going into battle. Kleomenes then seized a fort at Leuktron, 10kms (six miles) south of Megalopolis and then advanced upon the city to overtake it, giving Aratos no choice but to fight for its salvation. Initially, luck seemed to smile on the Achaeans. A part of Kleomenes' army was defeated and retreated to the Spartan camp. But soon, as the Achaeans were pursuing the enemy, they arrived in front of a deep ditch, where Aratos ordered them to stop, a prudent action as subsequent events proved. Lydiadas, the former tyrant of Megalopolis and now commander of the cavalry, refused to obey Aratos' orders. Dismissing Aratos as indecisive and cowardly, he crossed the ditch with his cavalry and continued the pursuit up to Ladokeia, a suburb of Megalopolis on the road to Asea. But there his troops were trapped in an area planted with trees and vineyards, filled with paddock and ditches that made them lose their cohesion and become easy targets for the nimble Tarantine horsemen and the Cretan archers that Kleomenes had launched against them.[58] Lydiadas himself was killed during the clash and soon the Achaean cavalry fled. In their flight, they fell upon the ranks of their own infantry spreading panic and confusion. As a result, the entire Achaean army took to their heels suffering heavy losses.

Kleomenes, showing magnanimity, returned to the Achaeans their dead while Lydiadas' body, decked in purple and wreathed, was sent to the gates of Megalopolis.[59]

The death of Lydiadas and the disaster at Megalopolis had a great impact on the Achaean League. Even though the reversal of fate was not caused by error on his part, Aratos was held responsible for the defeat of the League and so the next meeting at Aigion, voted not to give him money and not to maintain mercenaries for him; if he wanted to wage war, he would have to provide the means himself.[60]

In contrast, Kleomenes was convinced that the Achaean army was no match for the Spartan. Having finally acquired prestige and popularity on the battlefield, he could realize his ultimate goal and proceed to overthrow the regime in his city. But he was extremely cautious. His moves were carefully devised and made in complete secrecy since his opponents still had total control of power. Plutarch states that Kleomenes was forced to speed up his scheme for fear that his plans had been disclosed by his opponents and so he quickly put them into motion. Having succeeded in being assigned a fourth campaign, he again led a military force into Arcadia. But this time it was not merely a strategic move. In contrast to Agis, when Kleomenes departed from Sparta he took with him all the citizens whom he suspected would oppose his scheme.[61] He chose to invade the area of Megalopolis again. After the disaster at Leuktron[62] the Achaeans were unwilling to resist; therefore, Kleomenes was free to invade unhindered into Arcadia. Initially, he occupied the city of Heraia near the River Alpheios.[63] From there, he moved east, crossed Arcadia, and reached Argolis where at the hills southeast of Stymphalos he seized another city, Alsaia.[64] Then he moved to Orchomenos which was blockaded by the Achaeans[65] and after leaving food supplies for the city, he camped near Mantineia – which was still occupied by the Achaeans – with the intent of besieging it. For the uninitiated, his moves must have seemed excessively hasty. Eventually, his men weary of the tiring marches in the rough mountainous areas asked him to remain in Arcadia for a while. This was precisely what Kleomenes had been hoping for. He left them there. Relieved of those who might have opposed his aspirations, he set off for Sparta taking with him only his trusted friends, among whom two *mothakes*[66] and his mercenaries. He revealed his real purpose only to them and only after they had already set off for their return. He had to maintain secrecy up to the last moment. His own coup would not be bloodless.

The Overthrow

Kleomenes and his men arrived in Sparta at night and launched a surprise attack at the *ephors* during the evening *syssitia*. Four of the five *ephors* were killed and along with them a dozen of those who tried to defend them. The fifth *ephor*, Agylaios, although wounded, managed to crawl to the Sanctuary of Fear[67] and be saved. Kleomenes granted him his life. His triumph was so grand that it allowed him manifestations of magnanimity.

The next day, Kleomenes published the names of eighty wealthy Spartans who would be exiled. With this move he did away with the old aristocracy.[68] He then asked the Spartan Assembly to convene and addressed his fellow citizens openly. His speech, as cited by Plutarch, began with an attempt to justify the slaughter of the *ephors* and his coup.

Kleomenes claimed that the *ephors* had initially served the interests of the kings and substituted for them during their absence in the Messenian War. In support of his argument, Kleomenes referred to the ancient custom according to which when the *ephors* summoned a king to appear before them, he refused to go at the first and the second summons, and only at the third did he rise from his throne to appear before them.[69] In time, he said, the *ephors* managed to illegally impose their authority on Sparta. '... As long as, he said, the *ephors* kept within bounds, it had been better to bear with them; but when with their assumed power they subverted the ancient form of government to such an extent as to drive away some kings, put others to death without trial, and threaten those who desired to behold again in Sparta her fairest and most divinely appointed constitution, it was not to be endured. If then, it had been possible without bloodshed to rid Sparta of her imported curses, namely luxury and extravagance and debts and usury and those evils that breed all this, namely poverty and wealth, he would have thought of himself as the most fortunate king in the world to have cured the disease of his country like a wise physician, without pain.'[70] At this point, in order to justify his actions, Kleomenes thought it would be wise to invoke Lykourgos. 'Lykourgos himself had proved with his own actions that it was difficult to change a constitution without violence and fear. But he [Kleomenes] had used these two methods only moderately putting out of the way those who were opposed to the salvation of Sparta. For all the rest of the people he would be willing to make land available, cancel their debts to the debtors and test foreigners so that after they became Spartans, the best of them would fight for the salvation of the city and so Sparta would stop being considered an easy prey for the Aitolians and the Illyrians because of lack of defenders.'[71]

According to Kleomenes, the *ephors* were a non-Lykourgan institution whose abolition would be instrumental for restoration of the ancestral polity. This view was not new. In 395/4, Kleomenes' distant ancestor, the exiled King Pausanias, had written an essay blaming the *ephors* for being a non-Lykourgan institution.[72] It is possible then that Kleomenes' view of the *ephors* was based on the above essay.[73] The accuracy of this view, though, is a totally different issue. For the *ephors* had been an age-old institution whose abolition would appear as an outright infringement,[74] especially in the way it was done.

Then, Kleomenes further weakened the *Gerousia*[75] and created a new authority, a six-member body, the *patronomoi* who, as its name denotes in Greek, would see that the ancestral laws are properly observed.[76] Evidently, all these were non-Lykourgan measures that could be more or less justified. Kleomenes – as Agis had done before him – could have claimed that he infringed on the letter of the Lykourgan law in order to restore its spirit. Kleomenes proceeded to yet one more un-Lykourgan measure which could not be justified by any means. Under the pretext of restoring the *dual kingship*, he did not hesitate to place his brother Eukleidas on the vacant throne of the Royal House of Eurypontidai. This resulted in Sparta having two kings from the same house for the first time in history.[77] It is a foregone conclusion that Kleomenes intended to displace the House of Eurypontidai. For, if he genuinely wanted to restore the *diarchy*, he could have enthroned a Eurypontid relative of Agis as there were still several candidates such as Hippomedon. Appointing his own brother as co-ruler was nothing but a trick by Kleomenes in order to 'give the name of absolute power a less offensive sound'.[78]At this point he proved to be a worthy successor of his father, Leonidas II. The case of Eukleidas leaves no doubt that all state officials would consist exclusively of men imposed by Kleomenes. Therefore, Polybios rightfully describes Kleomenes as a 'tyrant'.[79] How else can we describe one who seizes power through a coup, overthrows the legitimate regime of his country with the help of mercenaries, and exerts power as an absolute monarch?

Having established absolute power, Kleomenes moved on to implement his social reforms in autumn 227. His two main reforms were the ones that Agis had attempted to implement before him. However, besides cancelling debts[80] Kleomenes proceeded to the redistribution of the 'civic land' in *kleroi*. With a gesture equivalent to that of Agis, Kleomenes 'himself placed his property in the common stock, as did Megistonous his step-father and every one of his friends besides; next, all the rest of the citizens did the same, and the land was parcelled out.'[81] Shares were given even to the eighty exiled citizens with the promise that they would repatriate in Sparta at a later time when the situation would be calmer. This was also a demagogic devise as it was obvious that none of the exiles was ever going to return to Sparta after losing his property.

So, how many new *kleroi* emerged from the redistribution?

Plutarch, who is the only source on this subject, states that after replenishing the manpower, Kleomenes raised a body of 4,000 hoplites.[82] This number does not necessarily correspond to the number of Spartan citizens and the question arises whether or not it included the approximately 600 'old' Spartans.[83] Most historians agree that it included them and that the total number of *kleroi* after the redistribution amounted to 4,000.[84] Some, however, argue that raising a 4,000 hoplite body is equivalent to the increase of the citizen body by 4,000 men. Thus, the total number of *kleroi* amounted to 4,600. This number is very close to that of the 4,500 *kleroi* that Agis had planned to distribute.[85] In any case, the number of *kleroi* emerging from land re-allotment must have been greater than 4,000 since, besides the eighty *kleroi* saved for the exiles, a part of them would go to senior citizens (over sixty years of age) who could no longer serve as hoplites.[86]

As a whole, 3,500 new citizens – of whom 2,000 came from 'inferiors'[87] and 1,500 from *perioikoi* and 'foreigners'[88] – were added to the existing Spartan citizenry.

Kleomenes once more restored the neglected *agoge* to its former status. It is worth noting that Kleomenes did not assign this project to a Spartan but to a foreign philosopher, Sphairos of Borysthenes, who undertook the task of educating and training the young men.[89] The *agoge* was not the only thing that was restored in Sparta at the time. Along with it was revived the austere way of life and the *syssitia* that resumed their essential role.

Undoubtedly, Kleomenes' new *homoioi*, who held *kleroi* and who shared a common lifestyle, living in barracks and participating in the *syssitia*, were politically equal. But were they also economically equal? Did they all share equal *kleroi* or perhaps, after land redistribution, *kleros* meant having the minimum stretch of land necessary to hold the status of 'equal'? Was it possible for some *homoioi* to possess more land or acquire more henceforward?

Kleomenes III silver tatradrachm, Sparta 227–222 BC. On the obverse the Spartan king is portrayed beardless and wearing a diadem according to the Hellenistic models. The reverse depicts the image of Artemis Orthia. (*Collection Alphabank*)

The most prevalent theory today is that Kleomenes tried, as Agis had done before him, to impose complete equality not only in the political but also in the economic life of Sparta. Now the new 'Spartans' would enjoy an unprecedented socioeconomic equality.[90] However, if this was Kleomenes' intention, then apparently one would expect that along with land redistribution he must have confiscated or redistributed movable property as well. Not only is there no evidence of that but there is evidence to the contrary. It appears that Kleomenes followed Areus' example and issued coins to facilitate monetary transactions. In these coins he is depicted beardless and with the royal diadem according to the standards of Hellenistic rulers of the time.[91] Yet, currency distribution does not contribute to the elimination of economic inequalities. Therefore, even if Kleomenes had intended to impose full equality on Spartan society, he must not have applied it. In the not so distant future, and according to all indications, the social and economic inequalities would reappear since Kleomenes had not taken any steps to prevent them.

The Spartan financial system could have functioned properly only if the number of Spartans had remained stable with continuous replenishment of annual losses. How feasible would that be with a constant population increase? The latter sounds very probable given that most of the new citizens were young and selected because of their excellent physical condition.[92] Thus, how would Sparta tackle the problem of allotting additional *kleroi* to prospective citizens? Was there additional land within the jurisdiction of the state to cover this prospect? How were the *kleroi* to be bequeathed? Were they from the state to the citizens or from the parents to their descendants? Were they to all the descendants, only to the sons or only to the first born son?

Unfortunately, like all the ambiguous questions regarding the nature, inheritance and role of *kleroi* in Classical Sparta, the questions on new *kleroi* in Kleomenes' Sparta remain unanswered as well. But whatever the relationship of the new owners was with their *kleroi*, the steady increase of the population of *homoioi* would sooner or later create the need to find new *kleroi*. This problem could be solved only with new conquests. So, Kleomenes was essentially forced to exert an expansionist policy constantly seeking new land for his new citizens.

Kleomenes' reforms had enormous resonance in Sparta. In the eyes of the newly enfranchised citizens, the king of Sparta was elevated to the status of a hero. There must have certainly been some dissidents – apart of course from the eighty exiles – such as women who owned large estates.[93] But these constituted only a small minority of the Spartan society who, after the consolidation of Kleomenes to power, did not dare express their opposition to the new regime. Kleomenes had the full support of the vast majority of his countrymen.

This was not owed to his reforms alone but also to his austere way of life and his exceptional personality. As Plutarch mentions: 'In all the matters Cleomenes was himself a teacher, his own manner of life was simple, austere and no more pretentious than that of the common man, and it was a pattern of self-restraint for all. This gave him a great advantage in his dealings with the other Greeks. For when men had to do with the other kings, they were not so much awed by their wealth and extravagance as they were filled with loathing for their haughtiness and pomp as they gave offensive and harsh answers to their auditors; but when men came to Cleomenes, who was a real as well as entitled king, and then saw no profusion of purple robes or shawls about him and no array of couches and litters; when they saw, too, that he did not make the work of his petitioners grievous and slow by employing a throng of messengers and doorkeepers or by requiring written memorials, but came in person, just as he happened to be dressed, to answer the salutations of his visitors, conversing at length with those who needed his services and devoting time cheerfully and kindly to them, they were charmed and completely won over and declared that he alone was a descendant of Heracles.'[94] His simplicity and frugality was, therefore, one of Kleomenes' most effective weapons. Projecting the ostentatiously 'lakonic' lifestyle, he broadcast to the world the message that Sparta had returned to her former virtue and was ready to take on her 'historic role'. However, he saw to putting aside his 'lakonomania' when diplomacy was imposed. As Plutarch states, he did not hesitate to scold a friend 'when he heard that in entertaining guest-friends he had set before them the black soup and barley-bread of the public mess-tables; 'for,' said he, 'in these matters and before foreigners we must not be too strictly Spartan'.[95]

It is high time the charismatic personality of the Spartan king was discussed. If his inscribed figure on the coins reflects reality, then Kleomenes must have been a very handsome man.[96] Decisive and dynamic, endowed with courage and strategic genius, he possessed qualities important for a leader, more so of a Spartan king thus guaranteeing the dedication and enthusiasm of his soldiers. If we believe Phylarchos' embellished description, Kleomenes was a loving husband as well, in love with beautiful Agiatis. Irrespective of this, however, Kleomenes' magnetism was unquestionable and recognized even by hostile Polybios, who despite his harsh criticism of Kleomenes as a political leader refers with admiration to Kleomenes the king and the man.[97]

On the other hand, there is no doubt that Kleomenes was tough and ruthless when he had to achieve his goal. Comparing him with Agis, Plutarch observes that Kleomenes 'was aspiring and magnanimous, and no less prone by nature than Agis to self-restraint and simplicity. He had not, however, the scrupulous and gentle nature for which Agis was remarkable, and his natural courage was always goading him on, as it were, and fiercely impelling him towards that which in any case appeared to be the honourable course. He thought it a most excellent thing to rule over willing subjects, but a good thing also to subdue such subjects as were disobedient, and force them towards the better goal.'[98] And the fact is that Kleomenes had a passionate temper and terrible tantrums which sometimes he was unable to fully control.

As noted, Kleomenes' reforms were merely the means to achieve the revival of Sparta. With his revolutionary innovations, he achieved to eliminate the chronic problems of the city in only a few months' time, cleansed her social structures and created a new army of citizens, perhaps the greatest in the history of Sparta. In fact, all of his socioeconomic reforms were aimed at the reorganization of the army in which Kleomenes made another radical innovation introducing Macedonian weaponry. The traditional spear was replaced with the long *sarissa*, whereas the hoplite shield, the *hoplon* which was held by an arm-band called *porpax*, with a lighter one which was held on the shoulder by a wide strap, the *ochani*.[99] Kleomenes took measures for the safety of the city by fortifying or strengthening existing fortifications of some strategic positions.[100] He did not stop there, though. Ignoring the tradition that wanted Sparta un-walled, he proceeded to construct walls for her protection.

The change in the appearance of the city was not achieved only with the construction of a wall. Kleomenes, as Areus I had done before him, followed the general trend of the Hellenistic kings of the time. He showed an interest in enhancing the city with statues of high aesthetic as is apparent by archaeological finds from the period. Two statue heads are attributed to Kleomenes' reign, the head of King Ptolemy III made from Parian marble (the first statue found in Sparta after the late Archaic period), and the colossal head of Herakles which belonged to a votive statue and draws on Lysippan prototypes.[101]

With the creation of a strong and dedicated army, equipped and trained with the latest military tactics, Kleomenes could finally realise the dream that for half a century was unattainable for all his predecessors: the restoration of the Spartan supremacy. Was this megalomania? Perhaps it was. But criticizing him as 'opportunistic'[102] is definitely excessive and unfair. For a Spartan king, the ambition to make his country great and strong was a sincere and noble ambition nurtured by a three hundred year tradition.

How feasible was something like this at the end of the third century? Did Sparta really have the opportunity to regain her lost hegemony or was it simply wishful thinking that had nothing to do with reality?

The truth is that with the exception of Sparta, the only significant power in the Peloponnese was the Achaean League. And as proven in battle, the Achaean army was significantly inferior to the Spartan one,[103] much less now that the modernized Spartan army was under Kleomenes' inspired leadership. The defeat of the Achaean League was tantamount to the domination of Sparta in the Peloponnese and her evolution as being the strongest power in southern Greece. The only serious threat to Sparta could come from Macedonia. However, having set the Peloponnese under her control, Sparta could confront Macedonia on equal terms. Besides, in 227 the threat from Macedonia was not yet visible so if Sparta appeared strong enough, she could always count on Ptolemy's support, since it was known that the Lagid dynasty was Macedonia's keen competitor in Greek affairs. Consequently, the Spartan dream for the resumption of her hegemony was no longer wishful thinking but a real prospect. Under certain conditions, Sparta could play a leading role in the political issues of her time. Even if winning the supremacy over Greece was questionable, its establishment in the Peloponnese and in southern Greece was almost certain.

Rising to Hegemony

The internal changes in Sparta did not go unnoticed by her opponents, especially by the leader of the Achaean League, Aratos. The complete dominance of a proven capable military leader in Sparta seriously jeopardized the position of the Achaean League, which after its recent military defeats could obviously not confront Sparta with its own forces. It needed the active support of a powerful ally. Such an ally could be the Aitolian League. But the opportunistic nature of the alliance between the two Leagues prevented them from having a mutual understanding. Therefore turning to the Aitolians for help was out of the question. Instead after the Aitolians' stance on the Arcadian Corridor issue, Aratos had good reason to worry about the possibility of a rapprochement between Sparta and the Aitolian League. Therefore, there were two main forces left that could effectively help: Egypt and Macedonia. But affiliating with both of them would be very difficult. Egypt was an ally of Sparta and the Achaean League, and it was unlikely that the Ptolemies, who generally avoided engaging militarily in southern Greece,[104] would help the Achaean League against Sparta.

The case of Macedonia was different. The Antigonids had always had aspirations in southern Greece and the Peloponnese, and in contrast with the Ptolemies, did not hesitate to intervene militarily in favour of their allies. Thus, Macedonia was the only credible force that the League could caution. But how could this be done when the current policy of the Achaean League was hostile to Macedonia? How would the Macedonian monarch react in a prospective attempt of rapprochement by Aratos whose name was associated with the expulsion of Macedonians inside and outside the Peloponnese?[105]

These issues were thorny. Nevertheless, Aratos was a great statesman endowed with the gift of coping with any situation. Due to his great diplomatic experience, he was able to understand that 'kings naturally consider no one to be a friend or a foe, but every time they weigh their friendships and enmities by measuring their own interest.'[106] Thus, all of Antigonos' reservations toward Aratos and his own policy until then would dissolve if he were persuaded that he had an interest in helping the Achaean League against Kleomenes.

Antigonos' affiliation presented an additional difficulty: most cities of the Achaean League were hostile to the Macedonian monarch and if Aratos approached him, he could well be described as a traitor. Moreover, the appeal of the League towards its old enemies would reveal its military weakness and would trigger separatist tendencies of its less ardent supporters.[107]

For all the reasons above, Aratos moved carefully and in complete secrecy. He knew well that among the cities of the Achaean League there existed some, such as Argos and Megalopolis that were mostly pro-Macedonian. In the case of Megalopolis, there was an additional particularity. Because of its significant geographical position, it was essentially the southern bastion of the Achaean League and had suffered the most from the war with Sparta. The defeats at Lykaion and Ladokeia had taken a heavy toll on the citizens and the frequent Spartan invasions had devastated the land.[108] The apparent inability of the Achaean League to defend Megalopolis forced many Megalopolitans to turn to Macedonia for help since they had had close ties with it in the past.

As a city member of the Achaean League, Megalopolis was not allowed to practise an independent foreign policy. The problem was overcome easily thanks to Aratos who used his influence on the Achaean League to send a Megalopolitan delegation to Antigonos. Towards the end of 227, two eminent Megalopolitan friends of Aratos, Nikophanes and Kerkidas, departed for Macedonia on a mission to seek Antigonos' immediate assistance for suffering Megalopolis. At the time, this did not necessarily entail that Macedonia would engage in war with Sparta simply by aiding Megalopolis.[109] Aratos assigned his two envoys an additional secret mission: beyond the formal request for Macedonian assistance, the two Megalopolitans were to feel Antigonos' intentions regarding the war between the Achaean League and Sparta. And because the possibility of a rapprochement between Macedonia and Sparta had to be avoided at all costs, the two ambassadors were to make clear to Antigonos that Kleomenean Sparta might become very dangerous. They were to recommend that it was in his best interest to actively assist the Achaean League in the war against Kleomenes since a possible alliance between Kleomenes and the Aitolian League would threaten not only the Achaeans but also the Macedonians. Once the Aitolians and Kleomenes defeated the Achaeans and got control of the Peloponnese, they would not be satisfied but would seek to conquer all of Greece. Therefore, Antigonos had to consider his options: should he confront Kleomenes in the Peloponnese for supremacy in Greece having the backing of the Achaeans and their Boiotian allies or should he fight alone in the region of Thessaly against the united forces of the Aitolians, Boiotians, even the Achaeans and the Spartans for the salvation of Macedonia?[110] If Antigonos agreed with Aratos' proposals, he would have to notify him and then Aratos would invite him at the appropriate moment.

Antigonos had no reason to reject the ambassadors' proposals. He had a unique opportunity to restore the lost sovereignty of Macedonia in the Peloponnese and did not want to lose it for anything. So he responded positively to the Megalopolitan request and to Aratos' clandestine proposals.

Antigonos' answer was obviously greeted with enthusiasm by the Megalopolitans. During the meeting of the League at Aigion in the spring of 226, the Megalopolitans requested that Antigonos be officially and immediately invited to come to their aid. However, Aratos had a different opinion. The general of the Achaean League did not yet share the impatience of the Megalopolitans. His plan had succeeded perfectly: he had approached Antigonos and had ascertained that the Macedonian monarch not only wasn't hostile towards the Achaean League but had no objections to intervening against Kleomenes if so requested by the Achaeans. There were still two major problems. Firstly, what would Antigonos ask in exchange for his help? Secondly, how would the Achaeans react since the majority of them were opposed to the intervention of Macedonia in the Peloponnese? For these reasons, Aratos chose not to reveal his true intentions. To the great surprise of the Megalopolitans, he declared in an eloquent manner that it would be better that the Achaeans confront Kleomenes alone and only if they lose all hope, should they resort to seeking the help of the Macedonians. As expected, the Achaeans applauded Aratos' stance and decided to continue the war under their own stream. In fact, this was a personal triumph for Aratos. He knew that the Achaeans trusted him as far as his genuine intentions were concerned and at the same time he knew that they would consent to his summoning Antigonos for help if needed.[111]

In the spring of 226, and obviously wanting to enhance his own prestige, Aratos decided to end his *strategia* by taking an aggressive initiative. He invaded Arcadia and succeeded in defeating a Spartan force near Orchomenos, which was commanded by Kleomenes' stepfather, Megistonous. 300 Spartans were killed and Megistonous was taken prisoner.[112] It was a small and temporary triumph for Aratos. He must have evaluated that the situation in Sparta was unstable after the latest developments and that Kleomenes would not have time to respond.[113] Yet, Kleomenes was determined to disprove him. In a display of power, he invaded defiantly the area of Megalopolis with his renewed army in May–June 226 and plundered it gathering rich booty. To provoke them even further, he called a wandering troupe and organized a theatrical competition for his men beneath the walls of Megalopolis while he and his soldiers watched the performance within the enemy territory. But his contemptuous behaviour did not stop there. He contacted the strong pro-Spartan faction of Mantineia and one night succeeded with the help of his supporters to take over the city. According to Polybios, the occupation of the city was accompanied by atrocities against the Achaeans who were arrested there.[114]

The taking of Mantineia was a major strategic success for Sparta. Her army was invigorated with new blood and, most important, the Arcadian Corridor was free again. From Mantineia, Kleomenes moved south, passed through Tegea and with a big manoeuvre invaded western Achaea and seized two of the oldest cities in the League, Dyme and Pharai. These cities did not hold particular strategic interest but their capture was a powerful, symbolic blow. The war was now moving into the heart of the Achaean League and was developing from border skirmishes into widespread conflict. No Achaean city was safe anymore. If the Achaeans did not want to abandon Achaea and their ancient cities to the mercy of Kleomenes, they would have to face him on the battlefield. At the end of 226, the Achaeans gathered all their forces and attempted to stop Kleomenes at Hekatombaion, a strong fortress in the plains south of Dyme.[115] No detailed description of the battle exists but it appears that the Achaean general, Hyperbatas, was deployed in such a way that he threatened to outflank Kleomenes' army. Yet, Kleomenes, confident of his army's supremacy, accepted the challenge. He was vindicated by the events. The Achaean army was completely defeated by Kleomenes' phalanx and suffered heavy losses. It was a crucial blow to the League.[116] After the battle, Kleomenes seized Lasion[117] and ceded it to the Eleians apparently hoping to win them over. The fact is that after his victory in Hekatombaion, Kleomenes' army was reinforced with fresh troops, thus depriving the Achaeans of their numerical advantage. The latter were now unable to counteract the superior quality of the Spartan army and the genius of Kleomenes. Moreover, the outcome of the battle seems to have convinced Ptolemy III that financial assistance to the Achaeans was wasteful and so he stopped subsidizing them.[118]

Under the pressure of the circumstances, the Achaeans sought to come to terms with Kleomenes. Kleomenes agreed to return the captives and conquered territories to them provided that he was entrusted the hegemony.[119] What exactly did he mean by that? Nothing less than set the Achaean League under the Spartan rule. Such a prospect would change the character of the League decisively, rendering it into Sparta's satellite.[120] But the destruction of Hekatombaion was still too recent to allow a dispassionate assessment. The earnestness to continue the war had substantially receded. Finally, a truce was signed, and Lerna,[121] a small town near Argos, was designated as the place to negotiate Kleomenes' demands. It was a foregone conclusion that in this meeting

Kleomenes' conditions would essentially be ratified. Under no circumstances would the rapprochement between the two forces be on equal terms.

In fact, a rapprochement between Sparta and the Achaean League on equal footing would have been a blessing not only for them but also for the whole Peloponnese. It would also have contributed decisively to its unification. In any case, it would have meant the end of devastating wars, the population decline and the destruction of its natural resources. But such a prospect would have been plausible only if the two rival leaders were not who they were. With Kleomenes and Aratos, this was impossible.

For Kleomenes, the unification of the Peloponnese was synonymous to Spartan supremacy. Consequently, the integration of Sparta to the League as an equal member was unthinkable. How could Kleomenes, the man who had repeatedly crushed the League's army and tarnished its name, put aside his Spartan ambition and compromise with the office of general of the Achaean League? Such a position might have been a great honour for someone like Lydiadas or Aristomachos, yet for a Spartan king this was a disgrace.

Aratos, from his perspective, was determined not to concede in any way the hegemony to the Spartan king under any circumstances. He had serious reasons not to. First and foremost, he had personal aspirations. The man who had devoted his life to the strengthening of the League, and after a point was identified with it, could not allow the destruction of his lifelong project.[122] Beyond this, Aratos acknowledged that the Achaean League as a political entity had no chance of surviving under Spartan rule. Evidently, the risks were no smaller under Macedonian suzerainty, either. Yet, for Aratos, the Macedonian supremacy was much more preferable than the Spartan one for two main reasons. Firstly, Macedonia was too far to exert its power effectively and consistently, while the Spartan supremacy would be absolute. Secondly, Aratos, like any genuine advocate of the wealthy class, saw in Macedonia the bulwark of social stability and security, while in Kleomenes' Sparta the threat of social revolution: 'the most dreadful of the evils for which he [Aratos] denounced Cleomenes, namely the abolition of wealth and restoration of poverty'.[123] The fact is that Kleomenean revolution had a great impact on neighbouring cities and especially on the poor masses who were craving for reform. Undoubtedly, the prospect of a general uprising by the poor caused intense concern among the rich. The ambient unease that prevailed at the time is evident in the poems (*meliambs*) of Kerkidas from Megalopolis, the same person who was sent as an ambassador to Macedonia to seek help from Antigonos in 227.[124] Kerkidas, who belonged to the ruling class of Megalopolis and was a personal friend of Aratos, criticized in his poems the excessive accumulation of wealth and urged the wealthy to indulge in charity to avoid the worst that is a social revolution. Kerkidas, who was fond of the Cynics but consciously belonged to the wealthy class, urged the rich not to flaunt their wealth so defiantly, so that they would not be overturned by the poor. His case indicates how pressing the social problems were at the time.

For Aratos, Kleomenes' domination was the worst option. In order to deter it, he was determined to ally himself with the devil, even if this meant 'expelling Satan by using Beelzebub'.[125] But after the disaster in Hekatombaion, the treaty of the Achaean League at Lerna was a possibility which Aratos could not afford to prevent. At this point, Fortune smiled upon him unexpectedly.

While everything was ready for the negotiations, Kleomenes suddenly fell ill. Plutarch says that it was a bad cold that occurred when he drunk cold water after a strenuous march resulting in bleeding and speechlessness.[126] As expected, the negotiations were postponed. There was an exchange of prisoners, among whom Megistonous who was handed over to the Spartans. Argos was designated as the new place of negotiations which finally occurred with nearly a six month delay in the summer of 225. Aratos immediately seized the opportunity. In the League's elections for generalship in the spring of 225, he renounced his claim to the post of general in favour of his supporter, Timoxenos. His decision seems inexplicable and Plutarch finds fault in it.[127] Amidst a whirl of mishaps, did Aratos want to evade responsibility of leadership when the existence of the League was threatened? Highly unlikely. What he wanted above all was to remain undistracted in order to achieve his objectives, that is, to thwart the negotiations and provide direct military support for the League. Antigonos had promised to aid but this was Aratos' last resort. He first tried to exhaust all his options until the last moment. He appealed to the Athenians, even to the Aitolians for help,[128] unfortunately to no avail. Therefore, the interference of the Macedonians in Peloponnesian affairs was the only, though the worst, option. Aratos understood very well that Antigonos would have great demands if he helped in ridding him of Kleomenes. Under the circumstances, the League was no longer in a position to negotiate anything with the Macedonian monarch. This would perhaps have been possible two years before when its weakness had not yet been revealed. In the summer of 225, though, the risk of total destruction was imminent. The ambassadors that Aratos sent along with his son, did not simply ask for help in a war that had evolved unfavourably for the League but appealed for its salvation. Antigonos' answer would confirm Aratos' worst fears.

While Aratos was waiting for Antigonos' response, the negotiations with Kleomenes were about to begin. Aratos wanted to undermine them in every way for fear that if there were a meeting between Kleomenes and the Achaeans, Kleomenes would persuade his interlocutors to recognize him as their ruler. As mentioned above, the place of negotiations was set in Argos. But for them to take place, Aratos succeeded in imposing the following terms on Kleomenes: according to one version providing that he agreed, Kleomenes would go to Argos with an escort of 300 men after having first accepted a number of Achaean hostages as collateral for his safety.[129] According to another version, Kleomenes could choose either to go to Argos alone after having taken with him 300 Achaean hostages or convene outside of Argos at the Kyllarabion gymnasium.[130] Apparently, these terms showed that Aratos was trying to prevent Kleomenes from occupying the city. But the mere fact that such conditions had been set (in any of the two versions) evidenced the change in the Achaean attitude towards him during these six months. Kleomenes realized this immediately and became outraged. This was something that Aratos must have anticipated when he set the terms. Kleomenes responded by sending Aratos a scathing letter. Aratos replied in the same manner thus outraging Kleomenes even more. Under these conditions, negotiations failed. The only solution was, therefore, to continue the war.[131]

After the failure of this overture, and while he was still at Argos, Kleomenes sent his messengers to Aigion, the capital city of the League, to announce the declaration of war. It was a smart, diplomatic move. Kleomenes knew that many cities were ready to defect from the League and aimed at prodding them to do so sometime between the moment the messengers would arrive in Aigion to make the announcement and the moment the Spartan army would appear in Achaea.[132]

These disruptive tendencies within the Achaean League began to appear immediately after the breakdown of negotiations. As Plutarch mentions, 'their [the Achaean] cities were eager to revolt, the common people expecting division of land and abolition of debts, and the leading men in many cases being dissatisfied with Aratos, and some of them also enraged at him for bringing the Macedonians into Peloponnesus.'[133] The leaders of many cities were opposed to Aratos' decision to invite Antigonos to the Peloponnese. Several of them, one being Aristomachos of Argos, had broken their relations with Macedonia (either in order to join the League or for personal reasons) and feared the consequences of the descent of the Macedonians on the Peloponnese. Some had traditionally good relations with Sparta, while others were Aratos' personal opponents.[134] At the same time, the poor masses believed that Kleomenes' social reforms would extend to their own cities.[135] In at least two major cities, Argos and Corinth there were professed *'Kleomenists'* and *'Lakonizers'*.[136]

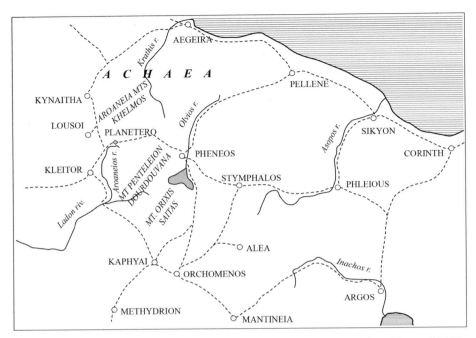

Map 4. Cities of Achaea. Kleomenes's operations in Achaea (Adapted from Tausend 1998). The locations are marked by their contemporary name.

Kleomenes' first strike was directed to the 'heart of the beast', Sikyon, the homeland of his great rival, Aratos. Kleomenes had a lot of supporters there with whom he had previously come to an agreement.[137]Although he was very close to seizing the city, his venture failed.[138] He turned westward and seized Pellene.[139] Then he moved to the interior ascending the course of the Olbios River (which flows into Lake Pheneos) and he seized Pheneos and the fort of Penteleion in Aroaneia Mountains, and Kaphyai.[140] With the occupation of Kaphyai, Pheneos and Pellene, the Arcadian Corridor extended into the territories of the League reaching the Gulf of Corinth. The League was split into two sections and Kleomenes with his army was interposed between them having the ability to attack in any direction he chose. To the west were the old Achaean cities and some Arcadian cities that continued to remain loyal to the League, while in the east were the largest and most important cities such as Sikyon, Corinth, Megara and Argos together with the cities of Argolis. Kleomenes decided to head east aiming precisely at those cities. Apart from their special importance, he knew well that in many of these cities there fermented trends of separatism very quickly so he stood a good chance of getting them on his side.

The state of the League had become extremely critical, as one after the other the cities fell under Kleomenes' possession and even in Aratos' homeland, Sikyon, many still sought a rapprochement with him.[141] Aratos reacted decisively and dynamically. At first, he succeeded in being given superpower by the Achaeans, who were called upon to declare him 'general emperor'[142] with special authorities and grant him a personal bodyguard. He thus achieved to stifle any separatist tendencies within Sikyon. Then he rushed to Corinth, where pro-Spartan trends had been manifested.[143] But while he was there, he was informed of the next major triumph of his enemy: Kleomenes, with the help of Aristomachos and the pro-Spartan faction of Argos, managed to capture the capital of Argolis. The operation occurred at the time when people were gathered to watch the sacred rallies of the Nemean Games.[144] Defying the sacred truce, Kleomenes drove his army at night to the walls, secretly invaded the city and once he had occupied the area around Aspis Hill, suddenly attacked from an inaccessible and unattended place located just above the theatre. The surprise attack was a total success. The Argives did not dare resist, the city surrendered to Kleomenes and a Spartan garrison was placed therein.[145] The terrible news spread like wildfire across the Peloponnese. It was the culmination of the triumphant march of revitalized Sparta. Kleomenes achieved something that no other Spartan had ever achieved: to take control of the age-old competitor city.

The news of the fall of Argos roused the '*Lakonizers*' in Corinth and no sooner than later riots erupted. The Achaeans were forcibly expelled and Aratos, who was in danger of getting lynched by the angry crowd, managed to save himself at the last moment and escape from the city on horseback. The Corinthians quickly summoned Kleomenes to their city in order to surrender it to him. He was in the area of Argolis, having just captured Phleious and Kleonai when he received the Corinthians' message. Yet, his enthusiasm for the accession of Corinth was significantly mitigated by two main reasons. Firstly, the Achaean garrison had not left but remained blocked in the citadel of the city, Acrocorinth. Secondly and most importantly, Aratos, the soul of the Achaean League, had managed to escape from the hands of the Corinthians. It was obvious that if Aratos had been arrested, any plans on the part of the Achaeans to resist would fall through and the Achaean League would surrender. The latter was of paramount concern to Kleomenes who at the time was struggling to catch up with developments knowing, obviously, what was common knowledge throughout the Peloponnese: the imminent arrival of the Macedonians.

On his way to Corinth, Kleomenes deviated east and seized Hermione, Troizen and Epidauros. Shortly before arriving in Corinth, he made an attempt to approach Aratos and, under his stepfather Megistonous' mediation, offered him a sum of money in exchange for the withdrawal of the Achaean garrison from Corinth.[146] Aratos refused. After his triumphant entry to Corinth, Kleomenes attempted to approach him again. Having taken all the necessary measures to keep Aratos' property in the city intact, he sent him the Messenian Tritymallos[147] and proposed a joint garrison by Spartans and Achaeans on Acrocorinth. He even promised to subsidize him with twelve talents a year, double the amount that Ptolemy had given him in the past.[148] Aratos again refused, alleging to Kleomenes an enigmatic excuse: that 'he did not control affairs, but rather was controlled by them.'[149] Kleomenes, who regarded the answer to be ironic, became furious. He confiscated Aratos' property in Corinth, then invaded Sikyon and, after ravaging the region, besieged the city.

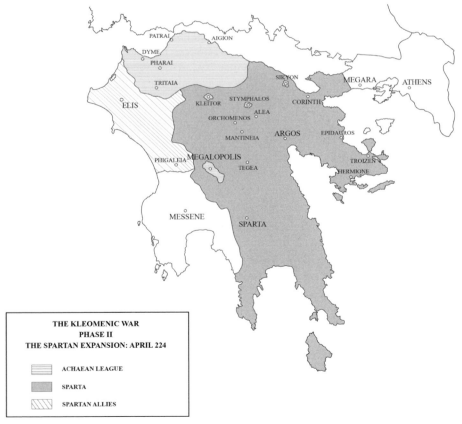

Map 5. The second phase of the Kleomenic War, Spartan Expansion.

Everything showed that Kleomenes' star was at its zenith. Within a few months, he managed to demolish the edifice that had been Aratos' life-long ambition. The Achaean League, with most of its cities under Spartan control, others preparing to defect and others desperately fighting for their salvation, seemed to be on the verge of collapse. In contrast, a revived Sparta emerged bright on the sky, ready to impose her hegemony on the Peloponnese after one and a half centuries. Had the moment finally come for Sparta's grandiose dream to become a reality?

Ostensibly, this possibility seemed inevitable. A sober assessment of the situation, however, would reveal that the outlook for Sparta and Kleomenes was not as optimistic as it seemed. The Achaean League had come to an extremely difficult position but it had not laid down arms. Under the robust leadership of Aratos, and despite the continued blows it had received, it still resisted. On the other hand, despite his impressive successes, Kleomenes did not have the strategic superiority that he displayed. He might have seized Argos and most Arcadian cities,[150] but the Achaeans possessed Megalopolis and thus continued to maintain a strong foothold in Arcadia. Moreover, as long as the Achaean garrison remained fortified in Acrocorinth, the possession of Corinth did not provide Kleomenes a serious strategic advantage. For the key of control of the Peloponnese was not Corinth, but rather the impregnable fortress on the top of that hill. 'For the Isthmus of Corinth, forming a barrier between the seas, brings together the two regions, and thus unites our continent; and when Acrocorinthus, which is a lofty hill springing up at this centre of Greece, is held by a garrison, it hinders and cuts off all the country south of the Isthmus from intercourse, transits, and the carrying on of military expeditions by land and sea, and makes him who controls the place with a garrison sole lord of Greece.'[151] The biggest problem of Kleomenes was that time was not on his side; he had to break the Achaean resistance before the Macedonians arrived in the Peloponnese. His repeated efforts to win Aratos over, both before and after the conquest of Corinth, as well as his explosive reaction when Aratos rejected him categorically, indicated that the Spartan king was well aware of how precarious his seemingly powerful position was and so was Aratos. Undoubtedly, the surrender of the Achaean guard at Acrocorinth, the fall of besieged Sikyon and, ultimately, the capitulation of the League was a matter of time. Yet, Kleomenes' time was waning. From the moment Antigonos and his army set off for the Peloponnese, the final countdown for him had begun.

The Turning Point

In April 224, Aratos, who was trapped in the besieged Sikyon, decided to mount a risky operation. Defying Kleomenes' blockage, he managed to escape secretly with ten friends and his young son, and reach Aigion by sea in order to attend a meeting of the representatives of the Achaean League.[152] There he announced Antigonos' terms to his countrymen:

The Achaeans would have to surrender the fort of Acrocorinth to the Macedonians and recognize Antigonos as *hegemon*, 'leader with full powers by land and sea'.[153] Moreover, the Achaean League would be bound to refrain from any diplomatic encounters without the consent of Antigonos[154] and swear allegiance to Macedonia annually.[155] Finally, the Achaean League would undertake to pay the expenses for the maintenance of Antigonos' forces.[156]

The conditions were harsh. Specifically, the return of Acrocorinth to the Macedonians formally and essentially sealed the Achaean League's submission to its old enemies. On the other hand, Acrocorinth was blocked by Kleomenes and Corinth had acceded to him with enthusiasm. In fact, the voluntary accession of Corinth to Sparta's sphere of influence acquitted the Achaeans from their commitments to the Corinthians and gave Aratos the ideal pretext of offering the fortress of Acrocorinth to Antigonos.[157] Regardless of any excuses, the fact is that the Achaeans were not in a position to negotiate Antigonos' terms. Faced with the risk of total destruction, they decided to send hostages (among whom Aratos' son) to Pella, the capital city of Macedonia, in order to validate the requirements and accelerate the advent of Antigonos to the Peloponnese.[158]

Antigonos' route to the Peloponnese was neither short nor easy. The Aitolians, motivated by their anti-Macedonian feelings, did not allow him to cross the Gates of Thermopylai. Antigonos who did not want to lose time trying to break this strong position, nor openly provoke the Aitolians,[159] decided to transfer his troops by sea to Euboia. He gathered his forces in fortified Chalcis, from there he arrived in Boiotia and through Mount Kithairon he ended up in Pagai of Megaris (modern Alepochori) where he met Aratos. Despite Aratos' doubts and fears, Antigonos received him cordially. The two men exchanged vows and sealed the terms of their alliance. Beyond what was already agreed upon, and evidently under Antigonos' pressure, the Achaean League agreed to cede Megara (which after the loss of Corinth was severed from the League's territories) to Boiotia.[160]

On hearing of the Macedonians' descent, Kleomenes who was already besieging Sikyon for three months, hastily resolved the siege and rushed to the Isthmus to organize his defence. At first the outlook was not favourable for him.

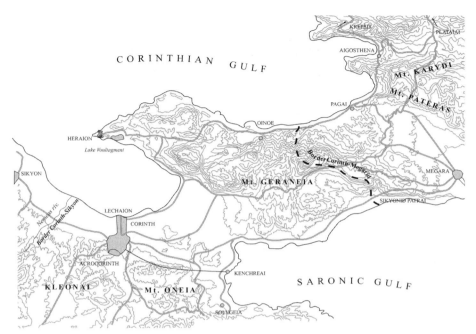

Map 6. Corinthian Gulf. As Kleomenes did not want to clash with the Macedonian army in the open, he withdrew from his advanced positions in the safe narrow Isthmus strip to an ample but strategically fortified position. His defence line started at Lechaion and stretched to Corinth and the Oneia Mountains all the way to the Saronic Gulf

In a pitched battle, the Macedonian phalanx was mighty and Kleomenes did not want to face it in the open. He chose to deploy behind the narrow section of the Isthmus, where he had originally developed his advanced positions.[161] He brought forward linear defence. The deployment of his defensive line ran from Lechaion, the Corinthian port which was connected by a wall to Corinth. The area around the citadel of Acrocorinth was entrenched thus completely blockading the Achaean garrison. A ditch reinforced with piles stretched from Corinth and reached up to Mount Oneia (modern Kakia Skala) in the Saronic Gulf thus completely blocking the entrance to the Peloponnese.

Kleomenes' strong defensive line made it impossible for Antigonos to penetrate it, nailing him there for days virtually immobilised. He could not afford to remain for a long period in the region because his supplies were limited and he had problems sustaining his army.[162] After a failed attempt to surprise attack Lechaion at night, Antigonos began to examine the possibility of transferring his troops by sea from Heraion (modern Perachora) to Sikyon. This was extremely difficult, because his fleet was moored at the Isthmus on the side of the Aegean Sea, so to reach Heraion he had to sail around the Peloponnese.[163]

Then, as Antigonos had come to total deadlock, an unexpected event occurred that changed the outcome of the war. One evening Aratos was informed that Aristotle, a friend from Argos, was preparing to instigate his countrymen to rebellion against Sparta. It appears that Aristotle had almost the entire population of the city on his side. What was happening with the 'Kleomenists' at Argos? What had prompted this unexpected shift? As Plutarch mentions, the main reason for Argos' rebellion was the people's discontent because 'Kleomenes had not brought about the anticipated abolition of debts.'[164] Aratos immediately seized this opportunity. Once he had alerted Antigonos of the developments, he boarded the ships with 1,500 men and sailed to Epidauros.[165] In the meantime, however, the Argives had already rebelled and with the help of an Achaean force that rushed from Sikyon and, under the command of general Timoxenos,[166] managed to block the Spartan garrison in the citadel of Argos.

The news stirred up unrest among Kleomenes' troops in Corinth. He tried to reassure his men but he knew that the recapture of the city was imperative. He could not remain in Corinth while the enemy forces were in his rear because they could plunder Lakonia unhindered at any moment and even threaten Sparta which had been left unguarded.[167] A force of 2,000 men under Megistonous was detached to retake Argos.[168] Unfortunately, in the ensuing fight Megistonous was killed and his force was repulsed. The Spartan garrison still held the citadel but it was obvious that sooner or later it would surrender. Kleomenes had no other option. Leaving Corinth hastily, he directed all of his forces to Argos. He managed to invade the city and join forces with the garrison in the citadel. He then tried to place the city under his control and managed to occupy some of its parts. It was too late though. Antigonos, who in the meantime had captured Corinth, rushed against him with all his forces and managed to arrive outside of Argos while Kleomenes was struggling to conquer it. When he 'saw Antigonos with his phalanx descending from the heights into the plain and his horsemen already streaming into the city, he gave up trying to master it'.[169] He gathered his forces and withdrew hastily from Argos; he returned by the shortest route from Mount Artemision through Mantineia to Sparta in May 224.

Argos was a fatal city for Kleomenes. Its conquest had catapulted his prestige to great heights, its loss, on the other hand, plunged it into the abyss and was the first step to his downfall. The reason for this was the shift of his supporters in the city because he did not implement the hoped-for reforms. Here lies the key point: Kleomenes had never expressed an intention to 'export' his revolutionary reforms. These were confined strictly within the boundaries of his homeland. They were designed to solve specific problems in Sparta, a warrior-landowner society based on a rural economy and the institution of helotage that made her unique among other Greek cities. The implementation of similar measures to other cities with different social structures, that is the 'export' of the revolution, was an extremely intricate matter and would create more problems than it would solve.[170] But regardless of the possibility of 'exporting' Spartan reforms, the truth is that if Kleomenes wished, he could have applied his social reforms in the cities that came to his grip. The fact is that he never did so because he did not intend to.[171]

A totally different issue is whether or not Kleomenes exploited the excitement and hopes of the poor in the Peloponnese for his own benefit. Many theories have been formulated on this question. Indeed, some have expressed confidence that Kleomenes' most effective weapon was propaganda and that his agents disseminated promises of land redistribution and debt cancellation to the poor citizens of the Achaean League, in order to win them over.[172] However, this is totally hypothetical. There is not the slightest indication that Kleomenes attempted to deceive the masses of the poor in the Peloponnese.[173] What is more likely is that Kleomenes was completely indifferent to the poor and made no attempt to win them over. He needed not to resort to false promises. In every city the impoverished were spontaneously attracted to him, spurred on by their own despair. Just the sight of the disciplined army of Sparta, a city which everyone knew had implemented 'land redistribution' and 'debt cancellation' was enough to rouse the waves of enthusiasm in his path.[174] Yet, Kleomenes did nothing to flame their enthusiasm. Thus, those who believed that he had a solution to their problems soon abandoned him as impulsively as they had embraced him.

Argos is a typical example. Kleomenes had supporters in this city not only among the poor but also among the most prominent citizens, like the tyrant Aristomachos, who sulked at the prospect of the arriving Macedonians.[175] Before taking control of the city, Kleomenes was able to address all social classes. From the moment he took control though, he had to either honour or fail the expectations he had created.[176] As it turned out Kleomenes did not keep his promises thus facing the fate of all those who take the 'middle road'. For the wealthy he was considered too rebellious and was not trusted, while the poor were disappointed because he was not revolutionary enough.[177]

His misfortune reached a peak when on his way to Lakonia, Kleomenes was informed about the death of his wife, Agiatis. He could not afford the time to grieve for her loss since he had to solve the urgent economic problems that arose after the sharp reduction of his territory. He immediately addressed Ptolemy and requested financial aid. Yet, after the loss of Argos and Antigonos' triumphant march, Kleomenes no longer inspired great confidence in the Lagid monarch. To offer assistance, Ptolemy demanded that Kleomenes send his mother and his children to Egypt as hostages. Proud Kratesikleia responded courageously to the dire task and departed with her grandchildren for Egypt. Kleomenes' separation from his family is movingly immortalized in Phylarchos' writings and has become the source of poetic inspiration for centuries[178] but did not help his cause in the least. What Kleomenes did not know was that Antigonos had already approached Ptolemy diplomatically and had requested that funding to Sparta be discontinued.[179]

At Argos, Aristomachos and his supporters were harshly treated by the victors. According to Phylarchos, Aristomachos paid for his opportunistic politics and was killed at Kenchreai after being horribly tortured.[180] His followers were massacred after Antigonos' departure from Argos.[181]

After Argos, Antigonos headed southwest and rushed to Megalopolis, ignoring the cities of the Arcadian Corridor. After expelling the Spartan garrison from the area of Aigytis and the border fort Atheneaum at Belminatis, he handed them over to Megalopolis. His goal was apparently to rebuild the traditional ties between Macedonia and Megalopolis. Yet, Antigonos did not attempt to seize Sparta. In any way, the operation was risky: her geographical position ensured her good natural defence and combined with Kleomenes' fortifications, it would be extremely difficult to take it.[182] Therefore Antigonos chose to ignore her temporarily. Having weakened Kleomenes sufficiently, he did not want to engage in a difficult and risky operation before consolidating his dominance in the Peloponnese. This, of course, was his true goal. Kleomenes was more of a pretext.

Having sent his men to winter at Sikyon and Corinth, Antigonos headed to Aigion to attend the autumn meeting in 224 where he was elected the commander of the allied forces. A century after Alexander, he founded a new 'Hellenic League' under the auspices of Macedonia.[183] Its difference from the first 'Hellenic League' was that this time it was a League of federations and not of city-states, which is indicative of third-century new dynamics in Greece. Moreover, the new alliance was by no means Pan-Hellenic. Apart from Sparta and her active allies, the Messenians, Eleians, Athenians, Aitolians and their allies did not participate in this alliance.[184] Nevertheless, the new 'Hellenic League' was a political triumph for Macedonia and guaranteed undeniable dominance in southern Greece. This must have been a bitter conclusion for Aratos if he ever believed that he could positively affect Antigonos' attitude towards the Achaean League. The friendly treatment he received by the Macedonian king in Pagai was nothing more than an expression of cordiality of a monarch towards his favoured courtier. Indeed Aratos now was in an awkward predicament. Plutarch reproaches him for his inconsistent behaviour reminding us that Aratos was the same person who had once taken the leading role in expelling the Macedonians from the Peloponnese but in order to eliminate Kleomenes he did not hesitate to 'cast himself and all Achaea down before a diadem, a purple robe, Macedonians and oriental behests'.[185] Aratos came to performing sacrifices and singing hymns (*paians*) in praise of his new ruler. The once-powerful leader of the Achaean League 'was no longer master of anything except his tongue, which it was dangerous for him to use with freedom'.[186] Moreover, Antigonos' condescending goodwill towards Aratos was in sharp contrast to the Macedonian monarch's contempt for the other Achaeans. Such behaviour caused their indignation. A typical example is what happened at Argos and Corinth. At Argos, Antigonos restored the statues of tyrants which the Achaeans had torn down after the city's integration in the Achaean League. At Corinth, he destroyed the statues of those who had expelled the Macedonian garrison from Acrocorinth. The only statue he left standing was that of Aratos who had repeatedly asked Antigonos to no avail not to demolish the other statues. Saving the Achaean League from Kleomenes came at a high price: twelve years later, when Aratos died, the Achaean League 'had become little more than a toy in the hands of the great powers'.[187]

The Months of Waiting

After the fall of Argos, Kleomenes found himself again in the situation in which he had been before the battle at Hekatombaion. The balance of power was reversed against him. However, he had not been completely weakened. Besides Lakonia, he still controlled several other cities, including the major Arcadian cities of Tegea, Mantineia and Orchomenos, while on the battlefield his army remained invincible. Yet, Kleomenes no longer projected the public image of the victorious leader he once was. His reputation had been severely tarnished.

Kleomenes was fully aware of his situation. He desperately needed a victory on the battlefield. Only this way could he reverse the situation to his favour, polish his prestige and revive the morale of his supporters. Consequently, he decided to take the offensive. On May 223, he ventured a daring – under the circumstances – operation: to seize Megalopolis.[188] However, this operation failed and – even worse – it caused an immediate reaction by Antigonos, who invaded and persistently besieged Tegea.[189] The Macedonian army was the best army of the era, it possessed the best equipment and had a long tradition in siege craft. The Tegeans, who quickly realized that they could not resist for long, chose to surrender in exchange for the Macedonians' forbearance. Antigonos then headed to Lakonia and Kleomenes rushed to confront him. But after the first skirmishes had started, Antigonos was informed that a force from Orchomenos was on its way in support of Kleomenes, thus threatening his rear. He swiftly turned, took Orchomenos' forces aback, crashed the enemy and then attacked the city of Orchomenos, seized it and plundered it. A permanent Macedonian garrison was placed to safeguard keeping a watchful eye over Orchomenos.[190] Antigonos then seized Mantineia which he handed

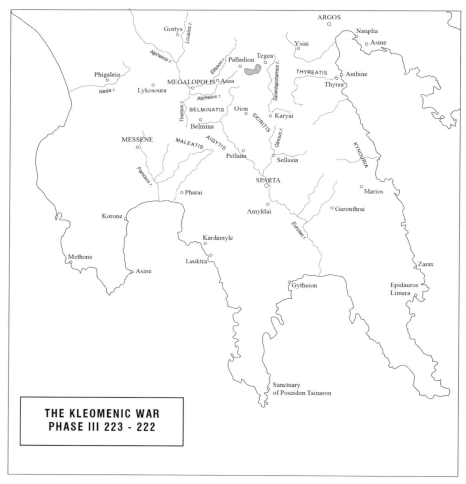

Map 7. The Kleomenic War, third phase.

over to the Achaeans giving them the opportunity to avenge the slaughter of the Achaean garrison by the Mantineians in 226. The city was looted and its inhabitants were slaughtered or sold as slaves on the market. The brutality of the Achaeans caused a stir that shook all of Greece. It was unprecedented for its time as nobody had inflicted a disaster of this size for a century on any defeated city.[191] The Achaeans abolished even the name of the city. When it was recolonized, it was renamed Antigoneia, a fact for which Aratos was held responsible by his opponents (August 223).[192]

With these military operations Antigonos succeeded in substantially constraining Kleomenes within the boundaries of Lakonia. In order to give the final blow to Kleomenes and his regime, Antigonos only had to invade Sparta. The project, however, was still overly dangerous. Kleomenes still had supporters in several towns and there was always the danger of a diversionary attack threatening to cut off his communication lines. Thus, Antigonos preferred to first deprive Kleomenes of his allies and weaken him; for he knew that his opponent was running out of time and was unable to maintain war for long. From Mantineia he proceeded to western Arcadia where the cities of Heraia and Telphousa surrendered to him. In Heraea, as he had previously done in Orchomenos, he placed Macedonian garrisons (which were to remain until 199/8) consolidating the Macedonian presence in the heart of the Peloponnese. Subsequently, and as winter approached (in November 223), Antigonos decided to dissolve his army and send the Macedonians, who were absent for more than a year-and-a-half from their homeland, to spend the winter at home.[193] He headed to Aigion to pass the winter there, taking only his mercenary forces with him, fully convinced that Kleomenes would be too weak to cause him any serious trouble.[194]

Undoubtedly, Kleomenes had fallen into serious trouble. After the loss of Heraia, Telphousa, and especially Orchomenos, Mantineia and Tegea, the number of his forces was dramatically reduced. In addition, after losing Ptolemy's subsidy, he was confronted with the serious problem of his army's maintenance.[195] Yet, Antigonos had underestimated his opponent. The Spartan king was not the sort of man to give up easily; he still had one last card to play. In order to overcome his difficulties and to replenish his meagre forces, he sought to mobilize a great pool of manpower: the helots. The liberation of the helots in order to enhance the Spartan army was nothing new. It had been applied in the past with much success.[196] This time, however, Kleomenes was in urgent need of money. Therefore he did not hesitate to put a price on their freedom. Specifically, he proceeded to emancipate those helots who were able to buy their freedom for five *attic minai*.[197] There was nothing revolutionary in doing so. It was clearly an attempt to increase his army and boost his funds. Kleomenes raised 500 talents[198] by emancipating 6,000 helots. Both the amount of money and the number of the emancipated helots seem large. Might this have been an exaggeration by Plutarch?

Firstly, the sole fact that Kleomenes put this specific price on the freedom of the helots reveals that he knew that many of them could afford it. From the fourth century, money was already playing an important part in the economic life of Sparta and social differentiation was apparently extended even among the helots.[199] For a quite long period, until Kleomenes' drastic reforms, the land that they cultivated consisted of vast areas of farm land, the majority of which belonged to a small plutocratic oligarchy. The yield from these large estates was much larger than farmers and owners needed to get by. It was, therefore, possible for helots to retain and exploit commercially a small part of their surplus production. Certainly, the five *attic minai* that Kleomenes requested would account for a helot's life savings. Large as the amount may appear, it may have been possible for someone to have saved it.[200]

Kleomenes armed 2,000 of the freed helots (probably after selection based on their good physical condition) in Macedonian fashion[201] 'as an offset to the White Shields of Antigonos'.[202] Of the remaining 4,000, a large part must have strengthened the light units of the Spartan army.[203] The result was that in November 223, the balance of power had been reversed in favour of Kleomenes. Antigonos was significantly weakened while Kleomenes was strengthened. This was a unique opportunity which the Spartan king could not leave unexploited. Once again, his target was Megalopolis.[204] This time Kleomenes decided to implement the following stratagem. Having gathered his forces and having taken five days of supplies with him, he moved to Sellasia suggesting that he intended to invade Tegea. Evidently he pretended to follow the 'straight route' from Sellasia which led north to the wet southern fringes of the Tegea basin via Skiritis. Kleomenes crossed obliquely the hills west of Sellasia without being noticed, followed an unpredictable path and emerged unexpectedly in the basin of Asea. From there, he surprise attacked Megalopolis and following the path along the River Elisson arrived in the city. It was a stunning 80kms (50 miles) course through rugged terrain that took Kleomenes and his army over a day and a night to cross.[205] A small force commanded by Panteus, rushed onto an unguarded side of the wall. With the aid of supporters within the city, they managed to penetrate therein, kill the guards and demolish part of the walls. This paved the way for the rest of Kleomenes' forces.[206] The Megalopolitans were taken aback. When they recovered from the shock, they counterattacked and attempted to repel the invaders. But it was too late. After fierce fighting, in which almost 1,000 Megalopolitans were killed or captured, the Spartans dominated the city.[207] Yet, the stubborn resistance of the defenders allowed most inhabitants, women and children, to evacuate the city and take safe refuge in Messene.[208]

Kleomenes did not allow his army to plunder the city. On the contrary, with the mediation of two of the most prominent citizens of the city, Lysandridas and Thearidas, he offered the Megalopolitans to ally and in return leave their city intact.[209] Yet, the Megalopolitans, motivated by a young compatriot named Philopoimen rejected Kleomenes' offer. His response was harsh. The city was severely ravaged and plundered to such an extent that it seemed as if it could never be inhabitable again. One could say that Sparta's accumulated rage for over one and a half century burst at once on the city which had been challenging her domination since its foundation. Kleomenes' anger is explained further by the fact that he realized his opponents' determination to continue the war at any price. Moreover, after his failure to win over the people of Megalopolis, the destruction of the city was strategically imperative. Prolonged occupation of a vacant city would require additional forces that Kleomenes could not afford to commit. Kleomenes had scored a spectacular success. He had managed to boost the Spartan army's morale and heal his injured prestige although strategically he had achieved nothing substantial. The plunder from Megalopolis was certainly not negligible. Yet, it did not suffice to meet the needs of war.[210]

In the winter of 223/222, while Antigonos remained inactive in Aigion, Kleomenes took all necessary measures to strengthen Sparta's defences and fortified all accesses in the event of invasion.[211] He was soon to take the offensive with a military operation equally impressive as the previous one. This time he would strike the fatal city of Argos. Of course, he would not try to take it. The Argives were fully aware of his imminent invasion and of course there were no 'Kleomenists' left in the city. Kleomenes wouldn't be able to repeat the stratagem by which he had placed Argos under his control two years before. Furthermore, he was hard up and could not possibly afford a long and costly siege. Despite these handicaps, in the early spring of 222, the Spartan army invaded Argolis undisturbed and ravaged the area.[212] No matter how risky it appeared, this venture was actually safe since the Macedonian forces had returned home. Moreover, Kleomenes, informed that Antigonos was in Argos with a small military force, was seeking to undermine the credibility of the Macedonian monarch to its allies or even push him into battle under unfavourable conditions. Antigonos certainly knew that at this stage an open confrontation with Kleomenes would be tantamount to destruction and so, despite the challenges of the Spartan king, he avoided the confrontation. He remained enclosed within the city walls ignoring the indignant protests of the Argives who saw in despair the Spartan army plunder Argolis undisturbed.[213] When the Spartan army later withdrew, Antigonos attempted to create a diversion. He moved his mercenary forces to Tegea threatening to invade Lakonia from there. Yet, Kleomenes, who knew the limitations of his opponents, ignored the hostile invasion. With a quick manoeuvre, he returned to Argos and continued to systematically plunder the land, in particular the wheat harvest.[214] Antigonos was forced to return and attempted to block Kleomenes in the plain of Argos by occupying all the passageways and by putting garrisons there. Such tricks did not worry Kleomenes. He knew well that without the Macedonian phalanx, Antigonos was not a serious threat. Therefore, the reaction of the Spartan king was similar to that four years before when, scorning his opponents, he organized theatrical performances in front of the walls of Megalopolis, in the heart of the enemy territory. Although blockaded in Argolis by Antigonos, Kleomenes sent messengers to the city of Argos, demanding the keys to the temple of Hera (Heraion) in order to sacrifice to the goddess. The Argives did not give him the keys but neither did they dare fight with him in an open conflict. Thus, Kleomenes sacrificed undisturbed outside the locked temple and then headed to Phleious. Antigonos' garrison tried to intercept Kleomenes in Oligyrtos but the latter easily dispersed the enemy troops and continued undisturbed via Orchomenos to Lakonia, leaving his enemies bewildered and his men filled with enthusiasm.

Once again Kleomenes had succeeded in polishing his image and in raising his men's morale. But that's all there was to it. As Plutarch descriptively presents it, the two opponents looked like two wrestlers with Kleomenes being skilful and Antigonos being much stronger and more promising.[215] Despite his spectacular success, Kleomenes failed to convince Ptolemy that he could reverse the outcome of the war. He did, though, succeed in convincing Antigonos that he remained an extremely dangerous opponent that had to be crushed in a pitched battle. Thus in the early summer of 222, Antigonos' forces gathered in the Peloponnese and joined his allies there reaching nearly 30,000 men.[216] This time Antigonos invaded Lakonia determined to finally finish Kleomenes. He had wasted a lot of time in this campaign and wanted to be disengaged from the Peloponnese in order to return to his homeland as soon as possible.

On the other hand, Kleomenes did not have the leisure to prolong a war of attrition with Antigonos. The maintenance of his army had exhausted all his resources for the recollection of which he had resorted to the most radical measures. Kleomenes had entrusted his last hopes on Ptolemy. He obeyed the royal command and had sent his own family to Egypt, waiting anxiously for the renewal of his royal subsidy. In the meantime, he 'could only meagrely and with difficulty provide pay for his mercenaries and sustenance for his citizen soldiers'.[217] Yet, when the official response by the monarch of Egypt finally reached him, its content was disappointing. Ptolemy unequivocally announced to Kleomenes the termination of his grant and advised him to make peace with Antigonos. Ten days after Ptolemy's ultimatum, in the summer of 222, Kleomenes hastened to confront Antigonos in the Lakonian territory, seeking as well the final reckoning.[218]

In fact, the opponents who would solve their differences in the forthcoming battle were not Kleomenes and Antigonos but Kleomenes and Aratos. The final battle was the climax of the struggle between these two men. In this ruthless fight, Antigonos was Aratos' trump card against which Kleomenes had no ace upon his sleeve. The following question must be asked: could Kleomenes have responded differently to Aratos' ultimate challenge?

Realistically speaking, there were two forces that Kleomenes could rely on: the Aitolians and Ptolemy. The former had rejected Aratos' appeal for help and had prevented Antigonos from passing through the straits of Thermopylai. Regardless of this, however, their attitude can be characterized more as 'unfavourably' neutral towards the Achaeans and the Macedonians. Was there a chance that they could actively support Kleomenes? This is doubtful. Kleomenes could not expect anything from Ptolemy apart from a frugal financial aid that would be granted to him only as long as he served Ptolemy's interests.[219] However, the kernel of the matter is not what the Aitolians or Ptolemy were willing to do for Kleomenes, but the fact that Kleomenes did nothing to ensure their active military support and their involvement in his war.

It is true that Kleomenes wrote repeatedly to Ptolemy requesting financial aid and did not hesitate to demean himself by sending his whole family hostage to Egypt. But once he faced the might of Macedonia, he needed much more than Ptolemy's money to win. Unfortunately, there is no reference in any source that he attempted to create a strategic distraction to Antigonos.

Herein lies the difference in temperament between the two men, Kleomenes and Aratos. As soon as he realized the inadequacy of the Achaean League to face Sparta militarily, Aratos did not hesitate to resort to an undesirable solution, the Macedonians. In order not to surrender the hegemony to Kleomenes, 'he cast himself and all Achaea down before a diadem, a purple robe, Macedonians, and oriental behests'[220] and so he was accused that he exchanged the Spartan hegemony for absolute monarchy. Between two bad choices this seemed preferable under the circumstances. Aratos chose to place the League under the authority of the distant Macedonians rather than place it under Sparta's direct control.

Unlike Aratos, Kleomenes conducted the war essentially relying on his own forces. At no stage of the war did he imagine compensating in any way the Macedonian threat or ensuring the active support of his allies. Despite his undeniable strategic genius, Kleomenes eventually lost the war while Aratos, a bad general but determined to win by any means, was pronounced a victor. Above all, Aratos' victory over Kleomenes can be attributed to the subtle but essential distinction between the two opponents, 'the distinction, in difficult circumstances, between the man who, as we say does his best, and the man who means to get the thing done and does it'.[221]

The Battle of Sellasia

The course of events was leading inexorably to the most decisive conflict. Antigonos, head of the Macedonian army and his allies, would attempt what he had methodically been preparing for in the last two years, the invasion of Lakonia. Having abandoned his diversionary tactics, Kleomenes decided that the time had come to openly confront the Macedonian king.

Kleomenes expected Antigonos to make the first move. The route the latter would utilize for the invasion depended on several factors, first and foremost on the location that he would use to concentrate his forces. Unfortunately, no such details are recorded in any historical account. If this location had been the plain of Tegea, Antigonos would have probably used one of the roads that led directly from Tegea to Lakonia and not the 'diagonal' route which demanded longer time because of its longer distance.[222] Possibly Tegea was considered far deeper in the enemy territory, thus also exposed to a surprise attack on the part

Sellasia. Panoramic view of the battlefield as seen from north to south. Olympos hill (an outgrowth of Provatares) is on the left, Oinous river (Kelefina) is in the centre and Evas hill with one of its two crests (Tourles) is on the right. The arrows on the photograph mark [from left to right] the respective positions of the Spartan phalanx, the positions of the forces in the centre and the positions of Eukleidas' forces.

of Kleomenes, especially in the early stages of the invasion when Antigonos' forces would lack in numbers and cohesion. In this case, the only other obvious location for this purpose was Argos.[223]

The tactical problem that Kleomenes faced was where exactly he would choose to confront Antigonos since he could not be sure which road his opponent would follow. Of course, these two routes were not of equal importance. A competent general such as Antigonos would quickly perceive the relative advantages and disadvantages and would choose the better option. If, for example, it was clear that Antigonos was following the 'straight' route from Tegea to Lakonia, Kleomenes could prepare successive surprise attacks and ambushes in appropriate places along this route in order to wear out and immobilize the opposing forces. Or, he could offer battle on the plain of Karyai at a place where the narrowness of space would work to his advantage.[224] On the other hand, Antigonos had the option to follow the path through Mount Parnon and find himself at the rear of the Spartan king, a possibility that Kleomenes could not overlook. Finally, a general of Antigonos' experience could send small detachments as decoy in more than one passage in order to deceive the enemy as to his intentions and to keep the path of his main force secret until the end.

Given the above, knowledge of the landscape indicates a single place from which it is possible to control an invading enemy's access to Lakonia from the north-northeast: Sellasia. In terms of tactics, this country was situated at the point where the narrow valley of Oinous widens enough for an army the size of the Spartan one to deploy and sustain forceful attack from major forces, such as that of Antigonos. From many aspects, Sellasia's advantage was obvious; its disadvantage was that there was not enough space for retreat. As a line of defence, Sellasia was literally the ultimate retreat, a location dangerously contiguous to Sparta. A possible unfavourable outcome of the battle meant that Sparta would be left defenceless.

Bearing all this in mind, Kleomenes paved the way for his defence. He blocked up the other passages with ditches and piles of tree trunks and placed garrisons so that he would be alerted if Antigonos chose one of the other roads to invade. Kleomenes and his army blocked the road to Sellasia, thus if Antigonos finally decided to break through one of the other passages, Kleomenes would have time to move to contain him.[225]

Therefore, the great battle that would judge the outcome of the Kleomenic war would be joined in Sellasia. What a strange coincidence, indeed! Sellasia was the strategic key point for Sparta's defence from the northeast, just as Athenaion was the equivalent key point from the northwest. Kleomenes' career traced its course in history starting with an offensive attack in Athenaion and ending in a defensive battle in Sellasia.

Opposing Plans and Opposing Forces

Fortune had there brought into competition two commanders equally endowed by nature with military skill

Polybios 2.66.4

Kleomenes carefully examined the battlefield. Experienced as he was, he chose the battlefield with an eye to making sure that it would guarantee the greatest possible advantages. He chose the spot where the road follows the flow of the River Oinous and passes between two hills, Evas in the west and Olympos in the east. He fortified the two hills with ditches and palisades[226] and deployed his forces there. He had fewer than 20,000 men.[227] Of these, 6,000 were 'Lakedaimonians',[228] who were armed according to the standards of the Macedonian phalanx[229] and were the strongest unit of his army. Along with the

View of Evas Hill from the plains near Oinous river.

light troops and mercenaries they reached a total of 11,000 men. They all took positions in Olympos under the command of Kleomenes himself.[230]

The *perioikoi* along with Kleomenes' allies, 5,000–6,000 men in total, were deployed west of the road on Evas Hill under the command of his brother Eukleidas.[231] Kleomenes' allies came from the few cities that remained loyal to him and even from the cities that were seized by his enemies.[232] The *perioikoi*, who constituted the bulk of this force, numbered around 3,500–4,000 men while Kleomenes' allies should not have exceeded 1,500–2,000 men.[233]

In the plain, between the two hills, Kleomenes deployed about 1,000 of his cavalry and part of his mercenaries[234] so that the forces of the left and the right wing could support each other mutually. Any attempt by the enemy to attack the centre of the Spartan army exposed him to a potential flank attack by the forces that would dash from the two hills and especially from Olympos.

Kleomenes selected the battlefield and planned the deployment of his forces very carefully. For, despite the fact that his army was one of the largest in the history of Sparta,[235] it remained inferior both in numbers and in quality compared with the forces of his opponents. Kleomenes had no illusions as to

Olympos Hill.

the outcome of a confrontation with the Macedonians in the open. Thus, he chose to deploy on a narrow and rough terrain, unsuitable for the development of Antigonos' heavy forces, where he could always take advantage of the slightest mistake of his opponent.

Kleomenes' assessment eventually proved correct. As he had foreseen, Antigonos chose to follow the route from Tegea to Sparta and so, in the middle of the summer of 222,[236] his army appeared in front of Sellasia. Polybios (2.65.1–5) gives a detailed description of Antigonos' army. It consisted of 28,800 men in total. Nearly half of his forces were Macedonians, namely 10,000 phalangites and 3,000 *peltasts*. The latter were an elite fighting force who fought as phalangites but were also able to perform special tasks when combined with lighter units.[237] There were also 1,000 Megalopolitans,[238] 2,000 Boiotians and 1,000 Epirotans[239] all armed by the Macedonian standards. Overall, Antigonos' heavy infantry amounted to 17,000 men. His lighter forces consisted of 3,000 mercenaries, 1,600 Illyrians led by Demetrios Pharios, 1,000 Galatians, 1,000 Agrianians, 1,000 Akarnanians, and 3,000 'picked' Achaeans, totalling 10,600 men.[240] Finally, Antigonos' cavalry consisted of only 1,200 cavalrymen of whom 300 were Macedonians, 300 Achaeans, and 300 mercenaries, 200 Boiotians, fifty Epeirots and fifty Akarnanians.[241]

The sight of the Spartan army waiting for the enemy on their fortified positions was awe-inspiring for Antigonos. Kleomenes had lined up in such a way that he made the most of the terrain features and from a distance it loomed large as a compact and impregnable front. His deployment with the flanks anchored on the two steep hills and his light troops in the centre was 'like that of skilled soldiers drawn up ready for a charge'[242] allowing him not only to repel enemy attacks but also to strike back at the right opportunity. In contrast, the lack of space deprived Antigonos of the advantage of numerical superiority and the rough terrain, along with Kleomenes' fortifications, deterred any charges by the Macedonian phalanx, which was Antigonos' main attacking unit.

Antigonos immediately saw the difficulty of the situation and did not rush to attack. He camped near Gorgylos, a small stream that ran at the foot of Evas, and using it as a hideout carefully watched Kleomenes' deployment for days, trying in vain to distinguish a weak point in his formations. He then tried to lure him to abandon his strong positions through feigned assaults and flanking moves in different spots. Yet, Kleomenes had fortified all the passages and had installed garrisons everywhere that warned him of every hostile move. By performing swift manoeuvres, he managed to neutralize every encircling attempt on the part of his opponent.

DEPLOYMENT OF THE OPPOSING FORCES

ANTIGONOS' FORCES

3.000 Macedonian "chalcaspids" under Alexander son of Alkmetos 1.600 Illyrians under Demetrios Pharios 1.000 Akarnanians 2.000 Achaeans 1.000 Epeirots (Kretans)	1.000 Megalopolitans under Kerkidas 1.000 Achaeans 1.200 Cavalry (300 Macedonians 300 Achaeans, 300 merce-naries, 200 Boeotians, 50 Epeirots, 50 Akarnanians under Alexander)	10.000 Macedonian phalangites of the phalanx under Antigonos Doson 1.000 Agrianians 3.000 Mercenaties 1.000 Gauls
TOTAL: 8.600 men	TOTAL: 3.200 men	TOTAL: 15.000 men

TOTAL FORCE: 26.800 men*

KLEOMENES' FORCES

Eukleidas		Kleomenes
3.500 - 4.000 Perioikoi 1.500 - 2. 000 Allies	1.000 Cavalry 1.000 Light armed mercenaries	6.000 Spartans of the phalanx 5.000 Light armed (mercenaries and emancipated helots)
Total: 5.000 - 6.000 men	Total: 2.000 men	Total: 11.000 men

TOTAL FORCE: 18.000 - 19.000 men

* The 2000 Boeatian infatry whom Polybios includes in Antigonos' forces are omitted in the above deployment since there is not the least reference of their participation in the battle.

The days passed and despite Antigonos' devices, Kleomenes' army remained firm in its strong positions. In the end, Antigonos realized that the only way to end the campaign was to give battle on Kleomenes' own terms: he would have to attack from his disadvantageous position at the foot of the Evas and Olympos hills and try to force Kleomenes to abandon his fortified positions on the high slopes. Thus in tacit agreement with Kleomenes, he decided to put an end to this pernicious hold and to finally carry out the battle that would determine the war.[243]

Opposite Evas Hill, Antigonos placed a strong but relatively flexible joint force that reached a total of 8,600 men. In particular, he deployed the 3,000 Macedonian '*chalkaspides*' ('Bronze Shields')[244] under the command of Alexander, son of Alkmetos, along with the Illyrians led by Demetrios Pharios so that their *speirai* would alternate with those of the Illyrians. His aim was to provide his units some flexibility so that their attack would be facilitated during their offensive in the rough uphill. In addition, the arrangement of the 'Bronze Shields' in alternating *speirai* with the Illyrians enabled the latter to attack and then retreat finding protection among the *speirai* of the 'Bronze Shields'. It was a tactic that had been implemented much earlier by Pyrrhos during his campaign in Italy when he adapted his army to Roman methods of combat.[245]

Alongside the Illyrians,[246] Antigonos lined up the Akarnanians and the Epeirots,[247] while further back 2,000 Achaeans were kept in reserve so that they cover the rear of the deployment.

In the centre, opposite Kleomenes' cavalry, Antigonos deployed his own cavalry, commanded by Alexander, namesake of the commander of the 'Bronze Shields'. Behind the cavalry he stationed the remaining 1,000 Achaeans and 1,000 Megalopolitans led by the aforementioned Kerkidas. Finally, Antigonos himself with 10,000 Macedonians of the phalanx, the *euzons* and the remaining mercenaries deployed opposite Kleomenes in front of Olympos Hill. Because of the narrowness of the terrain, Antigonos was forced to line up the phalanx thirty-two men deep instead of the usual sixteen.[248]

The Battle

This was an instance of the fantastic way in which Fortune decides the most important matters.

Pol. 2.70.2

Once he decided to attack, Antigonos had no choice but to attack on Evas Hill. Only there could he implement his plan successfully. Attacking Olympos and

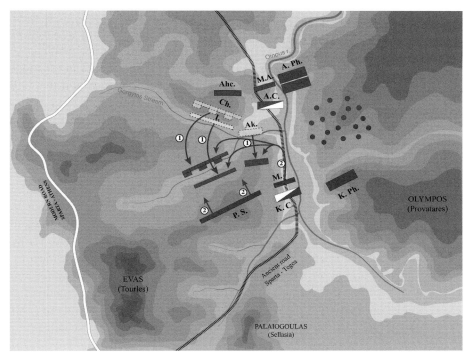

Ch	Macedonian Bronze Shields (Peltasts)
Ach	Achaeans
Ak	Akarnanians
I	Illyrians
M.A	Megalopolitans and Achaeans
A.C	Antigonos' Cavalry
A.Ph.	Antigonos' phalanx

P.S.	Perioikoi and Allies
K.C.	Kleomenes' Cavalry
K.Ph.	Kleomenes' Phalanx
M	mercenaries in the center
	Light troops of both sides on Olympos

THE FIRST PHASE OF THE BATTLE

Kleomenes' fortified defensive positions have been deliberately omitted on the map. Polybios only makes a general reference here and does not identify the exact location of Kleomenes' fortifications. Apparently, Kleomenes fortified only the most vulnerable accesses to the hill slopes. It turned out, though, that these fortifications did not significantly affect the evolution of the battle.

1. The Illyrians leave their hide in Gorgylos and storm Evas Hill followed by the Akarnanians and the Bronze Shields. The Achaeans who were in charge of covering the assault do not follow.
2. Eukleidas orders the mercenaries in the centre to assault the exposed flanks and rear of the attackers who are also being assaulted by the defenders of Evas Hill.

repelling Kleomenes' phalanx from its fortifications was practically impossible while any attempt to penetrate the centre would expose his flanks to attack by the forces on the two hills.

The problems were different on Evas. The attackers would not have to face the crack units which defended Olympos. However they had to cross the rough hillside and repel the defenders from their fortified positions. On Evas there was the additional problem of crossing the Gorgylos torrent that narrowly ran at the foot of the hill. In case the phalanx of the 'Bronze Shields' attempted to cross the torrent, it risked being trapped inside. There it would lose its cohesion and would be exposed to the attacks of the hill's defenders while unable to defend itself. To overcome these difficulties, Antigonos resorted to the following stratagem. The night before, he hid the Illyrians in Gorgylos in order to surprise attack Evas and pave the way for the phalanx.[249] The selection of the tough Illyrians for the implementation of the stratagem was not random. Their agility and experience in fighting in difficult terrain made them ideal for such an operation in order to cover the attack of the phalanx. The advancement of the Illyrians left gaps among the *speirai* of 'Bronze Shields' thus facilitating their own ascent of the hill. The Illyrians, on the other hand, were always able to return and fill in the intermediate gaps so that the deployment would appear to have a compact front. In accordance with the Illyrians, the 1,000 Akarnanians covered the left flank of the attackers. The 2,000 Achaeans who were stationed further back had to cover the rear of the phalanx, while the cavalry and the Megalopolitans in the centre were assigned to prevent any flanking attempt by the opposing enemy forces. A red flag raised on a *sarissa* from Antigonos' headquarters would signal the attack by the Megalopolitans and the cavalry in the centre.[250]

According to Phylarchos, whose opinion is reproduced by Plutarch, Kleomenes had suspected Antigonos' stratagem. Not seeing the Illyrians and the Akarnanians in the enemy right wing, he summoned Damoteles, the commander of the *krypteia*,[251] to monitor the safety of the rear of his deployment and the possibility of its encirclement by the enemy. Damoteles, though, having been bribed by Antigonos assured him that everything was under control. It remains uncertain whether this actually happened or whether it is 'composed' by Phylarchos.[252] The fact is, however, that with or without treason, Antigonos' stratagem succeeded. Once the signal was given with a white flag hoisted from Olympos,[253] the Illyrians sprang from Gorgylos and together with the Akarnanians charged the defenders of Evas. They were followed by the 'Bronze Shields' and at the end all of Antigonos' right wing began to advance on the slope of the hill. At that crucial moment, an unexpected event almost changed the course of the battle. Because of poor coordination, the Achaeans who had undertaken the task of protecting the attackers' rear did not move in time, thus creating a gap between them and the forces that had advanced on the slope of Evas.[254] This did not go unnoticed by Eukleidas who immediately sent the light infantry from the centre to attack the enemy flank.[255] The attackers suddenly became defenders. They had to confront their adversaries head on from a disadvantageous position on an inclined slope of the hill while at the same time they were being attacked from their sides and their rear.

The problems of the right flank were visible by the commanders of the centre of the allied forces. Among them was the thirty-year-old Megalopolitan Philopoimen, the man with the uncompromising attitude who had contributed decisively in preventing Kleomenes from seizing Megalopolis. In recognition of his stance, he was appointed 'honorary' commander of a small unit, that of the 300 Achaean cavalry. Anticipating the imminent destruction of the forces on Evas, Philopoimen asked Alexander and the other Macedonian officers to immediately attack their enemies opposite them. The young military commander's eagerness to distinguish himself on the battlefield was met with condescending smiles as they all waited patiently for the signal to attack. As long as the red flag did not rise from the side of Antigonos, there was not going to be an attack. What they did not do, Philopoimen dared do at the critical moment. Breaching orders, he attacked with his three hundred cavalry the forces that had been flanking the right of the Macedonians at Evas Hill. There followed a wild fight during which Philopoimen was seriously injured. Nevertheless, he had achieved his goal.[256] His example was followed by the other commanders of the allied centre resulting in the involvement of all of the forces of the Macedonian cavalry in the battle.[257] In the end, the pressure on the flanks and the rear of the attackers on the Evas stopped. Of the units that Eukleidas had sent against them, some scattered while others were forced to return to the centre in order to reinforce their cavalry which was fighting there.[258] Having secured its flanks and rear, Antigonos' right wing could now continue its offensive on Evas.[259]

Until that moment, nothing had been decided. As long as Eukleidas had control of the slope, the ascent of the hill remained closed to the attackers. In the rough slope, the 'Bronze Shields' were losing their cohesion and were unable to take advantage of their weapons and formation. Moreover, the defenders of the hill could get out of their fortifications every now and then, charge the attackers causing confusion in their battle line and then retreat to their fortified positions high on the hill.[260]

Rather than follow the above tactics, Eukleidas made a decision that proved fatal. He remained stationary at the hilltop leaving his enemies to approach

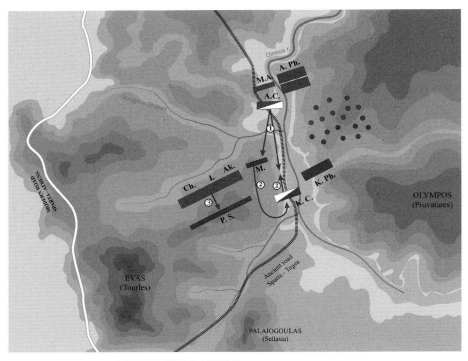

THE SECOND PHASE OF THE BATTLE
1. Philopoimen leads his cavalry against Eukleidas' mercenaries on his own initiative.
2. On Evas Hill the mercenaries retreat and rush to the cavalry's aid. The two cavalries clash in the centre.
3. All of Antigonos' right flank forces are now unhindered to assault Evas Hill. The defenders of Evas Hill attempt to confront them on the mountain ridge maintaining for themselves the advantage of the high ground.

undisturbed. According to Polybios, this was intentional by Eukleidas. He was confident that he would be able to easily repel his opponents once they reached him and so he preferred to wait for them at the top. After defeating them there, he would chase them along the steep slope in order to destroy them completely.[261] This is Polybios' view. More likely, though, Eukleidas had no better option than wait for the enemy in the higher parts of the hill. Given that the Macedonians, thanks to Philopoimen's initiative, managed to secure a firm foothold on the hill (while the Illyrians and the Akarnanians were covering the attack of the phalanx) the tactic of harassment by the defenders proved ineffective.

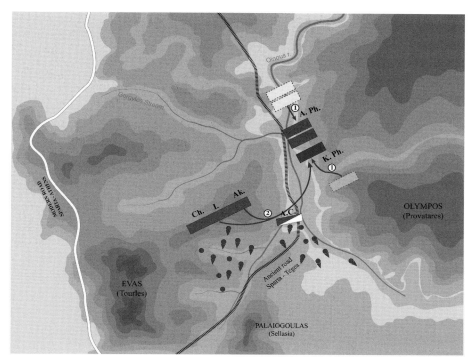

THE THIRD PHASE OF THE BATTLE

The attackers' supremacy on Evas Hill is overwhelming. The defenders are repelled and forced to retreat on the precipitous slope of the hill where they scatter.

1. Kleomenes attempts the ultimate assault with his phalanx in an effort to reverse the outcome of the battle. Antigonos counterattacks with the Macedonian phalanx. The two phalanxes clash inconclusively.
2. The forces of the victors of Evas hill now turn against Kleomenes. The Spartan phalanx is encircled and annihilated.

The conflict that followed proved the overwhelming superiority of the attackers. Despite Eukleidas' expectations, those who were repelled were not the enemy but his own troops who were forced to retreat from the top towards the reverse slope.[262] Thus they found themselves fighting on lower ground, while their enemies were stabilized at the top and then began to flank them.[263] No sooner had the entire left wing of the Spartan army been displaced from its new positions, than the retreat on the steep and precipitous slope caused them to flee in disorder. Thus Evas' defenders suffered exactly what (if we believe Polybios) they had been plotting for their enemies. Many died on the battlefield, among them Eukleidas.

During this time, Antigonos made no serious attempt to take Olympos Hill. He sent only his light troops and mercenaries there in order to harass Kleomenes who responded in the same way. So the conflict on Olympos became a series of skirmishes between the light units of the two armies but to no avail as neither of the two kings risked engaging his phalanx in a pitched battle. Kleomenes at some point realized the collapse of his left wing and was given the news of the death of his brother. He then became certain that the battle was decided. Between the two hills, his cavalry continued to resist but it was a matter of time before it also fled resulting in being encircled by the enemy. He then thought of playing his last card: he would throw in the battle his 6,000 'Spartans' in a forlorn hope to repel Antigonos' 10,000 Macedonians and to reverse the outcome of the battle. He certainly knew that an attack with a 6:10 ratio against him and against the best infantry of the time was doomed. The retreat from the battlefield while still time allowed would definitely have been wiser. Yet, Kleomenes chose to take the risk. The rescue of his army would make sense only if he defeated Antigonos. If he lost the battle, he would lose the war too.[264]

Determined to hold onto the slightest hope of success, Kleomenes gave the order to attack. If anything, he could rely on his men and their devotion to him. Most of his fighters were tested warriors who had stood by him since the beginning of his movement and had accompanied him across the Peloponnese without losing a single battle. Wouldn't they be able to accomplish this once again?

Seeing Kleomenes' phalangites emerging from their fortified positions and lining up for attack, Antigonos responded by mobilizing his own phalanx. The trumpets sounded the recall for the light troops of both sides and the two phalanxes lowered their *sarissai* and charged each other. At this last moment (acknowledged even by anti-Spartan sources)[265] all of Kleomenes' soldiers, regardless of origin proved to be true Spartans. Their attack was so fierce that the Macedonian phalanx was forced to retreat although it was more numerous and double in depth.[266] But that was not enough to reverse the outcome of the battle. The Macedonians rallied and counter-attacked repulsing the Spartan phalanx in return. The battle continued inconclusively with the two phalanxes pushing one another on Olympos, where 'the superior courage of the Lakedaimonians' succeeded for a while to counterbalance the weight of their opponents.[267] In the end, however, the impact of the Macedonian phalanx prevailed. At one point when they had the opportunity, the Macedonians changed formation to 'close order' and charged vigorously.[268] Taking advantage of the peculiar formation of the double phalanx, they managed to repel the Spartans and displace them even farther from their entrenched positions. Meanwhile, the victorious forces from

Evas had blocked every possibility of escape and, therefore, the 6,000 'Spartans' fell almost to the last man in the name of the traditions they were defending.[269]

There were, however, a few who escaped. Among them was King Kleomenes who, unwilling to accept defeat, chose to leave believing that he would have the chance to reverse the outcome of the battle in the future. Thus, another value of the 'Lykourgan' tradition was violated: for the first time in the history of Sparta, a Spartan king who had lost the battle and his army returned to the city alive.

The Aftermath

'In a sense,' notes Robert Browning,[270] 'all historical figures are tragic for us, since we know what was for them unknowable – the future.' In this respect, Kleomenes was perhaps the most consistent incarnation of the tragic hero precisely because of his stubborn refusal to accept his destiny. Beyond that, however, Kleomenes' tragic personality can be attributed to the fact that his only biography is based on the work of a predominantly 'tragic' historian who was also Kleomenes' fanatical supporter, Phylarchos. In the events that followed the fateful defeat at Sellasia, our only source, Plutarch's narrative, bears Phylarchos' strong influence and is steeped in dramatic and highly figurative style.

Phylarchos depicts the image of the defeated city in gloomy colours through the agony of the Spartan women who tried to soothe the exhausted fighters by taking away their weapons from their hands and giving them water. The main character of this drama, Kleomenes, is presented with the gentle glow of pure heroism: Phylarchos paints the picture of him refusing the tender care of his young female companion from Megalopolis, leaning on a column with his head hidden in his folded arm trying to put his thoughts in order.[271]

Certainly, many things would have concerned Kleomenes during that difficult time except for one: his violation of the Spartan code of honour that he had just committed. For fleeing from the battlefield was part of a well precontrived plan. Not only had Kleomenes foreseen the possibility of defeat but he had prepared his departure for this case. He advised his compatriots not to resist Antigonos and assured them that alive or dead he would continue to fight for Sparta. He left the city with a few faithful friends and rushed to Gytheion. There, they boarded ships that were 'provided for this very purpose'[272] and sailed for Alexandria.

This anti-heroic stance should somehow be justified. Phylarchos, loyal to the task of defending his hero, further cites a very touching passage that may well have been devised by Plutarch. This is the famous dialogue between Kleomenes and Therykion.[273]

Therykion, an old friend of Kleomenes, had a personal experience of the overthrow of the *ephors* in 227 and had a leading role in it. After the destruction of Sellasia, he fled with Kleomenes struggling between his devotion to him and his loathing of the idea of escape. When the ships moored in Aegilia (the present island of Antikythera), Therykion decided to talk to him and, taking him aside he said, 'O king, a death in battle, we have put away from us; and yet all men heard us declare that Antigonus should not pass the king of Sparta except over his dead body. But a death that is second in virtue and glory is now still in our power. Whither do we unreasoningly sail, fleeing an evil that is near and pursuing one that is far off?'

Some historians saw the above mention of suicide, which is clearly implied by Therykion, as Phylarchos' philosophical perception of Stoicism. According to the Stoic philosophical stance, suicide was the only honourable solution for Kleomenes.[274] Kleomenes' taking refuge at Ptolemy's court was equivalent to his being Antigonos' prisoner. 'But if we cannot consent to be ruled by those who have conquered us in arms,' Therykion continues, 'why should we make him [Ptolemy] our master who has not defeated us…? Or shall we say that it is on thy mother's account that we come to Egypt? Surely, thou wilt make a noble spectacle for her, and one to awaken envy, when she displays her son to the wives of Ptolemy, a captive instead of a king, and a runaway. Let us rather, while we are still masters of our own swords and can gaze upon the land of Laconia, here rid ourselves of Fortune's yoke, and make our peace with those who at Sellasia died in defence of Sparta, instead of sitting idly down in Egypt and asking every now and then whom Antigonus has left as satrap of Lacedaemon.' Kleomenes replied that death would be the easiest solution. Suicide, he said, 'Ought to be, not flight from action, but an action in itself. For it is shameful to die, as well as to live, for one's self alone…' 'I, however, think it right' concluded Kleomenes, 'that neither you nor I should abandon our hopes for our country; when these abandon us, death will be very easy if we wish it.' To this Therykion made no reply, but as soon as he got the opportunity to leave Kleomenes, 'he turned aside along the sea-beach and slew himself'.[275]

A glorious chapter in the history of Sparta closed permanently in this symbolic way. Another page would open in the life of Kleomenes and in the history of Sparta.

Alexandria

From Aegilia, Kleomenes arrived in Libya. The king's officials received him and accompanied him to Alexandria, Egypt. Kleomenes' lukewarm reception by Ptolemy must have been an unpleasant surprise. Later, the attitude of the Lagid monarch changed. Kleomenes still had the talent to enchant the people around him. The simplicity of his behaviour and the dignity with which he faced his fate quickly made Ptolemy appreciate and admire the defeated Spartan who, despite his misfortunes, had faith in himself and did not despair. He even regretted 'that he had neglected such a man and abandoned him to Antigonos, who had thereby won great glory and power'.[276]

Soon Kleomenes acquired Ptolemy's favour who assured him that 'he would send him back to Greece with ships and treasure and restore him to his kingdom'. Beyond the verbal assurances, Ptolemy gave him a substantial pension of twenty-four talents a year.[277] Kleomenes used this amount to increase his influence, making donations and bonuses to Greek mercenaries who were in Egypt.

He had no difficulty winning them over. His reputation as general and his personal charm were undeniable. All the Greek mercenaries were subject to his influence. In the meanwhile, Kleomenes kept a secret communication network with his homeland. We know of this because of the wife of Panteus who was one of Kleomenes' most loyal companions. Young Panteus had distinguished himself during his daring attack against Megalopolis. He was indeed the first to capture the city. To follow Kleomenes to Egypt, Panteus was forced to sever ties with his beautiful wife back home since her parents did not allow her to leave with him. One evening, however, she managed to escape and secretly arrived in Cape Tainaron. From there she boarded a ship bound for Egypt where she reconnected with her husband.[278]

Through his contacts in Sparta, Kleomenes was informed of the situation there. Antigonos had occupied the city but 'treated the Lacedaemonians humanely, and did not insult or mock the dignity of Sparta'.[279] He remained in Sparta for only a few days and then departed for Macedonia where the Illyrians had invaded and were pillaging.[280]

Another piece of good news was that Antigonos, for his own reasons, did not want to revive the institution of diarchy in Sparta. Therefore Kleomenes remained the sole legitimate king of Sparta and Sparta remained loyal to him.

Nevertheless, once again Fortune was not on Kleomenes' side. Before completing a full year of residence in Egypt, his protector Ptolemy III Euergetes died (221). He was succeeded by his son Ptolemy IV, who was later named Philopator. The death of Ptolemy III deprived Kleomenes of a strong supporter and changed the dynamics in the palace. Along with Philopator, a controversial figure emerged: Sosibios, Philopator's favourite.

From the beginning, the position of the new monarch was not entirely safe. His mother, the dynamic Berenice, planned to install to the throne her youngest son, Magas, who was governor of Kyrene and had the overall control of the mercenaries. Sosibios and Ptolemy began to plot their extermination in an effort to be one step ahead. In their conspiracy, they attempted to win over the mighty men of the court and, of course, they appealed to Kleomenes. The information we have about the latter's attitude is contradictory and unclear. According to Plutarch, Kleomenes tried to dissuade Ptolemy from murdering Magas.[281] Polybios argues instead that when Sosibios approached Kleomenes and promised to reward him in return for his cooperation, the latter sided with him.[282] Most likely Kleomenes tried to move diplomatically around the intrigues of the palace and exploit the situation to his advantage. When Sosibios confided to him his concerns regarding the mercenaries' attitude, Kleomenes reassured him and in a display of power, he said: 'Don't you see that there are 3,000 foreign soldiers here from the Peloponnese, and 1,000 from Crete? I have only to nod to these men, and every man of them will at once do what I want.'[283] His words impressed Sosibios so much that he decisively implemented his plans. At the same time, he realized that Kleomenes was aware of his power and was, therefore, dangerous.

With the murder of Berenice and Magas, Ptolemy IV managed to clinch his place in power. Polybios describes him as arrogant and indifferent to the problems of his people, 'absorbed in unworthy intrigues, and senseless and continuous drunkenness'.[284] Plutarch uses even harsher expressions. He says that even when he was sober, the young monarch was engaged in organizing orgiastic feasts: 'the king himself was so corrupted in spirit by wine and women that, in his soberest and most serious moments, he would celebrate religious rites and act the mountebank in his palace, timbrel in hand, while the most important affairs of the government were managed by Agathokleia, the mistress of the king, and Oenanthe her mother, who was a bawd.'[285] In reality, however, the one who ran the state was Sosibios, the most powerful man in the kingdom after Ptolemy. For Sosibios, Kleomenes' stay in Egypt equalled to the presence of a lion left alone with the sheep in the pen.[286]

In the same year (221), another event occurred which played a decisive role in Kleomenes' case. Antigonos Doson died[287] and was succeeded by seventeen-year-old Philip V. The rise of an adolescent to the Macedonian throne created the impression that Macedonian rule was weakened. The Aitolians took the opportunity to start raiding the Peloponnese and even defeated the Achaeans at Kaphyai. The Achaeans then sought Macedonia's help pleading alliance with them. This resulted in the outbreak of the Social War in 220. Evidently, the Achaeans were facing serious problems but Macedonia was not in a position to help them. The news soon reached Kleomenes who saw the new developments as an opportunity to regain his lost ground. Believing that the time for his return had come, he turned to Ptolemy IV and asked to be sent to Sparta with an army and fleet as had been promised by Ptolemy's father. To his surprise, the new monarch ignored him. Kleomenes insisted but Philopator continued keeping him in Egypt with various pretexts.

For Kleomenes, his return to Greece had become imperative. He tried to convince the king and his advisers to allow him to return if only alone to Sparta but without success. His appeals resulted in troubling the court and obviously embarrassing them regarding his case. The general assembly under Sosibios concluded that Kleomenes' withdrawal from Egypt was as unprofitable as his stay there.

Kleomenes' first request to send military power to Greece was rejected as an unnecessary expense. This would only have made sense if it caused some distraction to Antigonos' expansionist ambitions. The death of the latter, though, removed, at least temporarily, this danger for the Ptolemaic possessions in the Aegean and made this project unavailing.

Besides, Kleomenes' return to his homeland was risky. His influence and strategic genius made him superior to all his contemporaries, while his popularity, at least in Sparta, was undeniable. Knowing this, it would not have been difficult for him to extend his sovereignty even outside the boundaries of the Peloponnese. Ptolemy would then acquire a new and extremely dangerous competitor who, having lived long in the palace, knew the vulnerable spots of the regime.[288] The royal council then decided that Kleomenes no longer served the interests of the country. Even worse, he was a waste and keeping him longer in Egypt could be fatal due to his radiant personality and great power he had gained during his stay. Therefore, the only solution was to get rid of him. Yet, this would not be easy as evidenced by the way Sosibios and his supporters reacted; they did not immediately move against Kleomenes but they slandered him to Ptolemy using the following episode as an excuse.

It occurred in the harbour of Alexandria when Kleomenes was having a stroll with his two friends, Panteus and Hippitas. On the waterfront Kleomenes saw an old acquaintance disembarking, Nikagoras from Messene. He was the man who, after Agis' assassination, had hosted his brother Archidamos' in his home and had mediated to Kleomenes for Archidamos' return to Sparta. Nikagoras despised Kleomenes because (as Polybios confirms) he considered him responsible for Archidamos' murder.[289]

Plutarch, however, believes that Nikagoras' hatred had more humble motives. Nikagoras had sold Kleomenes an estate but had not been paid off for it.[290] Whatever was the case, the meeting of the two men was cordial. Nikagoras hid his real feelings from Kleomenes and Kleomenes cheerfully asked him the reason for his visit to Alexandria. When Nikagoras replied that he had come to bring war horses to Ptolemy, Kleomenes laughed and said sarcastically: 'I could wish that thou hadst rather brought *sambuka–girls* and catamites; for these now most interest the king.'[291] Thoughtlessly said, this was to be fatal for Kleomenes. Nikagoras laughed, of course, with the joke and did not comment. He later conveyed Kleomenes' words to Sosibios with whom he was doing business[292] who immediately seized the opportunity. Offering generous remuneration to Nikagoras, Sosibios persuaded him to write a letter stating that Kleomenes was allegedly plotting to overthrow the regime.[293] Sosibios arranged to bring the letter to Ptolemy four days after Nikagoras' departure so that the plot wouldn't be revealed. His plan worked out perfectly. No sooner had Ptolemy been informed of the content of the letter, than he ordered the arrest of Kleomenes and his friends. However, considering the severity of the accusation, Kleomenes' treatment was relatively lenient. He was given a large and spacious residence[294] where he lived in confinement with his companions from Sparta. His new residence had service staff and all the comforts he enjoyed before. He still had the opportunity for some indirect (presumably secret) communication with friends in the city.[295] In reality, however, he was in a lush prison facing charges of high treason with the death sentence pending.

This is how the Spartan king ended up three years after his arrival in the court of the Ptolemies. Was he a victim of conspiracy or were Sosibios' accusations valid? Polybios and Plutarch do not adequately respond to the above question while a critical analysis of the events leads to some scepticism.

Kleomenes remained in Egypt for about three years (222–219). His stay there, especially after Philopator's enthronement,[296] remains largely inexplicable. From February 221 and for more than two years, Kleomenes remained essentially inactive in Alexandria. Although he knew (as evidenced by the sources) that developments in Greece demanded his return, he wasted precious time initially trying to secure financial and military support from Philopator and later pleading permission to return alone. Yet, a man with Kleomenes' intelligence and with high connections in the royal circle should have been aware of the Lagid monarch's intentions. Consequently, the following question arises: Why did he not try to flee to Sparta? Certainly, the organization and implementation of an escape plan would have been extremely difficult but not impossible for Kleomenes, whose power and influence caused fear in Ptolemy's environment.

A man like Kleomenes who occupied such a prominent position in the court would certainly have found a way to secure the necessary means for his escape.

Moreover, Polybios and Plutarch agree that Kleomenes enjoyed great liberties in Alexandria. The episode with Nikagoras indicates that Kleomenes had the opportunity to walk in the port of the city together with friends and talk undisturbed with the visitors on the waterfront. Therefore, had there been any surveillance by Ptolemy, it would have been discreet enough to allow Kleomenes such freedom of movement.

Finally, Kleomenes must have had all the time to carefully arrange his escape. The presence of his family in Alexandria was certainly an added difficulty but Kleomenes always had the choice to leave alone. In this case, he would have left his relatives at the mercy of Ptolemy but this would not have been a problem for him since he had already done the same in the past. Therefore, according to all indications, Kleomenes' stay in Egypt was deliberate and was associated with some conspiracy. Were those who accused him of plotting to seize Kyrene[297] or even to overthrow Ptolemy right in doing so?[298] Unfortunately, these questions will remain unanswered although Kleomenes' subsequent attitude leans towards the second possibility. Whatever his plans may have been, it is certain that they were thwarted thanks to Sosibios' timely intervention. Unfortunately, for Kleomenes, Therykion's judgment was vindicated.

The Suicide

Among Kleomenes' high connections was a member of the palace, Ptolemy, son of Chrysermos. The two men had long since developed great familiarity and candour in their relationship. Wanting to investigate Philopator's intentions, Kleomenes asked Ptolemy, son of Chrysermos, to visit him. When he came, Kleomenes entrusted his concerns to him regarding the outcome of his case. The courtier tried to justify King Ptolemy's stance and reassured Kleomenes. Yet, his assurances did not persuade the Spartan king. Thus, as he was leaving, Kleomenes secretly watched him and listened to his conversation with the guards. The courtier severely reprimanded them and recommended that they guard Kleomenes more carefully describing him as a 'great wild beast that was so hard to keep'.[299] Kleomenes realized the Lagid monarch was up to no good. He called his companions and discussed the situation with them. He did not have to try very hard to convince them to escape. Their plan was facilitated by the fact that King Ptolemy was absent at that time in the suburb of Kanopos, outside of Alexandria. Kleomenes spread the rumour that the king planned to set him free. His friends in the city helped him in this. They sent him gifts and delicacies which supposedly were being offered by the king in prospect of his release. Kleomenes accepted them with feigned gratitude giving the impression to the guards that the time for his release was drawing near.

According to Plutarch, Kleomenes feared that his plan might be revealed by a servant and decided to hasten his escape. At the appointed day, he offered the guards a lavish meal and plenty of wine and managed to easily intoxicate them. He stripped the seam of his robe, let it fall free on his right shoulder and took the sword in his hand. So did his twelve friends. Then they went out to the streets of Alexandria. It was midday. Hippitas, who was lame and had trouble following them, asked to be killed so as not to delay the others. They grabbed the horse of a passer-by, put Hippitas on it and together continued their march. They did not head to the port, though, neither did they seek to move in secrecy. Instead, they proceeded in a blatant fashion to confirm all their heavy charges. Under the light of the midday sun, Kleomenes and his twelve companions started running in the streets calling on the people to unite with them against Ptolemy. Was this a desperate impulse or an organized plan that was implemented prematurely because of circumstances?[300] In any case, Kleomenes' estimation regarding the response of the city's inhabitants proved wrong. The Alexandrians were observing the reckless team in amazement and fear but did not respond to their appeals. As Plutarch notes sarcastically: 'These had enough courage, as it would seem to admire and praise the daring of Kleomenes, but not a man was bold enough to follow and help him.'[301]

Along the way, Kleomenes and his friends met the courtier Ptolemy, son of Chrysermos. Immediately, three of them fell on him and killed him. The same fate befell the governor of the city, who was also called Ptolemy. They saw him on his chariot coming against them with the city garrison. They then pounced on him and after scattering the guards and his entourage threw him from his chariot and killed him.

When Kleomenes realized that the Alexandrians were not going to follow him, it was already too late. He had wasted valuable time with his fruitless wandering up and down the streets and so the authorities managed to mobilize against him. Even if he had meant to escape, he was no longer able to do so. Yet, until the last minute, Kleomenes insisted on his original plan to overthrow Ptolemy. Not being able to win the people over, he tried to get support from the prisoners. The thirteen Spartans ran to the citadel of the city where the prison was located in order to liberate the prisoners. It was a desperate attempt which also resulted in dishonourable failure. Arriving at the jail, they found the gates well locked and the guards on full alert.[302]

After this, Kleomenes realized that it was all over. His only option was to carry out the plan that Therykion had recommended three years earlier. So the Spartan king and his twelve comrades committed suicide one after another with their own daggers. The suicide scene and its aftermath are described vividly by Phylarchos and are escalated to an emotional climax like the last act of a tragedy. Panteus, Kleomenes' dear friend took on the sad duty of killing himself last after making sure that the others were already dead. 'At last all the rest lay prostrate on the ground, and Panteus, going up to each one in turn and pricking him with his sword, sought to discover whether any spark of life remained. When he pricked Kleomenes in the ankle and saw that his face twitched, he kissed him, and sat down by his side; at last the end came, and after embracing the king's dead body, he slew himself upon it.'[303]

Phylarchos ends his story with a description of the massacre of Kleomenes' children, women and companions. The women hold, as in the case of Agis, the role of the tragic heroines. Shortly before her execution, Kratesikleia who had been informed of Kleomenes' death, sees her dead grandchildren and exclaims: 'O children whither are ye gone?' His wife was left last, like her husband, to casually cover the corpses of the other women in an effort to maintain their decency until the last moment.[304]

Unfortunately, Kleomenes' body was not spared the pillory. Ptolemy ordered that the corpse be hanged on a cross and left exposed to the sight of the Alexandrian mob.[305]

'In War'

'History must regret that Cleomenes had not died with his Spartans at Sellasia' William Tarn sombrely notes.[306] Undoubtedly, if Kleomenes had fallen on the battlefield, he would have had an end worthy of his career and his fame. Nevertheless, this is the last in a series of questions arising from the fatal battle of Sellasia.

Kleomenes lost everything at Sellasia. This battle is a dismal landmark in Spartan history since it resulted in the capture of the city for the first time in her history.

There are many questions concerning the events even before the start of the battle. Both Plutarch and Polybios[307] assert that if the battle had been delayed a few days, it would not have occurred at all as Antigonos would have returned to Macedonia to confront the Dardanian invaders. But then again, the coincidences are too important to go unnoticed. If at the start of the battle Kleomenes had perceived Antigonos' stratagem, if Philopoimen had not taken the initiative to lead the attack in the centre thus reversing the result of the battle, if, in other words, Fortune had not turned her back to Kleomenes, perhaps the outcome of the battle may have been different and Sparta may have been saved. What would have happened in this case, though? What were the odds of Kleomenes taking control of the Peloponnese again in order to materialize on behalf of Sparta what Aratos had dreamed for the Achaean League? Would such a prospect have been fruitful? Could Kleomenes' Sparta have functioned as a unifying power that could solve the problems of the Peloponnese, or even Greece?

As attractive as such a prospect may seem, the answer is emphatically negative. No, Sparta did not have the potential to bear the burden of such a mission. It is true that the city had regained much of her former power and radiance but she still remained a city-state with limited capabilities. Although Sparta scaled large for Peloponnesian standards, she was no match for Macedonia. Therefore, even if Antigonos had withdrawn from the Peloponnese for any reason, the Macedonians sooner or later would have returned (as they did later with Philip V) and Kleomenes would have had to confront them again under worse conditions since the Macedonians retained the support of their allies while Kleomenes had lost it.

Surely things would have been very different if Kleomenes had had the support of the Peloponnesian cities provided he extended the social reforms outside the boundaries of his homeland. But this was not the Spartan king's intention. The problem was that Kleomenes was not a social revolutionary to the same extent that he was a Spartan. His reforms were aimed solely at reinforcing Sparta's hegemony. Yet, the Greek cities had experienced the Spartan hegemony and had later abolished it with great relief. No one longed for the time that Sparta treated the Greek cities as subordinates imposing on them despised *decarchies* and Spartan *harmosts* and launching punitive expeditions against anyone who did not comply with her orders. Only Sparta would benefit from Kleomenes' victory; for the other Greek city-states 'it would be a setback of two centuries'.[308] Certainly, this was not what the poor citizens of Peloponnese – who had supported Kleomenes and Sparta – were seeking, for what they needed was 'land redistribution' and 'debt cancellation'. They had been enticed to support Kleomenes in hope that these two reforms would be implemented in their cities since they already had been implemented in Sparta. When they were disillusioned, they abandoned him. On the contrary, the fear that Kleomenes' social reforms would extend outside Sparta turned the affluent leaders of the Achaean League against him resulting in a devastating war that ended with Antigonos' intervention and the Macedonians becoming the regulators in Peloponnesian affairs.

"Olbiadas in war." A typical tombstone dedicated to a Spartan warrior who fell in battle. The tombstone was excavated from Pellana, Sparta and is now exhibited at the Museum of Sparta.

In fact, the only positive outlook for the Peloponnese was the reconciliation between Sparta and the Achaean League. But Kleomenes' obsession in securing Spartan hegemony combined with Aratos' intransigent attitude and his aversion to any social reform, rendered such a prospect impossible.

After all, the above hypotheses come to an end knowing the result of the battle. Sellasia was perhaps the greatest disaster in Sparta's history, so her failure in the struggle for hegemony looms as the least harmful effect. In Sellasia Sparta lost everything but her king who preferred to seek his fortune elsewhere, abandoning her to the mercy of her enemies.

It is true that nothing would have changed for Sparta if Kleomenes had been killed at Sellasia instead of committing suicide three years later in a foreign land. For him though, it would have made a great difference if he had been buried in the soil of his homeland under a marble headstone bearing the brief inscription: 'Kleomenes in war.'[309]

Chapter Three

Eclipse

*Defeat steels the hearts of the brave; it sorts them out; it selects all that are pure
and strong and makes them even purer and stronger. But it accelerates the fall
of all else or it devastates them. And so it separates the submissive masses from
the brave souls that continue their march.*

Romain Rolland, *Jean Christoff*

The destruction of Sellasia brought Sparta back to the state she was
a century before, just after her territorial mutilation by Philip II in
338/337. Once again the city lost her strategically important border
areas of Belminatis in the north, Dentheliatis in the west and all the areas on
the east side of Mount Parnon. Nonetheless, Polybios and Plutarch praised
the 'generosity' and 'philanthropy' that Antigonos showed to the defeated
city.[1] It is true that Antigonos did not retaliate and Sparta was not ransacked as
Orchomenos had been before nor did she suffer atrocities as Mantineia.[2] In this
sense, his behaviour towards Sparta can certainly be described as 'magnanimous'.
After stifling the Kleomenean *stasis*, Antigonos had no particular reason to
act vindictively against the Spartans.[3] His goal was more the restoration of
Macedonian rule in the Peloponnese and less the destruction of Sparta since,
although weak, she was still an obstacle in the expansionist ambitions of the
Achaean League.[4]

Before departing from Sparta, Antigonos saw to ensure that the city would not
cause any further problems. Sparta joined the 'Hellenic League'[5] and Antigonos
assigned her a garrison under Brachyllas from Boiotia who was 'charged with
cleansing Sparta of the Cleomenean virus'.[6] By and large, Kleomenes' political
reforms were abolished and the institution of the *ephors* was restored.[7] The
new pro-Macedonian leadership of Sparta, combined with the presence of the
Macedonian garrison, guaranteed her stability and her future pro-Macedonian
stance.[8] In fact, the situation was very different and much more complex than
what Antigonos would have wanted. It is understood that a number of Spartans
were positively predisposed towards him. Most of them belonged to the wealthy
minority that Kleomenes had sought to eliminate. Some others may simply have

benefited by the new realignment.[9] The losses of Sellasia left many *kleroi* vacant. A large percentage of them may have been incorporated with the properties of the exiled wealthy proprietors who, after their return from exile, had formed the new ruling class.[10]

However, the supporters of Antigonos' restoration consisted only a small minority of the inhabitants of Sparta because from the moment they saw their king leave for Egypt, most Spartans yearned for his return. Polybios cannot hide his bitterness at the fact that the Spartans resented the Achaeans and were ungrateful towards the Macedonians out of love for Kleomenes: 'Their motives for doing all this, for incurring the enmity of the Achaeans, for their ingratitude to the Macedonians, and generally for their unjustifiable conduct towards all, was before everything else their devotion to Cleomenes, and the hopes and expectations they continued to cherish that he would return to Sparta in safety.'[11] For Kleomenes' followers, a compromise with the restoration of the 'old regime' was impossible. Moreover, the memories of the time when Sparta dominated the Peloponnese were too strong and too recent to be obliterated. All Spartans, especially the youth, desired the restoration of the military and political power of their homeland.[12] It is probable that even among the socially privileged from the new regime there were many who resented the idea of surrendering to the Achaeans and the Macedonians. One thing was certain: behind the apparent calm and restoration of order, Sparta was a boiling cauldron. And it burst at the first opportunity.

In 220, the Peloponnese was shaken by a new great war referred to as the Social War. The main adversaries were the Achaeans and the Aitolian League. In an effort to ensure allies in the war with the Achaeans, the Aitolians came to a secret agreement with the anti-Macedonian faction in Sparta, since after all it was the most powerful faction in the city.

Similarly, the Achaeans appealed to the Macedonians requesting the activation of their mutual alliance. At the same time, they officially requested assistance from Sparta. The force that she sent them was purely symbolic. The city essentially did not participate in combat operations.[13] On the contrary the new king of Macedonia, the young Philip V, acted with surprising energy. He moved south, arrived in Corinth where he met with members of the Hellenic League and hearing from them that the situation in Sparta was tense rushed there. Philip's imminent arrival resulted in an outburst of riots between the pro-Macedonian faction and the anti-Macedonian one, which controlled three of the five *ephors*. Adeimantos, one of the *ephors*, as well as some other supporters of the pro-Macedonian faction were slaughtered, while others fled seeking refuge with the Macedonians. When the Spartans finally came to understand that they were dangerously playing their hand and as Philip had arrived in Tegea, they rushed to come to a compromise with him. They sent him a ten member delegation which tried to put the blame on the murdered Adeimantos and assured Philip that Sparta remained loyal to the League.

After the Spartan ambassadors had left, the royal advisers suggested two solutions to Philip: to either eradicate Sparta, as Alexander had done to Thebes, or to put her under direct Macedonian military control.[14] He thought that it would be wiser not to retaliate and as a good will gesture he left, considering that a sworn ratification of allegiance by the Spartans would suffice. He also acted on grounds of political expediency. At this time, Philip wished that the involvement of the Greek states in the Hellenic League be voluntary and not coercive.[15] Furthermore, the absolute weakening of Sparta would have rendered the Achaeans rulers of the Peloponnese, something that Philip, like Antigonos before him, wanted to avoid.[16]

The situation in Sparta was now bursting with hostility and would soon lead to open conflict between both the pro-Macedonian and anti-Macedonian factions. The following year (219), the Aitolian Machatas came to Sparta officially invited by Kleomenes' supporters and proposed an alliance with the Aitolian League. When the powerful pro-Macedonian faction in control of the city expelled him, Kleomenes' supporters decided to follow their exiled king's example and move forcefully to overthrow the regime. The conspirators, the majority of whom were 'young', suddenly attacked the *ephors* during a ceremony and slaughtered them along with some of the *gerontes*. This time the massacre occurred in the sanctuary of Athena Chalkioikos that had never been violated before.[17] All other supporters of the pro-Macedonian faction were exiled. New *ephors* were elected and Sparta formally allied with the Aitolians. It is around this time that Kleomenes attempted to overthrow Ptolemy in Egypt.[18] When the news of his death reached Sparta in 219, the *ephors* decided to restore the dual kingship. The new kings were Agesipolis III of the Agiadai[19] and Lykourgos of the Eurypontidai. Since the first was a minor, the power passed essentially to Lykourgos.[20] According to Polybios' testimony the latter had no relation with the royal house and attained the throne by bribing the *ephors* giving each of them one talent.[21] If this is not an exaggeration coming from Polybios' resentment, then the fact that Lykourgos was extremely wealthy is indicative of the socio-economic changes that had taken place in Sparta in the last three years. Kleomenes' system of equality was now history.

However, already from the beginning it appeared that the new king sought to emulate Kleomenes, at least in foreign policy. He sought to retrieve vital areas that Antigonos had detached from Sparta. Amongst them were Dentheliatis as well as the entire area east of Mount Parnon. Thus, in the summer of 219, three years after the defeat of Sellasia, the Spartan army resumed offensive activity.[22] Lykourgos invaded the eastern area of Mount Parnon and captured several *perioikic* cities among which were Polichne, Prasiai, Kyphanta and Leukai. Then, following in Kleomenes' footsteps, he attacked and recaptured Athenaion, thus ensuring control of Belminatis to a big extent. The Achaeans, who were pressed by the Aitolians and Eleans, seemed completely unable to confront him.[23] For the second time, Philip V took them out of this difficult position and immediately rushed to help. The Macedonian army invaded Peloponnese again and, after first occupying Triphylia, arrived in Megalopolis in mid-winter of 219–218.

In the meantime, Lykourgos was overthrown by an internal conspiracy. A man named Chilon, also a descendant of the Eurypontidai royal house, considered Lykourgos' election to the throne unfair and so attempted to seize power. Following what had by then become common practice, he slew the *ephors* and tried to assassinate Lykourgos. The latter managed to survive at the last minute and took refuge in Pellana. Chilon then appealed to the people and tried to ensure their support by reviving the 'Kleomenean' promise of social reform. However, not only did the population of Sparta not live up to his expectations of support, but when he and his two hundred followers went to the *agora*, they were faced with hostility and forced to flee secretly from Sparta.[24] According to Polybios, Chilon sought refuge in Achaea, a rather strange and somewhat suspicious choice.[25]

The overthrow of Lykourgos and the presence of the Macedonian army in Megalopolis resulted in the withdrawal of the Spartans from Athenaion but only after razing it. Once again, Philip did not move against Sparta. Having removed the threat to the southern border of his Achaean allies, he spent the rest of the winter in Argos and then departed for Macedonia.

After the failure of Chilon's *stasis*, Lykourgos returned to Sparta and continued his aggressive policy. In the summer of 218, the Spartan army invaded Messenia and later seized Tegea forcing the residents to seek refuge in the acropolis of the city.[26] These operations, which did not seem to follow any overall strategic planning, had no notable effect. Yet, they triggered an intervention by Philip for the third time, and this time it was decisive. Philip marched to the Peloponnese once again and, moving with surprising speed, appeared with his army at Tegea. From there he invaded Lakonia. This time the Messenians were among his allies. Their forces moved to Tegea in order to unite with Philip's army, however, they did not manage to reach Tegea in

Menelaion, the shrine of Helen and Menlaos.

time but were attacked and scattered by Lykourgos, who gained many spoils.[27] Meanwhile, Philip invaded Lakonia and moved along the valley of the River Eurotas plundering and destroying the area up to Cape Tainaron. He then headed back towards Sparta and arrived at her southernmost *kome*, Amyklai. Lykourgos, emboldened by his recent success, decided not to allow Philip to leave Spartan territory without a fight.[28] The battle took place at Menelaion, a sacred area standing on rough and difficult hills, a few miles outside of Sparta. Lykourgos had posted 2,000 men around the Menelaion Hill commanding all the area between the River Eurotas and Sparta. The rest of his forces were ordered to wait in Sparta and attack at his signal. Lykourgos had also blocked the flow of the Eurotas, so as to make it flood the valley between Menelaion and Sparta. Coming from the south, the Macedonians would have to move through the muddy ground, therefore being exposed to flank attacks from Sparta and from the Menelaion Hills. However it turned out that Lykourgos' stratagem was not good enough to match the superior Macedonian tactics. Philip first attacked Menelaion and with a combined attack by his mercenaries, his *peltasts* and the Illyrians, he managed to dislodge the defenders from the hills. Lykourgos' defence collapsed almost immediately and the Spartans fled, leaving 100 dead

THE BATTLE OF MENELAEION

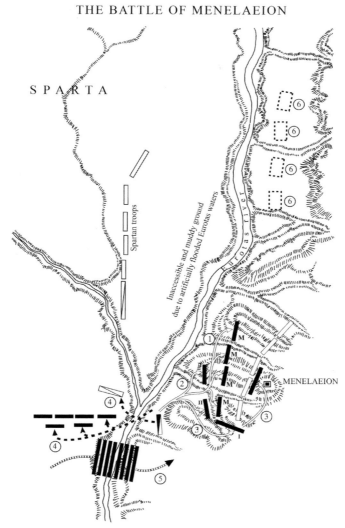

The battle of Menelaion. Philip V's assault at Menelaion is a typical example of Macedonian tactics for the occupation of a strong fortified position. It was a combination of light and heavy infantry. During the assault at Menelaion, Philip V used light infantry of mercenaries (M), Illyrians (I) and the renowned unit of "peltasts" (P). The mercenaries assaulted the slope frontally (1) followed by the peltasts (2), while the Illyrians attempted to encircle the defenders' positions forcing them to flee (Pol.5.23.4). Next, Philip left the Illyrians on the hill and crossed Eurotas river with his mercenaries and peltasts in order to cover the slow advance of the Macedonian phalanx (5). After his victory, Philip with his army marched to Menelaion hill and camped right across from Sparta (6).

and an even greater number of captives on the battlefield. Philip posted the Illyrians on Menelaion and with his *peltasts*, the light infantry and part of his cavalry quickly crossed the Eurotas in order to cover the slow advance of his heavy phalanx behind them. The Spartans sortied from Sparta and attacked Philip's force in an attempt to stop him. Yet, they were forced to flee, and by sunset Philip was the master of the battlefield.[29]

Again Philip did not attempt to seize Sparta. It was enough for him to display his power by deploying his army provocatively in front of the city. Since the Spartans did not dare to confront him again, he retired to Sellasia, where he visited the battlefield. There he ostentatiously celebrated Antigonos' victory by sacrificing on Olympos and Evas hills and then departed, leaving Lakonia devastated and Sparta humiliated.[30]

These events led again to Lykourgos' overthrow. This time he was accused of attempting revolution. The *ephors* tried arresting him but he fled to Aitolia.[31] Later, however, he was recalled and in the summer of 217 he invaded Messenia once again at the head of a newly raised military force. At the same time the Aitolians and Eleians invaded Messenia from the north. While Lykourgos succeeded in seizing Kalamai, his allies were defeated, thus forcing him to return to Sparta empty-handed. Shortly afterwards the Social War ended and thus deprived Lykourgos of the pretext for any further aggressive activities.

No other facts are known regarding the controversial figure of Lykourgos, who reigned in Sparta for another seven years until 210. Some historians believe that the Kleomenean faction returned to power during his reign.[32] Others, however, regard Lykourgos as a prime representative of the reactionaries and of the interests of the well-to-do. To them it was Chilon who represented the Kleomenean faction and not Lykourgos.[33] Of course, these theories are rather conjectures since the available evidence is insufficient to support either of them. The only thing that is apparent from both Lykourgos' aggressive policy and Chilon's revolutionary declarations is the profound impact of the Kleomenean revolution, and its enduring appeal to the Spartans.

The peace that prevailed with the end of the Social War did not last long. Two years after making peace, Philip V took a decision that was to seal the fate of Greece in the future. Influenced by the spectacular victories of Hannibal at Lake Trasimene and Cannae, Philip decided to become his ally (215). In an effort to offset the threat, Rome sought support from Greece and in 212–211 an alliance was established with the Aitolians, the main enemies of the Macedonians. The Aitolians turned once again to Sparta to ask her to join the alliance. The prospect of joining an anti-Macedonian (and therefore anti-Achaean) coalition was something that Sparta could not ignore. Thus the following year she joined the Roman-Aitolian alliance and two years later resumed hostilities with the Achaeans (208). Leader of the Spartans at the time was a man named Machanidas, who had come to power the previous year, after Lykourgos' death (possibly as guardian of Lykourgos' underage son Pelops).[34] Little is known about him, and some sources characterize him as a tyrant who most likely began his career as the leader of the mercenaries of the Spartan army.[35]

In the beginning, Machanidas achieved successes that can be considered major achievements – under the circumstances – managing to recapture Belminatis and seize Tegea. His army invaded Argolis and even reached Argos. The Achaeans again requested the assistance of Philip V but this time the salvation came from the general of the Achaean League, Philopoimen. For the first time since 223, the Achaeans would face the Spartans without foreign aid. Philopoimen had realized early on that the Achaean League was in great need of a powerful army. This was the only way to detach itself from the guardianship of Macedonia. Two years earlier, when he was still serving as the cavalry commander (*hipparchos*) of the League, he had applied himself to the radical reorganization of the Achaean cavalry so that it would be effective and able to perform complex manoeuvres.[36] When he became general, he attempted to do the same with the Achaean infantry, devoting the first eight months of his *strategia* to this purpose. He replaced the old equipment of the light armed Achaean infantry with the heavy armoury of the infantry of the Macedonian phalanx. Then Philopoimen assumed himself the training of the Achaean infantry in the new battle tactics.[37]

In the spring of 207 Philopoimen's new Achaean army, with its morale restored and reinforced with a large number of mercenaries, faced Machanida's army in Mantineia. There are no reports of the rival forces, yet they were estimated to be equivalent, about 14,000 men on each side.[38]

The description of the battle comes from Polybios. It is animated and dramatic, yet extremely tinged with biases in favour of the Achaeans.[39] Polybios, violating the rules of historical writing that he himself had established,[40] openly supports his compatriot Philopoimen, presenting him as the defender of freedom of all residents of the Peloponnese against the oppressive aspirations of a loathsome tyrant.[41]

Philopoimen deployed the light armed mercenaries on the left flank. The heavy infantry of the phalanx was deployed in the centre, behind a broad and deep but dry and gentle sided ditch, and on the right flank the Achaean cavalry. Machanidas deployed his own mercenaries on his right wing opposite Philopoimen's mercenaries. On the left he placed the Spartan infantry of the phalanx. In the centre and in front of the rows of the phalanx he mounted catapults which he used against the phalanx of the Achaean army. This was a major military innovation which quickly put the Achaeans in a difficult position.[42] To avoid more damage from the enemy missiles, Philopoimen ordered the light units and the mercenaries to attack. Immediately Machanidas led his own mercenaries into a counterattack and after a fierce conflict succeeded in putting the Achaean units to flight.[43] The result was the collapse of the entire left flank of Philopoimen's army. At this point, however, Machanidas committed a fatal error: he proceeded recklessly to pursue the fleeing opponents, thus losing control of the situation. In his absence and of its own accord, the Spartan phalanx, emboldened by the retreat of the Achaean left flank, launched itself in an uncoordinated charge at the Achaean phalanx which was deployed behind the ditch.

Philopoimen calmly kept the Achaean phalanx drawn up behind the ditch, redeploying its ranks so that it could take its attackers in flank. As the Spartans were attempting to cross the ditch, their ranks naturally lost their cohesion. At that moment, Philopoimen ordered the Achaean phalanx to charge. The Spartans were caught trapped in a ditch that hindered both their advance and their retreat, and massively defeated. When Machanidas returned from his fruitless pursuit, he found his army in full retreat and himself trapped on the wrong side of the ditch, which was controlled by the Achaeans. In his desperate attempt to cross it, he was spotted by Philopoimen who, after an eventful chase, killed and beheaded him.[44]

It is certain, however, that the outcome of the battle was decided not by Philopoimen's strategy but, as acknowledged by Polybios as well, by the mistakes of his opponent. Machanidas' mindless pursuit of Philopoimen's light troops and the equally imprudent assault of the Spartan phalanx on the Achaeans centre, proved catastrophic. Undoubtedly, the Spartans greatly underestimated their foes and paid dearly for it. The Achaeans would not be easy opponents thereafter.[45] But after the defeat at Mantineia this fact was of little importance. In this battle, beyond her leader, Sparta had lost the greatest part of her army,[46] which would be extremely difficult to replace.

Immediately after the battle, Philopoimen captured Tegea and then invaded Lakonia, where his troops engaged in the plundering of the countryside. However, no effort was made to take Sparta, presumably because he knew that it was an extremely difficult task. It is remarkable that even Epameinondas avoided a direct assault on the city despite his overwhelming victory at Leuktra. Instead, he provided for her weakening by detaching Arcadia and Messenia from her domain. Yet again, as the Theban warlord foresaw – and Pyrrhos bitterly experienced a century later – Sparta had two advantages that counterbalanced her assailants' military superiority: her location that worked as a natural fortress and the determination of her defenders.

According to Errington, as impressive as Philopoimen's victory may have been, it was not a decisive blow to Sparta where a surprisingly large percentage of the Spartan population still believed that they had not been defeated by the Achaeans and remained adamantly anti-Achaean. If Machanidas had not perished, the Achaeans would have little more than a tactical victory to boast of.[47] However, this claim is not entirely correct. The defeat at Mantineia might not have bent the Spartans but the losses of the battle were so heavy that the city would never be able to recover. Thereinafter the Spartan army would strictly avoid confrontation with the enemy in an open field, while the few times it dared do so, it was easily dispersed. This fact, and the lack of historic references to heavy units, makes it likely that after Mantineia the heavy infantry of the phalanx ceased to be the main striking force of the Spartan army.

The fact that after the destruction of Mantineia Sparta maintained her independence was the only essential difference from the consequences of the destruction at Sellasia fifteen years earlier. Sparta became again a city without an army, unable to protect her territory and with her independence at stake.

It is truly remarkable that Sparta managed not only to survive but to recover her glory for a second time and reassert her leading role in Greece. This was exclusively the work of the last of Sparta's great kings, none other than Nabis, son of Demaratos.

Chapter Four

Twilight

Ancient history has little room and less sympathy for lost causes. When a lost cause does earn a paragraph, it is treated from the point of view of the prevailing order, and, consciously or not, writers distort the facts to accord with the sympathies of the prevailing order

Moses Hadas[1]

The 'Last of the Spartans'

If it is true that history is written by the victors, then Nabis is the most typical example. All the information that has reached us about him comes from his enemies' camp, the primary source being Polybios, whose hatred for Nabis permeates every reference to him. In his portrait of Nabis, Polybios uses the gloomiest colours, referring to him as a greedy and bloodthirsty tyrant, responsible for horrendous crimes and the inhuman murder of his opponents. Nabis is unfortunately defenceless against these accusations, since no counterarguments have been salvaged by a sympathetic historian. Unlike Kleomenes, Nabis did not have his own Phylarchos, and all information available on him comes from historians after Polybios who adopt the latter's views, leaving the indelible stigma of 'the abominable tyrant'.[2] But how impartial is the view of a historian who consciously sides with the opposite camp?

In his early years, the Megalopolitan Polybios experienced his homelands' war against Nabis' Sparta, during which the Spartan army attempted to seize his city.[3] Polybios was the son of Lykortas, the prominent general of the Achaean League. Like his father, he was a passionate admirer of Aratos and Philopoimen, the latter being the man who abolished the Spartan constitution. As in the case of Kleomenes, Polybios' animosity towards Nabis is easily understood: simply the fact that Nabis was a Spartan and an enemy of the Achaean League was enough.

However, Polybios' malicious criticism of Nabis is more overt and much more intense than the criticism that he directs at Kleomenes. This is no coincidence. Apart from being a Megalopolitan and an ardent advocate of the Achaean League,

Polybios was consciously a representative of his class, the wealthy oligarchy, and therefore an opponent of every social reform. Kleomenes' reforms were reprehensible in the eyes of Polybios, but were nonetheless confined within Sparta. But spreading to the other cities a revolutionary movement which appealed to the masses was something that Polybios could not forgive. Much more than Kleomenes, Nabis represented a deadly threat to all the values that the noble-born historian from Megalopolis believed in.[4]

The restoration of Nabis' reputation began only in the early twentieth century. Modern historians, free from prejudice and Polybios' hostility, rejected his portrait of the Spartan king 'as mere caricature'.[5] Some did not even hesitate to recognize in Nabis the 'last of the Spartans'.[6] But more than that, Nabis was a great politician who 'not merely achieved a measure of domestic stability and prosperity but also acquired an international standing which made him briefly the focus of 'big politics' in the entire eastern Mediterranean world.'[7]

The Climax of the Revolution

Little is known about Nabis until the year he came to power. According to all indications, he descended from the royal house of the Eurypontidai.[8] His birth is placed between 250 and 240,[9] which means that the first two decades of his life were marked by Kleomenes' revolution and that perhaps he fought under his command.[10]

For the fifteen troubled years that followed the battle of Sellasia, there is no documentation of his life or of his actions. Based on his subsequent politics, it is logical to suppose that this time must have been one of intense internal debate for him over how to overcome the crisis which had befallen his homeland. It is certain that when he came to power, he had already fully formed his own basic political principles. From the first moment he was faced with the problem of shortage of manpower, the everlasting plague of Sparta which had become more crucial than ever after the destruction of Mantineia. In a period of fifteen years, more than 10,000 warriors, most of whom were Spartans, perished in war.[11] The replenishment of human resources in Sparta demanded radical action, similar to that Kleomenes had applied in the past. Nabis targeted the class of wealthy Spartans, which had been re-established after the fall of Kleomenes.[12] Those who were regarded as prominent, either because of their wealth or their glorious lineage, were banished and their property was confiscated. On this point Nabis proved a worthy successor to Kleomenes' policy. But Nabis went further than that: the beneficiaries of the re-allotment of the confiscated property were not limited to 'inferiors'[13] and mercenaries,[14] but also to helots[15] who were given

Spartan citizenship. He even forced the wives and daughters of the exiled men to marry the new landowners in order to legitimize the rights of his supporters over the property of the previous owners.[16] Nabis' actions were revolutionary, unprecedented and in complete contrast with the Spartan traditions. Especially the integration of the helots in the citizen body had until then been unthinkable. Even their emancipation was a temporary measure which was taken under exceptional circumstances. When Kleomenes resorted to emancipating the helots in 222 apparently without giving them citizenship, he did it under the pressure of needing to increase his army's size in order to secure the means to face Antigonos. For Kleomenes, this measure was only a last resort, and in fact it reveals how desperate his situation was. On the contrary, in Nabis' case, it seems that it was intentionally done in the context of his general policy. In this way he managed in a short time to maximize the benefits of using the populous class of the helots to increase the population of the city and as a consequence the size of her army. The repercussions of this opening towards the helots were certainly much larger. There is no doubt that with this measure the institution of helotage received a decisive blow, while simultaneously it was an important step towards the elimination of the dividing lines between the restricted and strictly distinct classes of Spartan society.

An important question is whether Nabis liberated or even integrated all of the helots or only part of them. There is no unanimous consensus by historians on this subject, either. Some hold that Nabis enfranchised all the helots – and only them – to the Spartan citizen body. Thus the population of Sparta became more socially uniform, and the Spartan society was reorganized. At the top of the new social pyramid stood the king and his entourage, next came all the Greek population of Lakonia (the old Spartans, the former helots and the *perioikoi*), and in the base of the pyramid were the slaves of alien origin.[17]

However, the above hypothesis presents some serious flaws, such as the problem of finding *kleroi* for an excessively large number of new citizens. Equally serious is the problem of tending the land. Who would cultivate the *kleroi* after integrating all the helots? Would foreign slaves be imported or would the new citizens cultivate their own land?

According to another hypothesis, Nabis freed all the helots from servitude but included only a part of them in the Spartan citizen body.[18] The truth, however, is that there are references to the preservation of helotage. According to Livy, when Nabis was forced to confront the invading Romans in 195, he pre-emptively purged Sparta of the distrustful helots. This means that twelve years after his rise to power, the institution was still in effect.[19] The existence of the helots is corroborated by Strabo's account that the institution existed until the Roman conquest.[20] Moreover, Strabo mentions that the helots along with the *perioikoi* were the first to turn to the Romans for help, something which would logically not have happened if all the helots had become citizens or had been emancipated.[21]

The fact is that when Nabis proclaimed a general conscription in 195, he raised a force of 10,000 'Spartans' which included the former helots.[22] Given that the total number of helots before Nabis' reforms was much higher than 10,000, if most of them had been integrated in the Spartan citizen body, he would have been able to recruit a much larger army. It is, therefore, most likely that helotage was maintained to some extent. But who were the helots fortunate enough to become 'Spartans' after all? Most probably, only the helots who used to work on the estates of the wealthy – against whom the revolution had been directed – were emancipated.[23] Regardless of the above, the integration of a helot in Spartan society must have occurred after some form of evaluation that took into account his physical condition, as had happened under Agis' and Kleomenes' reforms: above all, the new citizens had to be capable soldiers.[24]

However, regardless of the extent to which the measure applied, the integration of the helots into the Spartan citizen body meant that in the long run the age-old nightmare of Sparta, namely her 'enemy within' would be neutralized. Respectively, the inclusion of a large number of mercenaries helped remove their threat to the safety and the internal peace of the city as well.[25] As it turned out later, the newly integrated citizens of any origin defended Sparta with passion and dedication.[26]

Nabis' stance towards the *perioikoi* is not known. There are some sparse references to this matter, which unfortunately are contradictory and provide no information on the integration of the *perioikoi* into the Spartan society. Some explain it in the context of Nabis' expanding his navy, which would have been manned with *perioikoi* coming from the coastal cities of Lakonia.[27] According to Livy, notably many of them were among Nabis' best troops,[28] and indeed most *perioikic* cities stubbornly resisted the Romans in 195. However, later on, some of these cities also resisted Nabis when he attempted to take them back under his control. One possible explanation is that there may have been both sympathizers and opponents to Nabis' rule in the *perioikic* cities, as it also happened in other cities of the Peloponnese. But certainly his social reforms 'did not affect the *perioikoi* as a body and did not essentially change their status'.[29]

Another revolutionary reform by Nabis was his attempt to introduce to Sparta financial activities other than agricultural production and exploit her economic potential to the fullest. By insisting on the model of agricultural economy, Sparta had always secured her economic self-sufficiency; the citizens had always yielded enough income from their *kleroi*, which was not affected by the economic upheaval of the outside world. But this exclusively Spartan trait came at a heavy price: it doomed Sparta to economic regress. Even in the period of her greatest peak, Sparta never managed to develop a robust economy. Two factors worsened the problem: the misallocation and mismanagement of her resources. Nabis attempted to solve the former by re-allotting the land and by replenishing the human resources by increasing the number of citizens. As far as the latter is concerned, he attempted to solve it by strengthening trade and broadly circulating money. It is telling that Nabis, like Areus I and Kleomenes III before him, issued coins with his name and profile on one side and Herakles, the traditional symbol of Spartan power, on the other side.[30]

In addition, Nabis wanted to develop the city's naval potentialities, focusing on the creation of a fleet. Under his rule, Sparta came to possess a sizeable fleet for the first time in one and a half centuries. Gytheion was turned into a powerful naval base and an important centre of commerce. At the same time, Sparta created ties with major commercial centres in the Aegean Sea such as the island of Delos, where Nabis was honoured as 'Benefactor' on account of 'his public services to the state and temple' of the Delians.[31] Sparta's naval activity expanded also to Crete, where Nabis cultivated friendly relations with some of its cities. The network he created on this island provided Nabis with constant military support. There is evidence that he also placed some Cretan cities under his control.[32]

Additionally, Nabis strengthened Sparta's defence by completing her fortifications. Some works had already been hastily constructed in 294 during the invasion of Demetrios Poliorketes and, as mentioned earlier, Kleomenes too had fortified many of the city's strategic points. Nabis expanded and added to these works, systematically surrounding Sparta with a defensive wall, strengthened by towers at regular intervals, a moat and rampart.[33] Apart from securing her, the walling of Sparta was the first step towards genuine urbanization since it included four of the five constituent towns of the city in an area of 200 hectares.[34] Apparently, this internal change did not come abruptly but occurred over time and was not as obvious as her external change. From this period come the first private monuments. Along with the austere Spartan tombs there appeared aesthetically impressive Hellenistic graves with long epigrams, as opposed to the traditional ones bearing simply the legend 'in war'.[35] So at the beginning of the second century, the walled Sparta started to visually resemble the other big cities of her era.

Another characteristic of Nabis' policy was the imposition of heavy taxes on the citizens. Polybios attributes it to the greediness of the 'tyrant' and devotes an entire chapter of his *Histories* to describe an instrument of torture, an 'iron maiden' named Apia after his wife, by which Nabis compelled the citizens to pay their taxes.[36] Apart from Polybios' propaganda, the enforcement of taxation was a natural consequence of Nabis' policy. The construction of the walls and the fleet and the salaries of the mercenaries[37] demanded huge sums of money which Nabis had no other way to collect.[38] By this measure he laid the foundations of an organized system of financial management in Sparta for the first time in her history. On the other hand, the tax was closely connected with the wide circulation of money in Spartan society and with the radical reorganization of her economy.[39]

In Nabis' times Sparta strayed from the principles on which she was founded. The integration of the helots and foreigners in Spartan society, the wide circulation of currency, the organized taxation, the development of commercial trading and her fleet, the systematic and organized walling of the city; all combined with the (formal or informal) abolition of the ancient institutions such as the dual kingship, the *Gerousia* and the *ephors*, show that Nabis' Sparta had little in common with that of Lykourgos and justify his reputation as 'the wrecker of ancient Sparta'.[40] Yet detaching herself from her past was the price that Sparta had to pay in order to ensure her strength. At the end of the third century, most of the features that shaped her identity also hampered her development and undermined her existence. The Spartans could no longer afford to ignore the inherent weaknesses of their city, solely to maintain a tradition which over the centuries had become a redundant burden. In order to survive, Sparta had to deny herself.

Nabis did not reign jointly and, therefore, his kingship may not be called legitimate according to the Lykourgan law.[41] Nevertheless, the dual kingship and most institutions had already received fatal blows, and had deteriorated to such an extent after Kleomenes' coup that they had lost their meaning. Kings, senators and *ephors* had been repeatedly assassinated, banished and called back, while for about twenty years (227–207) all power was practically concentrated in the hands of one king instead of two.

Nabis was recognized as 'king' not only in Sparta but also by others, at least by the citizens of Delos and by the Romans until 197. Therefore, questioning his title on the premise of his legitimacy is not valid.[42]

Considering the way his power was exerted, Nabis fully justifies Polybios' description of him as a tyrant.[43] His reign was despotic and had many similarities to the Hellenistic type of monarchy, which appears to have been his model. According to all indications, Nabis himself appointed all his associates, advisers and assistants. Some of them, such as his Argive wife Apia[44] and her brother

Pythagoras who was also Navis' son-in-law, all came from his close family environment and were associated with the monarch as always happened with the favourites, the so-called *philoi* (friends) of the Hellenistic monarchs. Unlike the strict and austere lifestyle of Kleomenes, Nabis ostentatiously displayed all the privileges of his authoritarian rule. He owned stables with expensive horses, had a personal guard of mercenaries and lived in a luxurious palace, a fact unheard of until then.[45] Although there is no information to suggest that Nabis had officially abolished the remaining institutions, such as the *Gerousia* and the *ephors*, it is likely that even if these institutions still existed he had absolute control over them. Between the monarch and the people, there was no intermediary supervisory authority. Above all else, Sparta's new citizens were Nabis' subjects.[46]

Nabis Silver tetradrachm. Nabis is portrayed wreathed and bearded but without a moustache according to Spartan tradition. On the reverse is the image of Heracles, also a Spartan symbol. (*London, British Museum*)

All this adds a different perspective to Nabis' social policy, especially concerning land re-allotment about which the sources are almost non-existent. How was land redistributed? Was all the *civic land* redistributed, or only the confiscated large estates? Did all the citizens, old and new, receive equal *kleroi* or not? Essentially, the only reference on this comes from Nabis himself. In his speech to Flamininus in 195, he claimed that by making all citizens equal, he acted in accordance with the requirements of Spartan laws that aimed at increasing the number of the city's defenders.[47] But whatever the reasons Nabis gave for his social reforms, it is likely that land redistribution did not occur in the context of a return to tradition but as a first step in meeting the needs of the new, Hellenistic-type of monarchy. The new *kleroi* must have been a reward by the monarch to his subjects for their military service, rather than the restoration of an institution of the past. In this sense, the *kleroi* of the new 'Spartans' were comparable to those that the Ptolemies ceded to their mercenaries and had little to do with the traditional *kleroi*.[48]

As ostentatiously as he displayed the privileges of his authority, Nabis highlighted equally his ties with Spartan tradition. On his coins, he is depicted bearded but without a moustache, in a typical Spartan fashion, while the reverse sides of the coins depict Herakles, the traditional symbol of Spartan power. Moreover, in the only speech of his that has survived to present days (and in fact was preserved by sources hostile to him), Nabis swears in the name of Herakles three times. He does not hesitate to invoke the name of Lykourgos, the Legislator of Sparta, to justify his reforms – even though these were completely against the Lykourgan spirit. This seemingly contradictory behaviour is actually easy to explain. That Nabis ruled as a Hellenistic monarch is something that cannot be denied. But his kingdom was Sparta. And Sparta was not a multiracial mosaic, like Egypt and the East, but a *polis* with a uniform, centuries-old tradition. Nabis could not overlook this. Tradition was the code of communication between him and his fellow Spartans. Its invocation was just one weapon out of his arsenal of symbols.

This must be the reason why two fundamental and ancient Spartan institutions, the *syssitia* and the *agoge*, were not abolished.[49] But it is more than likely that their nature did not remain completely unchanged. A centralized and overtly despotic regime like that of Nabis could not have allowed the independent operation of the *syssitia*, but must have preferred to assume direct supervision. Therefore, it is probable that the cost of maintaining the *syssitia* was undertaken by the state and not by the citizens, some of whom might not have been able to meet these financial obligations anyway.[50] With the *agoge*, things were different. This institution must have been maintained to the degree that it contributed to the development of a powerful army[51] yet it is unlikely that it remained the criterion for integrating new citizens.

In essence, Nabis' social policy included revolutionary innovations while at the same time it retained key elements of the Spartan tradition provided that they contributed to the reinforcement of Sparta's power. According to an insightful observation, Nabis 'was inspired by the ancient ideal of equality without committing the mistake of simply copying it, but deftly combining those traditional elements that could be maintained and assimilated with those that had to change radically, he reconstructed Sparta as a new model state, a city fully armed to face the challenges of her times'.[52]

Nabis has been accused of great cruelty regarding the means he employed. Polybios states that he did not hesitate to resort to torture, banishment, executions and assassinations of opponents, not only within Sparta but even in cities where they had sought refuge.[53] Despite the amount of exaggeration that they apparently contain, these accusations should be considered true. But in a period of intense internal crisis, the use of violence was the only way to stabilize the position of the new leader, as well as to suppress the inevitable reaction to his revolutionary reforms. The difficulties he faced are reflected in the fact that it took him three years to consolidate his reign and to solve the internal problems of the city. Yet in 204 Sparta was again ready to take aggressive action.

Argos

Despite their differences in tactics, Nabis' strategy remained identical to that of Kleomenes. Both aspired to increase Sparta's power and were motivated by the desire to restore her supremacy. Inevitably, this policy brought Sparta into conflict with the Achaean League. For this purpose Nabis attempted to ensure the support of a great power. Not having the support of the Ptolemies as Kleomenes did, Nabis turned to Rome, the new power emerging on the scene as a major political player. Sparta had already allied with Rome since the outbreak of the First Macedonian War in 210 and so in the Treaty of Phoenice in 205, which ended this war, she enjoyed the benefits of being an ally of the victors along with the Aitolians, the Eleians and the Messenians.

The war with the League began in 204 under the slim pretext of the theft of a horse from Nabis' stables. The thieves fled to Megalopolis, where they were granted sanctuary. The refusal of the Megalopolitans to surrender the criminals gave Nabis the opportunity to conduct a series of raids on their territory. The war continued into the next few years with border skirmishes on both sides. Based on the scarce sources available, Nabis' strategy, limited as it was within this scope, can be considered opportunistic.

In 201 Nabis suddenly attacked Messene and seized the city, except for its acropolis. His action is difficult to interpret because Sparta and Messene were allied in 205 and had participated in the Treaty of Phoenice along with Rome and Aitolia. Some historians try to connect Nabis' action with Messene's internal problems, specifically the conflict between the democratic and the oligarchic faction that existed in the city.[54] One assumption is that he acted in order to prevent the Achaeans from occupying the city.[55] Another is that he responded to a call for help by the city's democratic faction[56] aiming to increase the prestige of Sparta[57] and ensure a convenient ally in the event of widespread conflict in the Peloponnese.[58]

However, the most probable explanation is that this was an opportunistic venture and that Nabis tried to exploit the conflicts within Messene with the ulterior motive of conquering it.[59] In any case, his plans were thwarted by the timely intervention of Philopoimen. The latter, without waiting for reinforcement by the forces of the Achaean League, assembled a Megalopolitan force and moved decisively towards Messene forcing Nabis, who was surprised by such a swift reaction, to retreat. The following year (201/200), Philopoimen was elected general of the League and attempted to carry the war into Lakonia. Polybios is filled with admiration for the organization and conduct of Philopoimen's campaign in Lakonia, which reached up to Sellasia and defeated a detachment of Nabis' mercenaries near Pellana.[60] However, this success did not have any particularly significant results apart from suspending Nabis' aggressive activity. The following year (200), when Philopoimen was absent in Crete, Nabis resumed his raids. In one of these, he attacked Megalopolis and forced the people to barricade themselves within the walls of their city.[61]

That same year, only five years after the end of the First Macedonian War, the Second Macedonian War broke out. The frivolous policy of Philip V would bring the Romans for the second time to Greece, this time not as a diversion but in order to decisively defeat the Macedonians. Faced with these developments, Philip V found himself needing to mobilize all his forces and, among others, addressed his allies of the Achaean League. He even offered the Achaeans to dispose of Nabis in exchange for their participation in the war against the Romans. The negotiations took place at the meeting of the Achaean League at Argos in the autumn of 200. The Achaeans faced a dilemma: as members of the Hellenic League they naturally had an obligation to accept Philip's proposal and assist the Macedonians. Yet they knew well that Nabis was less dangerous than making enemies of the Romans would be. Thus they replied evasively and essentially rejected Philip's proposal.

Two years later, the Achaeans came up against another awkward prospect. This time it was the Romans who came to ask them to turn against their former ally. After some time hesitating, the Achaeans finally decided to side with the Romans. This was certainly an unexpected blow for Philip. Following the Achaeans' decision, all of the Peloponnese was now hostile to him. But Philip's disappointment was offset to some extent when Argos unexpectedly refused to follow the policy of the League and sided with the Macedonians. Philip knew that whatever advantage this gave him was fragile and potentially brief. The location of Argos, in the centre of the Peloponnese, made it vulnerable as a target, and he was unable to provide forces to guard it. But he did not want to abandon the city to be retaken by the Achaeans, who had sided with his enemy. The only solution was to hand Argos over to a third power which would be strong enough to protect it and simultaneously hostile enough towards the Achaean League to guarantee its independence. This force could be none other than Sparta. Therefore Philip approached Nabis and offered to put Argos under his control on the condition that if the outcome of the war were favourable for Philip, Nabis would return Argos to the Macedonians. Philip's proposal was an unexpected gift for Nabis, which of course he had no reason to reject. The agreement was sealed with marriage proposals between Philip's daughters and Nabis' sons.[62]

Nabis then asked the council of Argos to accept his entry into the city. The consent of the Argives would legalize possession of the city and strengthen his case diplomatically. Obviously, he counted on a faction of supporters within the city, where he had strong connections through his wife, Apia. She and her brother Pythagoras were nephews of Aristomachos, the old tyrant of Argos who had sided with Kleomenes in 225.[63] Unfortunately for Nabis, the anti-Spartan party of the council prevailed so, lacking an invitation, he decided to place the city under his control by force. With the help of his supporters from within the city he managed to invade secretly at night, and the next morning he was the master of Argos.[64] Quite unexpectedly, Nabis had repeated Kleomenes' triumph. He would not, however, repeat the latter's grave mistake of ignoring the social problems of the city. As Livy emphatically states:

'The tyrant was admitted to the city at night, without the knowledge of anyone; when day came all the commanding sites were in his hands and the gates were closed. A few of the leading men got away in the first confusion and their property was plundered in their absence; the gold and silver of those who remained was appropriated and heavy fines imposed upon them. Those who paid promptly were let go without insult or bodily injury; those who were suspected of concealing or holding back assets were punished and tortured like slaves. Then he called an assembly and proposed measures, one for the cancellation of debts, the other for a distribution of land to individuals, thus lighting two torches with which revolutionists could inflame the commons against the nobility.'[65]

If the redistribution of land in Sparta was a measure that was closely linked to the traditional polity, outside of Sparta 'this measure and even more the abolition of debts stirred the idea of revolution. And even in Sparta, in economic and social conditions of the late third century, the land reform included the triumph of the poor over the rich and the stripping of the latter.'[66] Thus the expansion of the Spartan revolution to Argos would eventually raise the hopes of the poor classes in the Peloponnese, motivate them to revolt, and turn Sparta into both an attractor and a beacon for the disillusioned and socially marginalized. For Polybios, these people were the dregs of society, so we can understand his resentment when he states that Nabis converted the state of Sparta 'to an inviolable sanctuary for all people who had committed a crime or for people whose impiety had driven them out of their homeland'.[67]

Modern historians, however, recognize that 'his action in Argos adds to his personality another dimension, greater than that of the reformer kings; it allows him to be considered the undisputed leader of all the revolutionaries of the Peloponnese, as the only alternative to the conservative Achaean League'.[68]

As subsequent events indicate, this policy was vindicated: Argos remained faithful to Sparta to the end.

The fact that Nabis had conquered Argos with the consent of the Macedonians did not prevent him from appealing to his opponents. Wanting to ensure the legitimacy of his new acquisition, Nabis invited Titus Quintius Flamininus, the Roman commander, and King Attalos of Pergamon to the city. The meeting finally took place in Mycenae (February–March 197) where it was agreed that Sparta would send a force of 600 Cretan mercenaries to serve as auxiliaries in the Roman army, and would accept a four month truce with the Achaeans. Thus, in return for providing a token military force, Nabis obtained recognition of his possession of Argos, while his truce with the Achaeans gave him the time he needed to consolidate his rule in the city. And Sparta's influence extended to the towns directly dependent of Argos, such as Mycenae, where Nabis implemented his reforms.[69] The prestige of Sparta rose to the skies. In 197 her influence stretched from Arcadia and Argolis all the way to the Aegean and Crete.[70]

Nabis' stance towards Philip, of course, cannot be regarded as anything other than a betrayal.[71] As an act of diplomacy, it may have been correct to the extent that Nabis astutely foresaw the impending defeat of Philip and managed to ensure that Sparta would be on the victors' side. And in the short run, his choice proved correct when Phillip was defeated at Cynoscephalae in June 197. However, the outcome of this battle had a decisive effect not only on Sparta but also on all of Greece. The retreat of the defeated Macedonians from the scene rendered the foreign power from the West as sole regulator of Greek affairs. This was something that Nabis could not have prevented, even if he had foreseen it. Given his limited options, he attempted to exploit every opportunity for the benefit of Sparta, while at the same time he tried not to antagonize the big powers. Unlike Kleomenes, Nabis not only avoided provoking their intervention, but had studiously attempted to keep equal distances. This balance on a tightrope, though lacking the admirable integrity of Kleomenes' uncompromising policy, was proved successful and culminated in the recognition of his possession of Argos by the dominant power of the era.

The fact that two years later, the 'liberation' of Argos from the 'tyrant' would be the battle cry with which the Romans would lead a 'Pan-Hellenic' campaign against him, was impossible to predict at the time. Certainly, Nabis should not be held accountable for failing to foresee this development.

The Clouds from the West

For if once you allow the clouds now gathering in the west to settle upon Greece, I fear exceedingly that the power of making peace or war, and in a word all these games which we are now playing against each other, will be so completely knocked out of the hands of us all, that we shall be praying heaven to grant us only this power of making war or peace with each other at our own will and pleasure, and of settling our own disputes.

Agelaos to Philip V[72]

In June 196 there began in Corinth a large Pan-Hellenic celebration of the Isthmia games. A year after Philip V's crushing defeat by the Romans at Cynoscephalae, the festival had acquired considerable importance. The Greeks had gathered there 'from the entire world' not so much to attend the games but to anxiously learn what the Romans' stance would be in Greek affairs. Their continuing presence in Greece a year after its release from Macedonian supremacy was disconcerting. The Romans retained in their possession, among others, the three key cities, which Philip V had described as the three 'fetters' of Greece: Chalkis, Demetrias and Corinth. But did this mean, as the Aitolians were already claiming, that the Greeks had simply put the Romans in place of the Macedonian rulers? Would the Romans finally withdraw? If so, from which cities? The answers to these vexing questions would be announced at the start of the races by the Roman consul who had defeated Philip V: Titus Quinctius Flamininus.

During the period of waiting, the discussions between the assembled representatives were heated:

'... Some said that from certain of the places and towns it was impossible that the Romans could withdraw; while others asserted that they would withdraw from those considered most important, but would retain others that were less prominent, though capable of being quite as serviceable.[73] Also they spent time trying to guess the Romans' intentions, and there was widespread speculation about the "places" that the Romans would eventually keep for themselves and those that they would give up.'

Finally the herald appeared and, after the trumpeter had imposed silence on the gathered crowd, he delivered the long-awaited proclamation. Its content exceeded even the most optimistic expectations, to the point where at the beginning the audience did not believe their own ears. According to the proclamation, 'The senate of Rome and Titus Quintus, proconsul and imperator' decided to grant the Greeks their freedom, without imposing garrisons or heavy taxation, and giving them the right to keep their long established laws. The Romans even offered to withdraw from the three key cities (Corinth, Demetrias and Chalkis). When the herald, at the request of the crowd, read the proclamation for the second time, 'a shout of joy arose, so incredibly loud that it reached the sea. The whole audience rose to their feet, and no heed was paid to the contending athletes, but all were eager to spring forward and greet and hail the savior and champion of Greece.'[74]

All of this frenzied enthusiasm was a confirmation of Greece's total inability to regulate its own fate. In June 196 it was clear that the Greeks had officially resigned from the settlement of their own affairs, acknowledging a foreign rule on them. Having accepted that whatever the Senate may decide would not be disputed, they awaited passively for its announcement and, when it finally came, no one was bothered by the fact that the Greek cities' freedom had been decided by 'foreigners' in Rome and that it had been delivered in the form of a proclamation at Isthmia. Remarkable as it may have been 'that the Romans and their leader Flamininus' had done so much 'for the sole purpose of freeing Greece'[75] in reality the Romans were the ones who made the decisions and the Greeks the ones who had to conform. Beyond this 'decree of freedom' loomed 'the clouds from the West', foreshadowing the storm that would lead to Greece's complete subjugation fifty years later.

The first thunderbolt would fall on Sparta.

When the initial enthusiasm for the proclamation at Isthmia subsided, the Greeks faced the new reality. Despite their promises, the Romans still continued to occupy the three 'fetters of Greece' maintaining garrisons in Demetrias, Chalkis and Acrocorinth. The Senate, concerned about the successes of the Seleucid Antiochus III in Asia Minor, as well as the turmoil in Aitolia and Thessaly, wanted to retain these three strategic points under its control. Flamininus, who had declared that the Roman troops would soon be withdrawing, could not enforce the Senate's decision without jeopardizing his standing with the Greeks and his title of 'saviour and champion of Greece' – unless he found a pretext for keeping the garrisons in place. He found this pretext in the Achaeans' demand that Nabis should evacuate Argos. Yearning for the return of Argos to the League, they argued that allowing the city to remain under the rule of the tyrant Nabis was a violation of the Senate's decision to grant freedom to all the Greek cities. Flamininus addressed the Senate which gave him *carte blanche* to handle the case. He then assembled representatives of all the Greek allies in Corinth (195) and raised the issue of the 'liberation' of Argos, appealing to their love of freedom. In fact, this was an example of disguising one's blunt intentions under the guise of fighting for freedom. Rome, which had guaranteed the *status quo* in Greece, did not hesitate to violate it at the Achaeans request and seek support from all the Greeks – except the Argives themselves – for its intervention to 'save' Argos from tyranny. In essence, Flamininus aimed at legitimizing his campaign against Nabis. At the end of his speech he diplomatically stated that it was a Greek internal affair and that he would comply with the decisions of the majority. However, his speech did not convince the Aitolians. Their representative did not hesitate to openly blame the Romans for still occupying the three 'fetters' of Greece and accuse them for using this dispute over Argos as an excuse to prolong their stay in the country. He added that, should the Romans withdraw from Greece, the Aitolians would ensure that Nabis would withdraw from Argos, either by negotiations or by force in cooperation with the rest of the Greeks. But the Aitolians' arguments were not well received. Everyone else agreed with Flamininus' proposal and decided to declare war on Sparta. It was the second time that an appeal by the Achaeans resulted in a great power of the era leading a 'Pan-Hellenic' campaign against Sparta. Thus began the war Polybios refers to as 'Lakonic'.

Flamininus originally ordered the concentration of his forces at Elateia, in Phokis, and when it had been completed he invaded the Peloponnese. At Kleonai, halfway on the route from Corinth to Argos, a powerful force of 10,000 Achaean infantrymen and 1,000 cavalry joined Flamininus' army and they all headed to Argos. The city was defended by Pythagoras, Apia's brother and Nabis' son-in-law. He acted purposefully, strengthening the fortifications of the city and violently suppressing an attempt by the oligarchs to seize power. Those of them who managed to escape persuaded Flamininus that merely establishing the encampment of his army near the walls of Argos would encourage the people of the city to revolt. But in this estimate they were completely mistaken. Argos remained loyal to Sparta and, apart from a brief skirmish, this action did not have any substantial outcome. Thus Flamininus decided to call a war council. Despite the fact that all the allies (with the exception of Aristainos, the general of the Achaeans) favoured Argos as the target of their campaign, Flamininus decided to attack the 'true enemy' and led them towards Sparta.[76] Following the common practice of the time, his army first harvested the mature crops, destroyed the rest and then entered Arcadia and headed to Tegea.

From Tegea, Flamininus took the straight route to Sparta that crossed Skiritis and proceeded to Karyai where he was reinforced with 400 cavalry from Thessaly and 1,500 Macedonians sent by Philip V.[77] His army was also strengthened by the addition of a large number of exiles and dissidents of the Spartan regime, led by Agesipolis III (Lykourgos' former regent who had been exiled in 217). What concerned Flamininus the most was not how to further increase his forces, but how to secure the supplies necessary to maintain them.[78]

In order to confront Sparta's naval power Flamininus' brother Lucius Quinctius gathered a large fleet. The forty warships of the Roman fleet were reinforced by eighteen ships of the fleet of Rhodes, and they would also be joined by the fleet of Pergamos, commanded by Eumenes from the Cyclades islands. When these preparations were completed, Flamininus decided to invade Lakonia with his army while his fleet would sail along the coast to Gytheion. It was the largest invasion that Sparta had ever faced in her history.

Any leader aware of his unpopularity would have been panicked by an invasion of such a magnitude. If Nabis were indeed a despised tyrant, as described by Polybios, and his power were based solely on brute force, he would certainly have reacted erratically. But he decided to resist. His first action was to strengthen the fortifications of the city with trenches and ramparts. Sparta had at her disposal about 14,000 men, of whom 10,000 were 'Lakedaimonians', 1,000 were Cretans and 3,000 were mercenaries. These forces were reinforced with 1,000 more Cretans who Nabis summoned immediately from their island.[79] In order to prevent any internal *stasis*, Nabis did not hesitate to resort to extreme measures. According to Livy, he forced the Spartans to gather outside the city and surrounded the crowd with armed guards. Speaking to the assembled, he announced the names of eighty people who were suspected of possible treason. They were arrested and were all executed the following day.[80] He then ordered the arrest and execution of a number of untrustworthy helots.[81] These harsh measures proved effective. Especially in view of the difficulties that Sparta faced, many would even consider them indispensable.

In the meantime, Flamininus' army passed through Karyai into Lakonia and headed to Sparta. Despite its overwhelming superiority, the Roman army did not arrive in front of the city undisturbed. Just outside Sparta the vanguard, led by Flamininus himself, was suddenly attacked by Nabis' light infantry. It was towards the end of the day's march, and at that time the main force of the vanguard was occupied with marking and preparing the site for their military camp, totally unaware of the imminent attack. There was confusion and panic for a while; the situation was reversed at the last minute and only after the intervention of the Roman legions.[82]

In any case the Spartan army was in no position to confront the enemy in an open battlefield. The following day, when Nabis' mercenaries attempted to attack the rear-guard of the Roman army, they suffered a heavy defeat and were forced to retreat and barricade themselves in the walls of Sparta. From there, along with the other defenders of the city, they watched passively the Roman army plundering the surrounding area undisturbed.[83]

During this period the allied fleet placed under its control the *perioikic* coastal cities of Lakonia. Some of these surrendered readily, while others resisted and fell only after an assault.[84] Then the leader of the allied fleet, Lucius Quinctius Flamininus, decided to seize the strongest *perioikic* city and Sparta's naval base, Gytheion. The operation was not easy because the city was surrounded by a strong wall, reinforced with towers at intervals, and had a strong garrison. The preparations for the siege and in particular the construction of the necessary siege engines required the engagement of the crews of all three fleets.

The city's defence was undertaken by two commanders of equal power, Dexagoridas and Gorgopas. The enemy attacks were initially repulsed. But soon the situation became difficult for the defenders due to the critical effect of their enemies' siege engines. Battering rams and catapults constantly pummelled the fortifications and finally caused the collapse of a tower, which dragged with it the adjacent parts of the wall. The Romans attempted to exploit their success and invade the city through the breach. To divide the defenders' forces, they simultaneously attacked from the harbour side as well. The operation, however, was not easy, and finally the Roman commander chose to stop the assault, and came to an agreement with Dexagoridas for the surrender of the city. But Dexagoridas had acted clandestinely, without Gorgopas' approval. When the latter discovered this plan, shortly before the city was to be surrendered, he did not hesitate to kill Dexagoridas and continued the resistance alone, with even greater élan. Under his guidance, the city resisted the Roman assaults and Titus Quinctius Flamininus had to intervene personally. He detached 4,000 picked men from the main force of his army and rushed to his brother's aid in

Gytheion. His arrival, along with the increasing pressure from land and sea, eventually persuaded Gorgopas that he was resisting in vain. There was no other solution but to negotiate the surrender of the city. Having first secured the free withdrawal of the garrison from the city, Gytheion was surrendered to the Romans.[85]

Throughout this period Nabis was barricaded in Sparta. The only thing he could do was anxiously watch developments without the possibility of any intervention. Despite the gravity of the situation, Gytheion's strong resistance still allowed him some optimism. When Pythagoras arrived in Sparta from Argos with 1,000 mercenaries and 2,000 Argives, the situation started looking even more optimistic.[86]

However, when the news about the fall of Gytheion reached the city, Nabis realized that the war had been determined. The loss of this great naval base denied Sparta any possibility of replenishing her supplies, while it allowed her enemies to concentrate all their forces and tighten the noose around her. The fall of Sparta was now just a matter of time. Wanting to avoid a calamity, Nabis tried to enter into negotiations with his opponents and managed to arrange a meeting, which was attended by the Flaminini brothers, Eumenes of Pergamon, the admiral of Rhodes Sosylos, and Aristainos, the general of the Achaean League.

Nabis took the floor first and courageously defended his policy before Flamininus. He initially supported the legality of his possession of Argos, reminding the Roman general of the alliance they had agreed upon in Mycenae, at a time when Nabis was already the ruler of the city. All Flamininus had asked then was military assistance, which Nabis had provided, and not the withdrawal of the garrison from the city. 'But, by Herakles, in the dispute which concerns Argos, I come out the victor both by the justice of my case, because I received a city which belonged not to you but to the enemy, received it by its own act and not through compulsion; and by your own admission, since by the terms of our alliance you left Argos in my hands. But my title of tyrant and my behaviour argue against me, because I summon slaves to the enjoyment of freedom and establish the needy commons upon the soil.'[87]

Subsequently and with the same courage, Nabis defended the validity of his regime and his social reforms. 'As to my title, I can give this reply, that, whatever I am, I was the same when you yourself, Titus Quinctius, made the alliance with me. At that time I recall that you saluted me as king; at this time I see that I am called tyrant. Therefore, if I had changed the title of my office, I should have to explain my inconsistency; since you are changing it, you must give reason for your own.' Regarding his social reforms, Nabis reminded Flamininus that he had already implemented them when they allied, stressing that his reforms were an internal affair of Sparta and had not hurt their alliance in any way: 'Do not weigh what is done in Lacedaemon on the scales of your own [the Roman] laws and institutions.' Stated Nabis: 'You desire that a few should excel in wealth and that the commons should be under their control; our law-giver ordained that the state should not be in the hands of the few, whom you call the senate, and that no one order should predominate in the state, but he believed that by equalizing wealth and rank it would come to pass that there would be many to bear arms for the country.'[88]

'I admit', Nabis concluded, 'that I have spoken at greater length than suits the traditional brevity of our speech; and I might have summed up briefly by stating that since I entered upon my friendship with you, I have done nothing to make you regret it.'[89]

Flamininus responded by unleashing against him a torrent of accusations which revealed that the Roman proconsul was speaking from a position of power. He brazenly denied allying with Nabis, demonstrating clearly that this was not a negotiation among equals. 'We have never made any treaty of friendship and alliance with you', he said bluntly. The alliance, according to Flamininus, had been established with Lykourgos' son Pelops, the legal heir of Sparta whose power was usurped later by tyrants.[90] But they had only succeeded in seizing power because the Romans, occupied with fighting the Carthaginians in Africa and the Gauls, had been unable to protect the legitimate king of Sparta. But how, Flamininus wondered, could the Romans, who fought to liberate Greece from Philip V, ally with a tyrant? And in fact 'the most savage and lawless tyrant that ever lived'? At this point Flamininus severely chastised Nabis for his despotic regime and the crimes he had committed in Sparta and Argos. 'Hold', he told him, 'a free assembly in either Argos or Lacedaemon, if you want to hear true accusations against a most lawless despotism.'[91] He then turned to undermining Nabis' claim that he had respected his alliance with Rome. He replied that his attempt to seize Messene, a city allied to the Romans, and his alliance with Philip V, an enemy of Rome, constituted a double breach of the treaty. Flamininus further claimed that the Spartan ships were attempting pirate raids on Roman trading and transport ships. 'Actually,' said the Roman general, 'the coast of Macedonia was safer than the Malea peninsula for the ships that were transporting supplies for our armies.' He concluded: ' Cease then, if you please, to utter fine-sounding words about loyalty and treaty obligations, and dropping your popular style speak as a tyrant and an enemy.'[92] After Flamininus, it was the turn of the Achaean general Aristainos to speak. He tried to convince Nabis, in the beginning with advice and then with entreaties, to relinquish his throne. He reminded him that other tyrants in the Peloponnese had done the same and thereby secured for themselves a safe and dignified life. Nabis was certainly completely indifferent to Aristainos' hypocritical interest, but was mainly concerned by Flamininus' speech. The Roman proconsul's arguments were not particularly compelling. However, it was impossible to ignore the presence of his legions outside Sparta. Flamininus had spoken like a victor determined to impose his terms. And Nabis anxiously wanted to know what these terms were.

The following day Nabis announced that he was ready to leave Argos and turn over the prisoners and fugitives. He then asked that he be given in writing any other claims by the Romans. Flamininus convened a meeting with his allies to decide on their position. The majority of the allies wanted to continue the war to the end. They stated that if Nabis retained power, the freedom of the other Greek cities would be threatened. If they did not overthrow the 'tyrannical' ruler of Sparta, it would be tantamount to legitimizing him. In this case, prospective 'tyrants' in other cities would be encouraged to imitate him.[93]

Flamininus had a differing opinion. Given his recent experience in Gytheion, Flamininus knew well how difficult it would be to seize Sparta, a city that was better fortified and defended by a bigger garrison. Such an operation would have had some hope of success if the appearance of the Roman army had caused disruption and caused internal unrest among the Spartans. However, 'when they saw the [Roman] standards almost carried into the gates, no one had stirred'. Therefore, it would take a siege to seize the city.[94] Flamininus announced to the assembly that he did not want to tie down his troops in Sparta since he had to confront Antiochos III, who according to the latest information had advanced into Europe with strong forces. According to Livy, Flamininus' aversion to a long campaign was also due to a personal reason, which of course he did not disclose to the assembly. The Roman proconsul wanted to quickly end the war with Sparta, fearing that should he be replaced, the new proconsul would claim the credit for the victory Flamininus' efforts had made inevitable.[95]

Despite Flamininus' suggestions, the allies insisted on their original positions. Sparta had to be conquered even if it took a prolonged siege to achieve this. The Roman then switched to a different argument: He declared that he had no objection to proceeding with the siege of the city, if this were the decision of the council members. But as they all knew well, such an endeavour 'often exhausts the patience of the besiegers sooner than that of the besieged'. The besiegers should prepare for the possibility of spending winter outside the walls of Sparta. Apart from all other difficulties, such a plan would require huge expenses to build the necessary siege engines and equipment, and to secure provisions for their large army. Therefore, the allies should first address their cities and decide whether they would be able to meet the demands of such an operation. 'The enemy's country already offers nothing but the naked soil,' concluded Flamininus. 'Besides', he added 'winter will soon be here, making it difficult to transport supplies from a distance.'[96]

Flamininus' perceptive argument worked as intended. Faced with their responsibilities and required contributions, the allies were quick to agree to enter into a truce with Nabis. Flamininus' terms, which were given to Nabis in writing, were as follows.

Within ten days Nabis was to surrender Argos and the surrounding villages in his possession to the Romans. All emancipated slaves of Argos would return to their former owners. Nabis was forced to return the fugitives and his prisoners to the Roman allies, and the spoils he had confiscated from Messene to the city's inhabitants. He also had to return the property of the mercenaries who had defected to the Romans or their allies. He had to allow the children and women of the exiles to return to their husbands if they so wished. He had to yield to the Romans all the cities of Crete that were under his control and to no longer interfere in any way in the internal affairs of Crete. He had to withdraw the Spartan garrisons and their supports from all the cities that the Romans would put under their protection, and to refrain from building more fortifications within or beyond the territory of Sparta. Nabis was additionally obliged to hand over to the coastal *perioikic* cities all ships that were still under his possession with the exception of two vessels. Finally, he had to pay 500 silver talents in compensation, of which 100 talents immediately and the rest in eight instalments of fifty talents. To guarantee the terms of the treaty, five hostages were to be delivered to the Romans, among them Nabis' son Armenas.[97]

Whichever way one examines these terms, it is evident they were extremely harsh. Yet there were some positive aspects. Sparta would keep her wall as well as some access to the sea (which is evidenced by her possession of the two vessels). More importantly, there was no mention of regime change in Sparta and there was no question of the exiles' return.[98] The latter must have been a pleasant surprise for Nabis, who would still retain full power in Sparta and what was left of Lakedaimonia. But the loss of her fleet and coastal cities was a decisive blow to Sparta, which had by now developed strong ties with the sea. Additionally, the loss of the *perioikic* cities deprived Sparta of a significant part of her military resources, both in quantity and quality.[99]

Initially, Nabis only shared these terms with his advisors, but soon the news spread and caused considerable concern among the citizens. All those who had appropriated the property of the exiles or had married their wives resented the idea of losing their vested interests 'as if they were to be robbed'. The helots and slaves that Nabis had released were terrified by the fact that, apart from the loss of their liberty, they would return to their already enraged former owners. The mercenaries also dreaded the moment they would have to return to their cities 'which were not more opposed to tyrants than to their servants'.[100]

The citizens began to slowly gather in groups to discuss the terms with one another. As they were quite agitated, the situation soon threatened to get out of control. Instinctively, many rushed to take up arms. Perceiving the rising wrath of the citizens, Nabis summoned the *ekklesia*. Following Spartan tradition, or at least selected aspects of it, he officially announced the terms the Romans were offering. Livy reports that Nabis misrepresented some of them so that they would appear even harsher and more humiliating than they originally were. But it is most likely that even if he had attempted to downplay the severity of Flamininus' terms, the crowd would have been outraged all the same.

At each of the terms being announced, the crowd furiously screamed their objection. At the end, when Nabis asked the Assembly what he should reply to Flamininus, with one voice they urged him to continue the war, and started to shout encouraging phrases like: 'Hold tight!', 'Do not despair!' and 'Fortune favours the brave!' Then on a massive impulse, everyone rushed to the walls to take battle positions.[101]

Flamininus must have been particularly surprised by the unexpected sight. Instead of the committee that would come to ratify his terms, he saw enraged Spartans stream out of the city, unleashing their javelins and arrows at his men.[102] The message was clear: Sparta was determined to resist.

The Battle of Sparta

For four days the opposing forces limited themselves to skirmishes in front of the walls. When at some point the Spartans attempted to engage the Romans in proper combat, they were easily defeated and put to flight. Since the city walls still had gaps in several places, some of the Romans caught up in pursuit of the routed Spartans managed to briefly penetrate into the city.[103] This fact did not escape Flaminus' attention who decided, before beginning a regular siege of the city, to attempt her capture by storm. The Roman proconsul rode with his staff along Sparta's fortifications in an effort to identify weak points in them. Nabis had not had time to completely fortify the city. The wall protected only the most vulnerable points, where the ground was flat and passable. In the hills, and otherwise inaccessible or rough areas, where the terrain provided a measure of natural protection, there was no wall.

Flaminius' biggest advantage was his superiority in numbers. He tried to benefit from it as much as he could by concentrating all his forces around Sparta. To increase the numbers of his army even more, he summoned to Sparta even the personnel of his naval forces at Gytheion. His army now numbered 50,000 men. The fact that not all these men were of the same calibre as the Roman infantry did not inhibit the effectiveness of Flamininus' plan in the least. What he needed the most, and they provided, was a feint for his legions. His forces developed around the city's circuit. His aim was to attack at several places simultaneously, in order to confuse the defenders and to force them to scatter their forces. This way he would divert their attention from the points where the main attack would occur, so that it would be impossible for the Spartan forces to reinforce them.

The Roman legions aimed their main attack at the three unwalled areas in the south of the city: Diktynnaion, Eptagoniai and Phoebaion.[104] It was there that the Romans would attempt to penetrate the defences.

When the signal was given, the attacking forces hurled themselves simultaneously at the city from all directions. The pressure was so strong and relentless that the defenders almost came to the end of their rope. Nabis constantly received agonized pleas for help from various areas of the city that were in danger. Whenever possible, he would send aid, while he himself would rush to the points which were under the greatest pressure. But the strain of such an intense the battle proved too much for his nerves, to the point where he lost control of the situation. As the battle was reaching its peak amid general confusion, Nabis became paralyzed and 'was unable either to order what was appropriate or to hear the reports, and not only lost his power of judgment but was almost bereft of reason'.[105]

The fighting reached its highest intensity in the three areas where Flaminius had directed his main attack. At Diktynnaion, Eptagoniai and Phoebaion, the defenders initially repulsed the enemy attacks. The Roman legions' advance was slowed by the concentration of such a great number of troops in a limited space. However, this limited space created problems for the Spartans as well. It drastically reduced the effectiveness of the javelins they were throwing at their enemy, since there was too little room for them to run and build up momentum before launching them. This made it easier for the Romans to defend themselves with their large shields.

Eventually the leading Roman troops managed to push through the unwalled areas and approach the first houses of the city. There they found themselves at a disadvantage, as they also came under attack from above by the Spartans. The defenders resisted stubbornly, even removing and throwing tiles from

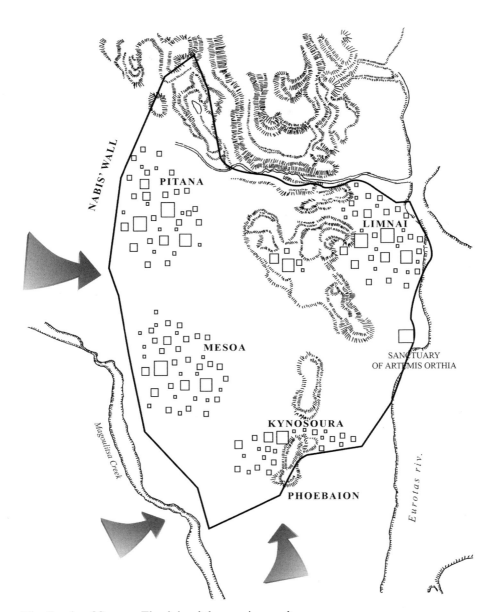

The Battle of Sparta. Flamininus' three main assaults.

the roofs of their homes at the invaders, while those who were still controlling the nearby hills tried to attack the enemy's most exposed flanks. At that point, the Roman infantry displayed its superb qualities. Reacting calmly and with exemplary discipline, the Romans '…held their shields above their heads and fitted them so closely together that no space was left for random shots or even for the insertion of a javelin from near at hand, and having formed their *testudo* they forced their way forward'.[106]

For as long as the fighting was confined to the narrow passages, the Spartans were able to hold their own against the Romans, who were not able to fully deploy their forces and exploit their numerical superiority. But when the Romans managed to move to wider thoroughfares and the open areas of the city, it was impossible to contain them. Some of the defenders retreated seeking cover and protection, while others fled the city spreading panic. When the Romans stormed into the city, most thought that Sparta had perished. Even Nabis himself 'trembling as if the city had been taken, looked about him for a way to escape'.[107] But against all odds, Sparta did not fall. Yet it was not the Spartan king, but the Argive Pythagoras who rose up to the challenge. Demonstrating the courage and determination of a truly great leader in that critical moment, he took initiative and saved the city: he ordered the torching of all the houses located near the gaps of the wall through which the enemy was pouring in. Dense clouds of smoke then spread throughout the city, creating a suffocating atmosphere. With no visibility and amidst pandemonium, the invaders could no longer keep their cohesion. The situation became even worse when parts of the burning rooftops started falling on them as they collapsed. The Roman army was cut in two. The fire prevented not only the retreat of those who had penetrated the walls, but also the advance of the forces that remained outside the walls. Considering the situation, Flamininus realized that the attack could not continue. Victory had literally slipped between his hands. Unable to do otherwise, he reluctantly ordered a general retreat. Sparta had been saved.

But this victory was only temporary. For the next three days, Flamininus continued to wear down the defenders of the semi-destroyed city 'sometimes harrying them with assaults, sometimes blocking open spaces with siege-works that no way might be left open for escape'.[108] Realizing that continued resistance would result in annihilation, Nabis decided to capitulate. This time he sent Pythagoras to negotiate with Flamininus in order to end hostilities. According to Livy, initially Flamininus sent him away from his camp scornfully, and Pythagoras was forced to fall to his knees and beg the Roman general to condescend to listen to him. Yet Livy then continues to state that while Pythagoras offered Flamininus the unconditional surrender of the city, in the end the negotiations ended in a truce under the same terms that the Spartans had initially rejected.[109] This unexpected turn, which certainly cannot be attributed simply to Pythagoras' diplomatic skill, is remarkable. Flamininus himself claimed that he simply showed magnanimity, 'when he saw that the destruction of the tyrant would involve the rest of the Spartans also in serious disaster'.[110] But it is obvious that the lenient attitude of the Roman proconsul to Nabis and his regime owed less to his vaunted love of the Greeks and more to the *realpolitik* Rome exercised. What concerned Flamininus the most was that potentially, a complete weakening of Sparta would lead the Achaean League to dominate the Peloponnese with unpredictable consequences for the relations between the League and Rome. Instead, as long as the threat of Sparta lingered, the Achaean League would remain dependent on Rome and a faithful ally.[111]

After this settlement, Flamininus headed to Argos to attend the Nemean festival and accept honours from the city's oligarchs, who had come to power in the meantime. Flamininus was also honoured in other cities, such as Gytheion where citizens erected a statue in his honour.[112] However, his allies did not show the same enthusiasm. When the news of the liberation of Argos was announced at the Achaean assembly, the general joy was tempered by the fact that Nabis had not been removed from power. The Aitolians, who were seeking an excuse to break their alliance with the Romans, took their resentment even further. In all their meetings they provocatively tore the treaty in pieces and declared that 'the Roman army had become the ready agent of Nabis' despotism.'[113] Despite these grudging reactions from the Achaeans and the Aitolians, the treaty was officially ratified by Rome in the winter of 195–194.

The End

After the Romans had withdrawn, Nabis made systematic efforts to complete the fortification of the city's walls. In light of the recent battles and of how the enemy had succeeded in penetrating into the city, this was necessary. Despite the fact that his son was a hostage in Rome, Nabis decided to resume hostilities with the Achaeans. The war was inevitable, as it was the only way to bring the coastal cities under his control again. This was vital for Sparta now that the city was heavily dependent on access to the sea for commercial trade. After their loss, and especially after that of Gytheion, Sparta suffered financially. Thus in 193 with the Aitolians' encouragement, Nabis tried to regain the lost territories. He activated his network of agents in the *perioikic* cities and started to entice them to rebel against the Achaeans. He soon managed to take them under his control, some peacefully while others violently. Gytheion, however, put up such sturdy resistance that Nabis was forced to besiege it. The Achaeans sent reinforcements to the city and asked for the Romans' help. The latter advised them not to move before the arrival of Roman troops, but Philopoimen, who was then general of the League, decided to ignore their recommendations. In his rushed effort to help the garrison of Gytheion, he chose to confront the Spartans at sea. This decision resulted in a massive defeat and nearly claimed his own life when his ship was sunk.

Philopoimen was luckier on dry land. With a surprise night attack he caught off guard and almost annihilated a detachment of the Spartan army that was encamped at Pleiai.[114] He then gathered his forces at Tegea and invaded Lakonia, attempting to draw Nabis away from the siege of Gytheion.[115] However, the Spartan king did not raise the siege, and only moved to confront Philopoimen after it had ended successfully. According to Livy who delivers a detailed description, the battle lasted two days. The two rivals first met on rough terrain in the mountainous and inhospitable area east of the Tegea–Sparta road. On the first day of the battle, Nabis' light infantry neutralized Philopoimen's army with a combination of ambush tactics and feigned retreats into narrow passages. The next day, however, Philopoimen executed a wide outflanking manoeuvre and led the main forces of his army to the rear of the Spartan army. In the slaughter that followed, Nabis lost three quarters of his forces. Along with the remains of his army, he fled to Sparta and hid behind the city walls helpless, while the army of the Achaeans plundered Lakonia undisturbed for a month.[116]

Then, with Flaminius' intervention, a truce was agreed.[117] Philopoimen and his supporters felt that in this way Flamininus reaped the fruits of the Achaean general's labour, since the latter had been the key agent in Nabis' defeat. Without ruling out the possibility of this personal rivalry as a cause, it is most likely Flamininus acted out of political motives. He primarily wanted to secure peace at his rear in view of the impending war with the Seleucid king Antiochos III. Additionally, he did not want Sparta to join the Achaean League.

On the other hand, Nabis lost everything he had managed to recover, and all that Sparta retained was her completed wall. But her prestige had been irrevocably damaged. For the Aitolians, who in the meantime had clearly become anti-Roman oriented, the agreement between Nabis and Flaminius made the former untrustworthy, to the extent that his power survived thanks only to the indirect tolerance of the Romans.[118] In addition, the Aitolians wanted to maintain a hostile power in the south of the Achaean domain, which would keep them occupied in the Peloponnese. But Nabis' Sparta could no longer play this role. Nabis himself was useless, and after his second treaty with the Romans he became untrustworthy in the eyes of the Aitolians. So they plotted to assassinate him and thereby eventually gain the control of Sparta. They were probably in contact with Nabis' political opponents in the city, and estimated that his popularity was low after his failed campaign and that the Spartans would herald them as liberators. This venture was entrusted to Alexamenos from Kalydon. He was dispatched to Sparta with 1,000 cavalry. Additionally he was assigned thirty picked cavalrymen who had been expressly instructed to unquestioningly obey the orders they would be given.

Alexamenos had carefully prepared his plan. He appeared in Sparta as a representative of the Aitolians, sent in light of their alliance to request Nabis' participation in the imminent war against the Romans. He added that Antiochos would soon arrive in Greece with powerful forces, that the Aitolians were ready and that their army would promptly march to reinforce Sparta as soon as it was required. Nabis' confidence was restored, and when Alexamenos suggested they should inspect together the joint manoeuvres by the Spartan army and his Aitolians, the king agreed enthusiastically.

The manoeuvres took place outside the walls of Sparta, near the River Eurotas. Nabis, unsuspecting of the ruthless Kalydonian's plans, inspected the troops on horseback accompanied by only two riders. This fact did not escape Alexamenos' attention as he sought the right opportunity to implement his plan. He had only revealed it to his picked men at the last moment, urging them to act quickly and decisively. Alexamenos relied on the element of surprise. The assassination would occur as Nabis was inspecting the Spartan army, before the eyes of his men and before they had time to react. Indeed, the assassins must have been quite audacious to form and implement such a plan.

According to military protocol of the time, Nabis' bodyguard was arrayed in the centre, while the Aitolians were deployed on the Right. Alexamenos had ordered the picked cavalrymen to level their lances and stand near him, fully alert. When he saw Nabis approaching from the left wing, he galloped quickly towards him and struck the king's horse with his lance. As the horse fell to the ground, throwing off its rider, the Aitolian cavalrymen swiftly pounced on him and started stabbing him with their lances. Nabis did not die immediately. His agony was prolonged because of his strong armour; it took many strikes before the assassins' lances pierced it. The last king of Sparta took his last breath under the eyes of his deployed army.[119]

At first, the Spartans were stunned, unable to process what had just happened before their eyes. When they recovered, it was too late. The Aitolians had reached Sparta, which the manoeuvres had left defenseless: 'Their leader shut himself up in the palace and spent a day and a night in going through the tyrant's treasures; the Aitolians, as if they had captured the city which they wished to seem to have set free, turned to plunder.'[120]

Eventually, the Spartans reacted. In an effort to restore the unity and continuity of the royal power, Nabis' supporters attempted to put on the throne Lakonikos, a youth who had been raised alongside Nabis' sons. With Lakonikos in charge, they attacked the Aitolians who were ravaging Sparta.[121] In Nabis' palace, Alexamenos and his companions put up some resistance, but in the end they were all massacred. Most of the rest gathered around the temple of Athena Chalkioikos where they were also killed. Those who managed to escape fled to Tegea and Megalopolis, believing that the cities of the Achaean League would treat the assassins of the 'Spartan tyrant' favourably. But they were gravely mistaken. They were treated as Aitolians: that is, as enemies. They were arrested and sold into slavery.[122]

After the death of Nabis, Sparta was a city mired in chaos. Whoever had the readiness to move with speed and strength would become master of the situation. This did not go unnoticed by the unrelenting enemy of Sparta, Philopoimen, who rushed to invade the city with strong forces. Acting decisively and taking advantage of the general disorganization, he achieved what the Aitolians had failed to do and what the Achaeans had always dreamed of: to occupy Sparta and integrate her into the Achaean League.[123]

It is true that compared to Kleomenes' noble figure, Nabis remains an enigmatic and somewhat controversial personality. This is in a large part due to the hostility of the sources; however we can't deny that Nabis was certainly a cruel tyrant. This trait of his is characteristic of his time, the age of Hellenistic monarchies. At the same time he was a great leader and a bold visionary. With his revolutionary changes, he finally succeeded to 'reconcile Sparta with her time'[124] and turn her into a strong state of international recognition.

The implementation of his revolutionary reforms even outside of Sparta, the creation of a strong fleet and the diplomatic opening abroad (Crete, Delos and Rome) suggest that, in contrast to Kleomenes, Nabis had aspirations that were not limited to the restoration of Spartan hegemony in the Peloponnese. Did he perhaps envision a greater state that could be extended beyond the boundaries of the Peloponnese?[125] Did he possibly desire to move even further? Was it his intention, as some believe, to create a 'Pandoric'[126] or a Pan-Hellenic union, where he would apply his revolutionary reforms? These assumptions are more or less pure guesswork. However, given his ambition and based on his overall politics, none of these can be ruled out. What the chances of success of such a venture were is a completely different issue. At a time when the future of the Eastern Mediterranean was being determined in the competition between the great Hellenistic empires and the rising power of the West, there was no place for city-states with limited resources and potential.[127] And Sparta, which remained a city-state above all, did not seem to be able to discard or overcome these inherent limitations. Furthermore, the constant wars and hostile raids had substantially worn out not only her own power but also those of the entire Peloponnese. This deterioration had a clear impact in warfare, where Sparta could not match her combined enemies' constantly increasing numbers. The 20,000 men Kleomenes deployed in 222 at Sellasia were one of the largest armies in the history of Sparta, but still not big enough compared to the 30,000-strong army of his adversaries. Three decades later, and despite his revolutionary reforms, Nabis failed to raise more men than Kleomenes had,[128] but he had to confront an enemy numbering 50,000.

In the beginning of the second century, every effort Sparta made to play a pivotal role in the developments of her times was doomed. Reality contrasted sharply with Nabis' ambitious plans. His brutal murder was an ending entirely unsuitable for a truly great Spartan, but it fittingly symbolizes the end of the Spartan revolutionary movement: all that remained of Sparta's grand attempt to resume her former power and glory was a trampled corpse in the valley of the Eurotas.

Chapter Five

Pax Achaica

After the torch–light red on sweaty faces
After the frosty silence in the gardens
After the agony in stony places
The shouting and the crying
Prison and palace and reverberation
Of thunder of spring over distant mountains
He who was living is now dead
We who were living are now dying
With a little patience

T.S Elliot
The Waste Land

The accession of Sparta into the Achaean League had no other repercussions for the city apart, of course, from the political ones. Philopoimen did not intervene in Sparta's internal affairs, did not impose the return of the exiles, nor did he claim any of Sparta's meagre territory. It sufficed him to simply install people in his confidence to power. Livy vaguely mentions that Philopoimen had come to an understanding with the 'leading citizens'[1] while Plutarch observes that he 'carried with him the principal men among the Spartans, who hoped to have in him a guardian of their liberties'.[2] What kind of people were these 'principal men among the Spartans'? Most likely, they were Spartans who had secured their survival in the past by pretending to be Nabis' supporters. One cannot rule out the possibility that among them there were some fervent supporters of Nabis' policies who had reconciled with the new reality. Naturally, the new partners of the Achaeans had no footing with the people as long as the memory of Nabis was still alive. A few months later, in the spring of 191, it became apparent that the Spartans were planning to leave the Achaean League. The Achaeans (under Diophanes, who was general at the time) decided along with Flamininus to invade Sparta, but they were deterred at the last moment by Philopoimen, who wanted to avoid getting the Romans involved in the internal affairs of the Achaean League.

Philopoimen rushed to Sparta and managed to ensure she would remain in the Achaean League by strengthening the authority of his pro-Achaean protégés. In a concrete demonstration of their gratitude towards him, Sparta's appointed leaders liquidated Nabis' palace and estate and offered to their patron the amount which they had raised, 120 talents. Plutarch states that the person who took the responsibility of delivering the money to Philopoimen was called Timolaos, and that he had a personal connection with him and had previously been a guest at his home.[3] Philopoimen refused the offer and suggested Timolaos should use this money to bribe his political opponents. However, shortly before the autumn of that same year, Nabis' followers managed to overthrow the pro-Achaean faction and expel them from Sparta. Thus the 'principal men' were added to the long list of the Spartan exiles.[4]

The Spartans did not limit themselves to this action. In the winter of 191–190 they sent a delegation to Rome asking to reclaim some *perioikic* cities, as well as the return of the five hostages that Flaminius had required from Nabis in 195. It was the first time – but not the last – that Sparta addressed Rome to request its mediation in resolving her problems. Behind these remonstrances hid Sparta's major social and economic problems: 'The state was kept in anxiety especially by the exiles, a great part of whom lived in the fortresses along the Lakonian coast, all of which had been taken away from Sparta. The Lacedaemonians, angered at this, in order that somehow they might possess free access to the sea, if ever they sent ambassadors to Rome or elsewhere, and at the same time that they might have a market and a place for the storage of foreign merchandise for necessary purposes.'[5]

The Senate finally approved the return of all the hostages but one: Nabis' son Armenas. The latter was kept in Rome for obvious reasons and later died there from an illness.[6] In 190, the rest returned to Sparta after a total of four years in exile. The return of these prominent members of Nabis' regime invigorated even more the anti-Achaean feelings of the Spartans, for whom the mere fact of forced membership in the Achaean League was humiliating. The situation was extremely tense after Rome's rejection of her request to reclaim the *perioikic* communities in which the exiled Spartans had defiantly settled.

In the autumn of 189, the tension that was simmering for a while burst to the surface. The Spartans unexpectedly attacked and occupied the city of Las, southwest of Gytheion, where their exiled compatriots had settled. The exiles, with the help of the *perioikoi*, eventually managed to retrieve control of the city and protested to the Achaeans about this incident. Philopoimen demanded that the Spartans hand over the instigators of the attack. The Spartans not only refused to comply with this demand, but killed thirty supporters of the pro-

Achaean faction in a wave of violence and declared the secession of Sparta from the Achaean League.[7] Livy asserts that the Spartans were so enraged that, if the city still had her former strength, she would have declared war on the Achaean League. But that strength was no longer there. Therefore, Sparta resorted to her only option, namely the search for a powerful patron. For the second time the Spartans appealed to the Romans. Their representatives travelled for this purpose to Cephalonia, where the Roman consul Marcus Fulvius was stationed, and asked for Sparta to come under Rome's protection.

As expected, the Achaeans reacted violently. They declared war on Sparta, invaded Lakonia and began to plunder it. However, the coming of winter obliged the Achaeans to recall their army. Meanwhile, Marcus Fulvius held discussions with representatives of both parties and referred the matter to the Senate that had now become the official arbitrator of Greek affairs. There, the Spartans defended their original position but the Achaeans appeared divided. A faction represented by Diophantos declared that the 'Spartan question' should essentially be settled by the Senate while another, represented by Lykortas (Philopoimen's friend and father of the subsequent historian Polybios) countered that the Romans had no reason to involve themselves in the Achaean internal affairs. As for the Senate, it answered evasively and ambiguously. 'The reply, however, was so ambiguous that both the Achaeans accepted it as a concession of freedom of action regarding Lacedaemon and the Lacedaemonians interpreted it as not granting the Achaeans full authority.'[8] But the underlying message was clear: Rome was unwilling to get actively involved in this dispute. Philopoimen was determined to resolve the long lasting 'Spartan question' permanently.

Thus, in May 188, at the head of an Achaean army with its ranks filled by a large number of the Spartan exiles, Philopoimen invaded Lakonia. The Achaeans camped in Kompasion, a location outside Sparta.[9, 10] Philopoimen's representatives arrived in the city, summoned the citizens and called the roll of those who were considered instigators of the riots. They then demanded that the instigators be handed over and tried, with the promise that during the period of their detention, they would be safe. These were the terms on which Philopoimen would leave the city unharmed.

The Spartans had no other choice but to comply with Philopoimen's terms. The presence of the Achaean army, together with a group of exiles of significant size, outside Sparta left no doubt about what would ensue if they acted otherwise. Given all this, those who heard their names called decided to surrender and trust their fate to the judgment of a negatively predisposed court. Other prominent Spartan citizens accompanied them to offer moral support and help them with their defence, which had now become a matter of vital importance. A total of eighty citizens, all members of Sparta's leading elite, left the city and headed to the Achaean camp.

None of them would ever return. Once they crossed the gates of the camp, they faced a threatening crowd. The exiles were gathered at the entrance awaiting them. At the sight of their defenceless enemies, they let all their hatred erupt. Verbal assaults soon turned into brutal violence and the situation got out of control. In vain the Spartans asked for protection, pleading with their assailants that Philopoimen had guaranteed their safety. The Achaeans deliberately delayed their attempt to intervene, thus allowing the exiles to take their revenge. The latter managed to chain a few of their rivals and then began to stone them. Seventeen were killed in this way, and the remaining sixty-three were saved only after Philopoimen intervened. But their fate was already sealed. Philopoimen had rescued them 'not because he was concerned for their safety but because he did not wish them to be killed by an angry mob, without a proper trial'.[11] The next day after a mock trial, all of the Spartans without exception were sentenced to death and executed.

The responsibility for the crime at Kompasion should be attributed entirely to Philopoimen. Even if he had not had a premeditated plan, it was obvious that the Achaean general did not hesitate to go back on his word in order to benefit from the situation and rid himself of the Spartan leadership. After the massacre at Kompasion, every thought for resistance in Sparta vanished. Philopoimen was determined to eliminate any possibility for Sparta to create problems for the League in the future. First, he ordered the demolition of her walls and the restoration of Belminatis to his homeland, Megalopolis. He then proceeded to institute radical changes in the organization of the state, abolishing all of Nabis' reforms. All of the freed helots and the mercenaries who had served in Nabis' army were expelled from Lakonia. Many tried to stay and hide in the region. The Achaeans chased them down, managed to arrest 3,000 of them, and sold them all into slavery. With the money they raised they erected a colonnade in Megalopolis, Sparta's relentless enemy city which had been levelled in the past by the Spartans. This monument would commemorate the event in the years to come. After disposing of the enemies of the Achaean League, Philopoimen restored the supporters of the pro-Achaean faction in Sparta. Additionally, he ordered the return of all exiles, restoring not only the recently persecuted pro-Achaeans but also all those who had been expatriated at different times by Nabis, Kleomenes and others. It was a carefully thought out plan. Philopoimen gambled that the gratitude of the repatriated former exiles would result in increasing sympathy for the Achaean League within Sparta. At the same time by encouraging the coexistence of many political factions, with conflicting interests, he kept Sparta focused on her internal problems and rendered her incapable of being a future threat to the League.

Nevertheless, Philopoimen did not intend to stop there. Certainly, the replacement of Nabis' remaining supporters in power by their rivals, the stripping of the city of her wall and of all the remaining territory, rendered her powerless and totally dependent on the League. But this time Philopoimen was determined to fully incorporate Sparta into the Achaean League. He knew that as long as Sparta maintained her distinctiveness, she would remain a foreign body at risk of seceding at the first opportunity. Consequently, the core of the 'Spartan Question' had to be crushed. Her traditions, the *agoge*, the *syssitia* and generally all of Sparta's unique traits had to be weeded out once and for all. Thus Philopoimen ordered the total abrogation of the Spartan polity and its replacement with the laws and institutions of the Achaean League.

The Spartans succumbed to this ultimate humiliation and let Philopoimen 'cut away, as it were, the sinews of their city'[12] without protesting. As Livy mentions: 'The Lacedaemonian state, thus, so to speak, emasculated, was long at the mercy of the Achaeans; yet nothing did them so much injury as the subversion of the discipline of Lycurgus to which they had been accustomed for eight hundred years.'[13]

If Kompasion were a disgrace for Sparta, for the Achaeans it was of course the ultimate triumph which sealed their dominance in Peloponnese. Expressing directly his approval, Philopoimen's compatriot, admirer and later biographer, Polybios, described Philopoimen's actions at Kompasion as a rare combination of 'good' and 'expedient' arrangement: 'The good and the expedient are seldom compatible, and rare indeed are those who can combine and reconcile them. For as a general rule we all know that the good shuns the principles of immediate profit, and profit those of the good. However, Philopoemen attempted this task, and succeeded in his aim. For it was a good thing to restore the captive exiles to Sparta; and it was an expedient thing to humble the Lacedaemonian state, and to punish those who had served as bodyguards to a tyrant.'[14]

But as evidenced by 'the day after', this settlement of the Spartan Question by Philopoimen was neither as 'good' nor as 'expedient' for the League as it initially appeared; and indeed, refuting his expectations, this regulation proved transient. His brutal behaviour helped unite all the Spartans (even the pro-Achaean faction) in a struggle that echoes the last gasps of the Spartan movement.[15]

The fact is that Sparta remained unrepentantly hostile to the Achaean League, still seeking her independence with all the meagre forces at her disposal.

The only thing she could easily do, and did with indomitable perseverance, was to keep up a stream of delegations carrying desperate diplomatic protests to Rome, thus forcing the Achaeans to account every so often for their policy before the Senate. The dream of her inclusion in the League 'turned into if not a nightmare, at least a persistent headache and sometimes an acute migraine'[16] with tragic long term consequences.

Sparta's first official protest against the events in Kompasion occurred a few months later, in the winter of 188/7. Despite the fact that the Senate did nothing more than express its disapproval of the event in writing, it set the ball in motion. The Spartan Question was reopened.

In the following years the Senate and its representatives in Greece continued receiving complaints from Sparta about their treatment by the Achaeans. The Achaeans, on the other hand, continued considering the issue an internal affair and ostentatiously ignored the suggestions of Quintus Cecilius Metellus, the Roman legate of Macedonia, to repeal the measures against Sparta.

Towards the middle of 184, Areus and Alkibiades, two of the 'old Spartan exiles' (those who had been banished by Nabis and had been repatriated by Philopoemen in 188),[17] appeared before the Senate to protest and argued with the Achaean ambassador, Apollonidas, in regards to the events at Kompasion. Their behaviour was considered an unforgivable betrayal by the Achaeans, who condemned them to death in absentia. At an emergency session at Kleitor in Arcadia, in the presence of Roman representatives and the two Spartans, the general of the Achaean League, Lykortas, attempted to justify the action of the Achaeans at Kompasion. Lykortas claimed that the Achaeans were not liable for the massacre of the hostages but instead the exiled Spartans were to blame, including Areus and Alkibiades, who were now protesting about the incident. Lykortas also noted that the wall of Sparta had not been built by Lykourgos but by tyrants in order to specifically abrogate Lykourgos' laws. 'If Lycurgus should rise from the dead today he would rejoice in the destruction [of the walls] and would say that now he recognized his home and the ancient Sparta. You yourselves, Lacedaemonians, should not have waited for Philopoemen and the Achaeans, but should with your own hands have torn down and destroyed all traces of the tyranny.'[18] Finally, he claimed that the Achaeans did not overthrow the Spartan polity since it had been abolished much earlier by the Spartan tyrants. In response, the Roman legate declared that the Spartans had every right to present their views to the Senate. However, beyond this, Rome did not want to do anything further regarding the Spartan Question.

The next Spartan delegation reached Rome in the winter of 184/3. This time, the Spartans asked for Roman arbitration in their internal problems. Four different views representing four ideological trends were expressed, and as all of them were represented before the Senate the confusion that prevailed in the city after the return of all the exiles was obvious. The conservative 'old exiles' demanded their property back and wanted the city to return to the state she was in before they were exiled, while others suggested a compromise solution that required land redistribution. The third view was expressed by a man called Serippos, who represented the pro-Achaean faction and sought to restore the state as it was in 192, when Sparta had joined the Achaean League on relatively favourable terms. Finally, a certain Chairon spoke on behalf of Nabis' supporters who had been banished and condemned to death in 188 after the events at Kompasion. Chairon requested that they be allowed to return to Sparta. As expected, the Senate was in an awkward position and was not able to understand the specifics of the problem,[19] so it ordered that the matter be examined by a special committee whose decision did not take long. It mandated the return of the exiles (Chairon's faction) to Sparta and forced the Achaeans to ratify it. The return of Nabis' supporters to Sparta in 183 caused turmoil and social upheaval. Once again a number of the 'old exiles' (the most conservative Spartans) were forced out of the city. The latter even sent a delegation to Rome in the winter of 183/2 to register their complaints, while the city was represented by Serippos (sent there apparently to oppose them). During his absence and while the Achaeans were busy suppressing the revolt at Messene,[20] it appears that Chairon attempted to detach Sparta from the Achaean League. However, his plans were aborted due to the timely intervention of the Achaean general, Lykortas. In the summer of 182, Sparta was again a member of the Achaean League.

However, the Spartan delegations continued appearing in Rome, in the winters of 182 and in 181 dealing with the issue of the restoration of the exiles who had been displaced by Chairon. In the winter of 181/180 Chairon seized power and tried to forcefully restore Nabis' reforms, announcing 'land redistribution'. Needless to say, his measures caused the immediate intervention of the Achaeans and his sentence to death.

In the history of Sparta, this was the last known attempt at social reform. After Chairon's attempts, it appears that Sparta finally resigned herself to her fate. All that was left to be done was to arrive at a 'historic compromise' in order to definitively resolve the Spartan Question. The man who history has recorded as finally achieving a solution to the problem was Kallikrates, the general of the Achaean League. In 180, the compromise that was reached under his *strategeia* included the definitive return of all the exiles to the city. In 179, permission was given to Sparta to rebuild her wall and restore part of her traditions.[21] It is not known which traditions and to what extent they were restored. How could Sparta possibly recover even a portion of her traditions while remaining embedded in the Achaean League, closely following the decisions of the Achaeans? Most probably, few things of minor importance were revived, such as those that had to do with the appearance of the Spartans, and although the city had maintained a certain military force, the *agoge* was never restored.[22]

And then there was silence. For the next three decades there are only sparse references – and quite minor indeed – to Sparta. Among the few significant events in relation to the history of the city are the visit to Sparta in 168 of Aemilius Paulus, the victor of Pydna, and her failed attempt – via diplomacy of course – to recover some territories from Argos and Megalopolis in 164. Despite the fact that the period from 179 to 150 is not mentioned in any sources, it is certain that if a significant event had occurred in Sparta, it would have at least been echoed in some surviving reference.[23]

The total absence of Sparta from the major historical events of the era should not be surprising. Sparta was now a negligible city of the Achaean League unable to affect developments in any significant way. Her fading away was the natural consequence of the eventual acceptance of her destiny even though for a time she struggled desperately to evade it. In the decade after Kompasion, the only way she stressed her presence was her persistent overtures to the Romans. But it appears that after 179 even these overtures ceased, or at least greatly dwindled, so Sparta sank into oblivion, forgotten by history.

Despite this, three decades later, Sparta came back on the world stage in a peculiar way. In 151, a Spartan, named Menalkidas, was raised to the highest post of the Achaean League. No details are known about how Menalkidas was elected general. Nevertheless the fact was indicative of the reconciliation of Sparta with the Achaean League. During Menalkidas' generalship, the Spartan Question returned to the spotlight as a result of his attempt to detach Belminatis from the Achaean League and integrate it to Sparta, as a true Spartan would. In 150, Kallikrates accused him of treason (obviously he was planning Sparta's secession from the League). Menalkidas managed to defeat this charge by bribing his successor in the generalship, Diaios. In his turn, Diaios, to exonerate himself from the bribery charges, tried to divert the attention of the Achaeans back to Sparta. With the excuse of Sparta's new remonstration with Rome about some territorial issue, Diaios accused Sparta of breaching her treaty with the League, which did not allow member states to send separate delegations to Rome, and so he invaded Lakonia. The Spartans, who were aware of their weakness in confronting the Achaeans, agreed to hand over to them twenty-four of their most prominent compatriots as responsible for the breach. According to Pausanias' testimony the Senate, at the urging of one of its members, Agasisthenes, allowed the accused to escape and then, to keep up appearances, sentenced them to death.[24] The accused travelled to Rome, where Achaean representatives arrived later. Not surprisingly, the debate between Diaios and Menalkidas before the Senate was marked by fluency rather than by decency on either side.[25] The Senate decided to send delegates to examine the case. Since the arrival of the delegates was delayed, there was enough time for Diaios to deceive the Achaeans and Menalkidas the Lakedaimonians. Diaios misled the Achaeans into the belief that the Roman senate had decreed that the Lakedaimonians should henceforth comply with all Achaean decisions; Menalkidas deceived the Lakedaimonians into thinking that the Romans had entirely freed them from the Achaean League.[26] The result was that in 148 Sparta seceded again from the League. The general of the Achaeans at the time was Damokritos who, ignoring the advice of the Roman general Metellus, declared war on Sparta and invaded Lakonia. This time the Spartans' effort to defend their homeland resulted in their crushing defeat by the Achaeans on the battlefield and the loss of the cream of their army. According to Pausanias, in this final confrontation with the Achaeans 1,000 of the youngest and bravest Lakedaimonians were killed.[27] After their defeat, the Spartans locked themselves in their walled city, while Damokritos, unwilling perhaps to provoke the Romans, did not proceed to besiege Sparta but only plundered the surrounding area. This decision was considered treasonous by the Achaeans, who imposed a fine of fifty talents and forced him to leave the Peloponnese. Diaios, Damokritos' successor to generalship, declared to the Romans that he would wait for the arrival of their representatives. In the meantime, though, he occupied the last *perioikic* communities around Sparta in order to use them as bases of operations against her. Menalkidas reacted by attacking and reoccupying the small town of Iasos, on the border of Lakonia and Skiritis. But Sparta had already exceeded the limits of her endurance. The Spartans 'were utterly unprepared for war, being especially ill-provided with money, while in addition their land had remained unsown'.[28] Menalkidas was considered responsible for this situation and, realizing the political impasse facing him, he took his own life by poison. 'Such,' Pausanias notes succinctly, 'was the end of Menalkidas, who was at the time in command of the Lakedaimonians, and previously he had commanded the Achaeans. In the former office he proved a most stupid general, in the latter an unparalleled villain.'[29] Menalkidas was justified shortly after his tragic end when the delayed Senate representatives finally arrived in Corinth in the summer of

147 to inform the Achaeans of Rome's decisions. Backing Menalkidas' version, the Roman representative Orestes officially announced to the astonished Achaeans that according to the Roman Senate neither the Lakedaimonians nor Corinth itself should belong to the Achaean League, and that Argos, Heracleia by Mount Oite and the Arcadian Orchomenos should also be released from the Achaean League.[30] Thus Rome was cutting back the territory of the League to the borders it had before the Kleomenean War!

Implicit in the announcement was, of course, another message. After the Macedonians, the Aitolians and the Seleucids, it was now the turn of the Achaeans to subordinate themselves to the will of Rome. But if the Senate representatives expected that the Achaeans would accept this decision without protest, they were gravely mistaken. The reaction was spontaneous and overwhelming. The first to suffer the Achaeans' wrath were of course the Spartans, who were held responsible for the intervention of Rome. The Achaeans vented out their just frustration on them ignoring the consequences:

'The magistrates of the Achaeans did not wait for Orestes to conclude, but while he was yet speaking ran out of the house and summoned the Achaeans to an assembly. When the Achaeans heard the decision of the Romans, they at once turned against the Spartans who happened to be then residing in Corinth, and arrested everyone, not only those whom they knew for certain to be Lacedaemonians, but also all those they suspected to be such from the cut of their hair, or because of their shoes, their clothes or even their names. Some of them, who succeeded in taking refuge in the lodging of Orestes, they actually attempted even from there to drag away by force.'[31] The lynching of the Spartans was only the beginning. The Achaeans were determined not to compromise with the Romans. Their general, Kritolaos, fatefully rejected any negotiation effort, thus causing the rage of the Romans and of course of Polybios who describes him as a 'demagogue'. In 146 the League officially declared war against Sparta, knowing that this would lead to Rome's intervention. In a desperate attempt to meet its military needs, the League imposed social measures such as debt relief for the poor and mandatory financial contributions by the wealthy, and these measures eventually extended to the release of 12,000 slaves. Despite the fact that they were not social reforms but rather emergency measures imposed by the circumstances, these measures were all revolutionary and they would be very difficult to revoke later. Openly expressing his resentment against the reforms, Polybios states that had the Achaeans not lost the war, their leaders, such as Kritolaos and Diaios, would have proceeded in many more measures against their wealthy fellow citizens:

'For my part, I think that Fortune displayed her resources and skill in resisting the folly and madness of the leaders; and, being determined at all hazards to save the Achaeans, like a good wrestler, she had recourse to the only trick left; and that was to bring down and conquer the Greeks quickly, as in fact she did. For it was owing to this that the wrath and fury of the Romans did not blaze out farther; that the army of Libya did not come to Greece; and that these leaders, being such men as I have described, did not have an opportunity, by gaining a victory, of displaying their wickedness upon their countrymen. For what it was likely that they would have done to their own people, if they had got any ground of vantage or obtained any success, may be reasonable inferred from what has already been said. And indeed everybody [the wealthy citizens] at the time had the proverb on his lips, 'had we not perished quickly we had not been saved.'[32] [A contradiction of nightmarishly enormous magnitude: if we had not perished so fast *as a nation* we would not have been saved *as a social class*!]

Regardless of Polybios' disapproval and despite it was certainly doomed to failure, the Achaean League succeeded in motivating the lower class, and in a combination of national and social rush, dared to confront Rome. History finally reserved for the Achaean League the role of the defender of Greek dignity, leaving for Sparta the pathetic role of the instigator of Roman intervention. A tragic irony. The traditionally conservative League, who had not hesitated in the past to turn first to the Macedonians and later to the Romans in order to stem Kleomenes' and Nabis' revolutionary movements, ended up incorporating the social and revolutionary elements of its time. In contrast, Sparta, which in Kleomenes' time was 'the leader of the national war against Macedon, and under Nabis the spearhead of social reform, supported the foreign oppressor. The wheel had turned full circle.'[33]

And to complete the paradox, this war that broke out against Sparta, a war conducted without her participation and resulting in the crushing defeat of her enemies and the subjugation of Greece to the Roman conquerors, led to the restoration of her 'Lykourgan polity' – although in a completely different form to the original.

Chapter Six

Pax Romana

*... And so in the little land-locked valley of the Eurotas the last Spartans
cultivated their fields in peace and strove to remember their ancient fame;
forgetting a little more as years passed, until Plutarch 'wrote them up' in the
lives of the various famous men of Sparta. And how much of what Plutarch
tells us is fact and how much legend it is difficult to tell.*

H.Michell[1]

The Museum City

Among the virtues that Virgil emphatically attributed to the Romans was their
tolerance towards the peoples they conquered. The way, however, in which
the poet's countrymen manifested this virtue was highly selective: those who
dared challenge the supremacy of Rome were doomed to perish. The ruins of
Carthage and Corinth are testaments that there was no mercy for cities that
attempted to confront them.

Sparta was a different case. From 188, she was considered Rome's protégé and
after the conquest of Greece she enjoyed a particularly favourable treatment.
The city maintained her wall, was spared (at least formally) the obligation to
pay contributions and, compared to other subjugated cities, she retained some
autonomy to the point of being called a 'free city'. She may have permanently
lost the *perioikic* cities, which united into a separate League –the *Koinon of the
Eleutherolakones* (Free Lakonians) – yet she was released from four decades of
Achaean occupation and finally regained her traditional system of government.
Thanks to the Roman conquest, the *syssitia*, the traditions and even more so
the *agoge* were restored 'so far as was possible after their many misfortunes and
great degeneration'.[2]

In the following years, the Spartans made serious efforts to revive the
'Lykourgan' traditions, resulting in their city earning the respect and recognition
of the Romans. For the latter, this strange and somehow eccentric 'Lykourgan
Sparta' was a very fascinating city. Her history, her glorious past and the
particularity of her inhabitants' eccentric lifestyle aroused Roman curiosity and

turned Sparta into a powerful attraction for a stream of visitors that increased in time. It is impressive that in 21, when Emperor Augustus visited Sparta, he honoured the Spartans by granting them the island of Kythera and by participating in the *syssitia*.[3]

The reputation of 'Spartan austerity' was so strong that when Apollonios of Tyana was invited to Sparta in 61 AD by the *ephors*, he sent them a letter in which he expressed his disapproval of the luxurious clothing and sophisticated ways of the Spartan ambassadors. Philostratos, who cites the event, claims that after Apollonios' insistence the *ephors* restored the ancestral practices, the wrestling grounds and the common messes 'and Sparta became like herself'.[4]

At the height of the empire's might, Sparta was found in the epicentre of the historic interest of the Romans, along with Athens. By that time, the Hellenistic civilization had completely been absorbed by the Roman upper class. Hadrian visited Sparta twice, in 124–5 AD and again in 128–129 AD, and there he was honoured for his building activity as 'founder' and 'benefactor'. In addition to his donations to the city, which included territorial concessions, Hadrian was given the office of *patronomos*, initiating a new tradition. Following his example, many rich and prominent foreigners aspired to enter upon this Spartan office which enabled them to link their name with the famous Spartan *agoge* in exchange for generous donations. Thus, during the Age of the Antonines, Sparta became a place to visit for many distinguished Romans as well as Greeks who wished to discover this historic city in person.[5]

Besides its beneficial effects on the economy of Sparta, the boost in what we now would call tourism greatly increased her reputation to a large degree. The result was an especially impressive effort by the Spartans to revive the 'purely Spartan' characteristics of their city, which had been greatly altered after Philopoimen's intervention.

One of the most interesting features of this effort was the reintroduction of the ancient Doric dialect. At a time when the *common* dialect (which was the Pan-Hellenic form that had evolved out of the Attic dialect) prevailed in Greece, in Sparta all the inscriptions associated with the famous *agoge* were written in the Doric dialect, sometimes even with obvious errors.[6] The fact reveals a 'deliberate and not always accurate archaism, which was intended to create an atmosphere of forged authenticity'.[7]

As a city, the Roman Sparta was certainly much more attractive than ever. She was surrounded by an impressive wall, she had many ancient temples and monuments and she was adorned with high quality artwork. But visitors would arrive there for another reason. What Sparta offered them was the unique experience of touring a living museum. The conservative city, which for many centuries had been inaccessible, holding out the rest of the world, finally opened her gates and invited guests to get to know her. 'We can imagine, if we are cynical enough, parties of tourists being conducted about, very interested in the *syssitia*, or in those that were preserved for show purposes; tasting the black broth; wondering at tales of antiquity of the *ephors* and the *patronomoi* and behaving like all tourists down the ages.'[8] The sports games of the adolescents were certainly the most popular attractions of the *agoge*. Among them were two activities known for their particular cruelty. The one was the 'battle' at Platanistas where, according to Pausanias, after a short ritual, teams of young people wrestled and using their arms, legs, kicks and bites tried to take their opponent's eyes out.[9] The other was the 'competition of endurance', which was held every year in honour of Artemis Orthia. According to ancient custom, which was supposedly 'revived', the teenagers had to steal as much cheese as they could from the altar, while the defenders of the altar tried to repel them by using whips.[10] In Roman Sparta, however, it seems that the custom was modified and took the form of bloody flogging, which the teen had to suffer silently at the altar. The winner was he who could endure the lashes the longest. The spectacle fascinated the Roman 'tourists', of course, who saw in it an original and high quality variation of the gladiatorial games. 'The sadistic pleasure to be got out of this miserable spectacle was so great that a theatre was built round the altar for the comfort of the spectators.'[11]

The image of 'traditional' Sparta, as it was developed and projected by her citizens during the Roman occupation, was in sharp contrast to her new reality. Although Sparta retained a special organization of her polity,[12] in most of her other characteristics she was minimally different from other contemporary cities. Undoubtedly the tide of 'tourists' who, motivated by their great interest for the Spartan history and *agoge*, visited Sparta was conducive to her becoming one of the major centres of Greek Heritage when the Roman Empire was at its zenith in the age of the Antonines. In this sense, the Spartans were considered to be the heirs of an ancient and glorious past which they endeavoured to maintain, and this conferred on them a special prestige within the territory of the Empire. As noted by a modern scholar of Roman Sparta, 'the prestige of the "revived" training and the tourism which it generated helped this otherwise fairly typical provincial Greek city to maintain a place in the world and allowed the Spartans to feel that they were still "special."'[13]

If Athens was the major cultural centre of the time, indispensable for the comprehensive education of the wealthy youth, then Sparta, demonstrating emphatically her 'Lykourgan polity', managed not only to ensure her identity in the Roman world but also to become a pole of attraction and an important landmark for travellers in Greece.

But there were two sides to the coin. Sparta had long ceased to be what she desired to display with so much tenacity. Her citizens, who used coins with Lykourgos' figure, who scrupulously observed their 'ancient' rituals, who proudly demonstrated their famous *agoge* in an effort to commemorate their illustrious ancestors, had nothing in common with them. For Lykourgos' traditions and laws were not commodities for tourist consumption, but the means by which Sparta created and maintained a strong army on which she based her dominance. In fact, the manifestations of *lakonomania* by the citizens of a small city of the Roman Empire were the requiem to an era that was irrevocably gone.

The Legacy

The character of the Spartan movement

The aim of this study, as indicated by the subtitle, is the description of the rise and fall of the Spartan revolutionary movement. While the terms 'revolutionary' and 'movement' have been used extensively by most historians in relation to both the leaders and the socio-political tides that prevailed in Sparta for more than half a century, in fact they have not been universally accepted. Since reservations or objections have been expressed at various times, a review of the matter and a 'reopening of the case' is essential upon the completion of the narrative part of this study.

It is true that the use of terms and expressions borrowed from contemporary reality in order to describe the socio-political trends of antiquity leads to an incorrect assessment more often than not. As has been pointed out, the dividing line that the ancient Greeks themselves drew between 'innovation' or even change and 'revolution' was much thinner than ours between 'revolutions' and 'reform'.[14] For this reason, some scholars have disputed that there was ever a Spartan 'movement', considering that there was no coherent ideological bond between the Spartan leaders of the period, while others doubt its revolutionary character either partially or completely.

An example of the first opinion, the denial of the existence of a 'movement', is the view that Nabis was the only true revolutionary who realized the essential problems of Spartan society and attempted to eliminate them, while Agis and Kleomenes were simply reformers who relentlessly chased anachronistic visions. This view argues that the restoration of the Lykourgan laws and the rebirth of Spartan power were minor issues and that the essential problem, which Nabis attempted to resolve, was to enable the residents of Lakonia to survive under the new socio-economic conditions of the Hellenistic era.[15] A similar view is expressed by Cartledge, according to whom Nabis 'surpassed the irredentist vision of Agis, Cleomenes and their imitators to embrace and realize a truly modern conception of Spartan state and society'.[16]

An example of the second opinion, denying the revolutionary character of the movement, is an emphatically expressed view that 'when we hear of seemingly radical-sounding schemes to abolish debts in Sparta, to redistribute the land on a massive scale, even to free helots, we should not be misled. Short term, these were pre-emptive, and sometimes desperate, measures designed to forestall and choke off a true revolution from below by making the fewest concessions possible. Long term, they were all promoted in furtherance of a paradoxically reactionary dream: the reestablishment of a strong and privileged elite, the purging of Sparta's new and effete luxuries, the return of the Lycurgan regime, complete with black broth, flogging, and barrack life; above all, the resurgence, in significantly increased numbers, of a matchless standing army.'[17]

There is certainly much truth in the statements above. But the Spartan movement was born out of the Spartan society and obviously it was intended exclusively for her. Its military objectives and limited nature do not contradict its revolutionary character. In the narrow context of the society which bore it, it was subversive and brought about radical changes in the structure of the Spartan socio-political system; in the literal sense it was genuinely revolutionary.

Some scholars have put forward even more extreme theories. According to Martinez-Lacy,[18] if a revolution requires the active participation of the masses to topple a regime, then obviously the Spartan movement was not revolutionary because the people did not actively participate in almost any subversive phase of the movement. Neither can this movement be described as revolutionary under the broader sense of the word: the overthrow of a regime and the imposition of permanent changes in society. For neither Agis' and Kleomenes' reforms nor Nabis' ones had a lasting effect. The first two were instantly abolished after the fall of the two Spartan kings, while Nabis' reforms were repealed four years after his assassination. Therefore, if somebody can be described as revolutionary in the broader sense, this is Philopoimen and the Achaean League! This conclusion is simply a hollow witticism.

But in respect to Martinez-Lacy's main argument, it should be noted that not all revolutions are successful or last long. A revolutionary movement is not limited to the 'ideal' type which this historian seems to have in mind, exemplified by the French or the Russian revolutions. Whether a revolutionary movement aims at restructuring society anew (referred to as 'progressive') or intends to restore a society to its former state (referred to as 'reactionary') does not undervalue the movement's revolutionary scope as long as it does not profess to improve minor structures of the existing system but intends to radically replace them. Twentieth century European history displays the characteristic reactionary revolutions of Italian and Spanish fascism and German Nazism, the revolutionary – and massive – nature of which is generally accepted.[19]

Although the aforementioned theories question it, the true revolutionary nature of the Spartan movement is supported by the narrative. To deny the existence of a 'revolutionary movement' is to overlook the fact that all historical records are inscribed into the frame of a unified ideological agenda. It is misleading to examine events in Sparta during this period in isolation, without taking note of existing interrelations. Instead the facts should be examined in the frame of a unified ideology with an obvious aim. This aim, none other than the reestablishment of the Spartan power and glory, contained two basic principles. Firstly, the restoration of '*Patrios politeia*', meaning a return to the traditional values of the Lykourgan constitution. This included the restoration of the *agoge*, the *syssitia*, the austere lifestyle and the unanimity of the citizens. Secondly, the restoration of an egalitarian regime through land redistribution and debt cancellation.[20] In addition, from a certain period onward, the effort to achieve the above objectives was motivated by the outright rivalry of Sparta with the Achaean League. Not only because they both strived for supremacy in southern Greece, but also because they struggled for the maintenance or the abolition of the status quo on behalf of the ruling class (as Polybios himself has admitted). These elements are obvious in all phases of the Spartan movement.

Equally consistent were the political programs of all the leading figures of the movement: Kleomenes effectively implemented Agis' political and social agenda, and even in the fifteen year period after the fall of Kleomenes (222–207) his ideas and his policy continued to influence the political life of Sparta. The existence of a 'Kleomenean party' might be a modern speculation,[21] but it is clear that, such a party existed, since all the protests and uprisings that occurred in Sparta during 220–219 originated from Kleomenes' supporters. His successor Lykourgos, whether he was a 'Kleomenist' or not, consciously tried to imitate him. His foreign policy was the same as that of Kleomenes: meaning it remained anti-Achaean, anti-Macedonian and, despite Sparta's obvious military weakness, firmly committed to the recovery of Spartan territory. The (usurper?) Chilon, who briefly overthrew Lykourgos, used the Kleomenean slogan of land reform in his desperate attempt to win over the Spartans. There is no doubt that Lykourgos' successor, Machanidas, continued the foreign policy of his predecessors and attempted to recapture the areas that Kleomenes had lost. Despite the vague picture, we can confidently conclude that the objectives, methods and basic ideological principles that characterized Kleomenes' movement were evident during the fifteen years from his fall until Nabis' appearance. Therefore it was still a vivid vision that was in decline rather than an ideological construct that had collapsed. At the same time, it is obvious that Nabis' radical reforms evolved from those previously implemented by Agis and Kleomenes. Land redistribution, debt cancellation, Sparta's opening to the world and the integration of the non-Spartans within her domain, the rebirth of Spartan power and Sparta's entry in the forefront of international policy were common goals for all three. It is impossible to consider Nabis' reforms separately, but only as a part of an evolutionary process in its extreme expression. Without Agis' and Kleomenes' precedent, it is difficult to comprehend Nabis.

Even after the fall of Nabis, the basic principles of the movement were evident in all the political sub-groups, even as they rushed to accuse each other and, together, the Achaean League before Rome, asking at the same time for the restoration of the 'Patrios politeia'. The ancestral polity, social equality[22] and hostility towards the Achaean League never ceased to exist and affect (in different ways) the views of the various fragmented political groups. Isn't it, perhaps, typical of all defeated movements to break up into smaller rival groups?

In fact the initiative and all revolutionary reforms originated from above and not from below. However, not all revolutions are initiated by the people. Moreover, it is true that beyond a certain point, the two most important leaders of the movement enjoyed the acceptance and support of the people.[23] Certainly, even in its most revolutionary expression, the Spartan movement never addressed the entire population of Lakonia, but only the population of a single city from which it sprang. Given the standards of its time and in relation to the closed society of Sparta which it addressed, this movement began as a reform effort and ended up completely subverting the political and social edifice of the Spartan society to such an extent that it has become a model revolutionary movement.[24]

'Sparta,' wrote William Tarn, 'offers us a picture of the three regular phases of a revolution; drastic reform, moderate or limited revolution and complete revolution, all within compass of about a generation.'[25] How positive the effect of this revolution was, is a completely different question which will be addressed next.

From Lykourgos to the Spartan Mirage (Revolution as Flight to the Past)

Throughout the course of the Spartan movement, Lykourgos' figure was a guiding force. Despite the fact that many a time the revolutionaries turned against most 'Lykourgan' institutions, at least at the level of declarations they aimed at restoring 'Lykourgan' values, which were the essence of the long established polity of their forefathers. In fact, Lykourgos' original revolution was an unfading source of inspiration and guiding principle for the Spartan revolutionary movement in all its phases. The similarities between the two revolutions are impressive.[26] Both emerged as a reaction to an intense social crisis and attempted to tackle the problem of major social inequalities through the expansion of the political body and land re-allotment. Citizen equality and austere military lifestyle were as fundamental to the Lykourgan revolution as they were to the revolution of the third century. Both prevailed with relatively little violence. Both went against the current of their time. The former aimed at Sparta's territorial expansion at a time when the trend among Greek cities was the establishment of colonies, while the latter was a bid to restore Spartan supremacy at the time when supremacy was the object of competition between large states or state-like entities: the Hellenistic empires, Rome, and the Leagues. This was the main cause for the failure of the second revolution: seen in the light of its time, the Spartan movement was nothing but a futile attempt to set back the clock of history.

Agis IV was not aware of that in 242 BC, when he implemented his reforms, aiming at regaining the lost radiance of his fatherland. Neither could he fathom the consequences of his actions in the long term. Unintentionally he initiated a disintegrating process, which concluded with the final overthrow of the Lykourgan constitution and Sparta's transformation to a museum.

Sparta was severely ailing when Agis undertook the responsibility of saving her. Yet, at the same time, the city still retained her identity. Until the moment when Agis carried out his coup, all the 'Lykourgan' elements of the Spartan constitution were still in effect. The *agoge* may have been downgraded, and no longer served the purpose for which it was created, the *syssitia* may have lost their original significance and turned into a showcase for a small minority, but they still existed and constituted basic components of Spartan society. Furthermore the institutions of the dual kingship, the *Gerousia* and the *ephors* were still functioning, after a fashion, and had never been doubted. The three classes (Spartans, *perioikoi* and helots) remained segregated, while Spartan society continued being closed to outsiders. Overall, the character of the city remained 'Lykourgan.'

With the violent overthrow of the *ephors* and his co-ruler, Agis dealt a crushing blow to these two ancient institutions, resulting in their weakening. The reaction to what he did led to his own overthrow and his deplorable assassination by the *ephors*. His fall signified the abolition of an essential Spartan institution: the dual kingship. In fact, Agis did not manage to implement but only a small part of his reforms. However, the path of subversion had now opened. Kleomenes proved a worthy successor of Agis, and was even more radical. Just as the *ephors* murdered Agis, so did Kleomenes murder the *ephors* and, invoking the name of Lykourgos, he abolished this institution. He then applied all of Agis' revolutionary reforms resulting in the opening of the Spartan society and, for the first time, the inclusion of non-Spartans. Kleomenes' Sparta 'while perhaps the best polity Sparta ever had, was certainly not the '*patrios politeia*'.[27] It hardly had anything to do with the Lykourgan polity which it supposedly was trying to revive. After his decline, *ephors*, *gerontes* and kings returned and were overthrown repeatedly; institutions continued weakening until eventually they lost their validity. The final blow was, of course, given by Nabis. His governance was nothing but a tyranny, disguised under the royal veil after the model of the Hellenistic monarchy, during which almost all Lykourgan traditions were abolished. Nabis' Sparta, which had successfully confronted numerically superior Roman forces and their allies, was a walled city, possessed a powerful fleet and an army of 10,000 'Spartans' most of whom were former helots and foreigners.[28] The confusion resulting from Nabis' fall is indicated by the fact that Spartans insisted on reconstructing their city walls, which had been destroyed by Philopoimen, and on restoring their ancestral polity when they convened at Kleitor in 184.[29] But the irony of fate should not go unnoticed: as pretentious, hypocritical and deceitful as Lykortas of Megalopolis' reply that the Spartans would have to destroy with their own hands the wall they were asking to rebuild may have been, he was historically justified. What the Spartans were asking, the walling of their city, was by definition contradictory to the Spartan traditions.

At least one of the main targets of the movement was realized even after Sparta was conquered by the Romans and turned into a 'museum piece'[30] and a Theme Park of her past:[31] Sparta had finally regained her ancestral polity. But to what extent and in what sense? For neither the *diarchy* nor the Spartan army, the two most important Spartan features synonymous to old-time power of the city, were recovered. The only elements that were revived were the 'ancient' way of life, frugal diet and *agoge*. But of these elements exactly which ones revived and how they were related to tradition is hard to say, since they had ceased to exist for more than four decades [188–146]. What memories of the 'Lykourgan' constitution – which supposedly they were trying to revive in 146 – could the

Spartans possibly have had since they did not keep meticulous records but relied solely on oral tradition? Much more since the regime which was abolished in 188 by Philopoimen was not 'Lykourgan' at all but a 'Kleomenean' or a 'Nabean' version of it. Understandably Polybios remarked that the constitution of Sparta during 227 to 188 was merely a disguised tyranny. But the Spartans would disagree with him. For eighty years after Kleomenes' coup the *patrios politeia* was now synonymous to the Kleomenean constitution in their consciousness. In 146 the only people who still preserved some memory of an independent and strong Sparta were those who had lived in Nabis' state.[32]

The problem with Sparta is that a huge amount of information about the city and her institutions comes from historians who lived during the first and second century AD and relied heavily on sources associated directly or indirectly with the Spartan movement. Pausanias' descriptions concern second century AD Sparta, while the numerous *Spartan Sayings (Apophthegmata Lakonika)* that Plutarch has collected and supposedly express 'Lykourgan' values uttered by famous Spartans are of dubious origin. Few of them can be considered authentic. As Tigerstedt aptly remarked, the *Spartan Sayings* do not reflect what the Spartans really were but what it was believed they were.[33]

All the above have naturally made us question the validity of the information on the origin of the Spartan constitution. This questioning begins as early as the mid-nineteenth century. In his classic work *A History of Greece*,[34] the British historian George Grote disputed for the first time the 'Lykourgan' land redistribution to equal *kleroi* considering that this perception was created in the third century under the influence of Spartan revolutionaries. By the mid-twentieth century, the French historian François Ollier[35] used the very accurate term 'Spartan Mirage' in order to describe this elusive and idealized image that Sparta came to represent through distortions, alterations and unsubstantiated additions to her true image. From then on, this expression was inextricably linked with Sparta,[36] so it is almost impossible to make any reference to her without referring to the 'Mirage', the misleading image surrounding Sparta which is a result of her idealization. The contribution of the Spartan movement to the formation of this mirage is considered crucial. The question that is raised is the following: What exactly happened in 227 after Kleomenes overthrew the legitimate regime? Were the Spartan traditions ultimately restored? Or, perhaps, were new traditions contrived so that they would serve the political and ideological goals of the Spartan king?

Recently, after having systematically reviewed the social and land tenure system of Sparta, Steven Hodkinson brought Grote's theory back into the limelight, arguing that the much celebrated social and economic equality of the

Spartans was concocted much later.[37] According to Hodkinson, the Spartans were not socially equal, nor were *kleroi* granted to them for a lifetime by the state; and despite the fact that Sparta did not have her own currency, the possession of gold and silver coins was allowed until the early fourth century, while even commodity-type trading was allowed to some extent. The phenomenon of corruption (or infection according to others) of the Spartan tradition began to evolve during the fourth century after the political and military weakening of Sparta. This led to her transformation 'from that of a political ideal whose merits could be argued and debated to that of a moral ideal whose merits were regarded as indisputable.'[38] Henceforth, most of the Greek intellectuals would treat Sparta as an exemplary society that was destroyed by the thrall of Mammon. To these theories were added by the end of the third century the theories of the Spartan revolutionaries, who incorporated their own views on equality into the existing literature and presented them as completely 'Lykourgan'. Even the enemies of the revolution fell victim to this perception. Polybios, who – despite his blatant hatred towards Kleomenes and his despise towards everything that smacked of the Spartan movement – described the Kleomenean version of equal allotment of Spartan *kleroi* as 'Lykourgan', is an undeniable testament to the power of the Kleomenean propaganda.[39]

Nevertheless, the person most responsible for the distorted view of Sparta and the definitive formulation of the Spartan Mirage was Plutarch. From a distance of four hundred years, this author from Chaironeia gathered a mass of scattered, contradictory information regarding Sparta throughout the centuries and transformed it 'into a coherent amalgam made up from a combination of fourth-century moralizing, early moral philosophy and revolutionary egalitarian propaganda.'[40]

It is noteworthy that Plutarch is the main source not only for both of the two major figures of the Spartan revolutionary movement but also for Lykourgos himself. Moreover, the lives of both third century Spartan kings and that of the legendary Lykourgos display some remarkable similarities concerning land re-allotment and equality of new *kleroi*. This calls into question the Lykourgan land re-allotment, which goes unmentioned by any source from antiquity up to Aristotle.[41] As Grote first pointed out, Agis' promises for land re-allotment are strikingly similar to the land re-allotment project realized by Lykourgos.[42] The description of Sparta before the Lykourgan reforms[43] is analogous to the decadent image of Sparta before Agis' and Kleomenes' reforms[44] which is proved to have originated from Phylarchos.[45] The citation that refers to land re-allotment by Lykourgos surprisingly resembles Kleomenes' speech to his fellow citizens the day after the coup.[46]

If we take into consideration the above observations, the previous proposition can be restated as follows: did the famous 'Lykourgan' revolution really occur or was it rather a myth fabricated by Kleomenes in order to justify his own revolution *in the name of Lykourgos*?

In seeking to answer the above, we first need to admit that the relationship of the revolutionary movement with the Spartan Mirage was reciprocal. On one hand, our understanding of the movement itself was affected by legendary Sparta through Plutarch's (Phylarchos') dramatic biographies, which present the leaders' idealized image. On the other hand, the Spartan revolution had a decisive role in shaping this Spartan legend and in particular the image of early Sparta and Lykourgos himself.[47] It is, therefore, no coincidence that the latest trend among scholars is to investigate the way in which tradition shaped the national identity of the Spartans. At the same time, researchers investigate the degree of her subsequent distortions that resulted in an idealized but illusive image of Sparta. In the context of raising various questions about Sparta, it is crucial to examine the role of the Spartan movement leaders, who exploited tradition or even concocted it in order to serve their political goals.

Many deliberately extreme theories have been put forward on this issue. The most subversive one is certainly that by Nigel Kennell[48] according to which the cornerstone of the Spartan edifice, the famous *agoge,* was nothing but a fabrication of Kleomenean Sparta (specifically philosopher Sphairos), which was completed during the Roman occupation. Kennell argues that the Spartan *agoge* is divided into three distinct periods: the 'Classical' period, which lasted until 270–250 when the *agoge* was abandoned; the 'Hellenistic' period which starts with its revival by Kleomenes under Sphairos' supervision and ends with its abolition by Philopoimen in 188; finally, the last period of the *agoge*, which began in 146 with the Roman conquest and lasted until the fourth century AD. During the first period, the *agoge* was merely a set of archaic customs, of rituals and initiations, which – as it also happened in other cities and especially in Athens – signified the transition from adolescence to young adulthood. The big change occurred during the Kleomenean revolution. At that time, philosopher Sphairos formulated a completely different image of Sparta with his theories and simultaneously transformed the *agoge* in what came to be regarded as the traditional training of the Spartan citizen.[49] According to Kennell, the dominant image of the Spartan socio-political system was developed almost entirely during the Hellenistic period by Sphairos, whom Kennell literally considers the inventor of the *agoge.*[50] The *agoge* of classical times had never been the foundation of the Spartan constitution. On the contrary, the *agoge* that Sphairos created in the second half of the third century was the foundation on which the Spartans rebuilt their traditional customs during the Roman occupation. '... From a set of initiatory rituals and customs slightly different from those anywhere else in Greece, Spartans in the Hellenistic and Roman periods constructed a unique institution, the *agoge*, through whose powerful re-enactments of an idealized cultural legacy, they claimed for themselves a lasting place in Greek culture and projected an image of Sparta that has endured for almost two millennia.'[51]

Despite the fact that Kennell's theory has been sharply criticized,[52] the questioning of the Spartan tradition's reliability, as evidenced in its falsification by the 'third century Spartan revolution', continues unabated. Flower, Kennell's successor to this theory, carries it even further. He claims that in their effort to legitimize their revolutionary reforms, Agis and Kleomenes did not hesitate to reconstruct or even reinvent certain 'Spartan' traditions in order to attribute all their radical changes to Lykourgos.[53] Both the equality of the inalienable *kleroi* and the presumed equality of the Spartans in the past[54] are considered to be entirely fabricated by the revolutionaries. The latter didn't hesitate to invent 'ancient' traditions and laws that allegedly prohibited dowries and procreation with foreigners. They even invented 'ancient' customs such as the observation of the starry sky by the *ephors*, in order to support their ideological positions always invoking the only absolute authority of Spartan history, Lykourgos.[55] Certainly, the objective was not a strict return to the Lykourgan constitution *per se* (with all its inherent weaknesses and flaws that led to its decline), but the creation of a renewed and strong Sparta. In order to legitimize this new Sparta in the eyes of the Spartans, it had to appear 'Lykourgan'; this was exactly what happened with the supposed return to the – 'restored' – past to which (according to this view) Sphairos' contribution was decisive.[56]

Given the above theories and the multiple distortions and reconstructions of the Spartan tradition (which did not happen only during the Hellenistic age but date back already in the Classical times) the research and study of Spartan history following the traditional methodology (i.e. combining evidence from Alkman, Tyrtaios, Xenophon, Polybios and Plutarch) is simply impossible. The reason for this is the fact that the Spartan tradition has been reinvented so many times and to such an extent that it is now impossible to describe any aspect of Spartan society through the infinite versions that she has taken during her long course of existence throughout the centuries. According to this theory, 'the only kind of Spartan history that one can write is one which traces the developmental stages of specific aspects of Spartan society...In a sense this kind of history is less satisfactory, because it does not allow us to imagine fully what it would have been like to live as a Spartan at a given time.'[57] This might create additional problems for the historian who is trying to reconstruct the Spartan history and also for the non-specialist who is trying to understand it. 'But it is preferable to face up to the limitations which our evidence imposes upon us, than merely to add another chapter to the Spartan mirage' concludes the author of this theory.[58]

Other scholars have objected to the above theories. Recently Figueira, investigating the nature of the Spartan *kleroi*, defended the idea of equal, indivisible and non-inherited *kleroi*,[59] and challenged the view that philosophers and historians of the third century were influenced by the revolutionary ideas of the Spartan movement. He claimed that the similarities in the numbers of the *kleroi* between the Lykourgan re-allotment and the re-allotments of Agis and Kleomenes are coincidental.[60] In a later work, he examined in detail all the philosophers of the Hellenistic times who had studied Sparta and concluded that they had not been affected by the Spartan movement. He maintains that the view according to which Sphairos should be held responsible for the systematic distortion of the Spartan tradition is self-contradictory. He criticizes contemporary historians for attributing to Sphairos two opposed roles: 'on the one hand, he has infected the programme of Kleomenes and his historiography with Stoic ideas, but, on the other hand, Kleomenean revolutionary policies influenced Sphairos' *politeia* creating fallacious precedents of Kleomenes that infiltrated Plutarch's work.'[61] (Let it be noted that Plutarch does not link Sphairos to Kleomenes' social programme in any way.) Finally, Figueira notes that 'the recent tendency to emphasize the influence of Hellenistic propaganda risks becoming a shibboleth that is deployed whenever we find ourselves at a loss integrating our data into meaningful reconstruction of Spartan institutions.'[62]

'The next book on Sparta will probably run to a single page, with one large question mark on it,' Toynbee wrote to Forest in 1969.[63] Nearly half a century later, the situation does not appear to have changed significantly. Questioning the accuracy and objectivity of sources regarding the Spartan socio-political system and, consequently, alleged land re-allotment, equality of Spartan *kleroi*, how they were distributed and inherited, and the role of the *agoge*, is a trend that has ebbed and flowed many times from Grote's time until the present. The extent to which the influence of the historians-intellectuals of the Hellenistic period has distorted what we know about the Spartan constitution, and how to remove this influence remains a popular and controversial subject of research for modern historians. It is difficult to decide on where reality ends and where fiction begins: truth and legend are so tightly interwoven that it is almost impossible to separate them. The Spartan movement casts its shadow heavily over Sparta.[64]

Having examined the Spartan revolutionary movement in relation to the Spartan tradition, we can now move on to a second, more difficult and controversial issue: if we analysed it on a Pan-Hellenic scope, how positive would the role of the movement have been? Was it conducive to the Pan-Hellenic unity and to what extent?

We proceed to examine this question without overlooking for a moment the fact that the concept of Pan-Hellenic unity had a totally different meaning in the ancient Greek world than it does today as examined by the national historiography in the context of a national Greek state. The sacrifice of each city-state's independence in favour of a superior 'national' interest, represented by a 'super state' was alien and often contrary to beliefs of the Greeks in Classical antiquity. The majority (with the possible exception of a small circle of intellectuals and politicians) identified national interest with the microcosm of their *polis* and set the boundaries of all national strategy within this narrow context. In this aspect, the Spartan movement was mainly a creation (possibly the last echo) of the Classical Greek world. It expressed the last attempt of a *polis* to assert its supremacy at a time when even the survival of such a small entity, not embedded in any larger (international) formation, was highly questionable. It is not a coincidence that the city which undertook this operation was Sparta. Certainly, there is a romantic side to this doomed attempt by Sparta to bring the world to her measures. This romantic side of the Spartan movement, combined with Plutarch's colourful charged descriptions, charmed writers and poets in the past and still continues to charm them in a special way.[65]

Nevertheless this feature, which was at the same time the movement's greatest weakness, exerted a negative effect on the political affairs of its time. Undoubtedly a city-state could not antagonize the Achaean League, a superior model of government in the Classical world, which Sparta fought to the bitter end. It is important to remember that even after Philopoimen's brutal intervention in 188 – and certainly to some extent because of it – Sparta remained a foreign body within the Achaean League and constantly sought the opportunity to secede from it. This stance echoed the last gasps of the Spartan movement, when the goal of the revival of the Spartan power had degenerated to the demand for restoration of the '*patrios politeia*'. This demand for 'Sparta's return to her paternal regime' was also the pretext for the final submission of the Peloponnese, the last independent territory of Greece, to the Romans.

In retrospect, the fate of Greece would not have been any different. But at the very least, if the Spartan movement had not erupted, the Peloponnese could have united much earlier, and been spared the bloody wars that tormented it for five decades (243–192) ruining the economy and decimating the population.

Reviewing the events 2,000 years later, one cannot but accept the historical verdict that the role of the Spartan movement in Peloponnesian affairs was negative. With respect to Sparta herself, it was devastating. However, the leaders of the movement were not in a position to know this, and even less those who followed them, wholeheartedly believing that they were fighting for righteousness and justice.

In 227, after Kleomenes' reforms, 4,000 people each received a *kleros* accompanied by membership in the Spartan citizenry, and along with it the conviction that they were now defenders of a centuries old tradition of which their *kleros* was the physical embodiment. For them, there had never been any doubt whether tradition was a fabrication or not. As a matter of fact, none of them ever doubted the legitimacy of their ideals. They were committed to the idea that Sparta could regain her grandeur and so they struggled to make her glorious. They could not have foreseen that the recovery of Spartan might, social justice and equality, the return to the values of the glorious past, and all these noble objectives which the circumstances of history were to convert to anachronistic hopes would exert a heavy price; in the short term, the destruction of Sparta, and in the long term to the destruction of the Peloponnese, thus becoming the pretext for the Roman conquest.

In conclusion, it was a revolutionary movement which, apart from the bloodshed it caused in the Peloponnese, stripped Sparta from all her Lykourgan features and dismantled everything that made her exceptional. Furthermore, it resulted in confusing reality and myth: the identification of the great socio-political revolution as the return to the traditional way of life, in other words the Lykourgan mantle in which the leaders of the Spartan movement consciously or unconsciously enveloped their reforms, contributed decisively to obscuring real Sparta and the Lykourgan revolution.

Several decades after the Spartan movement was eradicated, when the turmoil had subsided and the dust had settled, all that was left was an obsession to maintain the traditions and customs of Sparta, a kind of local folklore that during the Roman period resulted in Sparta becoming a living museum. All that this movement, with its claim of attempting to restore the true spirit of the law, accomplished in the end was merely to revive the letter of the law, and even that meaninglessly: a set of formalities without essence, seen behind the misleading veil of idealization.

If Roman Sparta ever had something in common with her old heroic self, this would not be the spirit but only the name of Lykourgos.

Appendix A

Military Roads of Lakonia

This is an attempt for a provisional reconstruction of the military roads of Lakonia according to the findings of recent scholars.

It includes the system of routes used by the Spartan army when it left the boundaries of Lakonia or by enemy forces when they invaded the Spartan territory. There were two major axes and their branches which served Sparta's road of communication with the cities in the north. These were, in order, from west to east as follows:

A) The road from Sparta to Megalopolis, most of which followed the Eurotas valley in a general north-western direction. Sources mention this route as early as the beginning of the fifth century. It was the route preferred systematically by the Spartan army in the days of great glory as it provided easy access to the territory of Megalopolis or the small basin of Asea to its east or, even further east, to the territory of Tegea. It followed the flow of the River Eurotas, bypassed Pellana and reached the area of Belminatis near the modern Lagonikos Inn. At the point where the watershed changes and the descent to the basin of Megalopolis begins, it divided into two branches along the left and right banks of the River Theious (modern Koutoufarina). The left (west) branch reached Leuktron (modern Leontari), a significant, fortified border town and from there it descended to the plain of Megalopolis. The right (east) branch passed through the area where today stand the villages of Skortsino and Boutsara and entered the territory of Megalopolis in the vicinity of the present-day village of Rapsomati. Reaching the plain of Megalopolis, the Spartan army had the ability to turn northeast, cross the small plain of Asea connecting Megalopolis with Tegea, climb the 'Kalogerikon' mountain pass and emerge at the Arcadian plateau coming from the west.

To reach Tegea, it was not necessary to follow the complete route through Megalopolis. Approximately where the route branches at Belminatis, another road began, heading northeast and following the foot of the mountain today known as Tsemberou. This road allowed the army to arrive safely – and shielded from being observed by the permanently hostile Megalopolis – to the border fort of Oreisthasion (modern Anemodouri), which was the last station for the

Spartan forces to assemble and reorganize before entering the basin of Asea and from there Tegea. As we know from ancient sources, this route offered the Spartan army the advantage of surprise and was utilized repeatedly.

In addition, there was a third alternative route to Asea, which avoided Megalopolis and was even shorter. It started from the nodal region of Belminatis, turned further east sinking into the steep ravine of northern Eurotas (modern Lagada), followed a meandering path seemingly difficult but actually walkable and arrived to the southern edge of Asea in the vicinity of the city of Eutaia (modern village of Lianou). It was easily controlled by a Spartan fort that was halfway along the route and could be used when good weather prevailed.

All these roads and their junctions constituted the military capital of Lakonia, the 'diagonal of Eurotas'. The apt name of this great military highway is coined by Y. Pikoulas who thoroughly examined the topography of northern Lakonia-southern Megalopolis region in his doctoral dissertation (Pikoulas 1988b p 203–216). The fact that it ran through the north Lakonic area in a north-western direction facilitated the gradual concentration of all military forces of the Spartan territory without delay in the event of general mobilization. A military force could begin its way from Sparta, assemble the Spartans and the *perioikoi* of the cities south of Sparta and on its march to the border incorporate at every stop units from the northern *perioikic* cities and, of course, the necessary supplies (Pikoulas 1988b p 202–203).

B) The stretch of 'straight' road from Sparta to Tegea which joined the Arcadian plateau with the Lakonia plain crossing the dry and sparsely populated region of Skiritis. It is approximately the same route as the current vehicular road from Tripolis to Sparta with minor local variations. The chain of steep hills that stand out in sharp relief against the terrain are formed by the merging of the extensions of Mainalon and the foothills of Parnon which are crossed by several streams. Two of them stand out for their size. They rise in the area of the villages Karyai (former Arachova) and Vourvoura at the watershed between Arcadia and Lakonia and they flow from north to south. One of them, the ancient Oinous (modern Kelefina) flows southward and merges with river Eurotas. The other, nowadays Sarantapotamos, flows in the opposite direction, i.e. northward, toward the Tegean plateau.

The road from Sparta rose towards Sellasia. There it branched off into two arms: the western one – which corresponds to the current vehicular road from Tripolis to Sparta-followed the Kleisoura Pass (modern name) to reach the small plain of Karyai; the eastern one, followed the riverbed of Oinous and met the western arm at the same place, Karyai. From there, a single road descended to the spring of Kryavrysi and following the course of Sarantapotamos it reached the plain of Tegea. The western arm is shorter and one would expect that in ancient times it was preferable for this reason but in fact this is how it looks on the map only. In reality, it is more arduous because of its many elevation changes and because it crosses a completely arid area. Loring (1895, pages 57–58) was the first to highlight this important condition, the presence of water sources required for regular use of a road. More than one hundred years later, Pikoulas noted in which roads there are water fountains and where.

A third route probably of secondary importance, belonged to the same axis, connecting Sparta with the main hamlet of Skiritis, Oion (modern Agios Ioannis Arvanitokerasias). The road ran from Sparta through Skiritis, reached Oion, and from there ended up at Tegea. A conspicuous fort was built on the hilltop of Khartzenikos (modern name) and controlled the road (Pikoulas 1987, pages 140–141, 146–147).

To have a full picture of the communication system of Sparta with its northern borders, we should also consider another road besides the two major routes, the 'big diagonal' and the 'straight road' from Sparta to Tegea. This road ran along the ridge of Mount Taygetos on the borders of Lakonia-Messenia following a north-to-south axis of direction that reached up to the border city of Leuktron. (Pikoulas 1988b pages 223–224).

Finally, there is evidence of a secondary cross street that connected Asea (from modern village Manari) with Oion (Loring 1895 pages 60–62). These two roads do not lend themselves to the movement of large armies and convoys.

It is remarkable that all these roads were suitable for chariot traffic. This is a safe conclusion based on the wheel ruts found in various place. The thought comes to mind that this entire transportation network, which evidence suggests stretched across almost all the Peloponnese and required planning and resources to maintain over the long term, is the result of a focused and systematic policy of Classical era Sparta when she was at the height of her power and prosperity.

Appendix B

Sphairos

The influence of Stoic philosopher Sphairos on Agis and Kleomenes is an extremely complex and controversial issue that has divided historians. Their views vary and are often contradictory, ranging from his recognition as a teacher of both Spartan kings to the outright rejection of any influence he might have had on them and on the revolutionary movement.

There is very limited evidence confirming Sphairos' presence in Sparta and his role as Kleomenes' teacher. Yet there are more than a few historians who detect a 'touch of stoicism' in Kleomenes' ideology. Kleomenes' revolutionary reforms show considerable similarity to Agis' reform programme. As David (1981, page 167) aptly observes, this has led the historians who regard Stoic philosophy as the driving force of the Spartan revolution to link it with Agis, despite the lack of evidence.

Tarn, who is strongly convinced that Sphairos was Kleomenes' teacher (Tarn 1923, page 135), argues that Agis 'must have known Stoic theories through Zeno's pupil, Sphaerus, who was at Sparta' (Tarn 1928, page 742). Ollier is also convinced that Stoic philosophy had a decisive influence on the Spartan movement, and he notes (Ollier 1936, pages 541–542) the apparent influence of the Stoics in many parts of the work of Phylarchos, who seems to have shared their views to some extent and relied on Sphairos' works on Sparta (for this see also David 1981, page 168). According to Ollier, the Stoic philosophy imbued the Spartan revolutionary movement with a special quality: 'Let us not doubt,' he says emphatically, 'that even without Sphairos' Stoic teachings, a more or less violent revolution would have inevitably erupted in Lakedaimon. But it would not have had the same splendour' (Ollier 1936, page 570). Ollier is certain that the Stoic philosopher Sphairos 'lived in Sparta at the side of King Agis' while acknowledging that Plutarch 'does not say a word of it' in his biography (Ollier 1936, page 546). Both the presence of Sphairos in Sparta during Kleomenes' youth (who was only a few years younger than Agis) as well as the zeal of the nineteen-year-old Agis for radical reforms led the French historian to conclude that 'if we did not accept Sphairos by his side, Agis seems less comprehensible'(Ollier 1936, page 546). According to Ollier,

Sphairos visited Sparta twice. The first time, he came to the city as the teacher of Agis and Kleomenes, leaving after Agis' assassination and returning after Kleomenes' victory to oversee the education of the Spartan youth.

Michell (1964, page 323) does not dismiss Ollier's hypothesis regarding Sphairos' first visit to Sparta but notes that only his second visit can be stated with certainty. According to Michell, Sphairos came to Sparta as a consultant to Kleomenes regarding the restoration of the *agoge* and the traditional polity.

Africa is more assertive, and completely rejects the hypothesis that Kleomenes was Sphairos' student considering it 'unlikely that King Leonidas who had lynched Agis, his mother, and his grandmother, would have tolerated a subversive instructor for his son.' (Africa 1961, page 18). However, the instruction of a philosopher who lived at the court of the monarch Ptolemy could not have been so subversive. Besides, Sphairos' preaching of the glorious past and the traditions of Sparta did not necessarily contradict the perceptions of the wealthy Spartans – King Leonidas among them – who 'invoked the traditions of Lykourgos, even if his interpretation of them was very different from that of Agis' (Oliva 1971, page 232). Africa further argues that the ideology of the Spartan revolution, if an ideological coherence could be assigned to it, is closer to the cynical than the stoic philosophy (Africa 1961, page 18). If Sphairos did in fact visit Sparta, this occurred only after Kleomenes had been established in power, meaning that he served Kleomenes 'as a propagandist in the halcyon days of the revolution when the king of Sparta could pay for publicists' (Africa 1968, page 10). Whatever 'cynical' features the Spartan movement may have had, they are also linked to the possible presence in Sparta of the cynic philosopher Teles from Megara (see Fuks 1962b). But the role of the latter is even more unclear than that of Sphairos. Moreover, the aspects of Sparta which supposedly charmed the stoics and cynics fascinated almost all Greek intellectuals of the time, with the exception of the Epicureans.

Sphairos' role as Kleomenes' teacher (and obviously Agis') has also been challenged by other historians such as Oliva (1971, page 232) and David (1981, page 167). Some are convinced about Sphairos' influence on Kleomenes (Rawson 2002, page 91, Shimron 1972, page 33, Erskine 1990, pages 123–149, Green 1993, page 143; the latter does not hesitate to consider Kleomenes 'a Stoic') but avoids taking a position as far as Agis is concerned. According to Cartledge (2002b, page 51) Kleomenes' Stoic influence 'remains more than a little doubtful' although the confidence with which he stood 'his Lykourgan ground may have owed something to the erudition of Sphaerus'. In a more recent study he maintains that 'Sphaerus might well have seen in Cleomenes a potential "wise man" and practical instrument of his ideas' (Cartledge 2009, page 118). There are still those, of course, who insist that Sphairos and his Stoic teaching influenced not only Kleomenes but also Agis, whose revolutionary reforms were directed against the Spartan traditions and harmonized with the universality of the Stoics (Ferguson 1975, page 132). Recently the theory of Sphairos' double visit to Sparta, first as a teacher of young Kleomenes and then after an invitation by the latter to undertake the education of young people and to help restore the *agoge,* has come again to the fore (Kennell 1995, pages 11 -12 and 101–102, 2010, page 174, Figueira 2004, page 56 and 2007, page 151). According to Kennell, the fact that Kleomenes was Sphairos' student was the main reason why he later assigned him the task of overseeing the *agoge* of the youth. According to Figueira, the return of Sphairos is mostly associated with the alliance between Sparta and Ptolemy: 'Sphairos may well have been Ptolemy III's agent in Laconia,' he stresses (2004, page 56).

Appendix C

The Modern Battlefield of Sellasia

The battlefield of Sellasia has been the subject of intense debate and controversy among historians since the mid-nineteenth century and especially during the early decades of the twentieth century to such an extent that a modern historian wrote of 'the new Battle of Sellasia'.[1] Of all historians of antiquity, Polybios is the only one who left a detailed description of the topography of the battlefield. Plutarch (*Kleom.* 28, Philop.6), Pausanias (2.9.2–3, 3.10.9, 8.49.4) and Livy (34.28.1) also provide meagre information.

The first person to have ever done a systematic verification of the site that Polybios describes was Captain (later Lieutenant-General) A Jochmus[2] during the first half of the nineteenth century. He carefully examined the area and provided a brief description of the battle accompanied by a detailed map showing the original layout of the opposing forces as well as their positions during the course of the battle. This map indicates the location of ancient Sellasia on Agios Konstantinos Hill. Jochmus identified Evas (which is mentioned by Polybios) with Mount Troules (also known as Tourles or Tourla) and Olympos with an outgrowth of Mount Provatares which is called Kokkina. The two mountains each rise on one side of the River Kelefina which has always been identified with Polybios' River Oinous. Tourles have two cone-shaped and sharp peaks, the higher of which is 784.30m or approximately 2573ft above sea level. Provatares consists of a set of hills, part of which is the aforementioned 'Kokkina'. Along the valley and parallel to the River Kelefina, Jochmus noted the existence of an ancient road marked by wheel ruts. Gorgylos, the tributary of the River Oinous which according to Polybios played a key role in the battle, is according to Jochmus a brook called Baraka. This flows at the foot of Tourles and ends in the River Kelefina at a point southeast of the ruins, where once stood Krevata's Inn. This brook has until modern times (April 2008) a steady stream of water during spring months. On the bank of the Kelefina opposite and a little bit south from its junction with the Baraka, at the foot of Provatares, the ground undulates forming a fold. Jochmus notes that this is an excellent defensive position, which is in line with Polybios' accounts of the battle.[3]

Jochmus' theory generally seems convincing. Its main disadvantage is that Eukleidas' deployment in Tourles is presented overextended: it begins from the position where Dagla's Inn (later also known as Pantazis') once stood, and extends deeply into rough and steep ground up to the highest northern summit of Tourles. Yet the possession of the whole of these locations was of no strategic importance, and furthermore fighting in this rugged region must have been practically impossible.

In the early twentieth century, Johann Kromayer (one of the later[4] researchers who visited the battlefield) formulated a quite different theory.[5] Specifically, he identified Evas Hill not with Tourles but with the much lower elevation of Palaiogoulas (637.75m high, approximately 2100ft), which is located further south on the west bank of the River Oinous (modern Kelefina). Kromayer also places Olympos on Kokkina's position but a little to the south from the position that Jochmus had suggested, that is on the southwest slope of Mount Provatares. According to Kromayer, the Gorgylos torrent is the shallow fold in the ground in the 'Kourmeki' passage north of Palaiogoulas, between the latter and Mount Tourles. South of Palaiogoulas, Kromayer discovered wheel ruts which – in his opinion – testify to the existence of the road he considered to be an extension of the Tegea road leading to Sparta.

This view was strongly contested by the Greek archaeologist George Soteriades, who repeatedly toured the battlefield and published his research on it.[6] Soteriades observed that if Kromayer's reasoning applied, then the ancient road from Tegea to Sparta should continue its course south for approximately 1,000m (3,300ft) past Kourmeki Passage before it turned west to Sparta, creating a pointless detour. According to Soteriades 'the ancient road along the Oinous does not run between the "Evas" and the "Olympos" hill cluster, but abandons the river and runs between Palaiogoulas and Tourla'.[7] If we accept Kromayer's view that Evas is identical to Palaiogoulas, then the road from Tegea to Sparta would not have passed between the two hills following the flow of the Oinous as mentioned by Polybios, but must have circled Evas Hill from the west.[8]

Soteriades cited two more compelling arguments to disprove that the Palaiogoulas is Evas Hill. Firstly, he stated that this hill is too small for a clash of 10,000 warriors to have happened on it. In addition, the northern slope of Palaiogoulas, where Antigonos allegedly attacked, is too steep to allow the tactics of Evas' defenders that is long range attacks followed by falling back to higher ground.[9] Moreover the south-western slope, down which the defenders of Evas were forced to retreat according to Polybios, is smooth and not 'steep and precipitous' as mentioned by Polybios.[10] Finally, Soteriades pointed out the existence of a strong wall on Palaiogoulas which he claims dates back to the fifth century BC or earlier. This wall had been identified for the first time by Jochmus who had noted the existence of a fortress on Palaiogoulas on the map which accompanied his work. Yet, in the description of the battle, there is not the slightest reference to a fort whose importance would have been decisive in the defence of the hill.

In response, Kromayer claimed that this fort was built later during the Byzantine era or even during the period of Ottoman occupation.[11] Soteriades then excavated Palaiogoulas and claimed in turn that he discovered shards (*ostraca*) dating to the fifth century, a wall that surrounded the hill, as well as traces of an ancient road at Kourmeki.[12] Kromayer's theory further displayed two major weaknesses: it places the Spartans on Olympos at a lower level than that of their opponents, thereby at a disadvantage, while Polybios clearly states that Kleomenes held all the advantageous ground on the battlefield. Furthermore, the Gorgylos torrent, which according to Polybios was an important landmark, according to Kromayer is a small and strategically insignificant stream.

Based on the above, Soteriades claimed that it is literally impossible to identify the area of the battlefield that Polybios described and that apparently the latter did not tour the battlefield himself but relied on vague and inaccurate information given to him by others who had been there.

Half a century later, W. K. Pritchett wrestled with the problem. As he states in his relevant work, his goal was to acquit Polybios of the contemporary historians' accusations of 'inaccurate' and 'contrived' description regarding the battlefield. According to him, any inaccuracies are due to the incorrect identification of the battlefield by Kromayer. Pritchett partly revived Jochmus' earlier theory, according to which Evas Hill is not Palaiogoulas, as Kromayer believed, but the opposite hill, Tourles. This hill is much higher and unlike Palaiogoulas its southern slope is steep and 'precipitous', a fact that explains the disastrous retreat of the defenders of Evas Hill as described by Polybios. Pritchett visited the area twice (in August 1962 with Professor Eugene Vanderpool and in January 1963). During his first visit to the battlefield, he discovered stone fortifications in the northern peak of Tourles Hill, extending from east to west, following the contour of the mountain facing north, built in such a way that access to the peak was denied. During his second visit, Pritchett found another stone wall at the lower parts of the northeast slope of Tourles Hill and at a distance of about 500m (1640ft) northwest of the abandoned Daglas' Inn. These stone walls, approximately 100m (330ft) long, also faced north and covered the smoother part of the slope. Pritchett argues that in both cases the wall must have been built by Kleomenes to fortify Evas Hill.[13]

Pritchett's most important differentiation from Jochmus is in relation with the findings on Palaiogoulas and Agios Konstantinos hills. Jochmus notes that Agios Konstantinos is the site of ancient Sellasia while Paliogoulas is the site of an ancient fortress. Pritchett argues the reverse: that Agios Konstantinos is an ancient fortress and Palaiogoulas is ancient Sellasia. Regarding Palaiogoulas Hill, Pritchett noted the presence of thousands of *ostraca* on the hill dated from the classical period. The number of findings convinced him (and obviously Vanderpool as well) that the ruins on the hill that Soteriades had found belong to ancient dwellings and not to a fortress.[14] According to Pritchett, this village is ancient Sellasia. Contrary to the prevailing theory until then, Sellasia's position is not in Agios Konstantinos[15] but on Palaiogoulas Hill. Pritchett discovered traces of an ancient road in Kourmeki, thus confirming Soteriades' views that the ancient road from Tegea to Sparta ran through that area.

In his conclusion, Pritchett confidently asserted that: 'My examination of the topography of Sellasia, finally, has failed to reveal any error on the account of Polybios. To the contrary, I know of no other ancient battle in which the account and the topography seem to accord so easily.'[16]

Pritchett's theory solves most problems regarding the morphology of the battlefield and is generally considered the most prevalent today. However, some comments and corrections should be made.

Based on Pritchett's description, Eukleidas commanded the centre of the Spartan army and also those forces that were deployed in the cone-shaped and inaccessible northeast summits of Tourles. Pritchett emphatically states that Kleomenes' deployment was linear except for the forces on Mount Tourles, which were cut off from the rest of his forces. Given Pritchett's authority, this view was not challenged by any contemporary historian.[17] Remarkably, Walbank revised his earlier position and, adopting Pritchett's views, represented Eukleidas' forces deployed on the two summits of Tourles.[18] However anyone who has visited the battlefield can easily understand that the specific deployment of the Spartan forces presented by Walbank cannot be correct. First and foremost, the northern slope of Tourles as well as the two cone-shaped peaks are extremely steep and would not allow the deployment of a significant number of men on them. Moreover, what could have been the purpose of removing such a sizable part of the Spartan force by detaching it to the inaccessible peaks of Tourles?[19]

Obviously then, Eukleidas' forces must have been deployed not on the two steep and remote peaks but on the north-eastern and smoother slope of Evas (the Dagla Ridge) in such a way as to be mutually supported by the remaining Spartan forces, specifically those of the centre. With that correction – as depicted on the map of the battle in the relevant chapter – Pritchett's view can be accepted as accurate.

G Morgan[20] attempted to correct Pritchett on another point, on the opposite end of the battlefield. He shifted the location of the collision of the Macedonian and Spartan phalanxes eastward to an enclosed smooth field situated at the gorge of Provatares north of Melissi summit, because of the flatness of the ground there (as the two phalanxes would have been expected to select for deployment). However in this case 'the engagement would have taken place far away and indeed out of sight of the rest of the action'.[21] To support this view, Morgan has the Macedonian phalanx reach this area by executing a complicated manoeuvre, moving up the rugged hillside, repeatedly changing its facing etc. These moves would have been unthinkable for the Macedonian army, deployed in close proximity and under constant observation of the Spartans.

Phylarchos, Polybios, Plutarch and the attack on Evas Hill

The most detailed and extensive description of the battle of Sellasia is undoubtedly that of Polybios. Yet it contains a very serious discrepancy.

Polybios refers to Kleomenes' defensive formation as mighty and impenetrable. He points out that Antigonos was confounded as he could not find any weakness in it. But from the development of the battle it becomes obvious that this mighty defence collapsed rather easily after a vigorous attack by Antigonos at Evas Hill. How can this be explained?

Polybios' explanation is well known: the man responsible for the collapse of the defence at Evas was Eukleidas, who, instead of exerting a flexible defence to prevent his enemies from ascending the slope, remained static on the ridge of the hill. He mistakenly believed that in the developing clash his troops would best their opponents and then would annihilate them as they retreated down the rugged slope. But is it possible for a Spartan warlord to have committed such a gross blunder?[22] Could a leader such as Kleomenes, who left nothing to chance,[23] have entrusted the command of his army's left wing to an incompetent general, just because he was his brother? Highly implausible.

Phylarchos (Plut. *Kleom.* 28) provides a completely different explanation according to which Antigonos with the help of traitor Damoteles managed to perform a successful outflanking manoeuvre with the Illyrians and the Akarnanians in order to attack the flank of Eukleidas' deployment on Evas.

At first glance, this version seems to answer quite comprehensively the question above, as it combines all the causes leading to the collapse of a strategically strong position: betrayal – concealment of a flanking force – outflanking – surprise attack.[24] Unfortunately this theory contrasts sharply with the other two principal accounts of the battle. There are no references to Antigonos' alleged outflanking manoeuvre in Polybios (2.65–69) and in Plutarch (*Philopoimen* 6).[25] Instead, they emphatically state that during the attack on the slope of Evas it was the attackers who were taken in flank and rear by the Spartans (Pol. 2.67.2 and Plut. *Philop.* 6).

Those who adopt the theory of the outflanking manoeuvre are obliged to reconcile two contradicting facts:

1. The encircling manoeuvre that the Illyrians and the Akarnanians allegedly performed against Eukleidas' left, secretly and after Damoteles' betrayal (Phylarchos).
2. The counterattack by the Spartan forces of the Centre against the assaulting Illyrians (Plutarch) and in fact against their rear (Polybios).

The issue becomes more complicated by the fact that Phylarchos does not mention at all the counterattack described by both Polybios and Plutarch, and conversely, both of the latter do not mention anything about the encircling manoeuvre Phylarchos reports.

Modern historians, in their attempt to reconcile the apparently irreconcilable, have formulated three theories, which rest on facts rather precariously.

According to the first theory, it was the Illyrians alone that turned Eukleidas' left flank. The Akarnanians did not participate in this manoeuvre. Instead they attacked frontally up Evas Hill, and once Eukleidas perceived this he sent his mercenaries to flank them (Errington 1969, page 21–23, Walbank 1957, page 283). According to this view, Philopoimen's attack at the centre was not crucial, but merely rescued the Akarnanians from annihilation. The battle was decided by the successful outflanking manoeuvre executed by the Illyrians.

Yet this reasoning is completely arbitrary and is not in the least confirmed by the available sources. Phylarchos clearly states that the outflanking was executed by the Illyrians *along with* the Akarnanians while there is not the slightest hint that the counterattack of the mercenaries from Eukleidas' centre was launched specifically at the Akarnanians.

The second theory, which was first formulated by Jochmus (1857, pages 39, 40) and was adopted by Pritchett (1965, page 69) fully accepts Phylarchos' version: that the assault on Eukleidas' left flank was executed by the Illyrians along with the Akarnanians. Therefore, the counterattack by Eukleidas' mercenaries could not have been directed at the aforementioned units (which according to Phylarchos were hidden), but at the Achaeans who were more exposed during the attack.

Both these theories overlook the following serious evidence. Firstly, Plutarch's emphatic statement (*Philop.* 6) that Eukleidas' counterattack was directed against the Illyrians, and secondly, the fact that the Illyrians and the Macedonian 'Bronze Shields' were deployed in alternating *speirai* from the start (Pol. 2.66.5). If Antigonos had intended to detach the Illyrians from the 'Bronze Shields' in order to turn Eukleidas' left flank, what was the point of alternating the Illyrian and the Macedonian *speirai* in a 'checkerboard' formation?

In order to bypass this difficulty, Walbank (1995, page 370) formulates another theory: that besides the Illyrians and the Akarnanians, the 3,000 *peltasts* (the 'Bronze Shields') also participated in the outflanking manoeuvre. All these warriors were hiding in the northwest part of Gorgylos. Moreover, Walbank claims that Eukleidas' counterattack aimed at the Illyrians 'and perhaps at the entire right wing of the Macedonians'. However, these manoeuvres seem impossible, especially to those who know the topography of the battlefield.[26] Additionally, the proposed concealed deployment of the 'Bronze Shields' and their participation in Antigonos' outflanking manoeuvre (which goes completely unmentioned in all descriptions of the battle) raises the following question: how could the Spartans have not noticed the sudden disappearance of 5,600 of their opponents (1,600 Illyrians, 1,000 Akarnanians and 3,000 'Bronze Shields') from opposite Evas Hill? This is highly unlikely, even if one accepts the theory of Damoteles' betrayal, which Walbank emphatically rejects anyway.

Finally, Walbank actually refutes his own theory by rejecting Damoteles' betrayal as fiction while accepting the theory of Eukleidas' encirclement by Antigonos. Since according to Phylarchos (who is the only source for this event), the encircling manoeuvre of the Illyrians and Akarnanians was only achieved through Damoteles' betrayal; without it the theory of encirclement collapses.

Regardless of whether the alleged encirclement (which even Plutarch does not adopt but only dutifully cites) occurred or not, its importance is exaggerated by Phylarchos in order to give a dramatic tone to his narrative. The topography of the battlefield (see above) and the historical evidence suggest that Antigonos' main attack at Evas Hill (in which his heavy and slow moving 'Bronze Shields' participated) was launched at the smoothest northeast slope of the hill and not on its inaccessible and remote summits.

Leaving Phylarchos aside, let us look more closely at what the other two sources provide us with regarding the attack on Evas Hill. According to Polybios' aforementioned view, during Antigonos' surprise attack on Evas Hill Eukleidas remained motionless on the ridge of the hill. However according to Plutarch, in the initial stages of the battle Eukleidas acted correctly. He exploited the weaknesses of his opponents' deployment in the best way and succeeded in flanking them.[27] And he would have certainly repelled them if it hadn't been for the timely intervention of Philopoimen, who at this phase of the battle gave the first indication of his undeniable military acumen.[28] Thanks to Philopoimen, the flexible Illyrian and Akarnanian units managed to establish themselves on the slope and the situation on Evas Hill turned against the defenders. The Illyrians did not allow the defenders of the hill to harass the 'Bronze Shields' phalanx and delay its advance. At the same time, the 'Bronze Shields' were considerably superior to Eukleidas' own infantry and their *speirai* provided protection to the Illyrians in case Eukleidas attempted to charge them. Undoubtedly, the defensive tactics described by Polybios (2.68.3), consisting of skirmishing assaults and falling back on higher ground, was ideal for the defence of Evas. However, after Antigonos' light units had established themselves on the hill's slopes, this tactic was unfeasible. In fact, after a certain point, the only thing left for Eukleidas to do was what he actually did: he waited on the mountain ridge keeping for himself the advantage of the higher ground, hoping to throw back his opponents with a forceful charge.

Consequently, in order to understand the collapse of the defence on Evas Hill, one does not need to resort to the theory of encirclement, or to underrate the strategic importance of Philopoimen's assault, or to accept the idea of a 'witless' Eukleidas remaining unaccountably idle. The key element for the defence of Evas Hill was Gorgylos stream, a fact that can be easily deduced from Polybios' accounts. The moment Antigonos succeeded in establishing the Illyrians' foothold on the slope beyond Gorgylos, he had taken an important step towards victory. After the failure of the defenders' counterattack, the attackers advanced up the hill and took complete possession of it, thanks to the effective cooperation of their light and heavy infantry, a regular and battle proven Macedonian tactic when faced with strong defensive positions on elevations.[29] These tactics required experienced and skilful troops as well as excellent coordination between participating units. Despite the fact that Antigonos possessed troops ideally suited for these tactics (Illyrians, Akarnanians and 'Bronze Shields') the attack on Evas Hill came very close to failure. Inevitably, this would not be the first or the last time in history where a mighty defensive position collapsed after a well-coordinated attack.

'From Crucified Kleomenes to Crucified Jesus':
An Extreme Theory by Arnold Toynbee

What's common between a Spartan king and Jesus of Galilee? Much, answers the renowned British historian Arnold Toynbee. Author of the much discussed but also controversial *Study of History*,[1] Toynbee believes that the legend of the Spartan king affected to a large extent the portrayal of the evangelical life of Jesus.

According to Toynbee, Kleomenes, Agis and other personalities of antiquity, such as the Gracchi brothers, belong to a class of aspiring 'saviours' of antiquity, who tried to solve the problems of their communities through a return to an ideal past. Toynbee characterizes them as 'archaists', juxtaposing them with the 'Futurists', (e.g. Aristonikos and Catiline), who attempted to do the same by creating an ideal future world.

Comparing the lives of the archaists and the futurists to that of Jesus, Toynbee finds a large number (eighty-nine in total) of similarities between them. Fifty-eight of them pertain to peculiar similarities and parallels between the lives of the two Spartan kings and the evangelical life of Jesus.

Toynbee points out that all three had royal lineage. Jesus was a descendant of David while Agis and Kleomenes of Herakles, while the criterion for inclusion in both Christian society and in Agis' and Kleomenes' 'new' Spartan society was not the *origin* but the *personal worth* of its members.

In particular, the following stand out among the common characteristics between Jesus' evangelical life and Phylarchos' biography of Agis.

Phylarchos cites a detailed genealogy before presenting each one's biography just as the Bible cites Jesus' lineage.

Both heroes are presented as leaving their opponents speechless in public discussion; Jesus with the Pharisees and Sadducees and Agis with Leonidas.

Both Jesus and Agis refused on principle to resort to violence.

Judas' betrayal resulted in the arrest of Jesus and his mock trial where he was accused of contempt of court. Similarly, Agis was deceived by Amfares, who with his two accomplices delivered him by force to a mock trial where Amfares reprimanded and threatened him when he laughed at the judges' hypocrisy. In both cases, the authorities' executors feared to carry out their assignment: the officers of the Sanhedrin did not dare arrest Jesus (John 18.6) as the servants and mercenaries did not dare kill Agis, either (Agis 19.9–10).

During their trial, Jesus and also Agis had one last chance to save their lives, the former provided he denied his messianic nature, the latter if he betrayed his associates. Yet, both remained true to their principles, resulting in their immediate death sentence.

Jesus' words to the women of Jerusalem, during his procession to Golgotha, 'weep not for me …' (Luke 23.27–28) bring to mind Agis' words to the grief stricken servant on the way to the gallows, 'stop weeping for me' (Plut. Agis 20.1).

Along with Jesus and also along with Agis, two more people were executed in exactly the same manner: two thieves were crucified beside Jesus, and Agis' mother and grandmother were hanged beside him.

Both biographies contain the scene of deposition.

The comparison between the lives of Jesus and Kleomenes also reveals many impressive similarities:

Jesus and Kleomenes defied the highest authority of their society, the former challenged the Pharisees and the latter the *ephors*, accusing them of usurping power and violating the laws.

Because of hostility towards them, Jesus' and Kleomenes' opponents went so far as to request the assistance of a foreign power against them, thus violating their own fundamental principles: the Jews accused one of their own, Jesus, to the Romans turning them into regulators of their inviolable internal affairs. The Achaeans asked the Macedonians to assist them against Kleomenes, thus bringing their homeland under the same Macedonian domination which they had struggled to shake off in the past. In both cases that was an unprecedented phenomenon.

The great popularity of both men embarrassed the authorities who wanted to but did not dare exterminate them, Jesus in Jerusalem (Matthew 21.46 and 26.3–5 = Mark. 11.18 and 14.1–2 = Luke 22.2) and Kleomenes in Egypt (*Kleom.* 33 = Pol. 5.35).

Before their dramatic end, Jesus and Kleomenes had one last supper with their twelve followers. Both were crucified[2] and their bodies remained intact on the cross. In the case of Jesus, his unexpectedly quick death made it unnecessary for the soldiers to break his legs (as opposed to the two thieves who had their legs broken in order to precipitate their death). In Kleomenes' case, a snake wrapped itself on his head and kept the vultures away from devouring his body (Plut. *Kleom.* 39).

The sight of Jesus' and Kleomenes' crucified bodies reversed the crowd's attitude and led to their apotheosis (deification). Toynbee points out that the description of the event displays even verbal similarity between the gospels and Phylarchos (Plutarch): 'He truly is the son of God' (Matt. 27.54, Mark.15.39) and 'addressing Kleomenes as a hero and a child of the gods' (*Kleom.* 39.2).

A loved one stands by the hero's mother during the ultimate suffering: Jesus' beloved disciple, John, supported his mother during her ordeal. Respectively, the wife of Panteus, who was Kleomenes' beloved companion, took care of Kratesikleia.

Jesus' and Kleomenes' scenes of torture end in a similar way: '... Jesus said, it is finished, and dropping His head, gave His last gasp' (John.29.30). 'At last the end came, and after [Panteus] embracing the king's dead body, he slew himself upon it' (Plut. *Kleom.* 37.7).

The bodies of Jesus and Kleomenes were punctured with a sharp weapon to determine if they were indeed dead. In both cases the jab caused an unexpected sign of life: after the piercing with the soldier's lance, blood ran from Jesus' body while Panteus' piercing with his sword caused a contraction in Kleomenes' face.

Is it possible that all the similarities listed above are merely coincidental? Toynbee disagrees:

'While the play of chance may, and indeed must be taken into consideration as one possible explanation of our correspondences between the gospels and the stories of certain pagan Hellenic heroes, this explanation cannot be pressed to extremes and will not offer us a complete solution of our problem.'[3]

Behind the similarities between Phylarchos' histories and the Gospels Toynbee perceives another source, a myth, which was formulated from oral tradition during the Hellenistic period when there was intense interaction between the Hellenic and the eastern cultures and their respective legends. Under the influence of these legends and through the channels of collective memory (folk memory), historical figures lost their identity and became anonymous heroes in time. At the same time, actual events of Greek history became associated with local beliefs and integrated various ritual elements, resulting in their full mutation. It would appear that both Phylarchos and the Evangelists were affected by such a myth, featuring a god-king who sacrificed himself for his people.[4]

Toynbee argues that Agis' and Kleomenes' stories spread by word of mouth from Lakonia to Galilee in the form of legends through Egypt which served as a communication bridge between the two areas. When Kleomenes fled to Philopator's court, he found 3,000 Peloponnesians and 1,000 Cretan mercenaries living there. Kleomenes had boasted to Ptolemy that it would take just a nod to make them follow him. It would be natural for such devotion to turn into a cult after the Spartan hero's tragic end. As Plutarch states '...those who were keeping watch upon the crucified body of Kleomenes, saw a serpent of great size coiling itself upon the head and hiding away the face so that no ravening bird of prey could light upon it. In consequence of this, the king [Philopator] was seized with superstitious fear, and thus gave the women occasion for various rites of purification, since they felt that a man had been taken off who was of a superior nature and beloved of the gods. And the Alexandrians actually worshipped him, coming frequently to the spot and addressing Kleomenes as a hero and a child of the gods.'[5] Plutarch adds that this devotion stopped because 'wiser' men managed to interpret the phenomenon in a convincing and scientific-like manner. But Toynbee observes that '... even if the Ptolemaic Government did succeed, by a deft combination of repression and propaganda, in driving underground an incipient worship of the dead Kleomenes among the populace of Alexandria, we may guess that the dead Spartan hero's admirers among the Peloponnesian and Cretan soldiery silently rendered to him the divine honours which it was their official duty to render to their living paymaster Philopator.'[6]

Shortly afterwards, Ptolemy proceeded to expand and radically reorganized his mercenary forces in order to effectively cope with the invasion of Antiochos the Great. Ptolemy's army, which besides the other forces also included 8,000 mercenaries, managed to defeat the invaders in 217 in the decisive battle of Raphia. Antiochos was forced to withdraw from all areas of Coele Syria, which he had occupied. These areas were once again put under the power of Ptolemy, who established new garrisons there. These garrisons were composed of mercenaries (a common practice of the Ptolemies in their possessions beyond Egypt) and must have included some of the 4,000 Peloponnesian and Cretan mercenaries who were in Egypt in 219. At the time, Ptolemy had dissolved their units and had created new ones, merging them with the new mercenaries.[7]

In this way, the legend of Kleomenes – just as the legend of Agis which was inextricably connected with him – was carried from Lakonia through Alexandria to the cities of Coele Syria. Evidently, the cult of Kleomenes, the man who attempted to overthrow Ptolemy, followed an underground route. The religious ceremonies performed in his honour were wrapped in a veil of secrecy and mystery. Apparently there were no shrines or statues dedicated to him. But there must have been some miniature scale figures of Kleomenes, reproduced on less conspicuous materials which circulated secretly among the initiated. Toynbee states that 'We know the shape of Pheidias' gold-and-ivory statue of Athena in the Parthenon thanks to the survival, far afield, of dwarf reproductions of it in coarser stone that were manufactured in the Imperial

Age.'[8] Similarly, rough images made of cheap material depicting historical or traditional scenes[9] may have circulated from hand to hand in the form of a secret cult among the members of the Hellenic internal proletariat. The proletariat resisted the oppression of the ruling minority by keeping alive the memory of the revolutionaries who had died for their people.

In addition to the mercenaries, the dissemination of the Kleomenic legend seems to have been carried through another remarkable social group, the educated slaves, who projected their personal aspirations onto every revolutionary personality. These slaves became 'a highly conductive medium of mental communication between a dominant minority to whom they were culturally akin and an internal proletariat of which they were judicially members'.[10] Through this process, some typical words and phrases of the two Spartan kings[11] passed to 'folk memory' and were transferred intact to the evangelical life of Jesus. Many of the similarities between the scenes in the gospels and in Plutarch's ('Phylarchos') biographies can therefore be explained by the fact that Agis and Kleomenes were the 'patterns' on which the evangelists were based.

Toynbee also highlights the fact that some of the scenes in the gospels seem to be incongruous, irrelevant and out of context, as opposed to the corresponding scenes in the lives of the two Spartans which seem totally reasonable. For example, the scene where Jesus' disciple violently hits the High Priest's servant and cuts off his ear, the reluctance of officials to arrest Jesus, the remark that Jesus' robe was seamless, the scene of the three victims on crosses, the preservation of Jesus' intact body on the cross, the piercing of Jesus' body by the soldier all seem unrelated to the texts in which they are contained. This happened because the evangelists felt obliged to include certain scenes in Jesus' story simply because these particular scenes were identified with the story of the 'Saviour' in the eyes of their reading audience. 'Whether the ultimate origin of these scenes was historical or mythical, they had come, we may surmise, to be regarded as an indispensable part of the credentials of any hero who was a candidate for recognition as being the Saviour par excellence. An author whose purpose in writing his book was to present as being the Saviour some hero of his own who had not yet won any general acknowledgment could not afford to leave these obligatory scenes out. So in they must go, however difficult it might be to piece them together with the particular story which this particular author was setting out to tell.'[12]

Thus, the evangelists included these 'mandatory' scenes changing them as much as possible in order to harmonize with the plot and the meaning of their own story: Kleomenes' bloody campaign in Alexandria became the unexpected assault of Jesus' disciple on the High Priest's servant in the gospel. And the grudging reluctance of the soldiers to arrest Jesus must have derived from the unwillingness of Agis' guards to kill a Spartan king.

The evangelists were certainly not the only ones who based their stories on pre-existing legends. A careful examination of Phylarchos' work reveals that he also sought to insert some scenes that he thought were necessary in order to adapt some indispensable stereotypes in Kleomenes' biography for the same obvious reasons the evangelists had done. So Kleomenes is portrayed ripping open the seam of his *chiton* and releasing his hand to more easily handle his sword. According to Toynbee, this is a clever trick by which Phylarchos conveys in Kleomenes' story the scene of the tragic end of Herakles where the hero was struggling desperately to pull Nessus' poisoned *chiton* off his body. Typical is also the scene in which Kleomenes and his companions run through the streets of Alexandria with lame Hippitas following them on horseback. According to Toynbee, Hippitas was not a cripple; his disability was 'constructed' by Phylarchos himself to justify his climbing on the horse and to add another 'mandatory' scene in his story derived from an eastern rite where the saviour-victim is on horseback. Respectively, the evangelists display the saviour-victim Jesus entering Jerusalem on a donkey with his followers accompanying him on foot. Finally, the scene where Panteus leans on Kleomenes' bosom echoes a ritual which also originates from some ancient eastern myth.[13]

This bold theory, however, presents some very serious flaws. One of them is the fact that Toynbee takes for granted that Phylarchos was not a 'historian' in the scientific sense but a skilled storyteller. A large part of Toynbee's arguments is based on this assumption. The association of Kleomenes' death with Eastern myths, Phylarchos' alleged reference to Herakles' poisoned *chiton*, the association of Hippitas on horseback with ancient rituals of the East assume that Phylarchos did not record the events with the accuracy of a historian but 'composed' them with the liberties of a novelist. Toynbee fully accepts Polybios' harsh criticism against Phylarchos, as well as the views of the historian Bux, who considers Phylarchos' work to be 'artistic' and not 'serious history';[14] he does not hesitate to present Plutarch's lives of Agis and Kleomenes as typical examples of the process through which biographies of historical figures are turned into novels.[15]

However – defying Polybios and Bux – it is certain nowadays that Phylarchos is a valid historical source and in no case can he be characterized as a fiction writer, despite his melodramatic style and his overt support of Agis and Kleomenes.[16] This fact refutes Toynbee's theory to a large degree.

Beyond this, many of Toynbee's analogies between Jesus and the two Spartans are fictitious and do not sustain a rigorous review. As noted by Thomas

Africa, Toynbee's attempt to associate unrelated people and events drives him to extremes: the fact that Kleomenes' companions and Jesus' disciples were twelve is a mere coincidence and so the sources overlook it. Jesus and Kleomenes were punctured by sharp weapons, but unlike the Roman legionnaire, Panteus *helped* Kleomenes commit suicide in order to avoid a worse death; Jesus' robe was seamless while Kleomenes'*chiton* wasn't; Agis urged the slave not to weep for him while Jesus said to the women of Jerusalem to weep for themselves; Jesus' arrest was the result of Judas' betrayal while Agis' arrest was a result of his naivety and of his incorrect assessment regarding his enemies' intentions. If someone is a fiction writer, this is not Phylarchos but Toynbee; his theory about the Spartan kings 'is an imaginative parody' as Africa succinctly states.[17]

An imaginative parody or an ingenious intellectual game? In any case, Toynbee's impressive theory remains an extreme example of the profound impact and the intense debate that two prominent figures of the Spartan movement continue to generate, fuelling imagination and interest throughout the ages.

Notes

Introduction

1. According to Plutarch (*Agesilaos* 28.5) the battle took place on the fifth of the attic month Hekatombaion, which in the current calendar corresponds to 6 July.
2. Xen. *Hell.* 6.4.16. This was the traditional annual celebration where groups of children, women and elders danced and sang in succession under the hot summer sun (Plut. *Lyk.* 21, see also Michell 1964 p 186–187, Parker 1989 p 149–50).
3. Plut. *Pelopidas* 23.4.
4. Plut. *Agesilaos* 28.5.
5. According to Xenophon (*Hell.* 6.1.1, 6.4.15, 4.6.17), four out of the six *morai* of the Spartan army fought at Leuktra. They included 700 Spartans, that is, the thirty-five age classes from twenty to fifty-five years old (Xen. *Hell.* 6.4.17). 300 of these were elite troops called '*hippeis*' (Hdt 8.124.3, Xen. *Lak. Pol.* 4.3). If the '*hippeis*' fought as a separate corps forming king Kleombrotos' bodyguard (Toynbee 1969 p 401–404, De Ste Croix 2005 p 516 and Cartledge 2002a p 251), then the remaining 400 Spartans would have been divided by 100 in each of the four *morai* thus the well-trained Spartan army (i.e. the '*hippeis*' along with the six *morai*) would not exceed 900 men. If the '*hippeis*' did not fight as a separate body and were divided in the four *morai*, then the number of Spartans in each *mora* would amount to 175 men, giving a total of 1,050 men (Jones 1967 p 129–130). Therefore, the total of the Spartan hoplites, along with five 'reserve' classes (fifty-five to sixty years old) that were mobilized at the aftermath of the disaster (Xen. *Hell.* 6.4.17), should have been between 1,200 (De Ste Croix 2005 p 514–516) and 1,350 (Jones 1967 p 130), or 1,500 men (Cartledge 2002a p 264). While even with the most optimistic estimates (Forrest 1980 p 134–5, who rejecting Xenophon's testimony, claims that the Spartans who fought at Leuktra were not 700 but 1,700) the number barely reached 2,500 men.
6. Xen. *Hell.* 6.5.28.
7. The term reveals how closely the Spartan constitution was associated with its putative founder, Lykourgos the legislator. Regarding the historicity of Lykourgos, there have been many theories from antiquity until today which still divide historians. There are those who recognize him as the founder of the Spartan constitution (e.g. Chrimes 1999 p 426–427, Forrest 1980 p 60 etc.) others even deny his existence (e.g. Toynbee 1969 p 277–278, Starr 2002 p 42, Africa 1968 p 7, Baltrusch 2003 p 20–22, etc.), while others accept the historicity of Lykourgos, but consider that the Spartan regime was not his own work but the outcome of a gradual development over time (e.g. Oliva 1971 p 70). However, for the Spartans, Lykourgos was the undisputed founder of their constitution and they ascribed him divine honours.

8. The chronology of the Lykourgan reforms is the subject of much controversy among historians. Some place them in the Late-ninth century. (Chrimes 1999 p 346–47, Fitzhardhinge 1980 p 166). Most agree, however, that they came to fruition during the seventh century, either at the beginning (e.g. Jones 1967 p 31–33, Forrest 1980 p 55–58) or in the middle, after the Second Messenian War (Toynbee 1969 p 260, Cartledge 2004 p 18).

9. Sparta was not a typical city-state. It was comprised of five villages, Pitana, Limnai, Kynosoura, Mesoa, and Amyklai – the latter was incorporated at a later stage. Unlike other cities, Sparta was not surrounded by a wall. The main reason for this was the fact that her defensive line was not confined to the city's perimeter but extended to the land of the *perioikoi* reaching up to the borders of the *perioikic* territory. Sparta functioned like a well-organized camp and her forces were able to mobilize and intervene anytime within and outside her territory (Kourinou 2000 p 243–246).

10. The most modern and comprehensive examination of this issue is that of Cartledge (2004a, 2004b). However, Toynbee's analysis (1969 p 221–239) still remains invaluable.

11. See Andrewes 1992 Chapter 3 and Chapter 6, Toynbee 1969 p 224–226, Cartledge 2004a p 74–75 and 2004b, Hanson 2003 p 59–65.

12. Only a part of the land was redistributed. A significant part of it was not distributed and was kept by the old aristocracy as its own. On this issue, which is one of the many vague and controversial issues on Sparta, see further notes.

13. The term '*homoioi*', meaning the 'equals 'or the 'peers' (Xen. *Lak. Pol.* 10.7, 13.1) describes the formation of new relationships between citizens while exposing the existence of inequalities before the Lykourgan reforms. '*Damos*' is called the citizen body in the Great Rhetra (Plut. *Lyk.* 6).

14. In Sparta there were two Royal Houses, the *Agiadai* and the *Eurypontidai*. According to tradition, the kings were descendants of Herakles.

15. The *gerontes* should be at least sixty-years-old, in order to be eligible for the *Gerousia*. This condition was severely criticized by Aristotle who stated sarcastically that 'there is old age of mind as well as of body' (*Pol.* 1270b 39–40). Although there appears to be no legal provision that required the noble lineage of the *Gerousia*, it is likely that such a restriction was informally applied. (Toynbee 1969 p 266–269, Cartledge 1987 p 121–122, Hamilton 1991 p 72 -73, with Xen. *Lak.* Pol.10.1, Arist. 1271a 9–18 and Pol. 1306a 18–19).

16. Some scholars (e.g. Chrimes, Oliva, Walbank, Baltrusch etc.) refer to the Assembly as *Apella*. Personally I am convinced by De Ste Croix's arguments (2005 p 538–541) that the use of the term *Apella* to represent the Spartan Assembly is inappropriate.

17. Certainly, the Spartan regime cannot be described as 'democratic', as modelled e.g. in Athens after the reforms of Kleisthenes. But for its time it was extremely progressive and the rights of the people were reinforced (Andrewes 2002 p 65–68).

18. See Forrest 1980 p 152: 'Sparta was the first state we know of to accept the idea that all citizens, *qua* citizens were equal, and to devise a constitution which allowed these citizens a defined and substantial say in running their city and Toynbee 1969 p 228: 'The key point in the "Lycurgan" constitution was that it vested the ultimate sovereignty

over the Spartan state to the *Spartiate Damos*, i.e. in the politeuma constituted by the *Spartiate 'homoioi'* (peers)'.

19. Although not as old as the institution of the dual kingship, of the *Gerousia* and of the Assembly (see Oliva 1971 p 123–131).

20. A typical example of this compromise is the oath exchanged every month between the kings and the *ephors*. The kings swore to obey the laws of the city and the *ephors* swore to the city that they would support the kings, as long as they upheld their vows (Xen. *Lak. Pol.*.15.7).

21. Andrewes 1992 p 100–103.

22. Despite the absence of figures, historians from the late-nineteenth century attempted to estimate the population of the helots as well as the Spartans. It is natural that these estimates differ, yet according to the most conservative numbers, the population of helots was 190,000 and the corresponding Spartans were 12,000 (Meyer in Andreades 1915 p 202, note 1). According to the boldest estimates, the number of helots reached 375,000 and the Spartan population at 25,000, meaning a ratio of 15:1 (Grundy and P.R.Coleman-Norton in Oliva 1971 p 53, note 3). What is certain is that the helots' population was considerably larger than that of the Spartans. It has been noted that during the Peloponnesian War, the Spartans did not hesitate to kill 2,000 helots (Thuc. 4.80) and release hundreds more (for military service under Brasidas), without seriously affecting the economy of Sparta (Powell 1989b p174 and 2002 p 255). Based on the testimony of Herodotos, in 479 at the Battle of Plataea, each Spartan was accompanied by seven helots (Hdt. 9.10.1, 28.2, 29.1), a population ratio of 1:7. This is now considered reasonable by Cartledge (2002a p 150 151) who estimates the population of helots to be 175,000–200,000 (Cartledge 1987 p 174). These estimates are very close to Hodkinson's in which the population of helots was estimated to be 162,000–187,000 (Hodkinson 2000 p 385–386).

23. Michell 1964 p 28.

24. The Doric form of the word *kleros* (see Cartledge 2002b p 42). The scantiness of the sources (the Spartans left no writings) leaves us in the dark about key points such as the social and economic realities of Sparta. Thus we cannot have answers to a host of questions: How was the land divided? What exactly were the *kleroi*? Were they equal to each other or not? Did they correspond to specific parts of land or to production quantities? Were they private property or state property? Did a *kleros* return to the state after its owners' death or could the owner bequeath it to his children? Could also daughters inherit? All these 'thorny' issues which arose during the middle of last century (Walbank 1957 p 728 to 729) but are still unanswered despite intense debate and controversy, are outside the scope of this study. Let it be noted that after the reforms, each Spartan was ensured a minimal piece of land, approximately of equal productive value. Yet, this does not mean that all the Spartans had equal fortune. The existence of strong social differences is therefore granted.

25. According to ancient sources (Plut. *Lyk.* 28, Myron = Athenaios 657d), the Spartans treated the helots inhumanly. It is interesting that, apart from the many humiliations to which they submitted them so that they wouldn't forget their position, the Spartan authorities entrusted groups of young people (who composed the famous *krypteia*) to

kill the most dangerous of the helots. Moreover, every year, the *ephors* declared war ritually against them thus legitimizing their killing by the Spartans (Plut. *Lyk*. 28, citing Arist. [fr. 538]). These reports may be exaggerated to some extent (see Michell 1964 p 79–82 and particularly Whitby 1994 p 105–111). On the other hand, the Spartans collected only a part of the production of their *kleroi* (Plut. *Lyk*. 24, *Moralia* 239e 41, Myron = Athenaios 657d) while the helots had the right to possess some goods and to have a family, which puts them at a higher position of subordination compared to other slaves (McDowell 1988 p 61–65, Ducat 2002 p210–211). According to Pollux's wording (3.83), their status was somewhere 'between free men and slaves'.

26. Thuc.1.6, Xen. *Lak. Pol.*5, Arist. *Pol.* 1294b20–40, Pol. 6.45.3–4, Plut. *Lyk*. 10. The only exception was the kings who were not forced to participate in the *agoge* and had certain privileges *ex officio* (Plut. *Agesilaos* 1.2, Herod. 6.56, 57, 58).

27. Reports on economic disparities between the Spartans have been evidenced in the late-seventh century. Poet Alkaios (around 600), for example, cites the case of the Spartan Aristodemos (Fr. 360, Campbell, in *Comments*. Pindar. *Isthmionikoi* 2.17.1), who protested because in Sparta, poor men had no dignity. Herodotos (7.134) characterizes Sperthias and Bulis, the Spartan ambassadors who went to the Persians in 480 as two Spartans 'of noble birth and great wealth'. On social inequalities in Sparta, see also: Hdt. 6.70, 7.134.2, Thuc. 1.6.4, 4.108.7, 5.15.1, Xen. *Lak. Pol.* 5.3, 6.4, *Hell.* 6.4, 10, 11, Arist. *Pol.* 1294b 20–30, Hadas 1932 p 67, Tarn 1928 p 741, Michell 1964 p 207, 219, Toynbee 1969 p 311–313, Tigerstedt 1965 p 77, 131, 1974 p 51, de Ste Croix 2005 p 219–220, Hodkinson 2000 p 76–81.

28. Around the middle of the sixth century, we observe archaeological findings which show that Sparta lagged behind in terms of material culture (luxury goods), artefacts and the arts. Although there have been voices denying such a regression, or at least feeling it is not noteworthy (Cook 1962), the difference from previous times, when Spartans participated in artistic creation and enjoyed a high standard of living is too striking to go unnoticed and unexplained. Holladay (1977) attributes this rupture to the tighter and fuller implementation of *agoge* and identifies the reason for this in the difficulties that Sparta encountered in her conflict with Tegea in the decades 580–560 and her need to establish a possible effective army. Cartledge (2002a p 133–134) notes that we can't talk of a sudden 'death' of the arts, which continued to flourish even after the second half of the sixth century in Sparta and Lakonia. He recognizes, however, the gradual decline and argues that this fact is connected with 'what Finley has called the "sixth century revolution", a complex and gradual transformation of the Spartan social system, designed to perpetuate Spartan control over the helots and *perioikoi* without abolishing the wide and growing disparities within the citizen-body itself' (Cartledge 2002a p 134).

29. See Andrewes 1992 p 92, Toynbee 1969 p 287–288, and recently Figueira 2002.

30. Finley 1981 p. 164

31. The contribution amount (Plut. *Lykourgos* 12.2, Athen. 4.141) was quite large but the income of a Spartan was also very high for its time (see Plato, *Alkibiades* 122d-123a). As Hodkinson has pointed out, the mean size of ordinary Spartan landholdings (18.4 ha) was much larger than that of the ordinary Athenian. Similarly, the average fortune

of the wealthy Spartans (44.62 ha) also exceeded that of most of the affluent Athenians (Hodkinson 2000 p 384). Figueira reaches the same conclusion in which the minimum income of a Spartan citizen was over 258 *medimnoi* (unit capacity of agricultural products). Therefore, the curve of distribution of property in Lakonia was displaced upward from the values prevailing in Attica (Figueira 2004 p 64).

32. Xen. *Lak. Pol.* 5.3.

33. Arist. *Pol.* 1271b10–20, Andrewes 1992 p 93–94, Baloglou 2011 p 184–189.

34. Andreades 1915 p 218–224.

35. Arist. *Pol.* 1271a 26–37.

36. Theoretically speaking, there might have been an opportunity to maximize the proceeds of his land by imposing an increase on the standard tax (*apophora*) on the *helots*. This was not prohibited by the state although one who did it was cursed upon (Plut. *Moralia* 239 d–e). Yet (at least until the fourth century) most helots lived in the confines of mere survival, which meant that their intensive exploitation would be tantamount to their extermination, and the benefits for the Spartan would be unrewarding (Cartledge 1987 p 174).

37. The sale and purchase of land in Sparta was not allowed. This, of course, was not enough to avert its trading in the form of donations and legacies (Arist. *Pol.* 1270a 20–25).

38. Toynbee 1969 p 308.

39. Pomeroy 2002 p 73–74.

40. In reality, the flow of 'new blood' was never ruled out, as seen in the strange case of the *mothakes*, who are thought to be sons of helot mothers by Spartan fathers (Michell 1964 p40–41, 89), or free born of inferior status, and brought up with the sons of wealthy Spartans (Hodkinson 2000 p355–356, Lazenby 2012 p26–27). The *mothakes* were trained through the *agoge* and if successful, they became Spartan citizens (see McDowell 1988 p77–83). However, this measure was applied individually and in exceptional cases. Thus, the number of new members was minimal and woefully inadequate to compensate for the gaps created by the low birth rate.

41. Arist. *Pol.* 1270b 15.

42. Arist. *Pol.* 1270a 40.

43. Diodoros Siculus (11.63) states that the victims reached 20,000, while Plutarch (*Kimon* 16) claims that the entire city was destroyed with the exception of five houses. According to Toynbee (1969 p 346–352), the results of the earthquake were devastating and had a lasting effect on the demography of Sparta. Instead, Cartledge (2002a p 190–91) believes that based on the available data, this view is exaggerated. Certainly, however, the sudden loss of a part of the Spartan population greatly exacerbated the problem of population decline.

44. According to Herodotos (9.35, 64), 300 Spartans were killed in a single battle. Hodkinson (1989 p 103–105) estimates that one year after the earthquake, at least 11.5 per cent of *homoioi* were lost because of their casualties in both the earthquake and the war. However, in a subsequent work, Hodkinson (2000 p 417–420) expresses his reservations as to these numerical estimates, noting that the worst outcome of the earthquake (and the Third Messenian War) was their effect on the distribution of

property. It accelerated the gradual development of the existing economic inequalities. Relatives of the deceased inherited additional land, but richer persons with deceased relatives gained considerably more property resulting in the accumulation of land to a few and an increase in economic inequality.

Sekunda (1998 p 15) considers the casualties from the earthquake and the Third Messenian War as the most possible causes for the decline of the Spartan population. Figueira provides a similar view and describes the earthquake as the first shocking blow to the Spartan system (Figueira 2002 p 160). In another study, he states that the earthquake and the uprising of the helots led to a dramatic and sudden reduction of the Spartan population (up to 40 per cent). A direct consequence of this reduction was the surplus of several *kleroi*, which were distributed to the relatives of the deceased. As a result, many Spartans gained greater wealth than they originally had. In this way, Figueira claims that Sparta managed to recover in population over the next year, up until the eve of the Peloponnesian War. But the price for this population rebound was the internal deterioration of the socio-political system which had long-term disruptive results (Figueira 2004a p 65).

45. De Ste Croix 2005 p 517. Cartledge (2002a p 191) contrasts the demographic decline of Sparta after the earthquake and the Third Messenian War with Argos' population recovery after the loss of 6,000 of its hoplites in the battle at Sepeia, around 494.

46. Thuc. *Hist.* 1.1.

47. From the middle of the Peloponnesian War and thereafter, Sparta used the '*homoioi*' carefully and sparingly. The bulk of the forces that were sent to campaigns abroad consisted of *perioikoi*, *neodamodeis* and mercenaries. After the war, the Spartan army was reorganized into six *morai*, consisting of both Spartans and *perioikoi*. Even so, the Spartans who took part in bloody battles (such as the battles of the River Nemea and the battle of Koroneia in 394) did not avoid casualties, which in some cases were very high (e.g. the destruction of an entire *mora* at Lechaion in 390). Cavaignac (1948 p 118–119) lists twenty-five cases of Spartan senior officers who fell on the battlefield between 404–371, among whom prominent leaders such as Lysander and seven *polemarchoi* (i.e. *morai* commanders). This is a clear indication of the high number of Spartan casualties during this period. It is important to note that ever since the beginning of the Peloponnesian war and afterwards, Sparta was in constant warfare. Lakonia was devastated by frequent Athenian invasions; many *kleroi* were probably wrecked and a considerable number of helots were lost; many deserted or were used in the growing needs of the Spartan army. Some scholars consider this phenomenon as the main cause for the disruption of the Spartan socioeconomic system and for the decline of the Spartan population (Lazenby 2012 p76–78).

48. The sudden influx of money caused inflation and an increase in the price of goods, such as iron which was a widespread commodity in Spartan society. This resulted in the disruption of her economy (Hamilton 1991 p 82–83).

49. Toynbee 1969 p 299. At the end of the sixth century until the early fourth century, the Spartans won the Olympic Games championship 12 times in the most expensive sport of the time, the chariot race. The winners, the owners of expensive horses such as Kyniska, the sister of King Agesilaos, spectacularly celebrated their victories often

by building grandiose monuments. This is an additional indication of the existence of a wealthy minority in Sparta during this period and an increase in their influence in city-state affairs (see De Ste Croix 2005 p 550–552, Hodkinson 1989 p 97–99 and particularly 2000 p 303–333).

50. Plut. *Lys.*17. See also Hamilton 1991 p 80–81, McDowell 1988 p 172–174; contra: Hodkinson 2000 p 429, who denies the existence of this law.

51. See McDowell 1988 p 174 and 222. However, in at least one case the law was applied and resulted in the execution of the Spartan *harmost* of Samos, Thorax. (Plut. *Lysandros* 19.4)

52. 'So that one can be pretty sure that those people [the Lakedaimonians] are the richest of the Greeks in gold and silver' (Plato *Alkibiades* 123a).

53. Arist. *Pol.* 1333b 10–35. Plut. *Moralia* 239F, Toynbee 1969 p 289 and p 299, Cawckwell 2002 p 251–252. Apart from the above mentioned case of Thorax, there was that of Gylippos who tried to embezzle money from the state (Plut *Lys.*16–17) and the *harmost* of Byzantion, Klearchos (Xen. *Anabasis* 1.19, Diodoros 14.12.2–9), who was exiled for similar reasons and became a mercenary along with Xenophon and the 10,000.

54. Andreades 1915 p 182.

55. Xen. *Lak. Pol.* 14.1–5. Derkyllidas is a typical case who, as reported by Xenophon (*Hell.* 4.3.2.), constantly wanted to travel abroad.

56. Xen. *Hell.* 3.3.4–11. See also David 1979.

57. Xen. *Hell.* 3.3.5.

58. The emancipated helots. In special occasions, helots were emancipated in return for military aid.

59. Xen. *Hell.* 3.3.6.

60. Plutarch (*Agesilaos* 32) mentions two further suppressed conspiracies to overthrow the regime after Leuktra. Both were crushed at their inception by Agesilaos.

61. Plut. *Agis* 3.1, 5.1.

62. Plut. *Moralia* 238e-f, Herakleides Lembos Exc.Pol. (Ed. Dilts) 373.12: The *ancient portion* [ἀρχαία μοῖρα] constitutes another obscure part of the Spartan land-tenure system. Most historians agree that it constituted one of the two types of land owned by the Spartans. Regarding to its recommendation and its identification of the site, various theories have been proposed, often quite contradictory. According to McDowell (1988 p 139) and others, the *ancient portion* represented the equal *kleroi* which occurred after the Lykourgan redistribution of land in Lakonia. In contrast, according to Cartledge (2002a p 144), the equal *kleroi* were in Messenia while the *ancient portion* was in Lakonia and represented the 'old land' owned by wealthy Spartans. Neither the size nor the number of *kleroi* that comprised the *ancient portion* is known, and some speculate that the term *ancient portion* does not signify land but the helot tribute to the Spartans (Hodkinson 2000 p 85–90 and Figueira 2004a: p51–52).

63. Plut. *Agis.* 5. The authenticity of the *rhetra* and the historicity of Epitadeus have been questioned by some historians, mainly based on a passage by Aristotle (*Pol.* 1270a 15 34) which refers to a similar practice without naming the legislator (see e.g. Jones 1967 p 41, Forrest 1980 p 137, Schütrumpf 1997, Cartledge, 2002a p 142 144 and p 271, Hodkinson, 2000 p 90–94, Flower 2002). Those who accept it (among whom

are Fuks, Toynbee, Oliva, Hamilton and McDowell), disagree as to the period it was implemented: Toynbee (1969 p 342–343) dates it after 371, Fuks (1962c p 245), Oliva (1971 p 188–192) Piper (1986 p28) and Hamilton (1991 p 84) after the end of the Peloponnesian War (404), while McDowell (1986 p 154) in the last third of the fifth century. My sense is that the economic changes associated with Epitadeaus' *rhetra* had already begun informally in the fifth century but were instituted towards the end of it.

64. Spartan women inherited a share of the paternal property either as a result of the reforms attributed to Epitadeus (Pomeroy 2002 p86) or as a given practice (Hodkinson 1989 p 81–82 and 2000, p 94–101).

65. Aristotle *Pol.* 1270a 24–25.

66. Perhaps, even worse, the loss of property for the Spartan woman would degrade her to an unwanted spinster. The case of Lysander's daughters, whose suitors left when they learned that they had no property (ignoring the glorious name of their father), is particularly revealing in this case (Plut. *Lys.*30.5).

67. Some historians go so far as to consider the loss of Messenia as the beginning of Sparta's social and economic decline (Piper 1986 p29–31). This view totally ignores Aristotle who asserts that the dearth of manpower was not the result but rather the cause of Sparta's decline.

68. Xen. *Hell.* 7.4.9, Oliva 1971 p 196.

69. Toynbee 1969 p 408. According to Cartledge (2002b p 14) up to Prasiai.

70. Philip's departure from Lakonia appears to be unexplainable. Some historians believe that Philip was no longer preoccupied with Sparta because 'Sparta was not worth the trouble' (Forrest 1980 p 139). Claude Mossé connects the departure of Philip to the power of the Spartan 'myth' which was so strong even in 338 that Philip II did not dare attack the city (Mossé 1989 p192). Cartledge suggests a completely different interpretation and emphasizes the political feasibility of Philip's attitude. By permitting Sparta to remain outside the Corinthian League, Philip could rightfully claim that no city was forced to be subjected to the Macedonian rule (Cartledge 2002b p 14.18).

71. Plut. *Agesilaos* 15. 4.

72. Kanellopoulos 1982 p 287.

73. Steinhauer 2000 p 316. The example was first given by Agesilaos who fought as a mercenary in Asia Minor (365) and later in the service of the Egyptian King Tacho (361). His son and successor, Archidamos, initially led a mercenary force in Crete and later in Italy. As it has been aptly pointed out (Oliva 1971 p 197), when the Greek cities battled for their independence at Chaironeia, the king of Sparta fell while leading his troops in their war against the Loukani and Messapii in Italy. Besides, prominent Spartans such as King Akrotatos I (315), Kleonymos, pretender to the throne (303), his son and King Leonidas II were all involved in mercenary activities. In the Late-fourth century, the port at Cape Tainaron, the southernmost tip of the Lakonian peninsula, evolved into an important market for mercenaries (Diodoros 17.111.2, Jones 1967 p 148–149).

74. Koliopoulos 2001 p 292–295.

75. For Kassander's expected invasion, see Justin 14.5, 5–7. Kassander finally invaded the Peloponnese three years later (in 315) in order not to control Lakonia but Messenia

(Cartledge 2002b p 26–27). Demetrios Poliorketes invaded Lakonia in 294 and intended to conquer Sparta, but was forced to withdraw due to problems within his territory (see Plut. *Demetrios* 35, Polyainos 4.7, 9–10).

76. Plut. *Pyrrhos* 28–29. It has been noted (Tarn 1928 p 214, Cartledge 2002b p 34) that in the description of Pyrrhos' attack on Sparta, Plutarch relies on the pro-Spartan historian, Phylarchos. He overemphasized the proud behaviour of the women as well as the heroism of the young prince Akrotatos, who had undertaken the defence of the city.

77. The rapprochement of Sparta and Macedonia was due to their need to confront their common enemy, Pyrrhos. A few years earlier, the opportunism and the lack of diplomacy of the latter had caused the coalition of two other traditionally hostile countries, Rome and Carthage, against him (Tarn 1928 p 214 and Koliopoulos 2001 p 307).

78. The case of Areus I inaugurates a new period in the history of Sparta. According to Phylarchos (= Athenaios 142a-b), Areus and thereafter his son, Akrotatos were responsible for the corruption of Sparta's traditional lifestyles and values. It appears that Areus attempted to govern by following the standards of the Hellenistic monarchy displacing the regent. In contrast to the standard practice of the Spartan kings, Areus signed his name on treaties, issued silver coins that also bore an inscription of his name, and had statues erected in his honour in many cities of the Peloponnese, including one erected by the monarch of Egypt, Ptolemy. All this certainly attests to his megalomania. At the same time, it is indicative of how Areus sought to be consistent with the trends in the international scene of his times and follow the Hellenistic models (Shimron 1972 p 6–7, David 1981 p 138 (but with some reservations), Cartledge 2002b p 34 -37). The lack of response to Areus' autocratic behaviour probably displays that the wealthy elite who supported him had full control of the situation so that 'if anybody objected, he either kept his objections to himself or was silenced' (Shimron 1972 p 7). The fact is also revealing of the deep shift in the Spartans' attitude in the third century if one considers that two centuries earlier they had strongly criticized Pausanias, the victor of Plataea, for similar behaviour.

79. Xen. *Lak. Pol.* 1.1.

80. Prosperity was not, however, widely spread and certainly did not affect all strata of the population in the same way. The release of the Persian treasure and the influx of large quantities of gold in Greece caused currency devaluation and major inflationary problems, such as the increase in commodity prices and the widespread use of slaves which led to a decrease in wages. These problems were intensified in the third century during which mainland Greece became the stage for constant warfare (see Tarn 1923 p 108–129, Rostovtzeff 1941 p 210–214, Walbank 1999 p 223–232, Green 1993 p 362–365 and 375–377).

81. Walbank 1999 p 83.

82. Wilcken 1976 p 384. It should be noted that the new cities had nothing in common with the economically and politically independent city-states but were fully integrated into the vast realms of state formations in which they were associated. Their wealth was concentrated to a few powerful citizens who were generally favoured by the Hellenistic monarchs.

83. Rostovtzeff 1941 p 206–208 and p 210–214. Unlike the past, the third century was marked by great social conflicts. Sixty social uprisings are registered in mainland Greece (especially in the Peloponnese) during the third century, compared to only five or six (of which none occurred in mainland Greece) during the Classical period. The revolutionaries demanded the redistribution of land and the cancellation of debts. These two requests were accompanied by one or more of the following measures: confiscation of the losing party's property, enlargement of the citizen body and liberation of slaves. The common demand in all these cases was the drastic change of the social and economic conditions (Fuks 1966 p 437–448).

84. A typical example of the decline of the city-state and its religion was the attitude of the Athenians towards Demetrios Poliorketes. They granted him the Parthenon to use as his personal palace and established their devotion to him. In the famous hymn sung in his honour, the descendants of the victors of Marathon raised Demetrios above the traditional gods of their city on the grounds that all their gods were either far away, did not listen, did not exist or did not care at all while Demetrios was standing alive before them (Athenaios 253e). Such a public declaration that the gods of the city were indifferent or did not exist or that they were useless idols and stones who were replaced by a living god would be unthinkable at any other time (Dodds 1996 p 152 and note 32).

85. It should be noted that, unlike the two previous philosophical schools, the Stoics were not indifferent to politics nor rejected the concept of the '*polis*.' But their contradictory political worldview theory was closer to the Hellenistic monarchy than the Classical city-state. The case of the Stoic philosopher Persaios, who was in the service of the Macedonian monarch Antigonos Gonatas as governor of Corinth is a typical (and not the only) example of the stoic stance towards the powerful men of their time.

86. Davies 1984 p 309–310.

87. Apart from the major transportation commerce centres, such as Corinth, Rhodes and Delos, it is particularly important that the two city-states, Megalopolis and Messene, experienced a great boom during this period. Therefore the claim that the third century *polis* 'was in the grip of a terminal malaise is at best a gross simplification' (Cartledge 2002b p 6).

88. Sakellariou 1973 p 472

89. Plut. *Aratos* 24.4 In order to preserve the democratic character of the Achaean League, it was forbidden to elect the same person for two consecutive years in the highest office of *strategos*.

90. According to Walbank (1933 p37), after the integration of Corinth 'the whole character of the League was changed; henceforward it was a political rather than an ethnic unit, and the word Ἀχαιός came to have the same kind of significance as *civis Romanus* or British citizen. Another scholar did not hesitate to stress the analogy between the Achaean League and the United States (Green 1993 p 248).

91. Walbank 1984 p 245–246.

92. Regarding this see Tarn 1928 p 739, Ranovic 2001 p 278, Walbank 1984 p 246 and specifically Errington 1969 p 6–8. Panagiotis Kanellopoulos' claim that the trip to the *synodos* must have been festive and attended by all citizens regardless of their social status is not convincing (Kanellopoulos 1982 v.3. Chap.1 p 56 and n.106).

93. Errington 1969 p6 n 3.
94. Ferguson 1973 p 41.

Chapter 1: Dawn

1. Shimron 1972, p 18.
2. Athenaios 142a-b, Cartledge 2002b p 42. The compulsory contribution to the *syssitia*, of course, still applied.
3. She still retained her importance until 272, when (even misleadingly) Pyrrhos stated that he would send his sons to Sparta to participate in the *agoge* (Plut. *Pyrrhos* 26.10). In the following years, the *agoge* languished but was not abolished (Shimron 1972 p 26).
4. This started after the official circulation of coined money by King Areus I in 280. Phylarchos (= Athen. 142b), who criticizes King Areus I and his son Akrotatos for disassociating themselves from the austere way of life, notes that in the following years some of the wealthy Spartans surpassed even them in luxury and opulence.
5. Plut. *Agis* 5.4. Regarding the problems in interpreting the above paragraph and the disagreements among historians, see Oliva 1971 p211. The most convincing is that of Fuks (1962c) according to which, there were 700 Spartan citizens of whom 100 had large estates and the remaining 600 were poor but managed to keep their *kleros* and pay their contribution to the *syssitia*.
6. Plut. *Agis* 5.4. (Translated by E. David). Phylarchos' bleak depiction of Sparta (which will be discussed below) is deliberately excessive in order to enhance the importance of Agis' and Kleomenes' reform project. Modern historians believe that, despite its excesses, this description corresponds in general terms to reality (Tarn 1928 p 739, David 1981 p 159, Cartledge 2002b p 42. etc.). How did 700 *homoioi* (even with the aid of mercenaries or other private slaves) maintain their dominance over thousands of hostile helots and '*hypomeiones*'? It was certainly a feat for the '*homoioi*'; yet, for the historians it remains an unsolved mystery …
7. The following analysis of the structure of Spartan society in the middle of the third century is based on David (1981 p 148–162).
8. According to some historians, the concentration of land into a few landowners marked a significant change in the role of the helots: they gradually ceased to be public slaves and came to form part of the property of the wealthy landowners (Mossé 1989 p 197, Cartledge 2002b p 69–70, Kennell 2003 p 83–85).
9. See Michell 1964 p 78, Africa 1968 p 4, Daubies 1971 p 675, Oliva 1971 p 259–60, David 1981 p 161, Cartledge 2002b p 56 and Kennell 2003 p 82–83.
10. See David 1981 Ch.IV n58 and n92.
11. David 1981 p 161.
12. See Fuks 1962c. Shimron (1972 p 151–155) considers that the figure should have been a little higher, but David disagrees (1981 p 159 note 48) and accepts Fuks' assessment as the correct one. The *hypomeiones* apparently belonged to the 'destitute and disfranchised mob' who resided in the city looking for an opportunity to overthrow the regime. According to Oliva, the 'mob' should have included not only *hypomeiones* and their descendants but also *neodamodeis* as 'the composition of free non-citizen population in Sparta had already become more complex by the beginning of the fourth

century' (Oliva 1971 p 212). In contrast, according to David (1981 p 149), the 'destitute and disfranchised mob' refers exclusively to *hypomeiones*.

13. David 1981 p 160. See also Oliva 1971 p178 note 2 and even more emphatically Lazenby 2012 p22–26 and 79–81.

14. A typical such case is that of Xanthippos, the Spartan who reorganized the army of the Carthaginians in the First Punic War and then returned to his homeland (Pol.1.32–34).

15. Cartledge, 2002b p 46.

16. David, 1981 p. 150.

17. David, 1981 p 152–3.

18. Plut. *Agis* 13.3.

19. Arist. *Pol.* 1270a, 24–27.

20. Plut. *Agis.* 7.5–6.

21. The only ancient source about Agis is his biography written by Plutarch. It is based on the lost work of historian Phylarchos, who wrote in the second half of the third century. Phylarchos' *History* covers the period from the invasion of Pyrrhos in the Peloponnese (in 272), until Kleomenes' death in Egypt (in 219). Despite the fact that Phylarchos was a contemporary of Agis and Kleomenes, his reliability is questioned by Plutarch, who considers him to be biased (*Aratos* 38.8) and accuses him of sacrificing the historic truth in order to move his readers in melodramatic narrative fashion (*Themistokles* 32.3). Long before Plutarch, Phylarchos had been severely criticized by Polybios (2.56), who accused him of sloppiness in historiography, for excessive emotive style and distortion of the historical truth. Polybios' criticism of Phylarchos is largely correct; unfortunately, Phylarchos 'rarely rose above the level of revolutionary propaganda' (David 1981 p 163). But is Polybios impartial? As shown by Africa (1961) in a thorough examination of this issue, Polybios' indignation against Phylarchos did not stem solely from his aversion to the historical methods of the latter but was mostly politically motivated. In fact, the Spartan movement that Phylarchos praised in his story was directed against all values of the Megalopolitan nobleman and pro-Achaean Polybios. Despite the excesses and overt prejudices which undoubtedly exist in Phylarchos' works and despite his melodramatic style (typical, though, of many historians of his time that can even be traced back to Herodotus (see Africa 1961 p 40 and 49, Walbank 1990 p 37)), Phylarchos should not be regarded as an unreliable historian. It is remarkable that even Polybios, despite his sharp criticism, did not hesitate to rely on Phylarchos for some passages of his *Histories* (Pol. 2.47.11, 2.70.6, 5.35–39. See respective comments from Walbank 1957 p 247, 290, 565–567 and Walbank 1990 p 79). On the other hand, scholars agree that Polybios 'violated the canons of scientific history as often as he professed them' (Africa 1961 p 36).

It is noted that Plutarch, although in many cases he often copies Phylarchos, does not always follow him blindly but seeks information so as to cross-check his source. (Africa 1961 p 41, Shimron 1972 p 11). In Agis' biography, in addition to Phylarchos' information, Plutarch shows awareness of the Memoirs of Aratos and of at least one other source, Baton of Sinope (*Agis* 15.4.). Therefore, Phylarchos' work could be checked for its reliability but 'the lives of Agis and Kleomenes, as told by Plutarch remain the principal source for any serious study of the reform movement in Hellenistic Sparta' (Oliva 1971 p 219).

Basically there are no other major sources referring to Agis. According to Fuks (1962b), there are only three minor references about Agis and his movement in Sparta; one is a vague reference in the work of the Cynic philosopher Teles who lived in the third century in Megara. Another reference is in Cicero's work *De officiis* (2.78–80) and the third is in Polybios (4.81,12 14). However, these three references 'do not add any facts to what we already know from Plutarch's life of Agis' (Oliva 1971 p 215 note 1). Finally, there is an odd reference by Pausanias (7.7.3, 8.10.5–8, and 8.27.13–14) whereby Agis was defeated and killed at Mantineia while leading his army against the Achaeans and Arcadians. Although it is likely that it is a completely unreliable reference (Africa, 1961 p 27, Walbank, 1984 p 247 note 68), some historians accept the battle as a historical fact. For example, Beloch (Beloch 1927 p.165) states that it was Agis IV's cousin and namesake who was killed and not the king. Jones (1967 p 151) and Cartledge (2002b p 40) date the battle around 250. An exception is Errington who unreservedly accepts Pausanias' report and places the battle 'sometime before 243' (Errington 1969 p 3).

22. Plut. *Agesilaos* 1.2.
23. Plut. *Agis* 4. For Agis' guardianship from Agesilaos see Beloch 1927 p 165.
24. Plut. *Agis* 7.1.
25. As pointed out by Cartledge (2002b p 46), the case of Agis was at least the fourth case since the seventh century when the name of Lykourgos was used as a pretext to resolve a major political crisis. In reality, the idealized image of Sparta (in the form that it took in the Mid-third century) was the development of a long-established concept which originated from her greatest adversary, Athens. Already in the Late-fifth century, as Athens' imminent defeat in the Peloponnesian War began to loom in the horizon, the youth of the aristocratic families of the city displayed their disenchantment with democracy openly, by behaving like Spartans (Aristoph. *Birds* 1281–1283). They showed off provocative clothing and hairstyle and exhibited their Spartan-friendly feelings in their overall behaviour (*lakonomania*). A typical example of this trend was Kritias, one of the subsequent Thirty Tyrants. The end of the Peloponnesian War marked the beginning of Spartan hegemony, an event which greatly affected the Greek intellectual life. The result was a flood of works that examined the institutions of Sparta, concluding with useful insights about how the Spartan socio-political system was so successful (Rawson 2002 p 33). Among the few that survived, the *Lakedaimonian Polity* by the Athenian Xenophon stands out wherein the author ascribes Sparta's strength and reputation to her institutions and polity. Unlike Xenophon, Plato did not share his contemporaries' '*lakonomania*'. To Plato, all the existing governments were greatly imperfect. Although he considered the Spartan polity to be supreme compared to its contemporaries, he found it to have serious flaws. Aristotle went even further, noting that these weaknesses were inherent and led inevitably to decline. This was the fiercest and most insightful criticism ever exerted against the Spartan regime (Baloglou 2006 p 311–327). Yet even Aristotle recognized that the Spartan constitution had many virtues (Schütrumpf 1994). With the death of Aristotle, the situation changed. Neither Plato's

nor Aristotle's students shared their teachers' criticism against Sparta. According to Aristotle's student Dikaiarchos, the Spartan constitution was a *mixed* regime that combined perfectly the three basic types of state: monarchy, democracy and oligarchy. As noted in the medieval lexicon Suda, Dikaiarcho's theories were taught to the young Spartans annually. At the end of the fourth century with the decline of Sparta's political importance the *polis* was no longer seen as the model polity it had been in the times of Plato and Aristotle. Sparta's decline was interpreted as the result of her corruption by the influx of money and the citizens' alienation from their austere way of life. This explanation has reached us through the widespread work of the historian Ephoros, who compared and contrasted the declining state of Sparta with the idealized image of a state which based its success on self-sacrifice for the common good and despise for material goods. During the Hellenistic age, influenced by the Cynics and the Stoics, these perceptions intensified the image of virtuous *Spartiate* refraining from wealth and luxury and devoting his life to the benefit of his city.

26. Euhemeros, Kassandros' protégé, wrote a novel dealing with an island called 'Panchaia' in which he referred to an imaginary state where there was neither property nor money. Iambulos wrote another Utopian novel about a people called 'The Children of the Sun' who lived on an island without slaves where all men were equal (see Ferguson 1975 p 102–110 and p 124–129).

27. Africa 1961 p 14.

28. See Tarn, 1923 p 127, Fuks, 1966 p 446–448.

29. Plut. *Agis* 6.1, Oliva, 1971 p 220.

30. Plut. *Agis* 4.2.

31. Oliva 1971 p 221.

32. Plut. *Agis* 6.3. Plutarch does not specify which wars Hippomedon participated in, nor what kind of wars they were.

33. According to Plutarch, the elder Spartans had long been submerged into corruption (Plut. *Agis* 6.2). It has been noted (Oliva, 1971 p 220) that Plutarch does not distinguish Agis' enemies from his supporters based on their social status or political beliefs but based on age. The contrast between the virtuous youth and the corrupt elders might be intended to emphasize the idealistic side of the movement, although there is no doubt that from the beginning, the youth responded with enthusiasm to Agis' reforms (see Shimron, 1972 p. 17–18).

34. Plut. *Agis* 8.1. Plutarch does not mention this directly, but it can be inferred by the text and Lysander's activities. The *eponymous ephor*, as respectively the *eponymous archon* in Athens, had enhanced powers including the ability to establish taxes and to add, at regular intervals, one month to the calendar (see Michell 1964 p 119). In the sixth century the Spartans, like other Greeks, had adopted in the *oktaeteris*, i.e. the eight-year-period. One year consisted of twelve lunar months. To make the lunar coincide with the solar calendar, three months were intercalated in every eight-year-period, in the third, fifth and eighth year respectively (Papachatzis 1971 p 10–11, Michell 1964 p 108 n.2 and Cavaignac 1948 p 14).

35. Plut. *Agis* 8.1. Unfortunately, the above region's limits were not clearly defined by Plutarch resulting in disagreements about its specifications. Chrimes (1999 p 286–287

and p 429–430) believes that the name 'Malea' does not mean the Malea promontory, the southernmost tip of Lakonia opposite Kythera, but an area in the north of Lakonia near Leuktron (present Leontari, see also Pikoulas 1988, p 129–135 about the locations of Leuktron and Malea) at the border of Megalopolis-Sparta. This interpretation, however, limits the land that was going to be redistributed to a narrow and barren area between Taygetos and Sellasia, with Pellana being the southernmost and Malea the northernmost point. From such a region, it would be difficult for the Spartans to get 4,500 *kleroi*; moreover, the most fertile part of the Eurotas valley would have been granted to the *perioikoi*. It is, therefore, preferable at this point to not rely strictly on Plutarch's description. As pointed out by Walbank (1951 p 99) 'whatever Plutarch originally meant (and wrote), the Pellana-Sellasia line must be the northern and not the southern limit of *Spartiate* land.' The land that would have been distributed to the Spartans apparently included all the 'civic land', that is all land in Sparta's dominion which would have stretched across the valley of the Eurotas, with the Malea Cape being its southernmost point (Oliva 1971 p 222 note 3).

36. Plut. *Agis* 8.2. As displayed by Fuks (1962c p 246), the number of '*hypomeiones*' who lived in Sparta and constituted the 'destitute and disfranchised mob' in the middle of the third century were 1,800–2,300. Those, along with the 700 existing citizens of Sparta totalled about 2,500–3,000 people. Therefore, the number of *perioikoi* and 'foreigners' who would be part of the new 4,500 Spartans should be at 1,500–1,800. The 'foreigners' were mostly mercenaries.

37. Plut. *Agis* 8. 2. It is probably in reference to the '*perioikic land*' as a whole, although Plutarch does not clarify it.

38. Plut. *Agis* 8.2. This measure was not only anti-Lykourgan but practically difficult to implement. Where would one house such large gatherings? (Michell 1964 p 294–296) According to Cartledge (2002b p 46), this was a conscious effort to unify the heterogeneous crowd of new citizens in the sense that massive gatherings would result in promoting the team spirit among the diners.

39. McDowell 1988 p 22–26 and Cartledge 2002b p 43.

40. Plut. *Agis* 9.1.

41. The choice of the oracle of Ino-Pasiphae in Thalamai as opposed to the oracle of Delphi is noteworthy. Cartledge (2002b p 44) suggests three possible explanations for this choice. Firstly, Delphi was under the control of the Aitolians and, therefore, Agis could not exert control over its oracle. Secondly, Agis had a different view of Delphi's role in the foundation of Sparta's constitution. Thirdly, he wanted to promote the status of the *perioikoi* by choosing a sanctuary that belonged to the *perioikic* territory.

42. Plut. *Agis* 9.3.

43. Plut. *Agis* 7.5.

44. Plut. *Agis* 10.1.

45. It is remarkable that Leonidas avoided referring to the land reform and the revival of the *agoge* despite the fact that they were key features of Agis' reforms. Obviously, he tacitly acknowledged their correctness.

46. Plut. *Agis* 10.2. It was certainly a demagogic argument; the fact that Leonidas had lived abroad did not constitute in any way a violation of *Lykourgos'* laws.

47. Plut. *Agis* 10.4.
48. Shimron 1964a p 151.
49. Ollier 1936 p 561.
50. (Plut. *Agis* 11.1) Majority 'by a single vote' in a total of thirty votes cast (twenty-eight elders and two kings) is mathematically impossible unless there were abstentions or unless someone vetoed. Perhaps it is used by Phylarchos figuratively in an effort to emphasize how close the reformers had been in their pursuits (Oliva 1971, p 224).
51. (Plut. *Agis* 11.2). This is Plutarch's only reference to this law. There are no other reports of such a law and possibly it was invented for this occasion. In Sparta, only the marriage of Leonidas with Kratisikleia was recognized. Marrying an Asian woman was not considered valid but until then no one had questioned the legitimacy of King Leonidas.
52. Africa 1961 p 53.
53. Leonidas was originally the guardian of the underage King Areus II and seized power after the latter's untimely death.
54. Plut. *Agis* 11.5.
55. Plut. *Agis* 10.1 and 11.1.
56. However, the period that *Agis* and his followers were in power should not have exceeded a few weeks since during this period Leonidas had sought refuge in the temple of Athena Chalkioikos. Of course, he would have been provided with food and water, but he could not have remained there for long period. It's really impressive that historians overlook this fact without a second thought. Nevertheless, it shows that the reformers did not have their compatriots' full support and it is closely linked to subsequent events.
57. Plut. *Agis* 12.1. Mandrokleidas was probably an *ephor* (see Africa 1961 p.14). Naturally, the allegations of the new *ephors* regarding the illegality of reformers were utterly justified.
58. Plut. *Agis* 12.2, see also Arist. *Pol.* 1271a. Despite the fact that Agis and his followers were blatantly violating the law, the interpretation of the law invoked was in general terms correct. As demonstrated recently by Carlier (2007), the Spartan kings had privileges (*gera*) which go back to Homeric times, where the political system operated under the following scheme: the people listened, the elders suggested and the king decided (Carlier 2007 p 55). The absolute power of the Spartan kings was cushioned by the fact that they were two. When there was harmony between them, their authority (at least until the reign of Kleomenes I) was unlimited but when they disagreed, it was necessary to have arbitration which came to be exercised by the people through the *ephors* (Carlier 2007 p 58).
59. Plut. *Agis* 12. 3.
60. Shimron 1972 p 21.
61. There is no reference to the participation of the people in the overthrow of the government. People remained completely passive throughout the duration of Agis' reform attempts (Shimron 1972 p 16, see also below).
62. Apparently conveying Phylarchos' view, Plutarch (*Agis*. 12.4), states that Agesilaos attempted to assassinate Leonidas but when Agis learned of this, he prevented the event and arranged for the safe transfer of Leonidas to Tegea.

63. Plut. *Agis* 13.3. The word refers to *klaroi/kleroi*. However there is no previous testimony of mortgages in Sparta (Mac Dowell 1988 p 156).

64. See Shimron 1972 p 22, Oliva 1971 p 226.

65. See previous analysis and Oliva 1971 p 229. Tigerstedt observes that Agis' ambitions did not coincide with the wishes of his countrymen. Those who had fallen into the status of a '*hypomeion*' wanted to recover their property and civil rights but were not interested in the expansion of the citizen body by adding non-Spartans in it (Tigerstedt 1974 p 53).

66. The common point between Sparta and the Achaean League was their opposition to the kingdom of Macedonia. Their alliance was forged around 244/3 for reasons that are not fully elucidated. A probable cause must have been the need to offset the potential threat from Megalopolis, ruled by the pro-Macedonian tyrant Lydiadas. Another possible explanation for the alliance may have been the temporary rapprochement (243–241) between Macedonians and Aitolians (Walbank 1984 p 250 and 253, 1995 p 324).

67. Plut. *Agis* 14.2.

68. Plut. *Agis* 14.3.

69. Aratos was proved right in his judgement. What he actually did was let the Aitolians invade and plunder Pellene, and, as they were scattered in the city, he surprise attacked and routed them (Plut. *Aratos* 31–32).

70. Plutarch cites another version originating from Baton of Sinope (*Agis* 15.4.) without adopting it, whereby Agis was the one who did not want to have a pitched battle. But it is unlikely that Agis changed his opinion at the last minute after the mobilization of his army and after he had arrived in Corinth. In addition, as Plutarch points out, Baton did not take into account Aratos' Memoirs in which he confesses that the decision to avoid the battle was his.

71. Regarding the nature of the Aitolian raids see Pol.4.3.1, Rostovtzeff 1941 p 198, Chaniotis 2005 p 136–137.

72. Forrest 1980 p 146, Cartledge 2002b p 47.

73. Plut. *Agis* 16.2. It should be noted that there is no mention as to whether the re-election of an *ephor* constituted illegality or not. Oliva (1971 p 228 note 1) notes the case of the *ephor* Endios who was elected in the year 413 and was re-elected in 404/3 in fact as an *eponymous ephor*. This, however, should be considered unusual especially if it happened immediately after the first tenure.

74. Shimron 1972 p 16–17. Moreover, the actions of Agis' opponents to reinstall Leonidas to power reveal that they knew that they would encounter no resistance.

75. Plut. *Comparison*. 3.1. This view is adopted by Tarn (1928 p 743).

76. According to Oliva (1971 p 228), the recall of Leonidas back to Sparta occurred *after* Agis' return from his fruitless campaign when he was no longer at the head of a well-trained army.

77. Plut. *Agis* 16.2. Most soldiers who followed Agis in his campaign were young and poor. They had been relieved of their debts and expected 'that they would receive allotments of land if they returned from the expedition' (Plut. *Agis*. 14.1).

78. Hippomedon later appears to act as a general of Ptolemy in Hellespont (Walbank 1957 p 484 and Fuks 1962b).

79. Shimron 1972 p 28. Polybios believes that Archidamos remained in Sparta and fled after Kleomenes' ascension to the throne (see next chapter for the murder of Archidamos). It is, however, surprising that the Messenians offered asylum to one who was seeking to make Sparta powerful. Perhaps, they still wanted to have the upper hand and planned to gain influence in Sparta later.

80. Plut. *Kleom.* 4.3.

81. Cicero De Officiis 2.80.

82. On the existence of this temple see Kourinou (2000 p 185–199). According to Cartledge (2002b p 47 and 48), it was the temple of Poseidon at Tainaron, where Kleombrotos went in an attempt to escape. But if Kleombrotos had managed to reach Tainaron, he would have also been able to escape.

83. Chilonis is displayed (apparently in Phylarchos' accounts) as a faithful and devoted wife, who followed Kleombrotos into exile, determined to share his fate. Previously, she – the faithful and devoted daughter of Leonidas – had followed her father to exile, where her husband Kleombrotos had banished him (Plut.*Agis* 17). 'Tragedy,' says Thomas Africa 'and tragic history are similar, in that they usually require heroines. Women are far more prominent in Phylarchos' work than they were in the world in which it was composed' (Africa 1961 p 43).

84. From the text (Plut. *Agis* 18.3) we get the impression that Agis knew them already.

85. Plut. *Agis* 19.5. It appears that Leonidas did not yet control all members of the *Gerousia*.

86. Plut. *Agis* 19.7. However, their request was clearly contrary to the Spartan tradition and practice where there was no public participation of citizens in trials (see Paus.3.5.2, 3.6.2 and McDowell 1988 s.193–194).

87. See Ollier 1936 p 540 note 6, Africa 1961 p 43.

88. Plut. *Agis* 21.1.

89. Plut. *Agis* 21.5, *Comparison* of 3.1.

90. Shimron 1972 p 23 note 35.

Chapter 2: Zenith

1. Ennead I Ch. 6.30

2. As Plutarch characteristically notes (*Kleom.* 2.1) '...as for practice in arms, self-restraint in the young, hardiness and equality, it was even dangerous to speak of these now that Agis was dead and gone.'

3. It should be noted that Agis had not banned the practice of loans (there is no mention of this) but had simply cancelled the existing debts (see Oliva 1971 p 244 note 2, Shimron 1972 p 26).

4. Shimron 1972 p 26. However, Plutarch's passage (*Kleom.* 2.1) suggests that the *syssitia* may have as well been banned. There may have been a policy of discouraging young people from participating in the *syssitia* lest they turned into a hotbed of rebellion as they were places of political debate and communal living.

5. Plut. *Kleom.* 2.1, 3.1.

6. Tarn 1928 p 742 believes that Phylarchos deliberately attempts to tarnish Leonidas' image in order to illuminate his hero Kleomenes and justify his subsequent attitude (see also Africa 1961 pp. 26, 37, 46).

7. Oliva (1971 p 230) and Shimron (1972 p 28) date the invasion in 240 or 239. Cartledge (2002b p 48) dates it at around 239.

8. For the invading Aitolians see Plut. *Kleom.* 18.3, Polyb. 4.34.9, 9.34.9; Oliva 1971 p 230 note2. The available evidence is not very informative as to the causes of the invasion. Shimron accepts Polybios' view and considers that the invasion of the Aitolians may have signalled the beginning of a strong and stable alliance between them and the Spartan movement (Shimron 1972 p 28).

9. Cartledge 2002b p 48.

10. Plut. *Kleom.* 1.1. With this action, Leonidas terminated the traditional diarchy and established a monarch coming from the House of Agiadai (see Oliva 1971 p 230, Cartledge 2002b p 49).

11. For Agiatis: Plut. *Kleom.* 1.2. For Xenares: Plut.*Kleom.* 3. 2.

12. The primary sources on Kleomenes are Aratos' *Memoirs* and the *Histories* of Phylarchos. Aratos and Phylarchos were Kleomenes' contemporaries and wrote about the events they experienced. Unfortunately, neither of these works has survived except as citations in other authors' works, namely Plutarch (specifically the lives of *Agis* and *Kleomenes, Aratos, Philopoimen*) and Polybios (especially his second and fifth book of *Histories*). The reliability of the primary sources is highly questionable. The dramatic style of Phylarchos' narrative and his overt admiration of Kleomenes, which leads him to excesses against the historical truth, have been mentioned (see prev. Ch.). Aratos' *Memoirs* are imbued with the subjectivity that characterizes all memoirs. Of the secondary sources, Plutarch relied heavily on Phylarchos to write Agis' and Kleomenes' biographies and on Polybios for the biography of Philopoimen. Polybios relies primarily on Aratos and in some sections Phylarchos. As displayed by Africa (1961), while Phylarchos exaggerated because of his style and his unabashed sympathy of Kleomenes, Polybios falsified history under the pretence of objectivity in a deliberate effort to adapt it to his political beliefs. Polybios' hatred of Phylarchos was due to the fact that the latter 'wasted' his talent to support Kleomenes. Therefore, Phylarchos 'remains a most important source, sometimes the only one. But biased he is and his statements must be checked as much as possible' (Shimron 1972 p 14). Other sources include certain passages by Pausanias, Justin and Diodoros Siculus, but they briefly touch upon what we already know on the subject.

13. Kleomenes must have been about 17 years old in 243. According to Plutarch, (*Kleom.* 1.1) when Kleomenes married Agiatis (between 241 and 239) he was not yet of marrying age (the legal marriage age for Spartans was between twenty and thirty years old). Thus he must have been born between 261 and 258, with the most likely date being 260 (as shown first by Beloch 1927 p 162. See also Ollier 1936 p 546, Shimron 1972 p 23, Cartledge 2002b p 50).

14. Plut. *Kleom.* 2.2.

15. Athenaios 141d, 334e. About Sphairos' life see Diog. Laertios 7.37, 7177–178. According to Diogenes, Sphairos was Zeno's and Kleanthes' disciple who lived for a time in Egypt in the court of King Ptolemy. It is not clear whether this is Ptolemy II Philadelphos (as it is believed by Ollier 1936 p 546, Michell 1964 p 323, Figueira 2007 p 145), or Ptolemy III Euergetes (per Africa 1961 p 17 , Ferguson 1975 p 132).

Unfortunately, 'the information we have about Sphairos' life in Alexandria is not better founded than what we know of his life in Sparta' (Oliva 1971 p 232 note 4).

16. Plut. *Kleom.* 2.2. It has been noted that the wording of Plutarch reveals the implicit doubt as to whether all this is indeed true (see p 232 1971 Oliva and David 1981 p 166).

17. Rostovtzeff 1941 p 1367 note 34.

18. For further discussion on these issues and commentary of relevant literature see appendix A.

19. Baloglou 2003 p 503.

20. David 1981 p 167.

21. Kennell 1995 p 58–59.

22. Plut. *Kleom.* 6.1. Although Plutarch mentions other supporters of Kleomenes, such as Therykion, Panteus, Phoibis and Hippitas, he does not provide us with any information about their social status.

23. Plut. *Kleom.* 3.4.

24. To honour Lydiadas for his initiative, the Achaeans elected him general of the League. He was a remarkable politician with a striking personality who quickly became a dangerous rival for Aratos.

25. Walbank 1984 p 449. Megalopolis' strong influence in the politics of the Achaean League is illustrated by the fact that from 235 onwards, most of the Achaean generals came from Megalopolis.

26. Walbank 1967a p 10.

27. Pol. 2.46.2. Polybios mentions only the first three cities but it is likely that the same thing happened with Kaphyai, as shown by Aratos' attempt to seize the city in 228 (Walbank 1984 p 451). The relation of these four Arcadian cities with both Leagues and Sparta is an extremely complex and controversial issue. (See Urban 1979p 79ff, Larsen1966 p51–54, Walbank 1984 p451).

28. The main reason for the alliance between the two Leagues just two years after the invasion of the Aitolians in Achaea was their common anti-Macedonian policy. This alliance, which lasted eighteen years, until 220, was directed against the Macedonians and King Demetrios. However, the rivalry between the two Leagues never ceased to exist.

29. Plut. *Kleom.* 4.1. The name of the settlement in the area can be found both as Belmina and as Belbina.

30. See Pikoulas 1988b p 24. Loring was the first to locate it, identify it, and trace its fortifications (Loring 1895 p 37–41, 71–72).

31. Chelmos' fortifications belong to various historical periods (up to the medieval times) and their condition complicates their identification and dating. Yet it is certain that the wall described by Loring (see above note 32) was not the hasty construction of 228 but must have been built later by Kleomenes to reinforce the defence network of Lakonia against the Macedonian invasion.

It should be noted that the fortifications that exist in the Athenaion and in Leukrtron, the other great border bastion, are late constructions. When Sparta was strong, the fortification of *perioikic* cities was forbidden; it was also unnecessary since she could quickly launch her forces at the border. When Megalopolis annexed the border areas, it barely reinforced Athenaion and Leukrton since its main focus was to densely populate the capital city, even at the expense of the regional settlements which had contributed to its rise. Kleomenes was the first to create substantial fortifications in the two places (Pikoulas 1988b p 184, 186).

32. Walbank 1984 p 456–457.

33. Plut. *Kleom.* 4.5. The number is high for Sparta's capabilities. Obviously a big part of this force consisted of mercenaries.

34. Methydrion (near the present village of Pyrgaki, 5–6 km (approximately three-and-a-half miles) south of Bytina) is the centre of a small basin on the north-western slope of Mainalon. It is clearly out of the axis connecting Tegea, Mantineia and Orchomenos which was the main part of the Arcadian Corridor that Kleomenes would have been expected to follow. Kleomenes certainly did not follow the straight road of Megalopolis – Methydrion since it passed very close to hostile Megalopolis. It was followed four centuries later by Pausanias (Pikoulas 1990 p 202 No. I), and it is where mud ruts have been identified. The road that Kleomenes followed is described by Pikoulas in No. IV (1990 p 203–204 and map p 206). It is a path passing through the present day villages of Silimna, Davia and Alonistaina where archaeologists have found mud ruts. For unknown reasons, Kleomenes deviated west from the strategic axis of the Arcadian Corridor.

35. The invasion of Argolis from Methydrion is strategically inexplicable as Kleomenes' manoeuvre was extremely difficult and risky. It is difficult to ascertain what exactly his plan was and what he was aiming at.

36. Plut. *Kleom.* 4.4. These may be exaggerated in order to emphasize the great numerical superiority of the Achaeans in relation to the forces of Kleomenes. According to Polybios (29.9.8.), in 146, when the League had all of the Peloponnese under its control and was able to mobilize all of its forces, it gathered 40,000 men. In 228 the 20,000 men should have constituted its entire army and would have been unable to mobilize under occasion. However, the Achaean League's forces clearly outnumbered those of Kleomenes (Walbank 1933 p 78).

37. It is located about 6km (four miles) south of present day Tripolis, between Tegea and Megalopolis. The fact that the two armies met at Palladion and not somewhere else in the area of Argolis, where the Spartan army was, is noteworthy. The explanation given by Walbank is that this time the Achaeans deliberately avoided following the Arcadian Corridor seeking to invade directly into Lakonia, but the rapid manoeuvres of Kleomenes thwarted their plans (Walbank 1933 p 78–79). It is, however, more likely that confronted with the numerical superiority of his opponents Kleomenes was forced to withdraw from Argolis and attempted to stop them at Palladion to defend the access to Lakonia.

38. Plut. *Aratos* 29.6. Similar details are reported by Polybios, Aratos' most ardent supporter (4.8). Plutarch describes the above accusations as slander, but recognizes that these stories were so prevalent that Aratos was always mentioned by name 'as one who was a good general, but always had these symptoms when a contest was impending' (*Aratos* 29.6).

39. Bikerman 1943 p 302 note 4.

40. Walbank 1984 p 456–457
41. Plut. *Kleom.* 4.5.
42. Walbank 1933 p 81. The friendly relations between Eleians and Aitolians had begun around 267. The good relations with the Eleians were necessary for the Aitolians to maintain access to the interior of the Peloponnese. In return for the cooperation of the Eleians, the Aitolians turned over to them some Arcadian cities. But in reality, the Eleians were so heavily dependent on the Aitolians that they were essentially their 'much abused subjects' (Larsen 1975 p 164).
43. Plut. *Kleom.* 5.1. Pol. 2.51.3. There is no reference to the number of combatants, nor to their losses.
44. Pol. 2.58.1. They are obviously those who helped Aratos take the city. The behaviour of the Achaeans towards the Mantineians at this stage was good (Walbank 1957 p 263).
45. Plut. *Kleom.* 7.3, and Walbank 1984 p 457.
46. The issue of Archidamos' murder is exhaustively explored in Oliva's 1971 p 234–242 extensive commentary on relevant literature.
47. In the meanwhile, Agis' underage son, Eudamidas III, had died. According to Pausanias (2.9.1), Eudamidas III (whom Pausanias names Eurydamidas) was poisoned by Kleomenes' supervisors. Who were the supervisors? The *ephors* or those who had custody of the child? As pointed out by Oliva (1971 p 240 note 5), it is difficult to come to any conclusions based on Pausanias' testimony because of the many inaccuracies in the text.
48. Plut. *Kleom.* 5.2. It was obviously the same tradition that *Agis* invoked, according to which, when the kings acted together, their power was raised above that of the *ephors*. As Chrimes observes: 'the history of Sparta in the past provided many instances in which the state was weakened in a crisis by the existence of regency in one of the royal houses' (Chrimes 1999 p 11).
49. Pol. 8.1b.3. This view is totally inconsistent with Plutarch's statement that Archidamos left Sparta because of Leonidas. Some historians (Beloch = Oliva 1971 p 235) attempted to reconcile the two views, assuming that Archidamos fled twice from Sparta. The first time was after Agis' murder and the second was after Kleomenes' coup. According to this extreme assumption, Kleomenes invited Archidamos to Sparta after the coup in order to assassinate him. Such contortions are nothing but attempts to reconcile the irreconcilable.
50. Pol. 5.37.5. The above version was probably fabricated by Kleomenes' opponents and is sourced from the Megalopolitan historian Ptolemy (*Athenaios* 246c). As pointed out by Walbank, 'A Megalopolitan, even living abroad, might well be hostile to Cleomenes of Sparta' (Walbank 1957 p 566).
51. See Africa 1961 p 31, Oliva 1971 p 239–241, Shimron 1972 p 36–37.
52. Plut. *Kleom.* 5.3. It is interesting that Plutarch does not adopt Phylarchos' view, while in his second version the killers are designated as Kleomenes' 'friends'. Some scholars (Gabba= Oliva 1971 p 242) consider Plutarch's second version to be accurate believing that Kleomenes initially was on the side of the oligarchy and cooperated with the ruling class and the *ephors*. This view is refuted by the fact that Kleomenes always followed a well thought out policy and refrained from opportunism (Oliva 1971 p 242).

53. Plut. *Comparison* 5.2
54. Cartledge 2002b p 51
55. See Oliva 1971 p 241.
56. See Oliva 1971 p 241 note 3, Africa 1961 p 31.
57. Plut. *Kleom.* 6.1.
58. Plut. *Kleom.* 6.3. Both these units consisted of mercenaries. The term 'Tarantine' does not indicate ethnicity but combat tactics and weaponry. Tarantines were a fairly common type of light cavalry or mounted infantry – an evolution of the ancient *hamippoi* – mainly using javelins or swords in close combat (see Griffith 1984 p 246–250). They were perfectly suited for the role that was entrusted to them by Kleomenes against the disorganized enemy cavalry particularly with the support of the famous Cretan archers.
59. As Walbank states (1933 p 83), Kleomenes had no reason to be pleased with the death of the Megalopolitan general, who would have become an ally either by intimidation or bribery. Instead, for Aratos, the death of Lydiadas was a fortunate event since it relieved him from a dangerous competitor.
60. Plut. *Aratos* 37.3.
61. Plut. *Kleom.* 7.5. Thus Kleomenes' supporters remained in Sparta.
62. Although no figures are available, the losses of the Megalopolitans were very high (Pol. 2.55.2–4).
63. Heraia (near the modern Heraia Baths) was located in the small plain at the confluence of the rivers Alpheios and Ladon, astride the road of Megalopolis, Gortyn, Heraia and Olympia. With the occupation of Heraia, Kleomenes cut off Megalopolis' connection with the northwest.
64. Plut. *Kleom.* 7.3. Walbank (1933 p 85) identifies it with Alea. However, such an expansive manoeuvre – from Heraia to Argolis – is quite impressive. On what pretext did Kleomenes justify his movements to his men?
65. Plut. *Kleom.* 7.5–6, and see Walbank 1933 p 82.
66. Plutarch states that these *mothakes* were 'two of the helots who had been bred along with Cleomenes' (Plut. *Kleom.* 8.1). See further notes. For Kleomenes' relation with the *mothakes* and the mercenaries see Marasco 1979 p 51.
67. Plut. *Kleom.* 8.2. Only Plutarch cites this specific information about the existence of such a temple.
68. Fifteen years before, the economic oligarchy in Sparta consisted of 100 wealthy Spartans. These 100 Spartans must be the eighty wealthy Spartans who were exiled by Kleomenes, the four murdered *ephors*, the ten defenders of the *ephors* [most probably Spartan citizens] and also a few of the rebels like Kleomenes himself and Megistonous. (see Fuks 1962a, 1962c).
69. Plut. *Kleom.* 10.3 The above statement is by no means a proof that the *ephors* had ever been subservient to the king as suggested by Kleomenes (Grote 2000 p 272). It must have been a mere demagogic argument in an effort to manipulate the people.
70. Plut. *Kleom.* 10.3–4 modified.
71. Plut. *Kleom.* 10.6 modified. This last comment resonates Kleomenes' traumatic experience from the Aitolian raids in 241, in which the Illyrians might have participated as mercenaries. It is interesting that in his speech, Kleomenes exhausts his arguments

in justifying the necessity of his coup rather than introducing his reform program to which he briefly refers. Moreover, as Shimron (1972 p.38) notes, Plutarch does not report any *rhetra* submitted by Kleomenes equivalent to that submitted by Agis. Apparently, Kleomenes took Agis' *rhetra* for granted and simply proceeded to its implementation, a fact that stresses the identical goals of the two kings.

72. Strabo 8.5.5. According to one theory whose origin goes back to the historian Ephoros, the institution of *ephors* was created by the kings and specifically by Theopompos. (cf. Plato Laws 691d-692a, Arist. Pol. 1313a 26–33. Rawson 2002 p 39, p 1971 Oliva 123–125, Tigerstedt 1974 p 78, Hodkinson 2000 p 28–29). For Kleomenes' descent from King Pausanias, see Plut. *Agis* 3.3–6

73. Africa 1968 p 8. More importantly, regardless of its origin, the aforementioned theory rejected the Lykourgan origin of the institution of *ephors* in the eyes of the Spartans and consequently its validity (1974 Tigerstedt p. 78).

74. Plutarch criticized severely the slaughter of the *ephors* by Kleomenes, and described it as illegal and unnecessary: '... Kleomenes... undertook his change of the constitution with too much rashness and violence, killing the *ephors* in unlawful fashion, when it would have been easier to win them over to his views or remove them by superiority of arms, just as he removed many others from the city.'(Plut. *Comparison* 4.1).

75. Paus. 2.9.1. Some scholars conclude that the *Gerousia* was abolished. Most probably its powers were revoked and thus *Gerousia* was turned into an annually elected body (see Oliva 1971 p 245–6, Daubies 1971 p 667 note 16 and Shimron 1972 p 39).

76. Paus. 2.9.1 (See also Oliva 1971 p 81 and p 245 note 3). The creation of the six-member body of *patronomoi* might be connected to the creation of the sixth Spartan village, the Neopolitai, which dates back to the late Hellenistic or Roman times (early imperial). The name of the village in Greek indicates an innovation; some scholars (Cartledge 2002b p 53) maintain that this village was founded by Kleomenes. On the other hand, the fact that the institution of *patronomoi* appears only in Roman times suggests that Pausanias' information may be incorrect (Walbank 1984 p 458).

77. Plut. *Kleom.* 11.3.

78. Plut. *Kleom.* 11.3.

79. Pol. 2.47.3, 9.23.3 and 23.11.5.

80. The abolition of debts is mentioned twice: First in Plut. *Kleom.* 10.6, Kleomenes' own declaration: '...debtors should be set free from their debts', and second in the implicit but clear reference in *Kleom.* 18.2. Since the debts were already cancelled by Agis, these were obviously *new* debts that were incurred during the years of restoration.

81. Plut. *Kleom.* 11.1. It is striking that Polybios does not refer at all to Kleomenes' reforms. Some claim that Polybios' silence is intentional. Polybios evaded referring to Kleomenes' social reforms due to his detest towards any social reform (Piper 1986 p55). Nevertheless, Polybios must have taken for granted that his readers knew Kleomenes' reforms either from another historian or perhaps from a section of Polybios' *Histories* that has been lost (Papastylou Filiou 1995).

82. Plut. *Kleom.* 11.2: «ὁπλίτας τετρακισχιλίους ἐποίησε» ('He created 4,000 hoplites'). Plutarch does not mention the 15,000 *kleroi* of the *perioikoi* that Agis intended to include in his reforms. It appears that Kleomenes did not proceed to such reform.

83. The 600 'old' Spartans derive roughly if one subtracts the almost 100 killed or exiled by Kleomenes from the 700 Spartans of the old aristocracy that existed in Agis' time (Plut. *Agis* 5.6)

84. Michell 1964 p 327, Jones 1967 p154, Forrest 1980 p146, Oliva 1971 p244, David 1981 p 249 p note 48, Cartledge 2002b p 52, Green 1993 p257.

85. Shimron (1972 p 151–155). Shimron believes that the verb 'created' in Plutarch's citation: 'he [Kleomenes] created 4,000 hoplites' (Plut. *Kleom.* 11.2) refers to newly integrated citizens (see also Fuks 1962c, Daubies 1971 p 667). This position has been disputed by David (1981 p 249 note 48). Particularly impressive is Walbank's view (1984 p 458) in which 'All landed property was put into a common pool, debts were cancelled and the land was divided into 4,000 Spartan lots. The citizen body was made up to perhaps 5,000 from the metics and *perioikoi*'. This view leaves 1,000 Spartans without *kleroi*, which is impossible for the Spartan society.

86. Daubies 1971 p 666–667. If the total of all new *kleroi* was strictly 4,000 (including the shares of the eighty exiles, as claimed by Cartledge 2002b p 52), the number of Spartan hoplites would probably be less than 4,000, which is in contrast to Plutarch's statement (Plut. *Kleom.* 11.2).

87. We must bear in mind that the number of 'inferiors' (*hypomeiones*) in the Mid-third century was 1,800–2,300. Plutarch does not mention them. Their inclusion is certain, however, since Kleomenes' programme was the same as Agis' who had clearly expressed that intention (see Fuks 1962c p 256–258, Shimron 1972 p 42–43, Cartledge 2002b in p. 52, Marasco 1979 p 51).

88. Plut. *Kleom.* 10.6 The 'foreigners' (*xenoi*) must have been mostly mercenaries who were loyal to Kleomenes (Cartledge 2002b p52, Kennell 2003 p83 and p91). Walbank calls them *metics* (Walbank 1984 p 458, see also Plut. *Aratos* 38.3 and Papastylou-Filiou 1997 p.79–84) both the 'foreigners' and the *perioikoi* were selected after evaluation. According to Cartledge (2002b p 52) their numbers amounted to 1,400. According to Griffith (1984 p 95), the integrated *perioikoi* encompassed the total of Kleomenes' Spartan soldiers. This view contradicts Daubies (1971 p 666), who, based on Plutarch (*Kleom.*10.6), argues that not only did mercenaries become citizens, but also their integration preceded the inclusion of the *perioikoi* (Daubies 1971 pp. 666–667). In contrast, Marasco contends that the mercenaries did not immediately become citizens. According to him, Plutarch's reference of the inclusion of 'foreigners' (*Kleom.* 10.6) signifies that Kleomenes had promised them they would become citizens, while for the *perioikoi* (*Kleom.* 11.2) this appears to be certain (Marasco 1979 p 51). Kleomenes, allegedly, carried out a second land redistribution by distributing new allotments to the mercenaries from the areas he had conquered 'during the period between the Battle of Dyme (226 BC) and the Macedonian invasion' (Marasco 1979 p 54). Despite the fact that this theory contains some pertinent observations, such as Kleomenes' special relationship with the *mothakes* who became citizens (Marasco 1979 p 51, note 30), it remains an assumption. There is nothing to suggest that Kleomenes ordered a second distribution of land other than the one he applied immediately after the coup.

89. Plut. *Kleom.* 11.2.

90. Fuks 1962b. See also Shimron 1972 p 41. According to Cartledge 'the 'civic land' was pooled and redistributed in equal portions to some 4,000 new and old citizens' (2002b p 52).

91. Kleomenes issued silver tetradrachms following the example of Areus I. His image is portrayed on the obverse, while the reverse depicts the image of goddess Artemis Orthia, protector of the Spartan *agoge* (Cartledge 2002b p 55). A second series of bronze coins is also attributed to Kleomenes. His image was replaced by Ptolemaic symbols, perhaps in recognition of Ptolemy III's financial assistance (see Cartledge 2002b p 55 and p 209, Palagia 2006 – 10). Note that some historians have reservations, as to whether he issued coins at all. If he attempted to revive the Spartan tradition, he was unlikely to issue coins (see Christien 2002 p 184, who attributes the above mentioned coinage to Kleomenes' successor, King Lykourgos).

92. Plut. *Kleom.* 10.6 and 11.2. According to Shimron (1972 p 151–2), the number of young Spartans must have increased at the rate of about 100 per year, due to births.

93. Obviously, after the redistribution of land, the women's rights on the *kleroi* must have been considerably curtailed and this was a serious reason for the former wealthy landowners to be against Kleomenes' regime.

94. Plut. *Kleom.* 13.1–2. The above account by Plutarch, is based almost entirely on Athenaios 142c-f and in some parts it seems that he has fully copied him. Throughout Kleomenes' idealized description that is reminiscent of the Stoic philosopher-king, there emerges the personality of a man who knew how to charm those around him.

95. Plut. *Kleom.* 13.3.

96. See also Plut. *Kleom.* 2.2.

97. Pol. 5.38.9–10, 5.39.5–6, 9.23.3–4 and 18.53.3.

98. Plut. *Kleom.*1.3 (See also *Comparison* 3.1 and 4.2). The fact is that the two Spartan kings' personalities are depicted somewhat schematically by Plutarch: the virtuous Agis, who voluntarily sacrificed himself for his ideals (*Comparison* 3.1), contrasted with the ruthless Kleomenes, who seized power by resorting to brute force (*Comparison* 4.1–2). Such an approach ignores the fact that Agis also seized power via a coup, deposed the legally elected *ephors* and expelled King Leonidas from Sparta. In fact, the only real difference between Agis and Kleomenes was that Kleomenes succeeded where Agis failed (Shimron 1972 p 38).

99. Plut. *Kleom.* 11.2. It is remarkable that, while other areas of Greece, such as Boeotia and Epirus had adopted earlier the Macedonian battle tactics, Sparta, despite her emphasis on military issues, did so with a delay of approximately one century. This reveals that the conservative Sparta had remained behind the developments of her era (Oliva 1971 p 246 and Cartledge 2002b p 53, Walbank 1984 p 458).

100. The fortifications included five main points: Chelmos Hill (= Athenaion in the area of Belminatis), the Khartzenikos (south of the modern village of Kollines), Aghios Konstantinos of Sellasia, Leontari (= Lefktron in the area of Megalopolis) and Aghios Konstantinos of Lianou (= Eutaia) (see Pritchett 1965 p 63 and especially Pikoulas 1988a p 478, p 186–187 Pikoulas 1988b).

101. Palagia 2006 p 210–215.

102. Africa 1961 p 26.

103. In fact, the Achaean army was badly organized and had a low morale while many Achaeans redeemed their military service by sending others to fight in their place. The Achaean infantry consisted mainly of the *thureophoroi*, a type of light infantry armed with small oval (but bigger than the *pelte*) shields, 'such as Celtic *thureoi* and Persian '*gera*' (Pausanias 8.50.1). *Thureophoroi* usually fought in open order using the tactics of the traditional *peltasts*, but were also able to fight in close formations (Pol. 4.8.11, 4.11.8). The cavalry of the Achaean army was badly commanded and (before its reorganization by Philopoimen in 207) unable to execute complex manoeuvres and change formations (Pol. 11.9.4–5, Plut. *Philop.* 9.1–7 Paus. 8.50.1, Errington 1969 p 63, Head 1982 p 47 and p 114).

104. A typical example of the Ptolemies' opportunistic attitude was King Ptolemy II's stance during the Chremonidean War (267–ca. 261), where he had openly sided with an anti-Macedonian coalition that included Athens, Sparta, and a large number of Greek cities. Although Ptolemy II sent his fleet to help his allies, he declined to engage it in (open) conflict with the enemy, a fact that contributed decisively to the defeat of the anti-Macedonian coalition.

105. It should be noted that unlike the Aitolian League, which was by definition anti-Macedonian, the Achaean League was not fervidly pro-Macedonian oriented until after Aratos came to power.

106. Pol. 2.47.5–6

107. Pol. 2.47.8

108. Pol. 2.55.2–4

109. Theoretically, Greek cities could apply the principle of *epimachia* to their diplomatic ties, whenever they had an interest in doing so (Thuc. 1.44.1, 49, 5.27.2, 48.2 Arist. Pol. 1280b 27). As Bikerman has indicated (1943 p 291–294), according to this principle, a country was entitled to help the victim of a hostile invasion without being involved at war with the invader.

110. Pol. 2.49. The potential risk resulting from Sparta's coalition with the Aitolians is obviously exaggerated by Polybios. Until then the Aitolians had been the Achaeans' allies and had not moved against the Achaean League in any way (Urban 1979 p 131 ff, Walbank 1984 p 462). Nevertheless, the possibility of an anti-Macedonian coalition was there, and it was certainly not contrived by Aratos (Bikerman 1943 p 302). Besides, the Aitolians were not known for being faithful to their allies, but for being strongly anti-Macedonian.

111. Plut. *Aratos* 38.7–8. Polybios notes that Aratos had a hidden agenda. He kept secret his communication with Antigonos, and did not mention it even in his own memoirs (Pol 2.47.10–11). Yet, if Aratos was so secretive, then how did Polybios know about his real objectives? One possible explanation is that Polybios relied on the testimonies of other Megalopolitan historians whom he does not name (Walbank 1995 p 357, Urban 1979 p.126 ff). Some historians (Gruen 1972), though, argue that Polybios' exclusive source was Phylarchos and do not hesitate to challenge both Polybios' and Plutarch's testimonies in order to support that Aratos was not involved in the negotiations between the Megalopolitan delegates and Antigonos. Their main argument is that Aratos' policy had always been anti-Macedonian and not anti-Spartan (Gruen 1972

p613–614). In fact, Aratos' reluctance to openly confront Kleomenes from the start, met with strong opposition on the part of the Megalopolitan leader Lydiadas and the Argive leader Aristomachos whose cities were traditionally hostile to Sparta. Gruen believes that Aratos has wrongly been perceived as a plotter and orchestrator of a clandestine rapprochement with Antigonos and that this biased view was originated from Phylarchos. Plutarch's and Polybios' accounts were based on Phylarchos, each in a different way: Plutarch accepted unreservedly the image that Phylarchos created for Aratos, while Polybios attempted to justify Aratos' attitude by accrediting him patriotic motives (Gruen 1972 p.619–620).

The main flaw of the above theory is that not only does it disregard Plutarch's and Polybios' testimonies on this issue, but it also underestimates the leadership skills of Aratos, who remained the absolute ruler and the soul of the Achaean League to the end of his life. Therefore, the assumption that the Megalopolitans sent an embassy to Antigonos without Aratos' prior approval is impossible. Moreover, Aratos' anti-Macedonian history does not rule out the possibility of approaching his former enemies. As most great statesmen, Aratos was insightful and politically flexible. In this respect, his attitude is perfectly understandable. Finally, seeking ulterior motives behind Aratos' reluctance to openly confront with Sparta is superfluous. His phobia during the battle (reported by Plutarch and Polybios) combined with his awareness of the Spartan military superiority and Kleomenes' strategic genius provide adequate explanation.

112. Plut. *Aratos* 38.1. It was probably the guard that Kleomenes had stationed in Arcadia before the coup (Oliva 1971 p 246 note 4).

113. Plut. *Kleom.* 12.1.

114. Pol. 2.58.4. On the contrary, Plutarch (*Kleom.* 14.1 and *Aratos* 39.1) states that the Achaean garrison was expelled. However, the subsequent brutality of the Achaeans towards the Mantineians attests to Polybios' version (see Oliva 1971 p 250 note 1, Walbank 1984 p 463).

115. Walbank (1933 p 90) locates it in the area where the present railway from Patrai to Pyrgos runs.

116. Plut. *Kleom.* 14.2, *Aratos* 39.1 and Pol. 2.51.3. Unfortunately there is no reference either of the numbers or the quality of the opposing forces.

117. Plutarch (*Kleom.* 14) cites that Kleomenes 'went up against Langon, drove out the Achaean garrison...' This probably refers to the city of Lasion in Elis (Walbank 1933 p 81, 90).

118. Ptolemy's decision was probably affected by the fact that Aratos had sent a delegation to his Macedonian rival (Walbank 1984 p 464). There is serious evidence that at that time Sparta and Egypt strengthened their ties: Besides Ptolemy's statue in Sparta that has already been mentioned and dates back to that period and also the Ptolemaic emblems depicted on Spartan bronze coins, there is also a reference to a votive of Ptolemy to Kleomenes at Olympia, which probably dates back to the period of 226–224 (Palagia 2006 p 210–212). The strengthening of ties with the Ptolemies may possibly be associated with the presence of Sphairos in Sparta, since the philosopher had previously lived in the court of the Ptolemies.

119. Plut. *Kleom.* 15.1.
120. In fact, Kleomenes did not only seek to impose the Spartan hegemony but also add a personal touch to it assuming the role of a mighty patron, as Ptolemy III had done earlier for the Achaean League. (Plut *Aratos* 24.4, Oliva 1971 p 251 and Walbank 1984 p 463). As Marasco highlights (2004 p 204), Kleomenes did not aim at simply reconstruct the old Peloponnesian League (in which the powers of the Spartan king were minimal). He wanted to create a coalition under the standards of the Hellenic League of Philip II of Macedonia and the Hellenistic kingdoms, whose leaders were universally recognized as supreme commanders.
121. In present day Myloi at Nauplion.
122. A contemporary historian (Shipley 2000) wonders whether behind Aratos' obsession with the Achaean League hid his desire for a Sikyonian empire (!) 'It is tempting to ask whether Aratos and his allies were seeking to create the biggest possible empire for their own ends, or to offer cities the chance of autonomous development and lift the fear of Macedonian rule' (Shipley 2000 p 138).
123. (Plut. *Kleom.* 16.5) see also Tarn 1928 p 756.
124. This can be deduced from the fact that the sixth *meliamb* refers to the stoic philosopher Sphairos by name, perhaps scornfully. Both the second and the fourth *meliambs* criticize the unfair distribution of wealth, and warn of the danger of revolution. It is striking that in contrast to the cosmopolitan nature of the Cynics and their contempt of wealth, Kerkidas deliberately sided with the ruling class of his homeland and did not hesitate to defend it even on the battlefield in 222 (see Africa 1961 p 20, Michell 1964 p 325–326, Oliva 1971 p 248–249, Ferguson 1975 p 134–135, Walbank 1984 p 466, Green 1995 p 387).
125. Shimron 1972 p 49.
126. Plut. *Kleom.* 15.2.
127. Plut. *Kleom.* 15.1.
128. Plut. *Aratos* 41.2. And Walbank 1984 p 466.
129. Plut. *Aratos* 39.2–3.
130. Plut. *Kleom.* 17.1.
131. Plut. *Kleom.* 17.2. At the time, general of the Achaeans was Timoxenos (225/4).
132. Plut. *Kleom.* 17.2. Kanellopoulos 1982 vol. II p 115.
133. Plut. *Kleom.* 17.3. It is significant that there was no established consensus among the cities of the Achaean League as they had not all joined with enthusiasm. As Polybios recognizes, some cities had been forced to join in: '…many were brought to share in it by persuasion and argument: some, though acting under compulsion at first, were quickly brought to acquiesce in its benefits' (Pol 2.38.7).
134. Walbank 1984 p 464
135. Plut. *Kleom.* 17.3
136. Regarding the followers of Kleomenes at Argos *(Kleomenists)* see Pol. 2.53.2. Regarding the Spartan sympathizers at Corinth *(Lakonizers)*, see Plut. *Kleom.* 19.1. Some historians (Urban 1979 p 166–213) claimed that the accession of the Achaean cities to Kleomenes was ascribed mainly to the political calculations and the opportunism of their leaders. This theory significantly underrates the appeal the Kleomenean reforms

had for the masses; however, it recognizes that the social pressures shaped to some extent the practices of each city's leaders.

137. Plut. *Aratos* 40.1

138. Plut. *Aratos* 39.3–4

139. Pellene was yet another purely Achaean city that fell into Kleomenes' hands, after Dyme and Pharai. Its importance was not negligible, as Pellene was a religious center for the area, second to Aigion, the capital of the Achaean League.

140. Kleomenes' campaign makes sense if we read Tausend's essay. Tausend (1998) identifies Mount Penteleia with the summit of Mount Aroaneia (Chelmos, modern Dourdouvana). On its western slope, is the village Planitero and according to Tausend the town Penteleion. On the map it appears that this fortified town oversees Kleitor and the road to Kynaitha (modern Kalavryta) and Aigeira on the Corinthian coast. Therefore, it was vital for Kleomenes to occupy Penteleion in order to seize Kaphyai and open the Arcadian Corridor.

141. Plut. *Aratos* 40.1.

142. *strategos autocrator*' Plut. *Aratos* 41.1.

143. Plut. *Kleom.* 19.1.

144. After Argos undertook the organization of the Nemean games in the third century, the games were held in the town of Argos and not in their birthplace, Nemea, anymore. Aristomachos had reluctantly joined the Achaean League succumbing to the pressures of Aratos, who had promised to offer him the generalship of the Achaean League. He sided with Kleomenes out of political ambition, resentment against Aratos and desire to regain influence in the city that he once dominated (Mandel 1979 p 304).

145. Plut. *Kleom.* 17.4–5 Walbank 1933 p 96 and 1984 p465.

146. Plut. *Kleom.* 19.2.

147. Plut. *Kleom.* 19.4 In his *Life of Aratos* 41.3. Plutarch calls him Tripylos. Surprisingly, the mediator in favour of Sparta was a Messenian. This rarity may be attributed to the appeal of Kleomenes' revolutionary reforms. It appears that there were several Messenians who set their resentment against Sparta aside and openly supported Kleomenes hoping for broader social reforms in Messene, too.

148. Plut. *Aratos* 41.3 Green (1993 p 798 note 96) claims that Kleomenes, whose own subsidy from Ptolemy must not have exceeded twelve talents, was facing such financial hardships that he could not afford bribery without any guarantee of success. Therefore, Kleomenes' proposals of cooperation to Aratos combined with Kleomenes' careful refusal to confiscate Aratos' property in Corinth reveal that Kleomenes' ulterior motive was to reduce Aratos' reliability and render him suspect of treason in the eyes of the members of the Achaean League.

149. Plut. *Aratos* 41.4 and *Kleom.* 19.4. The above phrase by Aratos can have two meanings: it was either an inept excuse for rejecting Kleomenes' proposal (in the sense that it was now too late for any negotiations), or it was an admission of failure to exert his power on the Achaean League and to conform to the decisions of the other leaders. The latter is consistent with Green's view that there were conflicting trends within the League in which the pro-Macedonian faction was almighty – despite Aratos' resentment against them (see note 111). However, the former is closer to reality. The man who

determined the League's policy was no other than Aratos who he had recently served as 'general emperor' of the League and was systematically re-elected every two years as its 'general'. Kleomenes' rage against him was, therefore, absolutely justified.

Moreover, Kleomenes' attempt to approach Aratos indicated that the Spartan King's exclusive intent was to put Corinth under his absolute control even if he had to cooperate with his bitter enemy to succeed it. Given that Aratos was double faced, he must have exposed Kleomenes to the Achaeans for attempting to bribe him. He claimed his integrity as an excuse for refusing to cooperate with Kleomenes.

150. Not all, though: certain cities such as Kleitor and Stymphalos remained loyal to the Achaean League until the end (Pol. 2.55.7–9).

151. Plut. *Aratos* 16.4–5.

152. Plut. *Aratos* 42.1–2 It is not clear whether this was the standard spring *synodos* or an emergency *synkletos*. Aratos' son had apparently returned from the trip he had taken to Macedonia the previous year. In reference to the date of the Achaean meeting in the spring of 224 (which others, such as Bikerman (1943 p 294) and Will (= Oliva 1971 p 256 note 2) place in late 225), see Walbank 1984 p 465 note 48 and p 467–468 note 54.

153. Plut. *Aratos* 38.6. This title had been formerly awarded to Ptolemy III. (Plut. *Aratos* 24.4) However, the Macedonian hegemony was much more direct and easier to impose on the Achaeans compared with that of the remote Kingdom of Egypt (Walbank 1995 p360 note 81).

154. Plut. *Aratos* 45.1

155. Liv. 32.5.4 and Walbank 1995 p 700 note 85. Later the Achaean League enacted a law prohibiting even the proposal of any measure or provision against the alliance with the Macedonian monarch (Liv. 32.22.3, also see Walbank 1995 p 360).

156. Plut. *Aratos* 45.2

157. Pol. 2.52.3–4.

158. Plut. *Kleom.* 19.4, *Aratos* 42.2.

159. Larsen (1966 p 56) points out that denying access to the Thermopylai passage must not have created any serious troubles for the Macedonians other than a small delay. Furthermore, it does not indicate anything regarding the Aitolians' intentions except an 'unfriendly attitude' toward the Macedonians.

160. Pol. 20.6.7–8. Walbank 1995 p 361.

161. Plut. *Kleom.* 20.1.

162. Plut. *Kleom.* 20.2.

163. Plut. *Kleom.* 20.3. Sikyon must have been the nearest safe harbour for massive transport of large military forces, since Kleomenes was in control of the Isthmus of Corinth.

164. Plut. *Kleom.* 20.3.

165. Plut. *Aratos* 44.2. Apparently, Epidauros was unguarded. Kleomenes' army could not be in Corinth, Sikyon and the Isthmus simultaneously. No wonder 1,500 men were transported to Epidauros by sea since it was a raiding force whose transport proved possible under the circumstances. Nevertheless, to transport 20,000 men along with their equipment and supplies to the enemy territory by sea was unfeasible.

166. Plut. *Kleom.* 20.4. According to Polybios (Pol 2.53.2), during this period (224/3) Timoxenos was *strategos* (general) of the Achaean League. However, this year should

have been Aratos' turn to be elected in the position since he was systematically re-elected every second year (Plut. *Kleom.* 15.1, *Aratos* 24.4) and in the previous year (225/224) he had not served as *strategos* but as '*strategos autokrator*' (general emperor) having special powers. Walbank explains this discrepancy by claiming that during Aratos' service as *stategos autokrator* (225/224), Timoxenos served as '*strategos*' of the Achaean League. Next year (224/3) Timoxenos remained in this position *de facto* since Aratos was absent negotiating with Antigonos (Walbank 1933 p 173–175, 1957 p 254 and 1984 p 467–468 note54).

167. Plut. *Kleom.* 21.2. Sparta lacked defenders but was not defenceless, since Kleomenes had provisioned for her walling. Plutarch clearly states that Kleomenes feared an eventual siege by his enemies. (see Kourinou 2000 p60, note 156)

168. Kleomenes held Megistonous responsible for the defection of Argos because the latter had persuaded him to trust the Argives and had deterred him from driving the suspects out of the city (Plut. *Kleom.* 21.1).

169. Plut. *Kleom.* 21.4. Plutarch remarks once again, Kleomenes' inability to confront the Macedonians in an open field. The superiority of the Macedonian infantry was undeniable. For the events see also Pol. 2.53.2–6. For the date see Walbank 1984 p 467 note 55.

170. Cartledge 2002b p 53, Koliopoulos 2001 p 330.

171. Walbank maintains that Kleomenes was not willing to implement his reform programme on Argos, Sparta's age old rival, as his reforms would render it powerful (Walbank 1984 p 468). But there is not the slightest reference regarding the implementation of any social reforms in any city under Kleomenes' control while there is strong evidence of the opposite: when in 226, with the help of the Mantineians, he won the city from the Achaean League he simply assigned to it its old regime (Plut. *Kleom.* 14.1, Pol. 2.57.) Later, when the Corinthians surrendered their city to him, he offered Aratos – a keen exponent of the wealthy class – a joint administration of Corinth. In both cases, Kleomenes was driven by his political interest and was indifferent to the social problems of the local population (Shimron 1972 p 45–46).

172. Africa 1961 p 26.

173. Shimron 1972 p 46.

174. Comparing Kleomenes' new Spartan army with the other 'Greek and Macedonian armies', Plutarch notes that it was the only army which 'had no players in attendance, no jugglers, no dancing girls, no harpists, but was free from any kind of licence, scurrility, and general festivity; while for the most part the young men practised themselves and the elder men taught them, and for amusement, when their work was over, they had recourse to their wonted pleasantries and the interchange of Spartan witticisms' (Plut. *Kleom.* 12.3). This is certainly an idealized image owed to Phylarchos. However this image reflects the feelings of anticipation that Kleomenes' promising army inspired in the dispossessed people. In their eyes, it embodied the hope for the oncoming revolution.

175. Aristomachos had abandoned the Macedonians in order to join the Achaean League. It was reasonable for him to fear retaliation by the Macedonians. This, of course, does not justify his opportunistic policy (see Mandel 1979 p 302–307).

176. Walbank 1984 p 467–468.
177. Tarn 1923 p 138.
178. This event has inspired, among others, two of K.P. Kavafy's finest poems: *In Sparta* and *Go, O King of the Lakedaimonians.*
179. Plut. *Kleom.* 22.7
180. Pol. 2.59 Polybios emphatically denies the accounts of the torturing of Aristomachos; however, he considers his killing fair
181. Pol. 5.16.6
182. Pol. 5.22.1–5, Kourinou 2000 p60
183. Pol. 2.54.2–5. Walbank, 1933 p 104
184. Tarn 1928 p 759 and Walbank 1933 p 104 and 1984 p 468
185. Plut. *Kleom.* 16.5
186. Plut. *Aratos* 45.4. Antigonos was honoured in special celebrations, the famous 'Antigoneia.'
187. Errington 1969 p. 26
188. Pol. 2.55.5. To determine the date of the attack, see Walbank 1995 p 367 and p. 702 n.130
189. Pol. 2.54.6–7.
190. Plut. *Aratos* 45.1–2.
191. Tarn 1930 p. 44.
192. Plut. *Aratos* 45.4–6. The events were vividly described by Phylarchos. In an attempt to justify the Achaeans' and Aratos' behaviour, Polybios argues that Phylarchos tried to impress his readers by overemphasizing and distorting the facts (Pol. 2.56.1–9). He also claims that what the Achaeans had sustained was retaliation for the massacre of the Achaean garrison by the Mantineians in 226. According to Polybios, the Mantineians deserved to suffer a worse fate than the looting of their property and their enslavement (Pol. 2.58.10–12). But Polybios' arguments (obviously based on Aratos' excuses in his *Memoirs*) were not enough to reduce the Greeks' abhorring of the events (Rostovtzeff 1941 p 194).
193. Pol. 2.54.13–14 see Walbank (1995 p.355 note 6).
194. As pointed out by Walbank (1995 p 367) Antigonos, who probably knew that Kleomenes had lost his Egyptian subsidy, was counting on wearing his opponent out.
195. Kleomenes, who had already sent his family to Egypt as hostages, was anxious about the renewal of his subsidy as promised by King Ptolemy. The impressive military operations he conducted subsequently aimed at convincing Ptolemy that Sparta was still able to reverse the course of the war and, therefore, his financial support was not futile.
196. Helots had been emancipated by the Spartans several times in the past for this purpose by the Spartans. Michell (1964 p 251) lists at least seven known cases when the helots volunteered to serve in the Spartan army: in 425 (Thuc. 4.80), in 413 (Thuc. 7.19), in 412 (Thuc. 8.8), in 400 (Xen *Hell.* 3.1.4), in 396 (Xen *Hell.* 3.4.2), in 394 (Xen *Hell.* 4.25), and even after the destruction of Leuktra 6,000 helots rushed to fight for Sparta at the prospect of liberation from the Spartans (Xen. *Hell.* 5.6.29).
197. Plut. *Kleom.* 23.1.

198. Plut. *Kleom.* 23.1

199. One such connotation is found in the Lexicon of Hesychius (fifth-sixth century AD): «μονομοιτῶν Εἰλώτων ἄρχοντες» (Hesychius μ 1626). Cartledge compares these helot-foremen, to the Russian *kulaks*, the *muzhiks* who became proprietors of their own farms. A *monomoitos* was probably 'the overseer who made sure that the work on the *kleros* was done regularly and properly, particularly where vines were cultivated, who negotiated for equipment, repairs to buildings and so on, and who arranged for the payment of the stipulated rent and for the disposal of the remainder including any surplus for sale outside the *kleros* – all with a sharp eye to personal gain' (Cartledge 1987 p 174). See also Hodkinson 2000 p 124–125.

200. This amount was also equivalent to the fee for the liberation of slaves from the Late-third century until the middle of the first century in the entire Greek world (Daubies 1971 p 675, Cartledge 2002b p 56, Ducat 2002 p 210 note 27).

201. Plut. 23.1. This is the prevailing view (Toynbee 1969 p 389, Oliva 1971 p 259, Shimron1972 p 50, Walbank 1984 p 470, Cartledge 2002b p 56, Kennell 2003 p 85). However, a number of other theories have been put forward. Africa (1968) argues that the 2,000 helots must not have been used only in military service, but also they must have acquired civil rights. This view is problematic for two reasons: firstly, the inclusion of the helots in the citizen body contrasted with the Spartan tradition and secondly, it entailed the problem of finding 2,000 new *kleroi* for the new citizens. Africa's assumption (1968 p 11) that Kleomenes might have promised to the helots' new *kleroi* taken from the enemies' territories is nothing but a contrivance in order to support his farfetched theory.

  A diametrically opposing view is expressed by Daubies who claims that Kleomenes did not arm in a Macedonian-like fashion 2,000 helots but 2,000 *perioikoi*. His main argument is that the translation of Plutarch's respective citation is incorrect and misleading. According to his interpretation, the text does not specify whether the 2,000 armed men were helots or not (Daubies 1971 p 668 ff.). Additionally, Daubies (1971 p 670) claims that Kleomenes was in need of skilled and experienced warriors in order to man his phalanx, so these men can't have been former-tillers. However, the phalanx was used as a striking force, and at that time its impact was owed to the heavy pressure it exerted on the enemy lines, which did not need particularly skilled men: 'only the first five rows and the rearmost were composed of trained men, while the other rows were filled up with half-trained men who just pushed' (Tarn 1930 p 28). On this issue, I'd rather follow the *communis opinio*, according to which Kleomenes included in his phalanx 2,000 newly emancipated helots [i.e. the *neodamodeis*] who were allowed to fight but had no civil rights. This view does not solve all the problems of Plutarch's obscure phrasing. Yet, it is the least problematic of all.

202. Plut.23.1. There is no further reference to the 'White Shields' neither by Plutarch nor by Polybios in his detailed description of Antigonos' forces (Pol. 2.65.1–5). Polybios only refers to 'Bronze Shields' (Pol. 2.65.5) and some scholars (Daubies 1971 p685–688) identify the two units. See also below.

203. Obviously, a number of the newly emancipated helots couldn't have offered any military services because of old age or poor physical condition.

204. Pol. 2.55.3–4 and 2.61–63 Plut. *Kleom.* 23.2–4, Philopoimen). Kleomenes' actions were not opportunistic but very well thought out: the Great City (Megalopolis) was much extended in relation to its population and, therefore, difficult to guard (Walbank 1957 p 258). According to Polybios, during the war (particularly after the losses at Lykaion and Ladokeia) its population had further declined (Pol 2.55.2–4). Moreover, seizing it would boost Kleomenes' tarnished reputation.

205. Walbank 1933 p 108.

206. According to Polybios, Kleomenes' supporters in the city were Messenian exiles (Pol. 2.55.3). This contradicts both the subsequent attitude of the Megalopolitans who fled to Messene and the traditional hatred of the Messenians toward the Spartans. On the other hand, it is known that Kleomenes had Messenian supporters such as Tritymallos (Plut. *Kleom.* 19.8, *Aratos.* 41.3). According to Walbank, this can be explained by the existence of intense internal rivalries between the democrats and the oligarchs in Messene. The 'Messenian exiles' and Kleomenes' supporters must have been followers of the Messenian Democratic Party who believed in Kleomenes and his revolutionary reforms (Walbank 1957 p 258).

207. Plut. *Kleom.* 24.1.

208. The big size of the city and the fact that Kleomenes used a relatively small number of men for the attack played an important role in allowing the civilians to escape safely. Such a difficult and secretive operation could not have been carried out with numerous forces.

209. Plut. *Kleom.* 24.3–5. Polybios claims that it was Kleomenes' initiative and avoids naming the two Megalopolitans (Pol 2.61.4). One possible explanation for this is that Thearidas was Polybios' grandfather (Errington 1969 p 17). However, Kleomenes' attitude is remarkable: here, as well as previously in Mantineia, Argos and Corinth, he did not announce social reforms. Instead, he sent two prominent Megalopolitans to negotiate with their fellow citizens and he simply promised that he would return Megalopolis to its citizens intact. In this case also, his motives were purely political (Shimron 1972 p 45–46).

210. Polybios is indignant with Phylarchos' exaggeration, who increases the value of the loot from Megalopolis to the incredible amount of 6,000 talents in order to polish Kleomenes' image. With convincing arguments he refutes Phylarchos' excessive estimates and decreases it to a reasonable 300 talents (Pol 2.62).

211. Kleomenes fortified certain hilltops with trenches and palisades in carefully chosen positions that guarded the potential invasion passages.

212. The Macedonian garrison at Tegea was certainly not able to intercept Kleomenes' march. Besides, Kleomenes must have utilized some of the routes from Lakonia to Argolis through Mount Parnon on the right side of the Tegea plain. On the year of the invasion, see Walbank 1995 p.368. Cartledge (2002b p 56–57) places the campaign in early 222 while Walbank (1995 p 356) more plausibly in early spring 222.

213. Tomlinson (1972 p 161) points out that Kleomenes' main goal was to cause a major uprising in the city of Argos, which Antigonos might not be able to stifle (Plut. *Kleom.* 25.4). This view is reinforced by the fact that Kleomenes allowed no atrocities beyond land destruction. According to Plutarch, Kleomenes prevented the burning

of Kyllarabion gymnasium and attempted to justify the destruction of Megalopolis attributing it to a momentary burst of anger (Plut. *Kleom.* 26.2). However, Kleomenes' risky actions at this stage of the war were mainly associated with the discontinuation of Ptolemy's subsidy: both the seizure of Megalopolis and the ravage of Argolis indicate Kleomenes' effort to convince Ptolemy that he was powerful enough to deserve a subsidy renewal.

214. Plutarch (*Kleom.* 26.1) states that the Spartans destroyed the harvest of the Argives using wooden staves and not knives or sickles. The use of wood for the destruction of grain indicates that wheat was ripe but not ready for harvest, otherwise the invaders would have burned it. Consequently, the plundering took place towards the end of the spring (see Chrimes 1999 p 434 note 1).

215. Plut. *Kleom.* 27.2.

216. Plut. *Kleom.* 27.5. For a detailed description of Antigonos' forces see notes 244–8.

217. Plut. *Kleom.* 27.2.

218. Pol. 2. 63.1–2.

219. As Africa notes (1968 p 3), Ptolemy III was frugal of his subsidies. As long as the Achaean League served his interests against Macedonia, Ptolemy gave Aratos a meagre subsidy of six talents a year. Remember that in 224 Kleomenes had offered Aratos twice the amount in order to win him over (Plut. *Aratos* 41.3).

220. Plut. *Kleom.* 16.5.

221. Tarn 1930 p 49.

222. For a description of the two accesses to northern Lakonia see here, at p. 40–42.

223. In this case Antigonos would have had more options at his disposal:
    i.   He could follow the route from the Argos plains northwest to Mantineia and then he could make his way to Tegea.
    ii. He could follow a southern route from Argos through Mount Artemision and Mount Khtenias to Mantineia.
    iii. Another way, which Pausanias refers to as 'Trochos', began from the modern village of Elliniko and through two alternative uphill routes ended in the plain of Hysiai (modern Achladokampos). From there he could reach the Tegean plain. Loring (1895, p 80), Petronotis (2001 p 50), Pikoulas (1990b p226–236).
    iv. He could also turn south, then enter the Thyrea plain (part of Kynouria) and follow the route that Pausanias refers to as 'Anigraia' all the way to Astros. From there he could climb Mount Parnon, pass the ancient Hermai and end up at Karyai. However it would have been difficult for an army to cross the western slope of Mount Parnon as it was covered by a dense forest of oaks referred to as Skotitas (Loring 1895, p 54–55,57).

224. Incidentally, Colonel Leake placed the battlefield of Sellasia approximately in this location (Loring 1895, p 59, note 131).

225. The main sources for the battle are Polybios (2.65–69), who provides a detailed description of the battle, and Plutarch's two biographies of Kleomenes (28) and Philopoimen (6). As Walbank has pointed out (1957 p 272 – 273), Polybios (as seen in 2.66.4, 2.70.3) and Plutarch were based on Phylarchos. Polybios, however, also used another source, probably a Megalopolitan informant from Philopoimen's circle. Of

course, as is the case with many other issues concerning the history of the Spartan Movement, there is no absolute certainty concerning the battle of Sellasia. Following his usual tactic of sitting on the fence, Cartledge does not even bother to investigate the events simply stating: 'as with almost all ancient and many modern battles, precise details of the battle site and of the number, disposition and evolutions of the opposed forces are more or less controversial. In one sense, this is immaterial. Cleomenes' cause was lost before even battle was joined …' (Cartledge 2002b p 57). Such a disdainful view of one of the greatest battles in the history of Sparta is-in the present writer's opinion- extreme, even if Kleomenes' cause was indeed lost before the battle was joined. For this reason, this study will try to shed light on all 'controversial' issues concerning the battle of Sellasia.

The question of the battle date has been resolved by Walbank. There were three possible dates: 223, 222 or 221. The first had been previously proposed by Ferrabino and initially accepted by Walbank (1933 p 197). Beloch's and especially Tarn's (1928 p 863) proposed date was 222. Some considered 221 (e.g. Chrimes 1999 p 433–434) to be the most probable date, because Polybios (2.70.4) reports that after the battle, Antigonos went to Nemea to celebrate the Nemean games, which were celebrated in 'odd' years (the second and the fourth year of the Olympiads). Yet, more recent evidence clearly indicates that the death of Ptolemy III Euergetes (in whose court Kleomenes fled after the battle) occurred in February 221 (Walbank 1957 p 272). Consequently, Walbank does not hesitate to reject both 223, which he had proposed earlier, and also 221 arguing that obviously the celebration of the Nemean games was postponed due to the war. He concluded: 'Hence Sellasia was in 222' (Walbank 1957 p 272). For a detailed account of this see Oliva 1971 p 262 note 2. The latter, however, claims that the battle took place in early 222. This view conflicts with Polybios' testimony (2.65.1), according to which Antigonos began his campaign in early summer. Therefore, the battle must have taken place in late June or early July 222 (Walbank 1995 p703 note 140). This chronology is now generally adopted (Shimron 1972 p 51 note 107, Cartledge 2002b p57). For a detailed topography of the battle site, see Appendix C. For 'the number, disposition and evolutions of the opposed forces' see next chapter.

226. Pol. 2.65.8–9 «…τάφρον καί χάρακα προβαλόμενος» A palisade (χάραξ) was a strong fence made of stakes driven into the ground to enclose an area, especially for defence.

227. Pol.2.65.7 and Plut. *Kleom.* 27.11. Unfortunately there are no detailed figures for Kleomenes' individual units thus their estimate is problematic. Toynbee (1969 p 388–389) and Walbank (1995 p.369 and n.148) believe that Kleomenes' forces amounted to 20,000 men. However, the force that Kleomenes deployed on the battlefield must have been smaller, since a substantial part of it was busy guarding the camp and other passages to Lakonia (Pol 2.65.6, 2.65.12). According to Daubies (1975 p 386–387), the army that Kleomenes deployed on the battlefield could not have exceeded 18,000 men, a view that, despite the objections of other historians (e.g. Marasco 1979 p 48 note 17), seems more realistic.

228. This term is used by Polybios to describe Kleomenes' forces on Olympos Hill (Pol 2.65.9). The term 'Lakedaimonians' is used in a broader sense than the term 'Spartans' and includes the Spartan citizens together with the *perioikoi*. But since Polybios makes

a separate reference to the *perioikoi* who were deployed on Evas Hill (Pol 2.65.9), it is probable that in this case the term 'Lakedaimonians' only refers to the 4,000 newly integrated 'Spartans' after Kleomenes' reforms (Toynbee 1969 p 389). Combining the citations *Kleom.* 23.1 and *Kleom.* 28.8, most historians conclude that 2,000 *neodamodeis*, who bought their freedom and were armed as *phalangites* according to the Macedonian model, should be added to the 4,000 Spartans (see Walbank 1957 p 279, Toynbee 1969 p 389 note 5, Pritchett 1965 p 68). This view was challenged by Daubies, according to whom the terms 'Spartans' and 'Lakedaimonians' cannot possibly refer to helots-former or freed ones (Daubies 1971 p 680). It is true, however, that these terms are not used in their strict sense neither by Plutarch (see Africa 1968 p 5) – as admitted even by Daubies in a later paper (Daubies 1975 p 390) – nor by Polybios, who uses the term 'Λακωνικῶς' (Lakonic) meaning 'Σπαρτιατικῶς' (Spartan) (Pol.5.39.5.). Therefore, Daubies' interpretation of the two terms is invalid.

Marasco's theory reaches extreme conclusions despite the fact that he accepts the inclusion of 2,000 helots in Kleomenes' phalanx. According to the Italian historian, 4,000 Spartans who were reinforced by 2,000 helots armed by the standards of the Macedonian phalanx were deployed on Olympos. But Marasco (1979 p 50–54) argues that the number of the Spartans who fought at Sellasia was much greater than 4,000. The extra number of Spartans did not come from the 2,000 freed helots, but from the mercenaries who were naturalized by Kleomenes during the period 226–223. According to Marasco (1979 p 50), a significant number of Spartans must have been arrayed in other parts of the deployment: many of them may have belonged to the cavalry and may have been deployed on the plains between the two hills, while several Spartans may have also been on Evas Hill under Eukleidas' command (Marasco 1979 note 24). The above theory remains an untenable speculation as there is no reference to confirm it.

229. They were armed with the long *sarissa* (Pol.18.29.2 and Snodgrass 1999 p 118 and p 120–121) and they carried a shield hanging from their shoulder by a strap (*ochani*) (Plut. *Kleom.* 11.3–4.).

230. According to Polybios (2.69.3), the total number of light armed *euzons* and mercenaries on Olympos was approximately 5,000. Toynbee however (1969 p 389), claims that the number of Kleomenes' mercenaries should not have exceeded 1,000 since Antigonos, who unlike to Kleomenes had no shortage of funds, had no more than 3,000 mercenaries in his service. In order to explain the remainder 4,000 *euzons* on Olympos, Toynbee identifies them with the 4,000 [out of the 6,000] emancipated helots who were not included in the phalanx. The assumption is that all the helots who had been emancipated for five *minai* were also fit to fight. Most likely though, the opposite is true: the helots who could afford such an amount must have been relatively old and therefore unfit for war. Perhaps the elder parents might have paid the five *minai* for their sons' redemption. Even so, only a small percentage of the emancipated helots must have been able to fight. Thus a large number of the *euzons* on Olympos must have been mercenaries. The large number of mercenaries in the Spartan army is not contradictory to Kleomenes' financial problems. On the contrary, paying mercenary wages must have been the main source of his difficulties.

231. Pol.2.65.9. According to an assessment by Kromayer (= Walbank 1995 p 704 note148) the total number of soldiers on Evas did not exceed 5,000. Walbank observes that in this case all of Kleomenes' forces together were only 18,000 (11,000 on Olympos plus 5,000 on Evas plus 2000 in between) and not 20,000, as reported by sources. Therefore, the number of defenders on Evas should have been 7,000. As mentioned, however the number of forces that Kleomenes deployed in battle was much smaller than 20,000 since a considerable part of them were busy guarding the passes and his military camp.

232. Walbank 1957 p. 278 and 1984 p. 471.

233. According to Daubies, the overall number of Kleomenes' allies came to 3,000 men. This figure is an exaggeration. Daubies' claim that Kleomenes still had supporters among the Argives and Megalopolitans is not convincing. Instead, at this stage of the war there should not have been many allies left determined to fight alongside Kleomenes (Toynbee 1969 p 389). Daubies (1971 p 679 and p 691) further argues that the *perioikoi* were only 2,000 men. He specifically identifies them with the '2,000', whom (according to Plutarch's controversial passage *Kleom.* 23.1) Kleomenes had equipped 'in Macedonian fashion' to confront Antigonos' 'White Shields'. However, Daubies' estimate is wrong because the *perioikoi* were always the majority in the Lakedaimonian army. As Urban points out (1973 p 95), in 243 Agis intended to divide the 'civic land' of Sparta in 4,500 *kleroi* and the *perioikic* land in 15,000 *kleroi* (Plut. *Agis* 8.1).This number denotes that the *perioikoi* were more than three times the number of Spartans. To this, Daubies responded (1975 p.383–386) that the *perioikic* population significantly dwindled in the years after the fall of Agis for two reasons: first, in 240/239 the Aitolians captured 50,000 slaves (Plut. *Kleom.* 18.3, Pol.4.34.9) and second, in 227 Kleomenes integrated a number of *perioikoi* into the Spartan citizen body. Nevertheless, Plutarch's' estimate of 50,000 slaves is obviously excessive and it is uncertain whether it refers exclusively to the *perioikoi* (Rostovtzeff 1941 p 203). As for Kleomenes' reforms, he did not integrate more than 1,000 *perioikoi* in the Spartan citizen body. Consequently, there is no reason to assume that the number of the *perioikoi* had dramatically dwindled as claimed by Daubies. Completely contrary to the above estimate is Toynbee's, who argues that since the usual ratio of Spartans to *perioikoi* was 4:6, there must have been 4,000 Spartans and at least 6,000 *perioikoi* in Kleomenes' army (Toynbee 1969 p 389 -390). In this case, the number of defenders on Evas Hill along with their allies must have been 7,000 men (see Walbank 1995 p 704 note 148). But it would be very difficult to repel such a large number of defenders on a fortified slope, most of whom were heavy infantry according to Toynbee. Although the attackers on Evas Hill were fewer than 6,000, they easily prevailed as evidenced by the course of the battle. Therefore, the defenders of Evas Hill must have been numerically outnumbered by the attackers and even lighter armed than them. There are no reports on the armour of the *perioikoi* and the allies. The former fought traditionally as hoplites alongside the Spartans, using spear and the large round shield called *hoplon*. While there is no reference to a change in their armour either before or after Kleomenes' reforms, some researchers believe that the *perioikoi* kept their traditional armour (Toynbee 1969 p 389, Head 1982 p 7). During the course of the battle, however, the tactics of the defenders of Eva's Hill did not seem to be those

of a hoplite infantry, but rather those of light armed units (see Pol. 2.68.5–8 and the following note. This is certainly true for Kleomenes' allies who were deployed on Eva's Hill. Most of Kleomenes' sympathizers probably came from the lower social strata and certainly could not have the means to maintain heavy infantry equipment.

234. Pol. 2.65.10–11. The number of cavalry is conjectural (see Walbank 1995 p 369), as there is no reference to the number of troops at the centre. Polybios (2.67.2) describes the mercenaries as *euzons*, implying that they were light armed.

235. According to Toynbee's estimates, Kleomenes' heavy infantry was 12,000 hoplites (4,000 Spartans along with 2,000 former helots armed in the Macedonian fashion and 6,000 *perioikoi* armed with the traditional hoplite equipment). As Toynbee states (1969 p 390) the last reference to a similar Spartan military force was in 479 at the Battle of Plataea. The number of *perioikoi* and their armour is overestimated by Toynbee (see above). But in any case, the force that Kleomenes deployed on the battlefield of Sellasia is remarkably strong for Sparta's military potentialities.

236. See note 225.

237. Daubies (1971 p 683 ff), erroneously identifies the specific unit with the light armed *peltasts* of the Classical age. After Iphicrates' reforms in the fourth century, *peltasts* had already acquired heavier armour, even a medium-sized spear suitable for close combat (Snodgrass 1999 p 110–111, Warry 1980 p 67). Moreover, Antigonos' '*peltasts*' did not serve as auxiliaries but rather they consisted a 'crack' unit of the Macedonian infantry and fought with *sarissa* alongside the phalanx as did earlier the unit of *hypaspists*' in Alexander the Great's army (Griffith 1984 p.71, 119, 319, Walbank 1967a p 290–293 and 1995, p 567).

238. '1,000 Megalopolitans armed in the Macedonian manner' (Pol. 2.65.3). After the plundering of their city by Kleomenes, the Megalopolitans could not provide their men with equipment and so Antigonos provided it for them (Pol 4.69.5–6, see also Walbank 1995 p 368).

239. The Boiotians had already adopted the tactics of the Macedonian phalanx by 245 (Walbank 1957 p 275), while the Epeirotes had adopted them even earlier, from the time of Pyrrhos.

240. Although there is scanty information about Antigonos' mercenaries from the battle description it appears that they fought alongside light units (Pol. 2.69.3). Demetrios Pharios had participated in the campaign as Doson's personal ally and not as a member of the Hellenic League (Pol. 3.16.3). The Gauls are likely to have forged another treaty or alliance with the Macedonians, but were probably paid for their services as were the Agrianians also (Walbank 1995 p 368 and p 704 n.142). The Akarnanians were notorious slingers (Steinhauer 2000 p 315) and, like the Illyrians, they were also allies of the Macedonians. The 3,000 Achaean 'picked men' were descendants of noble families of Achaea. However, the fighting value of the Achaean army, until its upgrade by Philopoimen, was poor (see above note 107).

241. The ratio of infantry to cavalry in the Macedonian army was more than 20:1 while the corresponding ratio in the army with which Alexander crossed the Hellespont was 6:1. The small proportion of cavalry in Antigonos' army, especially in an age when this force played a key role in the battle, is striking to Walbank (1995 p 368). However, in

the difficult terrain of the Peloponnese, the efficiency of cavalry was very limited and certainly Antigonos knew this.

242. Pol. 2.65.11.

243. Pol. 2.66.4.

244. Pol. 2.66.5. Walbank notes that Polybios uses the term *chalkaspides* ('Bronze Shields') to refer to the aforementioned 3,000 '*peltasts*' (see Walbank 1957 p 280 and 1995 p 704 n.150). Daubies (1971 p 691–92) identifies the 1,000 Gauls and the 1,000 Agrianians with the heavy infantry of Antigonos' phalanx specifically with Polybios' 'Bronze Shields' and Plutarch's 'White Shields'(see above note 386). This is obviously wrong. The tactics of the regular and disciplined phalanx were completely different from those of the wild and undisciplined Gauls and of the light armed Agrianians who carried javelins, slingshots or bows (Arrian *Anabasis* 1.14, Walbank 1957 p 274).

245. Pol. 18.28.10. The strength of every *speira* of the Antigonid phalanx was approximately 250 men strong in five files of fifty men deep to advance up the slope. From the Mid-third century the Illyrians were organized in *speirai* following the Macedonian example and, apart from skirmishing, they also charged the enemy lines. Their *speirai* were of course less regular than the Macedonian ones (Head 1982 p52, Walbank 1957 p280).

246. 'ἐπὶ δὲ τούτοις' (Pol. 2.66.6). The translation of the above phrase from Greek is problematic. Does it mean 'alongside' the Illyrians (Walbank 1995 p370, Pritchett 1965 p69) or 'behind' the Illyrians? (Schweighaeuser, Paton, Treves = Walbank 1957 p280) However since the Akarnanians participated with the Illyrians in Antigonos' stratagem, they must have been deployed alongside the Illyrians and on their left. For the Epeirotes see next note.

247. Polybios doesn't mention 'Epeirotes' but 'Cretans'. Since the Cretans are nowhere mentioned in Antigonos' forces (Pol. 2.65.2–5), some scholars believe that the correct term is 'Epeirotes' (Schorn = Walbank 1957 p 280). But the participation of Cretans in Antigonos' army is possible. As noted by Griffith (1984 p 70), the Cretans may have been included in Antigonos' 3,000 mercenaries (Pol 2.65.2–3). Antigonos is known to have made treaties with some Cretan cities and Macedonians were probably authorized to recruit mercenaries from them (Walbank 1957 p 280–281 and 1995 p 370 and note 153). The Cretans were famous archers and their role may have been to cover the attack on Evas Hill, shooting over the attackers (Head 1982 p75). It is noteworthy that, besides the position of the Epeirotes, Polybios does not indicate the position of the 2,000 Boiotians either. Walbank (1957 p 280–281 and 1995 p 370 and note 154) accepts Kromayer's theory (1903 p 233 note 3) that they were assigned to guard the camp. But it is unlikely that the heavy infantry of the phalanx was in a subordinate role instead of reinforcing the attack on Evas. And it is also strange that Walbank lightheartedly disables 2,000 Boiotians, leaving them in Antigonos' camp. In addition, he fails to deduct from Kleomenes' forces a number of men that may have been used to guard his own camp as well as the passes and entries to Sparta.

248. Pol. 2.66.9 see also Walbank 1957 p 281. As Pritchett observes, the normal sixteen- by-sixteen Macedonian phalanx changed in Sellasia; the width was halved to eight files and the depth was doubled to thirty-two ranks. Therefore the Macedonian phalanx required a front of about 312 yards (285 meters). Antigonos was forced to this awkward

deployment in order to avoid moving higher on the rough slope of Olympos (Pritchett 1965 p.69 note 50).

249. Pol. 2.66.10. The 'Bronze Shields' (or the *peltasts*') phalanx was more flexible than the Macedonian one which was completely unsuitable for an attack on the rough inclined slope. Nevertheless, the 'Bronze Shields' were heavy infantry of the line and during their slow ascent of the slope, they were always vulnerable to the assaults of the mobile light troops. Therefore, it was essential that they be covered by the Illyrians.

250. Pol. 2.66.11, Plut. *Philop.* 6.2.

251. Plut. *Kleom.* 28.3. It is interesting that Phylarchos refers to the *krypteia* as a scouting unit. This fact indicates that during this period the *krypteia* was not simply a part of the Spartan *agoge* and that it was not limited to 'policing' the helots, but had developed to a combat unit on a scouting mission. However, this reference to the *krypteia* is too important to overlook, or else how could Phylarchos have known of its existence? Obviously there is a grain of truth in that there indeed was such a unit and even in the role ascribed to it by Phylarchos. (Regarding the contradictions surrounding the character of the *krypteia* see Chrimes 1999 p.375, 390, and especially Levy 1988 p 249–250, Birgalias 1999 p97–117, Ducat 2006 p 281–332).

252. It is worth noting that Plutarch (*Kleom.* 28.1) simply states, without adopting the information given by Phylarchos, that there had been an act of treachery. Walbank (1957 p285) dismisses it as a 'silly story' and considers it to be a pure invention by Phylarchos, who tried to excuse his hero, Kleomenes by displaying him as victim of betrayal. On the contrary, others are more sceptical (Africa 1961 p49). Moreover, Gorgylos was a natural trench and guarding it would be a prerequisite for the defence of Evas. The fact that a major enemy force managed to hide in the stream bed, leaves open the possibility of betrayal. However, Phylarchos does not associate Damoteles' betrayal with the hiding of the Illyrians in Gorgylos but rather with a successful outflanking manoeuvre which Antigonos had supposedly carried out with the Illyrians and Akarnanians encircling the far left of Eukleidas' deployment. (On this see Appendix C).

253. Pol. 2.66.10.

254. In Plutarch's version (where a red flag is the common signal for attack for both the Illyrians and the allied centre) the gap was created because the Illyrians attacked without waiting for the signal unlike the Achaeans who remained steady at their post waiting for the order to attack (Plut. *Philop.* 6.2). Therefore, the flank and the rear of the Illyrians were left uncovered due to the premature attack and not due to the reluctance or hesitation of the Achaeans. According to Walbank the above version misrepresents the facts in an effort to exonerate the Achaeans' behaviour during the battle (Walbank 1957 p.282).

255. Plut. *Philop.* 6.2, Pol. 2.67.2. 'θεωροῦντες τὰς σπείρας τῶν Ἀχαιῶν ἐρήμους ἐκ τῶν κατόπιν οὔσας'. There are two different interpretations concerning the counterattack from the Spartan centre which derive from two different translations of Polybios' account (Pol. 2.67.2). According to the first translation (Shuckburgh, Paton): '[the light troops from the centre] observing that the Achaean lines were not covered by any other troops behind them...' This is accepted by Pritchett (1965 p 69) and Jochmus (1857 p.39). According to them during the advance of Antigonos' right wing, the

Achaeans must have moved to higher ground and so it was *they* who suffered the attack on their left flank and on their rear by the opposing forces of the centre. The second translation is Kromayer's (presented by Walbank 1957 p282, 1995 p 370 and note 158) 'when [the light troops from the centre] saw that the units [of the attackers] were not covered in the rear *by the Achaeans...*' This is consistent with Plut. *Philop.* 6.2–3. As Walbank (1957 p282) observes, since the Achaeans were in reserve, their rear cannot have been exposed by the advance of the Illyrians and Akarnanians. His argument seems convincing.

256. According to Plutarch (*Philop.* 6.4), Philopoimen, who had left his horse and fought on foot on a difficult ground, was injured by a barbed javelin, a dangerous weapon that pierced his thighs through and remained wedged preventing him from moving. It is said that Philopoimen, anxious to join the battle as it was at its hottest, broke the shaft of the weapon in two in the middle by moving his legs backward and forward and then ordered that each fragment be drawn out separately. This story comes from Philopoimen's circle, or even by him, and is probably exaggerated. His injury, however, which is also mentioned by Polybios (2.69.1–2) shows that Philopoimen fought with vigour. In fact, he was later praised for his initiative by Antigonos (Pol.2.68.1–3, Plut. *Philop.* 6.7, see also Errington 1969 p.22).

257. Plut. *Philop.* 6.6

258. Pol. 2.67.6

259. Pol. 2.67.7

260. Pol. 2.68.3–5 Such tactics, in which masses of fighters rush over their fortifications to harass the enemy lines and return to their original positions avoiding close combat, are not those of the heavy infantry hoplites, but obviously those of skirmishing, the usual tactic of the light infantry. This suggests that a large part of the defenders on Evas must have consisted of light infantry. In any case, they were lighter armed than their opponents.

261. Pol. 2.68.6–7. See also Appendix C.

262. The attackers' supremacy is stressed by both Polybios and Plutarch. Polybios (2.68.9.) clearly states that the defenders on Evas were repulsed because of the superior weapons of the heavy armed phalanx (see also Pol. 2.68. 5). Apparently, he refers to the arms and formation of the 'Bronze Shields' and not of the Illyrians. Plutarch makes a similar statement on the outcome of the battle attributing Kleomenes' defeat to the superiority of the armour and to the impact of the heavy armed phalanx of his opponents (Plut. *Kleom.* 28.1).

263. Plut. *Kleom.* 28.6

264. Pol. 2.69.6. Tarn (1928 p 762) holds a completely opposite view. He accepts Plutarch's view (*Kleom.* 28.3–4), according to which the Spartans charged the enemy from Olympos upon the start of the battle and were not driven to it by despair. Walbank (1933 p 111–112 and 1957 p 285–6) claims that Kleomenes' phalanx attacked at the moment the ambushed troops were assaulting Evas, but before the Illyrians had scaled the brow of the hill. In a later work, however, Walbank revises his views and accepts that Kleomenes attacked *after* having realised that the battle on Evas was lost (Walbank 1995 p 371). Most likely this is what actually happened. Had Kleomenes intended to

charge the Macedonian phalanx, he would not have placed his own phalanx behind fortifications. But Kleomenes was always unwilling to confront the Macedonian phalanx in a pitched battle. Two years earlier at Isthmus, he chose 'to fortify thoroughly not the Isthmus but the Oneian range of hills and to wear out the Macedonians by a war of posts and positions rather than to engage in formal battle with their disciplined phalanx' (Plut. *Kleom.* 20.1). Again when he was fighting to regain Argos, the sight alone of the Macedonian army was enough to force him to leave the city (Plut. *Kleom.* 21.4).

265. Pol. 2.69.8.
266. According to Plutarch (=Phylarchos), the Macedonians were repulsed approximately five furlongs (1,100 yards). Such a large repulse is certainly excessive, especially considering the great depth of the Macedonian phalanx. If such an incident had indeed happened, the Macedonian phalanx would essentially have been scattered (Walbank 1995 p 371 and note 163).
267. Pol. 2.69.8.
268. (Pol. 2.69.9): '*closing up the ranks of their pikes*'. This was a special tactic of the phalanx called *pyknosis* (Walbank 1957 p 286–287).
269. Regarding the losses of Kleomenes' forces, there is only a brief but clear reference in Plutarch according to which 'many of his mercenaries fell, as we are told and all the Spartans, 6,000 in number, except 200' (Plut. *Kleom.* 28.8).
270. Browning 1978 p 224.
271. Plut. *Kleom.* 29. Regarding the young Megalopolitan, Plutarch states that she was a free woman and had voluntarily followed Kleomenes after her hometown's occupation by the Spartans.
272. Plut. *Kleom.* 29.3 The fact was also attested by Polybios (2.69.11).
273. Plut. *Kleom.* 31. (See also Walbank 1957 p 287). It cannot possibly be verified whether this dialogue ever occurred and to what extent it is true, or whether it is entirely Phylarchos' fabrication.
274. Ollier 1936 p 542.
275. Plut. *Kleom.* 31.6.
276. Plut. *Kleom.* 32.2.
277. Plut. *Kleom.* 32.2. This amount of money was exorbitant for Ptolemy, so can we assume that Phylarchos had intervened?
278. Plut. *Kleom.* 38.4.
279. Plut. *Kleom.* 30.1 also see Pol. 2.70.1.
280. Pol. 2.70.1. Plutarch (*Kleom.* 30.1) states that Antigonos departed on the third day due to an invasion by 'barbarians', who were probably rebellious tribes east of Illyria, akin to the Dardans (Walbank 1957 p288).
281. Plut. *Kleom.* 33.3.
282. Pol. 5.36.1–6. As pointed out by Walbank, Polybios and Plutarch used as Phylarchos as their basic source. Polybios also used some other source, hostile to Kleomenes, which Plutarch considered unreliable (Walbank 1957 p 566).
283. Pol. 5.36.4 also see Plut. *Kleom.* 33.6.
284. Pol. 5.34.10–11

285. Plut. *Kleom.* 33.2. Such a representation may be excessive because, on the other hand, it is attested that during the campaign against the Seleucid King Antiochos, Philopator showed stamina and vigour.
286. Pol. 5.35.13 and Plut. *Kleom.* 33.6.
287. Probably from tuberculosis. Polybios states that after a decisive battle against the Illyrians (222) where Antigonos defeated them, he began spitting blood and soon expired (Pol. 2.70.6). Plutarch also mentions that Antigonos broke a vessel and bled to death after shouting loudly 'O happy day' after the victory (*Kleom.* 30.2). Walbank (1995 p372) estimates his death approximately one year after his victory in Sellasia, in early autumn of 221.
288. Pol. 5.35.10.
289. Pol. 5.37.5–6.
290. Plut. *Kleom.* 35.1. As pointed out by Walbank (1957, p 568–569) Plutarch and Polybios each relied on different sources. Plutarch relied on Phylarchos, while Polybios relied on the Megalopolitan historian Ptolemy, son of Agesarchos. As a Megalopolitan, Ptolemy was certainly biased against Kleomenes (Walbank 1957, p566).
291. Pol. 5.37.10 (also see Plut. *Kleom.* 35.2). The *sambuka* was a musical instrument, similar to the harp.
292. Pol. 5.37.11–12, Plut. *Kleom.* 35.3. In his version of the incident, Plutarch states that Nikagoras had previously asked Kleomenes to settle up with him for the estate he had bought. When Kleomenes claimed that he had no money, Nikagoras was infuriated and, in an effort to avenge him, mentioned Kleomenes' ironic comment on the king to Sosibios. However, the story about the estate does not seem convincing (Walbank 1957 p568). It also appears unlikely that Kleomenes the inventor of inspired revolutionary reforms, would reduce himself to real estate transactions in Messene or anywhere else.
293. There are two different versions regarding the content of Nikagoras' letter. According to Plutarch (*Kleom.* 35.3), the letter stated that if Ptolemy gave Kleomenes vessels and troops, he would seize Kyrene. In contrast, in Polybios' version (5.38.5–6) Kleomenes was accused that in case he was not sent to Sparta along with sufficient supplies and funds, he would overthrow the regime of the Ptolemies in Egypt.
294. Pol. 5.38.7 and Plut. *Kleom.* 35.4
295. Plut. *Kleom.* 37.1.
296. His enthronement occurred between 5 February and 16 February 221 (Walbank 1957 p 564).
297. Plut. *Kleom.* 35.3.
298. Pol. 5.38.5–6.
299. Plut. *Kleom.* 36.2
300. Both Polybios (5.39.2) and Plutarch (*Kleom.* 36.4) report that Kleomenes acted on impulse. However, Kleomenes' subsequent attitude implies that it was all pre-fabricated.
301. Plut. *Kleom.* 37.4.
302. Pol. 5.39.4–5, Plut. *Kleom.* 37.5. Polybios and Plutarch state that Kleomenes harboured no illusions about the success of the venture but he did so to appear worthy of his name and of Sparta. Both historians praise his action (Pol.5.38.8–10, 39.6 and Plut. *Kleom.*

36.4). However, Kleomenes' attempt to liberate prisoners and the fact that he did not try to escape even at the last moment, both indicate that he was plotting with Ptolemy IV's political opponents against him. Their plan was poorly organized and hastily executed (see Shimron 1972 p66, Kanellopoulos1982 volume 2 p129–30).

303. Plut. *Kleom*. 37.7.
304. Plut. *Kleom*. 38.
305. Plut. *Kleom*. 39.1. Phylarchos adds that a snake coiled itself around Kleomenes' crucified body and prevented vultures from devouring it. The Alexandrians thought it was a miracle and came to the place of crucifixion as if to a shrine to worship him. However, the association of the dead hero with the snake is not accidental, as seen from the closing words of Plutarch's narrative: 'the ancients associated the serpent more than any other animal with heroes.' The association of heroes or gods with snakes had ancient origins. In Greece and especially in Sparta, as evidenced by the numerous relief columns, gods and heroes-patrons are depicted either in the form of snakes like the Dioscuri or along with snakes. In the evolution of this trend, the influence of Egypt was significant (see Mitropoulou 1977 p 49–94 and Voutiras 2000 p 377–384).
306. Tarn 1928 p 762.
307. Pol. 2.70.3, Plut. *Kleom*. 27.5.
308. Walbank 1933 p 165.
309. According to Lykourgan laws, Spartans were prohibited from erecting funerary monuments. Only those who fell in battle and women who died in childbirth had the honour of an austere *stele* bearing the name of the deceased. The kings were the exception; unlike other citizens, their funeral was splendid and their burial majestic. Kleomenes' victors, though, would certainly have not allowed such an honour to the fallen king. But what would be the point of Kleomenes having a royal funeral when he could have had the honour of sharing his Spartans' fate obeying, as they had done, 'their forefathers' laws'?

Chapter 3: Eclipse
1. Pol. 2.70.1, 4.34.9, 5.9.9, 9.31.3–4, 9.36.2–5, Plut. *Kleom*. 30.1.
2. Another city which was not lucky enough to witness Antigonos' generosity was Sellasia, whose population was sold into slavery by the victor of the battle before his triumphal entry to Sparta (Paus. 2.9.2).
3. Africa 1968, p 5. Moreover, the Kleomenean revolution was dangerous only for the Achaean League; it was not a serious threat for Macedonia (Shimron1972 p 63).
4. Aratos' anti-Macedonian stance in the past could not be easily forgotten by Antigonos. For him, the Achaean League remained an unreliable ally (Shimron 1972 p.60).
5. Pol. 4.24.4–6 and 4.34.10. Most historians agree on this point (see Tarn 1928 p 762, Walbank 1957 p 288 457 and 470, 1984 p 472 and Oliva 1971 p 264). Shimron (1972 p 66–68) argues that Sparta was not a full member but simply an ally of the League and that she was in a special and extremely relaxed relationship with it. Cartledge seems rather indecisive: '… the added humiliation for Sparta of forcible incorporation in – or at any rate – alliance to Doson's Hellenic League is very likely but cannot be proven.' (Cartledge 2002b p 57). However it is unlikely for a leader of the calibre of Antigonos

to miss the opportunity of Sparta's compulsory integration in the Hellenic League, which would help both strengthen the League and weaken her rivals.

6. Cartledge 2002b p. 61–62.

7. Pol. 2.70.1, 5.9.9, Plut. *Kleom.* 30.1. There is unfortunately no reference regarding the fate of Kleomenes' reforms, nor is it known whether the eighty exiled Spartans returned home in 227. It is generally considered more likely that Kleomenes' reforms were abolished and that the old order was pretty much restored (Tarn 1928 p 762, Ollier 1943 p 123). This view, however, is not unanimously accepted. Chrimes (1999 p 20–21) argues that Antigonos allowed the maintenance of certain Kleomenean institutions such as the *patronomoi*, the *Gerousia* and the *ephors*. She maintains that Antigonos had no time to deal with complex issues such as land redistribution. Shimron (1964a, 1964b and 1972 p 53–63) considers improbable that the eighty exiles ever returned. This view has been criticized by Oliva (1971 p 264–266) and Texier (1975 p.7, note 25). Walbank (1957 p 288, 1984 p 472 and 1995 p 371) is certain that Antigonos abolished the 'Lykourgan' (i.e. the political) reforms of Kleomenes and that the eighty exiles returned but questions whether Kleomenes' social and economic reforms were revoked. (The abolition of debts, for example, was impossible to revoke.) Cartledge (2002b p 57–58) accepts that some of Kleomenes' reforms, such as the institution of the six *patronomoi* and the sixth *kome* of Neopolitai (founded by Kleomenes) 'were apparently allowed to survive'. On the issue of Kleomenes' social reforms and on the return of the eighty exiles, he avoids taking a stand. Walbank's view, however, seems more convincing.

8. However the Macedonian garrison and its commander Brachyllas did not stay for long. In 220 they left Sparta (Cartledge 2002b p.61). What was the fate of the 6,000 slaves freed by Kleomenes? Sources unfortunately do not mention anything. 2,000 of them fell on the battlefield with the Spartan phalanx. The others, who were unable to escape, probably returned to their former state. Yet, how the reduced number of Spartans still controlled their helots is still a big unanswered question.

9. Walbank 1995 p.371.

10. On the other hand, as pointed out by Oliva (1971 p 266), 'it would be absurd to suppose that all the free land came into the hands of the enemies of Kleomenes. There may have been a compromise solution.' This solution, however, was to prove short-lived.

11. Pol. 4.35.6.

12. The dedication of the youth to Kleomenes was absolute. It is significant that almost all subsequent uprisings were spearheaded by young Spartans (Pol. 4.22.8, 4.35.1–3, Oliva 1971 p 267).

13. Pol. 4.9.6.

14. Pol. 4.23.8–9.

15. Hammond 1995 p. 381.

16. Shimron 1972 p 72–73. Polybios (4.24) claims that it was Aratos who persuaded Philip to ignore the opinion of his *Hetairoi* and to show clemency towards Sparta (also see Plut. *Aratos* 48.3–4). This view is accepted by some historians such as Walbank (1933 p 123, 1967a p 31) and Gruen (1972 p 615). The latter argues that this confirms his theory that Aratos sought a peaceful coexistence with Sparta and not her destruction.

But whatever Aratos' influence on the young king of Macedonia may have been is obviously exaggerated by Polybios. Hammond (1995 p.708 note 16) questions the reliability of Polybios' information. It is more likely that the young but dynamic King Philip V made the decision himself without being influenced by anyone.

17. Pol. 4.35.2–4

18. It appears, although not certain, that Kleomenes' death occurred just before the violent events in Sparta (see Chrimes 1999 p 23, Walbank 1957 p 484, Oliva 1971 p 268, Shimron 1972 p 73).

19. Pol. 4.35.10. Agesipolis was the grandson of Kleombrotos, King Leonidas' son-in-law, who usurped his throne in 242 (Bradford 1977 s.v. Agesipolis).

20. According to Livy (34.26.14), Lykourgos banished the young Agesipolis, usurped power and reigned alone.

21. Pol. 4.35.14–15. The views of modern historians remain controversial on this issue. Chrimes argues that even the name 'Lykourgos' refers to the period of Agis IV's reforms: Lykourgos belonged to the family circle of the young king, as did his most enthusiastic supporters (Chrimes 1999 p.23). Jones (1967, cited in the table of the genealogies of the Spartan kings) considers Lykourgos to be the legitimate king of Sparta. In contrast, Mossé (1989 p 195) characterizes him a usurper, who merely claimed to originate from royal blood. Texier (1975 p 8) agrees and states that with the rise of Lykourgos to the throne 'an illegal reign in Sparta was established and a dynasty of usurpers was founded.' Lastly, according to Walbank (1967 p 484), Oliva (1971 p 269) and Cartledge (2002b p 62), Lykourgos belonged to the house of Eurypontidai but did not have the strongest claim in the line of succession.

22. It should be noted that the Spartans were a small minority in Lykourgos' 'Spartan' army since Sparta's heavy infantry was annihilated at Sellasia (Pol.4.36.4 and 5.20.6). As pointed out by Griffith (1984 p 95), 'from this time on Sparta becomes, as never before in her history, a power relying mainly upon mercenary soldiers.'

23. Pol. 4.60.2.

24. Pol. 4.81. 3–10.

25. Chilon is a strange and highly controversial figure. The slaughter of the *ephors* and the announcement of land redistribution are very reminiscent of Kleomenes. So how 'Kleomenean' were Chilon's intentions? According to Shimron (1964b p 236–237), the hostility of the majority of the Spartans towards Chilon and his abortive coup show that the reforms he announced were unpopular. But land redistribution had become also a 'dangerous' declaration and its rejection by most Spartans may have been due simply to the presence of the Macedonian army in Megalopolis, and the fear of a possible invasion in Sparta. On the other hand, this slogan could have been used by Chilon simply to win over the masses. His escape to Achaea suggests that he had connections with the Achaeans, the enemies of Kleomenes' reforms (Shimron 1972 p.75). Some historians (Texier 1975 p.10) consider Chilon a genuine expressor of the Kleomenean faction, while others do not hesitate to characterize him as a 'provocateur' and 'agent' of Philip, who deliberately incited riots in Sparta in order to get a pretext to invade Lakonia (Ferrabino = Oliva 1971 p 270 note 5). However all of the above

theories are essentially speculative. The only available source is Polybios' (4.81. 3.10) brief mention, which does not allow for reliable conclusions.

26. Pol. 5.17.1–2.
27. Pol. 5.20.1–10.
28. Pol. 5.20.11.
29. Pol. 5.23.1–10. The combined use of light and heavy infantry in order to seize strong defensive positions of the enemy was a traditional tactic of the Macedonian army. This was the same tactic already applied by Antigonos Doson at Sellasia against Eukleidas on Evas Hill (see also Appendix II).
30. Pol. 5.24.
31. Pol. 5.29.8–9.
32. Shimron 1972 p. 72–78.
33. Some historians maintain that Chilon's attempt at revolution indicates that he was an ardent supporter of Kleomenes (Tigerstedt 1974 p 66). Texier (1975 p.10 note 41) goes so far as to wonder whether the 200 supporters of Chilon were the 200 Spartans who according to Plutarch (*Kleom.* 28.8) survived the battle of Sellasia.
34. Lykourgos, who died in 210, had superseded the Agiad King Agesipolis by 217, thereby finally ending the institution of dual kingship in Sparta. As there is no evidence as to how Machanidas ascended to power, some speculate that he was the guardian of the underage Pelops (Walbank 1967 p 255, Oliva 1971 p 272), while others are sceptical on this (Cartledge 2002b p 65).
35. As leader of the Tarantine mercenaries (Texier 1975 p.11). Some historians (Oliva 1971 p 272–273) attempt to connect him to a socio-political reform similar to that of Kleomenes and Nabis. On the other hand the available information is too scanty to allow such conclusions (Texier 1975 p.12 note 51).
36. Plut. *Philop.* 7.3–5, Pol. 10.23.
37. Pol. 11.9.4–5, Plut. *Philop.* 9.1–7, Paus. 8.50.1, Errington 1969 p. 63.
38. Walbank 1967 p. 282.
39. Pol. 11.11–18. And Plut. *Philop.* 10, who is based entirely on Polybios.
40. See Pol. 1.14.5–7 and especially his famous critique of the 'tragedy writer' Phylarchos (Pol. 2.56.11–12), where Polybios contrasts objective historiography, (which aims to teach the 'lovers of wisdom'), with tragedy, (which aims at sensationalism and entertainment of the public).
41. As recently noted (Chaniotis 2005 p 193–196) the description of the battle brings to mind contemporary Hollywood epic blockbusters, with Philopoimen and Machanidas as 'good' and 'bad' respectively: 'The war, which started as a struggle between tyranny and liberty, ends in a close up, where Hellenistic historiography meets the epic war films of Hollywood. The battle culminates in a face-to-face combat between the two protagonists: the tyrant and the champion of liberty' (Chaniotis 2005 p 195).
42. The existence of a large number of catapults in Machanidas' army indicates his intention to besiege Mantineia. It seems that this is what Philopoimen sought to prevent, and the reason he gathered his forces in front of the city (Walbank 1967 p 283).
43. It is worth noting that in the battle, Machanidas had command of the mercenaries and not of the Spartan infantry of the phalanx, as would be expected. In fact, his mercenaries 'did all that soldiers could do' (Griffith 1984 p 95).

44. Pol. 11.17.7–18.7. Plut. *Philop.* 10. The vivid and almost poetic description of the duel between Philopoimen and Machanidas is obviously based on descriptions by eyewitnesses and even by Philopoimen himself (Chaniotis 2005 p 195). But this idealized picture seems to not have been accepted by all historians of Polybios' time. There were those who believed that Philopoimen did not display in battle the required vigour, which is revealed by Polybios' need to defend him by stating that Philopoimen initially remained stationary behind the ditch, 'not to avoid fighting, as some supposed, but from a very accurate and scientific calculation of strategic advantages' (Pol. 11.16.4–5). However it is likely that, had Machanidas returned from his pursuit earlier, he would have attacked the Achaeans from the sides and rear. This attack, combined with the frontal assault of the Spartan phalanx, would have destroyed the Achaean army (Walbank 1967 p 292).

45. For the Achaean League the battle of Mantineia was a milestone. Apart from a triumphant victory on the battlefield which the League won based solely on its own effort, the event marks the beginning of the end of its manipulation by the kingdom of Macedonia (Errington 1969 p 66–67 and p.75).

46. According to Polybios (11.18.10), the losses of the Lakedaimonians were more than 8,000 warriors: 4,000 fell on the battlefield and even more were captured. These numbers may be exaggerated, and obviously the losses not only concerned Spartans but the *perioikoi* and the mercenaries (Chrimes 1999 p.27 note 2) as well, perhaps even helots (Cartledge 2002b p.67). But still the losses of the Spartans must have been very large since the Spartan phalanx was trapped in the ditch and almost annihilated by the Achaeans.

47. Errington 1969 p. 65.

Chapter 4: Twilight

1. Hadas 1932 p.74.

2. No biography of Nabis by ancient historians has survived to present day. Information about him is found only from references within the narrative of events in which Nabis happens to be involved. The most extensive references come from Polybios, Livy and Pausanias. The surviving citations of Polybios regarding Nabis are: 13.6–8 16.13 and 18.17. Livy (59 B.C. – 17 A.D.) wrote almost two centuries later and knew little of the Hellenistic history. As he confesses (Liv. 33.10, 36.19.), for matters relating to the period of Hellenistic history he relied on Polybios, whom he considers utterly reliable. In his description of the relevant events (Liv. 31–38), Livy essentially copies Polybios and he therefore reproduces the latter's views on Nabis. Pausanias, who wrote much later, sketchily refers to Nabis. References of him are in 4.29.10, in 8.50.5, 51.2 and in 7.8.5, 7.9.2. The other surviving references (few in number and all of them fragmentary) also come from historians later than Polybios i.e. Diodoros of Sicily (27.01, 28.13), Strabo (8.366), Plutarch (*Philopoimen* 12.4–6, 13.1–3, 14, 15, *Titus* 13.1–4, *Comparison* 3.1–2) and *Justin* (31).

3. This incident occurred in 200 when Polybios was still at a very tender age. According to some scholars, the future historian was six-years-old at the time (Hadas 1932 p 75 and Michell 1964 p 330), although Walbank (1990 pp. 6–7) maintains that Polybios was

two-years-old at the most in 200. It is even possible that this year was the year of his birth. But even if he did not have personal experience of these turbulent events, it is certain that Polybios was raised in their shadow.

4. Hadas 1932 p 75, Michell 1964 p 330, Oliva 1971 p 274, Shimron 1972 p 81–82, Cartledge 2002b p 60, Texier 1975 p 104–105.

5. Cartledge 2002b p. 61–62. As presented by Polybios was the result of a long process during which many extreme theories were expressed. Some historians drew an analogy between the regime of Nabis' Sparta and the communist regimes, (Holleaux 1930 p 147, Hadas 1932 p 75–76, Griffith 1984 p 96), while others (Ollier 1943 p 123, Aymard 1938 p 33 ff.) considered his movement to be an unsuccessful repetition of Agis' and Kleomenes' movement. (For a detailed presentation of the theories which have been published about Nabis see Oliva 1971 p 274–277).

6. See Mündt 1903 p 79 according to whom if Philopoimen is recognized as 'the last of the Greeks' (Plut. *Philop.* 1.4, *Aratos* 24.2), then Nabis must be recognised as 'the last of the Spartans.'

7. Cartledge 2002b p60.

8. IG XI. 4,716. Most historians agree on this. It appears that he was a distant descendant of the exiled King Demaratos who had fled to Persia in 491–90; Demaratos' descendants returned to Sparta around 300 (Hadas 1932 p 75, Chrimes 1999 p 27, Forrest 1980 p 148, Shimron 1972 p. 83, Bradford 1977 sv 'Nabis', Texier 1975 p 16, Cartledge 2002b p 68).

9. In 197 Philip V suggested to Nabis that he give his daughters in marriage to Nabis' sons (Liv. 32.38.3). For Nabis to have sons of age appropriate for marriage (twenty-thirty years old) in 197, he must have been born in the decade between 250 and 240 (Hadas 1932 p.75), or between 245 and 240 (Walbank 1967 p 419–420, Shimron 1972 p. 84 and Texier 1975 pp. 16–17), or even between 250 and 245 (Cartledge 2002b p 68).

10. Even if one considers the date of his birth to be in 240 at the latest, this would make Nabis eighteen-years-old at the time of the Battle of Sellasia. Shimron (1972 p 96) is almost certain that Nabis served in Kleomenes' army. On the other hand, the fact that Nabis was Kleomenes' contemporary does not necessarily imply that he was his supporter. As Cartledge points out, the mere fact that he descended from the Eurypontidai royal house and could have laid claim to the royal house which Kleomenes had displaced, made his position precarious in Sparta. Therefore, he might have been opposed to Kleomenes but not manifested it openly in order to ensure his survival (Cartledge 2002b p 68). Texier proceeds into flights of fantasy, claiming that the name 'Nabis' (which he does not consider Greek, and which is not found anywhere in Demaratos' genealogy) must have derived from the Hellenization of the Jewish word 'nabi' (= enlightened). This extravagant theory has Nabis follow Kleomenes to Egypt, 'the land of divine names', where he chose (according to the trend of the time) a second name for himself, one that symbolized his revolutionary ideas (Texier 1975 p. 17). The above theory is, of course, ungrounded. The name Nabis (–Nabidos) is indeed Greek. It is a diminutive abbreviation deriving from another name, just as Agis is the abbreviation of Agesilaos. The full form of the name must have begun with the prefix Nau – (NaF -), as did those of the Spartan *ephors* Nau-atis (late-fifth century) and Nau-kleidas (early-

fourth century), or that of the commander of the Spartan army contingent against Epaminondas, Nau-kles, to mention but a few examples. For more information on how the Lakonic letter F becomes B, see Buck (1955 p 47), the most eminent specialist on dialects.

11. As already mentioned, the battle of Mantineia completed the destruction of Sellasia: there is no mention of the Spartan phalanx thereafter (see above and Texier 1975 p27, note 31).

12. The reappearance of the rich and distinguished Spartans is probably connected with the return of the oligarchy after the defeat of Kleomenes in 222 (Walbank 1995 p 371). However, Texier considers it unlikely that all those who had been exiled by Kleomenes returned to Sparta and claims that the number of rich citizens persecuted by Nabis must not have exceeded a few dozen (Texier 1975 p.29). Shimron dismisses the idea of the return of the eighty exiles to Sparta and believes that Kleomenes' social reforms were never abolished. He claims that social differentiation occurred slowly and steadily during the fifteen years from 222 to 207 (Shimron 1972 p 85 and p 87–88). By the end of this period, the beneficiaries of Kleomenes' reforms had become the new ruling class in Sparta. He concludes that all of the Spartans banished by Nabis must have been the beneficiaries of Kleomenes' reforms (Shimron 1972 p 137).

13. Liv. 34.31.11, 34.31.14, 34.32.9. Although Livy does not use this term, it is likely that he refers to them (or perhaps to *perioikoi*) when he writes about the 'poor' who received the confiscated estates of the wealthy.

14. Pol.13.6.3. Oliva argues that this measure was a great innovation and marks one of the differences between Nabis' policy and that of Kleomenes (Oliva 1971 p280). But it has already been mentioned that the inclusion of mercenaries in the citizen body was first implemented by Kleomenes (Plut. *Kleom.* 10.6, Marasco 1979 p 54 note 38, Cartledge 2002b p 52, Kennell 2003 p 83 and p 91).

15. Pol.16.13.1. Liv. 34.31.11, 34.31.14, 38.34.6. The fragmentary nature of the sources and the fact that both Polybios and Livy refer to the release of 'slaves' and not 'helots', have caused serious disagreement among modern historians regarding the interpretation of this particular measure taken by Nabis. According to Tarn, Nabis freed slaves, while 'part of his army was composed of liberated helots' (Tarn 1923 p 139). The release of the helots on a wide scale is discussed also by Toynbee but he remains undecided about whether they were incorporated in the citizenry or not (Toynbee 1969 p 203 and note 4). In contrast, Jones argues that Nabis 'freed and enfranchised many slaves but not apparently the Helots, who were the necessary base of the Lycurgan system' (Jones 1967 p 158). After a systematic review of the sources Kennell postulated a similar view according to which Nabis freed 'slaves' and not helots. He indicates that there is no mention anywhere on the integration by Nabis of the helots to the Spartan citizen-body. The view that the word 'slave, οἰκέτης (*oiketis*) or *servus* are equivalent to the word 'helot' when used in connection with Sparta, is according to Kennell simply speculation (Kennell 2003 p 91). In a later work he states that Nabis is sometimes credited erroneously with deliberate abolition of helotage (Kennell 2010 p180).

It is true that private slaves existed in Sparta as early as the fourth century (Plato *Alkibiades* 122d), but their numbers were small in comparison with those of the helots (Oliva 1971 p 280, Cartledge 2002b p.70). Furthermore (and despite Kennell's reservations), when the ancient Greeks referred to Sparta, they frequently used the term 'slaves' to suggest the helots (Ducat 2002 p 196). It is significant to compare that in Kleomenes' biography (23.1) Plutarch states that he set free the *helots*, while in the *Comparison* (5.1.) he states that he set free all the *slaves*. Finally, as already noted, after the third century the position of helots changed compared to what it had been in the past. The helots were no longer 'common slaves' but apparently belonged to the owners of the large estates which they cultivated (Mossé 1989 p 197, Cartledge 2002b p 69–70, Kennell 2003 p 83–85). And even if Kleomenes' revolution restored the state's ownership of the helots (Kennell 2003 p 85, 90), after his fall they were probably returned to their former (or newly created) landowners. Therefore, most historians agree that most probably Nabis enfranchised and integrated helots and not – or not only – slaves (See Hadas 1932 p 75–76, Oliva 1971 p 280, Shimron 1972 p 89 Mossé 1989 p 197–198, Texier 1975 p 34, Cartledge 2002b p 69–70, Mendels 1979 p 323–324).

16. Pol. 13.6.2–4, 16.13.1, Liv. 34.31.11, 34.31.14, 34.35.7, 34.36.5, 38.34.6. It has been noted that the Spartan women had rights to their ancestral property and undoubtedly some of them must have possessed great fortunes; therefore, Nabis' action was significant. But since this information comes from Polybios, it is also likely to be incorrect or distorted. It is possible that, as Nabis' implacable enemy, the historian exaggerated events to emphasize the radical nature of his reforms and, therefore, their 'criminal' nature (Oliva 1971 p280).

17. Texier 1975 p. 35.

18. Cartledge 2002b p. 70.

19. Liv. 34.27.2, 34.27.9. According to Oliva, the 'suspected helots' mentioned by Livy could have been former helots who were integrated in the citizen body but were simply unwilling to resist the invaders (Oliva 1971 p 280–281). However, he acknowledges that 'we have no reason to suppose that Nabis freed all the helots' (Oliva 1971 p 281).

20. Strabo 8.4.365.

21. Strabo 8.5.5.366.

22. Livy 34.27.2–3.

23. Mossé 1989 p 198, also see Pol. 16.13.1.

24. All of Nabis' policies suggest that, above all, he was interested in strengthening the Spartan army. Thus the new citizens he created should have been effective soldiers (Liv. 34.31.18, Oliva 1971 p 282).

25. As noted, after the battle of Sellasia the majority of Sparta's combat forces consisted of mercenaries. The risk of having a disproportionate number of mercenaries to the citizens was already evident from the fourth century. In a treatise attributed to Aeneias Tacticus (*Poliorcetica* 12.4–5), the author draws attention to this very fact and cites the example of the city Heracleia in Pontos, which was seized by its own mercenaries. Another example is mentioned by Polybios (2.5–7), who refers to Phoenice in Epeiros. The city had hired 800 Gaul mercenaries to protect her but they delivered her to her enemies. 'My object, in commenting on the blind folly of the Epeirotes, is to point out

that it is never wise to introduce a foreign garrison, especially of barbarians, which is too strong to be controlled.' (Pol. 2.7.12).

26. Liv. 34.36.5–7, 34.39, 35.36.4–10. Typical examples of the strengthening bonds between mercenaries and Spartan citizens are two funerary epigrams of mercenaries dating from this period. The first concerns Botrichos from Arcadia (I.G.V.1.724) and the second the Illyrian Plator (Steinhauer 1992), both of whom fell in battle. They are dedicated to them by their Spartan wives, Timo and Aristonika respectively, and refer to the bravery of the dead and the feelings of their wives towards them. The tender tone of the epigrams is in sharp contrast to the austere 'in war' epigrams of Spartan tradition, and underscores the deep social and ideological changes that had occurred in Spartan society at the time (Steinhauer 1992 p.243).

27. Oliva 1971 p 282 Mendels assumes that the number of *perioikoi* had been reduced significantly in the meantime because of the frequent wars, and especially their participation in the disastrous defeats of Sellasia and Mantineia (Mendels 1979 p 322).

28. Liv. 34.36.3 Among Nabis' senior officials there were also *perioikoi*, such as Timocrates of Pellana, who was assigned the administration of Argos in 195 (see below).

29. Shimron 1972 p. 88

30. The evolution of the Spartan coinage is a characteristic sign of times: It is notable that the first coins Areus I had issued bear his name but do not feature his portrait. The coins issued by Kleomenes display his portrait but do not carry the king's name. Nabis was the only king of Sparta who dared issue coins with both. In time, the Spartan kings shed their austere appearance and looked more like Hellenistic monarchs (Palagia 2006 p 209 note 35).

31. Ditt. Syll³. 584

32. Liv. 34.35.9. It seems that Nabis exploited the conflict between the cities of Knossos and Gortys, which had erupted from 204 and supported the former against the latter (see Errington 1969 p 34–48 for details). His opponents even accused him of piracy. This is something that cannot be denied since the Cretans were famous for their pirate activities. However, his recognition as a 'man of virtue' (ἀνήρ ἀγαθός) by the commercial centre of Delos (see previous note) shows that his activity in the Aegean Sea was not limited to piracy.

33. Pausanias 7.8.5. Livy 34.34.4, 39.37.1–2. Toynbee 1969 p 171 note 2. According to Kourinou, the wall was probably constructed in two stages: the first involved a hasty perimeter fortification of Sparta with ditch and palisades in order to counter the invasion of 195, and the second involved the strengthening and expansion of the walls in the years between 195–192 (Kourinou 2000 p 57–62).

34. The wall of Sparta, built to protect her from a possible siege, is closely linked to the organized provision of the city's water. Votive reliefs from the Late-third and Early-second century (Museum of Sparta No. 5343 and no. 6747) document the existence of offices concerning the water supply of Sparta, such as the water commissioners (*hydragos* and *hyphidragos*), making a convincing case for the existence of an organized water supply system (Kourinou 2,000 p 225–226, Cartledge 2002b p 71–72).

35. Cartledge 2002b p 72.

36. Pol.13.7. This story has been characterised as a flagrant fabrication of pro-Roman propaganda (Chrimes 1999 p.35) or 'ascribed to the overheated fantasies of embittered exiles' (Cartledge 2002b p 72) and has been generally dismissed as fiction (Oliva 1971 p 287). However, as in every historical question there are those who seek to differentiate themselves from the prevailing views. Peter Green states that the information about this device is so intriguingly detailed and explicitly described that despite the widespread reservations of the majority of scholars, he suspects it might have actually existed (Green 1993 p 302).

37. There were quite a few mercenaries who had not been enrolled in the citizen body: in 195 there numbered at least 6,000. This number is arrived at by taking account of the 3,000 mercenaries and 1,000 Cretans in Sparta, the 1,000 who came from Crete as reinforcements (Liv. 34.27.2) and the 1,000 mercenaries who accompanied 2,000 citizens of Argos who arrived in Sparta under Pythagoras (Liv. 34.29.14.) Obviously, there may have been additional mercenaries deployed in cities such as Gytheion and also in the garrison that remained in Argos under Timokrates. Griffith estimates the number of Nabis' mercenaries to be 7,000–8,000 men (Griffith 1984 p 98).

38. Shimron 1972 p 86. Shimron also notes that Nabis could not hope for subsidies from abroad, since during that period the great powers had no political interest in southern Greece. According to Pausanias, Nabis went so far as to sell the valuables and dedications of temples (Paus. 4.29.10). If this reference is valid and is not a concoction of hostile propaganda, it is revealing both of the revolutionary nature of Nabis' reforms and of his pressing need for funds.

39. It is noteworthy that there is no mention of debt cancellation in Sparta. However, this is indirectly inferred by the reasonable assumption that most of the creditors would have been the wealthy and prominent citizens whom Nabis had expelled from Sparta. Moreover, there is clear reference by Livy that when Nabis occupied Argos, he cancelled debts and applied to the city all the other reforms that he had implemented in Sparta (Oliva 1971 p 280 note 3). Others, however, oppose to this reasoning and claim that as the socio-economic structure of Argos was very different from that of Sparta, Nabis was faced with a different set of problems- and therefore applied different solutions. Moreover, in order to become more easily accepted by the Argives, Nabis would have needed to implement more radical measures than in Sparta (Mendels 1979 p 325–326). Cartledge argues that Nabis deliberately avoided cancelling debts in Sparta, as part of his effort to encourage financial transactions within the city (Cartledge 2002b p70–71).

40. Ehrenberg RE Nabis col. 1481 (= Shimron 1972 p 97). It has been noted that in contrast to Agis and Kleomenes and despite his declarations (Liv.34.31.17–18), Nabis did not seek (or even pretend) to enforce equality of property and restoration of the austere way of life. Properly speaking, he applied the usual practice of the time, which entailed seizure of a rival factions' property and its distribution among the supporters of the winning faction. In this sense, Nabis was a typical Hellenistic revolutionary and his social policy differed substantially from that of his predecessors (Mendels 1979 p 311–317).

41. According to Diodoros, Nabis usurped power after the assassination of Pelops, Lykourgos' son (Diod. 27.1). However the reliability of this information is questionable,

as it is possibly based on one of the rumours that were being propagated by Nabis' enemies against him (Chrimes 1999 p 27, Oliva 1971 p 279 note 4, Texier 1975 p 28, Cartledge 2002b p 68).

42. The few archaeological findings emphatically support that Nabis' royal title was recognised both in Sparta and abroad. Three stamped tiles of the roof of the Spartan wall have been discovered, bearing the inscription 'of King Nabis' (IG V 1 885, a–c, Kourinou 2000 p 53). The silver tetradrachms depicting his figure and bearing his name have been already mentioned, as well as the many inscriptions referring to him or the period of his reign. Among them stands out his recognition as 'King of Sparta' by the Delian Assembly (SIG 3 584). For his recognition by the Romans, see Liv. 34.31.12–14.

43. As Mossé observes, Nabis's policy is not interpreted simply by the traditions of a city that had always been an exception to the Hellenistic world, but furthermore seems to also embody what his opponents saw in him, the type of the revolutionary tyrant (Mossé 1989 p 198). Cartledge compares him with the famous tyrant of Syracuse, Dionysios (431/0–367), noting the striking similarities in their policy (Cartledge 2002b p 69).

44. Polybios (13.7. [2] And 13.7.6, 18.17.2–5) refers to her as 'Apega'. But as Roussel indicates, the euphonic 'g' must have been added to 'Apia' which must have been her real name. This is probably the daughter of the tyrant of Argos, Aristippos II and niece of Aristomachos II who had joined Kleomenes' cause in 225 (Roussel 1922 p 431 and Bradford 1977 sv 'Apega'). Apia radically differed from the traditional image of a Spartan king's wife: instead of living in Nabis' shadow, she was actively involved in state affairs and supported her husband's policy. According to Cartledge (2002b p 74) she was 'Sparta's first real queen'. Her brother Pythagoras was Nabis' chief of staff. In an effort to strengthen family ties, Nabis married one of his daughters with him thus Pythagoras was simultaneously Nabis' son-in-law and brother-in-law. The practice was not uncommon in Sparta providing that intermarriage occurred between Spartans. However, the case of Pythagoras and his sister Apia, resonate the change in morals of their time, for they were Argives.

45. For Nabis' stables and selected horses, see Pol.13.8.3. For Nabis' palace, see Liv. 35.36.1, Plut. *Philop.* 15.4. For his bodyguard, see Pol. 13.6.5 (also see Cartledge 2002b p 69).

46. Mossé 1989 p 199, Texier 1975 p 26, Shimron 1972 p 86. There are two gatherings of the Spartan Assembly by Nabis reported in 195. In the first case the gathering was made by force, with the intent to arrest and execute suspected traitors (Liv. 34.27.4–6). The second was when Nabis was confident that the assembled citizens would approve of his political decision (Liv.34.37.2 -3). These were merely irregular gatherings, rather than institutional functions to determine or debate and validate decisions.

47. Liv.34.31.17–19. But is that statement sufficient evidence for us to accept that the new *kleroi* were equal? On the other hand, the imposition of taxation and the circulation of money, in combination with the presence in the city of the king's favourites, provide serious evidence for the preservation of economic inequalities (Mendels 1979 p 314–318, Taiphakos 1995 p 115).

48. The provision of *kleroi* as a reward for the services soldiers rendered to a powerful despot was a well-known and accepted practice. Dionysios, the tyrant of Syracuse, had adopted it in the past, and so had all the Hellenistic monarchs. It is this practice that Nabis most likely implemented, since his regime can be classified either as 'tyrannical' or as 'Hellenistic monarchy', and has very little in common with the traditional Spartan way.

49. Their preservation is indirectly inferred from the fact that all Spartan traditional institutions were abolished after Nabis' reign, by Philopoimen (see Plut. *Philop.* 16.6 also Liv. 38.34.3 and Paus. 8.51.3).

50. Shimron (1972 p 86) seems to imply this when he claims that 'with the liberation of many helots, the state had to pay at least part of the *syssitia*.' Much more important, however, is the fact that Nabis sought to have complete and total control of the lives of his subjects. One of his strongest weapons must have been the power to confer citizenship to anyone whom he favoured and remove it at will.

51. However, the contribution of the *agoge* in this field was disappointingly minimal since according to all indications, the quality of the Spartan army fell dramatically in the following years. There is not the slightest mention of heavy infantry in Nabis' army. Instead, it is frequently mentioned that Nabis relied almost exclusively on mercenaries (Liv. 34.27.2, 34.28.8, 35.27.15 and Griffith 1984 p.97).

52. Texier 1975 p. 36

53. Pol. 13.6.7–10. These accusations are reiterated by Diodoros, Livy and Pausanias. According to Ollier, Nabis' frequent use of brutal violence and the historical sources' exaggeration of it end up depicting him as a flawed copy of Kleomenes (Ollier 1943 p 123). The truth is that there is no specific reference to a named person eliminated by Nabis, and even his main political rival, the deposed King Agesipolis, was not targeted by Nabis' assassins (Aymard 1938 p 36 note 33). But this does not mean that the revolutionary reforms were imposed solely by peaceful means of persuasion. On the contrary, we should assume acts of violence 'even without their being attested in the sources' (Shimron 1972 p 84).

54. For the internal problems of Messene, see Plut. *Aratos* 49.2–3, 50.1

55. Chrimes 1999 p. 30

56. Shimron 1972 p. 87 note 23

57. Mosse 1989. 198

58. Texier 1975 p. 39

59. Oliva 1971 p 284. For the facts regarding the capture of Messene, see Paus. 4.29.10, 8.50.5, Paul. 16.13.3, Liv. 34.32.16, 34.35.6, Plut. *Philop.* 12.4.

60. Pol.16.36–37. It should be noted that one of the achievements Polybios praises Philopoimen for is that he succeeded in mobilizing his forces and moving with secrecy to Lakonia without being noticed by Nabis' extensive spy network. What can be inferred from the point above is that Nabis maintained a considerable number of supporters in many cities outside of Lakonia, who informed him of the movements of his opponents. This fact, combined with the use of Cretan assassins to kill political opponents in the cities where they sought refuge (Pol.13.6.7–10), suggests the existence of a well-organized clandestine network spread across the Peloponnese. Here again, another

essential difference is implied between Nabis and Kleomenes. The latter probably did not even imagine creating such a network.

61. Plut. *Philop.* 13.1
62. Liv. 32.38.3. The reference is completely vague. It is not known how many children Nabis had. There survived just the name of a son, Armenas.
63. Texier 1975 p. 17–18 and p. 108 (genealogy).
64. Liv. 32.38.4–6.
65. Liv. 32.38.6–9.
66. Mosse 1989 p. 201.
67. Pol. 13.6.3–6, 16.13, also see Diod. 27.1.
68. Texier 1975 p. 66.
69. Liv. 34.35.3 also see Cartledge 2002b p. 74.
70. Shimron 1972 p 97. Tomlinson (1972 p 170) argues that Philip gave Nabis not only the city of Argos but all of Argolis. He also believed that Nabis attempted to renew the ancient ties of friendship between Sparta and Argos, while at the same time weakening the nobility of Argos and restoring the city of Mycenae into prominence.
71. Shimron 1972 p. 91, Cartledge 2002b p. 74.
72. Pol. 5.104.10–11.
73. Pol. 18.46.2.
74. Plut. *Titus* 10.5.
75. Pol. 18.46.14.
76. Liv. 34.26.6–8. Apparently Flamininus realized that, all the assurances of the oligarch fugitives to the contrary, the citizens of Argos would passionately defend their city on the side of the Spartan garrison (see Oliva 1971 p 289 note 4).
77. Liv. 34.26.10–11. After the defeat in Cynoscephalae Philip V was obliged, as an ally of the Romans, to assist them. Of course his righteous anger against Nabis and his desire to avenge the betrayal of Argos may have been an additional incentive.
78. Liv. 34.26.10–14.
79. Liv. 34.27.1–3
80. Liv. 34. 27. 8.10. The gathering took place under the threat of arms and was not convened to reach decisions. Its only purpose was to terrorise the gathered Spartans. It cannot therefore be described as an Assembly.
81. Liv.34.27.2, 34.27.9. As mentioned, the presence of helots in 195 suggests (though does not assert) that the institution of helots still existed.
82. Liv. 34.28.3–6.
83. Liv. 34.28.9–12.
84. Liv. 34.29.1.
85. Liv. 34.29.8–13. Beyond Dexagoridas' initiative to deliver Gytheion to the Romans, Livy says nothing further. His action can be classified either as treason (to his king, Nabis) or patriotism (to save his city from destruction). Some consider the event to reveal the existence of two competing political groups in Gytheion 'none of which seemed to be fond of the Romans' (Taiphakos 1984 p 116 note 32).
86. Argos naturally remained on the side of Sparta, under the command of Timocrates of Pellana (Liv 34.29.14).

87. Liv. 34.31.9–12.
88. Liv. 34.31.17–18. The above references by Nabis, regarding equality, land distribution and replenishment of the population with the liberation of slaves (34.31.14) is closer to Kleomenes' reform agenda than Lykourgos'. According to Shimron (1972 p 97 note 44), it is very likely that Nabis (or whoever put these words in his mouth) had Kleomenes in mind rather than Lykourgos as a model legislator: *'noster legum lator.'*
89. Liv. 34.31.19. Nabis' speech to the Roman governor is the only surviving case of comparison between the Roman and the Spartan constitution, in which the latter is shown to be superior to the former. Moreover, Nabis' arguments seem more convincing than those of Flamininus'. This event possibly indicates the origin of a pro-Spartan source, which Polybios followed and then Livy copied. According to Taiphakos (1984), this source is the Lakedaimonian historian Sosylos. Why would Livy accept reproducing such a clearly anti-Roman speech? It would be naïve to attribute this event to Titus Livy's objectivity – more so for someone like Texier to believe (1977 p 151) that Polybios, from whom this dialogue essentially derives, demonstrated in this case an unprecedented impartiality. Taiphakos (1984 p 125–136) attempts to give a more convincing explanation, according to which Nabis' speech gives Livy a wonderful opportunity to exercise indirect criticism of the existing social system of his country, criticizing through the words of a tyrant and enemy the unequal distribution of wealth and the social disharmony that prevailed in Rome in his time.
90. Liv. 34.32.1–2. It is interesting that Livy himself, in an earlier reference to King Lykourgos, characterizes him as 'tyrant' (Liv.34.26.14.). Therefore Flamininus contradicts himself when he calls the son of a 'tyrant' the legitimate King of Sparta (Texier 1975 p.12 note 51).
91. Liv. 34.32.10.
92. Liv. 34.32.20.
93. Liv.34.33.8. It is obvious that the Achaeans and their allies were afraid of Nabis' revolutionary reforms spreading throughout the Peloponnese. It has been noted that the main cause of the Achaeans' resistance to the possibility of Spartan hegemony was that it could enforce Nabis' social revolution upon them (Briscoe 1967 p.10).
94. Liv. 34.33.9–11
95. Liv. 34.33.12–14. The probability of Flamininus being replaced is low, given that he had proved his ability in handling Greek affairs and the Senate had expressed their absolute confidence, giving him complete freedom of movement in the war against Nabis. Therefore the cause of Flamininus' stance should be sought more in his concern over the impending invasion by Antiochos than in his personal ambition (Wood 1939 p.100).
96. Liv. 34.34.6
97. For Flamininus' terms see Liv. 34.35.3–11.
98. It is interesting that the exiles' wives and children were not forced to return to them, but given a choice to do so. Judging by subsequent events, they did not show any willingness to return (Pomeroy 2002 p 91).
99. Livy 34.36.3.
100. Livy 34.36.7.

101. Livy 34.37.4–6.
102. Livy 34.37.6.
103. Livy 34.37.8
104. Only Phoebaion's location has been identified so far; it is south of Sparta (Kourinou 2000 p 200–210).
105. Liv. 34.38.7
106. Liv. 34.39.6.
107. Liv. 34.39.8. This anti-heroic description of Nabis can be attributed to Polybios and is obviously exaggerated.
108. Liv. 34.40.1.
109. Liv. 34.40.2.
110. Plut. Titus 13.3.
111. See Briscoe 1967 p 9.
112. Its base has survived which bore an honorific inscription: 'the town of Gytheion to its Saviour Titus Quinctius general consul of the Romans' (SIG³ 592=SEG XI.923). Gytheion had serious reasons for this great honour to Flamininus, who was not a consul but a proconsul. Thanks to the treaty which he had imposed on Nabis, Gytheion together with all coastal *perioikic* cities, gained full independence from Sparta and formed the League (*Koinon*) of the Lakedaimonians (Taiphakos 1974 p 23–24, Cartledge 2002b p 77).
113. Liv. 34.41.6.
114. Pleiai are located in the current village of Apidia (Taiphakos 1974 p.25 note 2).
115. Liv. 35.12, Plut. *Philop.* 14.4–6, Paus.8.50.8–9, Just.31.3.21.
116. Liv. 35.27–30. Livy lists names of locations (Mount Barbosthenes, Pharai, and Pyrrhos' Charax) which are not referred to anywhere else and are completely impossible to identify. (Loring 1895, p64–65)
117. Plut. *Philop.* 15.2, Paus. 8.50.10. It is quite possible that the status quo of 195 was restored (Cartledge 2002b p 77), although there is no clear reference. Also, it is not certain whether Nabis lost Gytheion or not. According to Errington (1969 p.108) Nabis continued occupying the city until his assassination. But if the terms of the treaty of 195 were imposed anew, this possibility must be ruled out. It is also unlikely that Nabis was allowed to occupy such an important port and naval station. Therefore, either the city was recaptured by the fleets of Rome and Pergamon (Oliva 1971 p 295, Cartledge 2002b p.77) or Nabis agreed to withdraw his forces.
118. Errington 1969 p. 109.
119. Liv. 35.35.10–19
120. Liv.35.36.5–6. Some historians claim that there was a rumour about the existence of fabulous riches in Nabis' palace and that their acquisition was the main motive for his murder by the Aitolians (Holleaux 1930 p.207). Others consider this to be an exaggeration but admit the existence of treasures (at least in the form of war booty) stashed away inside the palace (Aymard 1938 p316 note 13 and note 17 p317). The fact remains that the rumour proved false. Alexamenos did not find the tyrant's legendary treasures, simply because they did not exist. As shown later, when Timolaos and other Spartan collaborationists liquidated the palace along with all of Nabis' assets, they did

not collect more than 120 talents (Plut. *Philop.* 15.4). Nabis' personal property, which apparently composed only a part of the above amount, can hardly be called a 'treasure' (Texier 1975 p.100).

121. Liv. 35.36.8. This is the one and only reference of Lakonikos in history. Nothing else is known about him. Evan Sage, (Livy' translator in Loeb series 1967 p110), highlights the peculiar occurrence of the name and speculates that perhaps Livy mistook the adjective 'Λακωνικός' in Polybios' text as a noun or that the text is corrupt. However, the desperate attempt of Nabis' followers to enthrone a king even by random selection, is indicative of the personalised kind of regime that Nabis had established, as well as of the chaotic situation in which Sparta was reduced.

122. Liv. 35.36.9–10. According to Livy (35.36.3–5.), if the Aitolians had tried to convene the Spartan Assembly instead of proceeding to loot Sparta, they would have been indeed welcomed liberators. This is of course an exaggeration but it indicates that there were quite a few dissidents in Sparta, whose full support the Aitolians had taken for granted. As it turned, out this support was overestimated.

123. According to Livy (35.37.1–3.) at the same time a roman fleet of twenty-four quinqueremes under the command of Aulus Atilius reached Gytheion, therefore facilitating Philopoimen's plans. However we would expect the Romans to not assist Philopoimen in his plan of occupying Sparta, since their policy was to prevent let the Achaean League from completely ruling the Peloponnese. We can consider this particular incident as an attempt by Livy to emphasize the Romans' influence and their participation in Greek affairs (Oliva 1971 p 297 note 3).

124. Texier 1975 p. 40.

125. Shimron 1972 p. 98

126. This at least is Texier's view (1975 p 63) according to which Nabis sought to unite the Dorian tribes into a 'pandorisme', in an effort to protect his revolutionary reforms from his opponents.

127. Thirty years earlier, when the political scene was different, there were still probabilities for success in such schemes, provided that Sparta would have rallied the people of the Peloponnese. While Kleomenes had this opportunity but let it slip through his fingers, this opportunity was never given to Nabis. When he came to the throne of Sparta it was already too late.

128. Recall that in 195 Nabis' army numbered 10,000 Spartans, 2,000 Cretans and 3,000 more mercenaries (Liv. 34.27.2). Along with the garrison of 1,000 mercenaries from Argos and 2,000 Argives who rushed to the aid of Sparta (Liv.34.29.14), his forces amounted to 18,000 men. Of course, the garrisons of Gytheion and of the other *perioikic* cities as well as the forces of his fleet must be added to this number, too. But again, his army must not have been much greater than 20,000 in total.

Chapter 5: Pax Achiaca

1. *Evocatis principibus (*Liv.35.37.1–2*).*

2. Plut. *Philop.* 15.3.

3. Plut. *Philop.* 15.4–6, Oliva 1971 p. 298, Cartledge 2002b p. 78, Errington 1969 p. 110–111.

4. The Spartan exiles consisted of those who had been banished for the first time by Kleomenes in 227, by Lykourgos in 219 and mainly by Nabis in 207. This last category was certainly the most numerous. Regarding the problem of the exiles and political factions inside and outside of Sparta: Errington 1969 p 134–136 (for the 'old exiles'), pp. 140–148 and p. 288–291 (for the period 183 to 178). Also Shimron 1972 p 135–150, a critique of Errington. Generally, the question of the origin of Spartan exiles is highly controversial since the available sources are incomplete.

5. Livy 38.30.6–7.

6. Pol. 21.3.4.

7. Liv. 38.31.4.

8. Liv. 38.32.9.

9. 677

10. This specific location is referred only by Livy and its position is not determined.

11. Liv.38.33.11. Plutarch (*Philop.* 16.3) mentions the view of the Spartan historian Aristokrates according to which Philopoimen killed 350 Spartans. Is this an exaggeration by a biased historian or was Kompasion followed by other massacres in Sparta, about which Polybios stays silent? The issue is highly controversial and all cases are possible (Cavaignac 1948 p 206, Errington 1969 p 145 pt 1 Oliva 1971 p 301 note 1).

12. Plut. *Philop.* 16.6

13. Liv. 38.34.9, also see Paus. 8.51.3–4

14. Pol. 21.32c.3

15. The assassination of Nabis may have signalled the end of the Spartan revolutionary movement, as applied by historians since they have the luxury to observe events from a distance and after the fact. This was not the case with those who lived it. For them nothing had been decided. Thus 'the various groups and factions that were created in thirty years of revolution still exist and compete for power, require an equitable solution to the issues of property and restoration of the constitution and resist domination by the Achaeans' (Shimron 1972 p 101).

16. Cartledge 2002b p. 80

17. Pol. 22.11.7–8, Shimron 1972 p. 137–138.

18. Liv. 39.37.4–5

19. Pol. 23.4

20. Messene, which had joined the Achaean League in 191, had defected under the guidance of Deinokrates. To bring it back within the League, the Achaeans initially appealed to their Roman allies. The latter not only refused to assist, but informed them that they would not reconsider even if other cities like Sparta, Corinth and Argos defected (Pol. 23.9.12–14). The Achaeans then undertook to forcefully reintegrate Messene into the League on their own and, after bloody clashes in one of which Philopoimen was killed, they succeeded thanks to General Lykortas (Plut. *Philop.* 18.5–21.3). Only then did the Romans, for the sake of appearances, decide to impose an economic blockade on Messene (Pol. 23.17.3). As aptly noted 'this incident is an illustration of Rome's claim to exercise a protectorate beyond what clearly defined in treaties and documents' (Larsen 1935 p 209).

21. Paus. 7.9.5 and also Oliva 1971 p. 311–312

22. Cartledge 2002b p. 84
23. Shimron 1972 p. 129–130
24. Paus. 7.12.7–8
25. Paus. 7.12.8
26. Paus. 7.12.9
27. Paus. 7.13.3
28. Paus. 7.13.7
29. Paus. 7.13.8, modified.
30. Paus. 7.14.1.
31. Paus. 7.14.2–3.
32. Pol. 39.11.
33. Shimron 1972 p. 134

Chapter 6: Pax Romana

1. Michell 1964 p. 337
2. Plut. *Philop.* 16.6.
3. Cassius Dio 54.7.2.
4. Philostratus Vita Apollonii 4.31.3.
5. Spawforth 2002 p. 113–114.
6. Spawforth 2002 p. 143–176 and Kennell 1995 p. 87–93.
7. Todd 2003 p. 69.
8. Michell 1964 p. 336.
9. Paus. 3.14.10.
10. At least this is how Xenophon describes this custom (*Lak. Polity* 2.9).
11. Michell 1964 p 336. Michell's bitter remark caused the indignation of Taiphakos (1974 p 38 note 3). However, Plutarch (*Lykourgos* 18), who describes this custom and its evolution until Roman Sparta, mentions cases of youths who died during the whipping. Regarding the theatre, see Piper 1986 p 182–184, Todd 2003 p 69–70, and Spawforth 2002b p 122–123 and p 205.
12. Which, of course, was very different from the original 'Lykourgan' one (see Piper 1986 p145–147, Spawforth 2002b p 160–175).
13. Spawforth 2002b p. 210.
14. Cartledge, 2002b p 39. In the early twentieth century there were some historians (G. Kazarow 1907, E.Bux 1925, von Pöhlmann 1925, as listed in Oliva 1971 p 216–217), who characterized Agis and Kleomenes as 'socialists'. They claimed that the two kings became the leaders of the poor Spartans influenced by the Stoic philosophy. Noting the weaknesses and excesses in Phylarchos' dramatic narrative, these scholars have totally rejected him as a historical source and have accepted Polybios as the only reliable source, considering the effects of the stoics on the revolutionaries to be certain. Bux and von Pöhlmann have gone so far as to compare third century Sparta with Germany after the First World War, and the Spartan movement with the German Social Democrats of 1918. There were those who connected Stoicism with the communist ideology. Toynbee (1939a p 179–180) compares the Stoic philosopher Blossios and the revolutionary Aristonikos with Marx and Lenin respectively. According to Tarn,

Agis' ideology leaned towards 'stoic communism' (Tarn, 1928 p 742). Similar views were expressed on Nabis; some historians have not hesitated to call him a 'communist' considering him a model social revolutionary surrounded by Cretans and 'Red Guard' mercenaries (Holleaux 1930 p 147 and p 189). Today, these theories have been discarded. Moreover, the ideologies of Stoicism and Marxism show no substantial similarities apart from some very general analogies. The Hellenistic philosophy faced the major social and economic problems of its time in a completely different way than modern philosophy does. Moreover, the comparison of the Spartan revolutionary movement or any revolutionary movement of antiquity with contemporary socialist movements is meaningless. Socialism as a concept is inseparably connected with capitalism and industrial society and, certainly, nothing can be said about socialism in ancient societies of relatively primitive economic structures lacking factory infrastructure and real productive capital (Tigerstedt 1974 p 73–74).

However, the fact that current research practices avoid comparing the historical events of so dissimilar societies and cultures does not preclude some historians from referring to Hellenistic Sparta using expressions borrowed from contemporary political terminology. Recently, a historian did not hesitate to ascribe to Agis' reform attempt 'hidden fascist incentives' (Green 1993 p 252) and claim that Kleomenes 'may have learned some things about primitive (and elitist) communism from his wife or from Sphairos or even in some general way from the cynics …' (Green 1993 p 257).

15. Texier 1975 p. 6
16. Cartledge 2002b p 60. However, it should be noted that in the same essay, Cartledge (2002b p 39) recognizes – albeit somewhat reluctantly – that both Agis and Kleomenes should be regarded 'as revolutionaries rather than (merely) reformists'.
17. Green 1993 p. 251.
18. Martinez-Lacy 1977.
19. The term revolution is used not in the strict Marxian sense but rather broadly in the light of modern scholarship of the last decades, cf. among others Herf (1984), Sternhell (1994), Neocleous (1998), Griffin (2004), Breschi (2012).
20. These two basic principles of the movement have been identified by Shimron (1972 p 125).
21. This term was introduced by Shimron (1972 p 69 ff.). It was Cartledge who identified it as a modern one (2002b p 61).
22. Irrefutable evidence for this is Chairons' failed attempt of land redistribution.
23. For Kleomenes and Nabis, there is no room for any doubt. It is true that Agis did not appear to have on his side the majority of his fellow citizens. This however does not justify Martinez-Lacy (1977) when he reduces Agis' reform attempt to the level of a conspiracy among members of the Spartan ruling class.
24. This is, in general terms and with individual differences, the prevailing theory. See Tarn (1923), Hadas (1932), Ollier (1943), Africa (1961), Forrest (1980), Shimron (1972), Tigerstedt (1974), Ferguson (1975 p.131–137) and David (1981). Walbank (1999 p240) considers the movement of the Spartan kings, Agis IV, Kleomenes III and of their successors to be typical example of temporarily successful revolutionary movement of the period.

25. Tarn 1923 p. 128.
26. David 1981 p. 170
27. Shimron 1972 p. 126.
28. After the inclusion of *perioikoi* and foreigners, originally by Kleomenes and especially by Nabis, the Spartan population was altered to such an extent that it permanently changed its composition. The 700 residents of unmixed Spartan ancestry became the minority of the general population and the purity of their origin ceased to exist (Shimron 1972 p 127).
29. Liv.34.37.
30. Shimron 1972 p. 134.
31. Todd 2000 p. 66.
32. Those were nearly twenty years old in 192, were approaching seventy in 146.
33. Tigerstedt (1974 p 18). Tigerstedt goes so far as to wonder whether the Lykourgan Sayings reflect merely Sphairos' philosophical concepts. He does, however, leave the question unanswered recognizing the great difficulties of such an answer (Tigerstedt 1974 p 82).
34. G.Grote, *A History of Greece*, 10 vols, London, edition 1872. See Grote 2000, p 308–333 and especially p. 320–330. However Grote was not the first to question the 'Lykourgan' land redistribution. As he acknowledges, the question had begun a little earlier – unbeknownst to Grote – by other academics like Lachmann and Kortum (Grote 2000 p 322 note 1).
35. Ollier 1933 and 1943.
36. See Hodkinson 2000 p. 4, Whitby 2002 p. 11.
37. Hodkinson 2000. The issue of the ownership of Spartan *kleroi* as shown in Plutarch's biography of Lykourgos is remarkably contradictory. Plutarch speaks of donations of *kleroi* to new-borns. Yet only Spartan citizens had the right to obtain *kleroi*, i.e. those who had (successfully) passed the stage of *agoge* and had been admitted to the *syssitia*. This inconsistency reveals Plutarch's effort to reconcile two opposing theories: the hereditary transfer of *kleroi* and the existence of equal and undivided *kleroi* owned by the state (Cartledge 2002a p 144). The fact is that the only ancient source that mentions the famous Spartan communal land ownership is the above reference by Plutarch (*Lykourgos* 16). In his paper entitled 'Five words that shook the world' Hodkinson refers to Plutarch's famous words 'Κλῆρον αυτῷ των ενακισχιλίων προσνείμαντες' (*Lykourgos* 16) and notes that the famous theory that 'a Spartan was the exclusive owner of his property for life and that the city would recover his property after his death' (Hodkinson 2007) is founded exclusively on these five words.
38. Hodkinson 2000 p. 37.
39. Grote 2000 p317. Polybios believed that Lykourgos had introduced equality of property and he expressed his great surprise how the best informed ancient authors (such as Plato, Xenophon, Kallisthenes and Ephoros) compared the ancient Spartan polity to that of Crete, where there was no equality of property (Pol.6.45–48). According to Grote, this fact marks the difference between the views of earlier authors and those of the third century, who Polybios was based on. The earlier authors compared Spartan

and Cretan institutions 'because they did *not* conceive equality of landed property as a feature in old Sparta' (Grote 2000 p 317 note 1).

40. Hodkinson 2000 p. 60

41. Grote 2000 p 311–312. Regarding land redistribution in Plutarch, see *Lyk.* 8, *Agis* 8, *Kleom.* 2. Unlike Lykourgos' land reallotment, the land reform that Agis proclaimed and Kleomenes implemented is confirmed by the testimonies of Phylarchos and Polybios.

42. According to Plutarch (*Lykourgos* 8), Lykourgos divided the *perioikic* land into 30,000 *kleroi*. Concerning the redistribution of Spartan land, Plutarch mentions three different versions: a) that *Lykourgos* divided the land into 9,000 *kleroi* b) that he distributed it into 6,000 *kleroi*, in addition to which King Polydoros established 3,000 more and c) that he divided them into 4,500 Spartan *kleroi*, which Polydoros doubled later. For Grote (2000 p 318) the last version is very similar to Agis' proposal (Plut. *Agis* 8) for the redistribution of Spartan land into 4,500 *kleroi*. Africa (1968 p.10) considers it a certainty that Plutarch received the number of 4,500 *kleroi* from Phylarchos' history. He grounds his beliefs on Phylarchos' description of Agis' reforms and argues that the previous version of the distribution of 6,000 *kleroi* is related to Kleomenes' 6,000 Spartans (4,000 citizens + 2,000 freed helots). Marasco makes similar remarks (1979 p 50). Jones (1967 p.40) notes that the land reform which Agis sought to implement included 4,500 *kleroi* for the Spartans and 15,000 *kleroi* for *perioikoi*, i.e. half the *kleroi* of the 'Lykourgan' redistribution because Sparta had lost Messenia. Tigerstedt supports similar views (1974 p79 and note 251). Hodkinson (2000 p 43–45 and 69–71) argues that the numbers of *Lykourgos*' 4,500 and 6,000 Spartan *kleroi* reflect Agis' and Kleomenes' social programs respectively.

43. Plut. *Lyk.* 5.

44. Plut. *Agis* 5.4–5.

45. Hodkinson 2000 p 54. Hodkinson points out that all *Laconic Quotations* that refer to *Lykourgos* place particular emphasis on the concept of equality (Hodkinson 2000 p 45), which dominated the ideology of third century revolutionaries: this fact confirms the influence of the Spartan movement in the misrepresentation of the Spartan tradition (Hodkinson 2000 p.70).

46. Plut. *Lykourgos* 8.: '[*Lykourgos*] determined, therefore, to banish insolence and envy and crime and luxury, and those yet more deep-seated and afflictive diseases of the state, poverty and wealth, he persuaded his fellow-citizens to make one parcel of all their territory and divide it up anew, and to live with one another on a basis of entire uniformity and equality...' (cf. Plut. *Kleom.* 10.4. and Hodkinson 2000 p.93).

47. Tigerstedt (1974 p. 76–77).

48. Kennell 1995.

49. Critically examining the '*Instituta Laconica*' Kennell finds grammatical errors, signs of altered phrases and later additions, which reveal Stoic influence on the first seventeen of them (Kennell 1995 p 104–106). Based on the above, Kennell claims that this work, which allegedly outlines Sparta's constitution, is in fact a set of excerpts deriving mainly from Sphairos' lost work (Kennell 1995 p 107).

50. Kennell 1995 p. 102

51. Kennell 1995 p. 148

52. Some historians (Cartledge 1997) observe that in his effort to support his theory, Kennell makes oversimplifications that degrade and misinterpret the testimonies of ancient historians and especially Xenophon's. According to others (Keen 1996), many of Kennell's arguments are not based on facts but on his own speculations: 'too often K. will make a proposition and then treat it as a fact to base a further proposition.' Besides, the fact that Agis and Kleomenes wanted to restore the *agoge* does not mean, as Kennell erroneously assumes, that the *agoge* had ceased to exist but that they simply wanted to change the particular form which it had in the third century (Keen 1996). Among others, Ducat has severely criticised Kennell's theory. He challenges all of Kennell's positions and in particular his theory that the first seventeen of the '*Instituta Laconica*' belong to Sphairos (Ducat 2006 p ix–xvii and p27–30).

53. Flower 2002.

54. As Flower points out, the meaning of the Greek word ὅμοιοι (*homoioi*) is 'similar' and not 'equal', since 'equal' means 'ἴσοι' (*isoi*) in Greek. Therefore, when Spartans called themselves *homoioi* they did not mean that they were 'equal' but 'similar'. 'Individuals who are similar, dress alike, act alike, eat alike but are not necessarily equal in terms of possessions and status. Individuals who are equal not only have the same habits, but the same possessions as well…But we should realize that the concept of equality was alien to the way Spartans thought about themselves in the archaic and classical periods' (Flower 2002 p 197).

55. Flower 2002 p196–197.

56. Flower 2002 p 199–200. Flower aptly observes that if Kleomenes had only meant to re-establish the constitution of ancient Sparta, he could have relied on the known works of Kritias, Xenophon, Aristotle and Dikaiarchos. However, this was beyond the scope of his interest. What he really wanted was to create a constitution which would meet his political ambitions and which he would present as a reconstruction of the Lykourgan constitution. Undoubtedly, this was none other than Sphairos' 'Spartan constitution' as described either through his work or through his teaching. Besides, the simple fact that the revival of the Lykourgan *agoge* (a project of paramount importance for Sparta) was assigned to Sphairos of Borysthenes and not to a Spartan highlights the degree of Sparta's alienation from her traditions (Green 1993 p 257). For Kleomenes' conscious distortion of the Spartan tradition, see also: Marasco 2004.

57. Flower 2002 p. 209

58. Flower 2002 p. 209

59. Figueira 2004a. According to Figueira, the Spartan *kleroi* were kept broadly unchanged at least until the great earthquake of 464. (For earlier versions of this theory see Michell 1964 p 205–232, McDowell 1988 p 133–161, etc.).

60. Figueira considers it unlikely for Kleomenes' 6,000 'Spartans' to be associated in any way with Spartan *kleroi*, since obviously the 2,000 freed helots did not receive any *kleroi*. He also notes that the number of 4,500 Lykourgan' *kleroi* included in Agis' reform agenda may well reflect the influence of the Lykourgan tradition on Agis and not *vice versa* (Figueira 2004a p 59 and p 70 note 84). Similar views had also been presented before (see Ehrenberg = Oliva 1971).

61. Figueira 2007 p151 The existence of two diametrically opposite trends in historical research that consider the Kleomenean revolution to have been inspired by Sphairos' Stoic ideals and Sphairos to have been an apologist of the Kleomenean revolution had been previously identified by Tigerstedt, who concluded that it is impossible to rule on the legitimacy of one or the other (Tigerstedt 1974 p.70).

62. Figueira 2007 p 153.

63. Forrest 1980 p. 7

64. It is significant that despite the conflict of the historians regarding the degree of the deterioration of the Spartan tradition due to subsequent influences, the Spartan mirage still holds an undiminished appeal through popular literature and cinema. The huge commercial success of the film *300* (a transfer of Frank Miller's famous and similarly commercially successful graphic novel) as well as the plethora of historical novels with themes on Sparta e.g. the *Gates of Fire* and *Winds of War* by Steven Pressfield, *The Shield of Sparta* by Valerio Massimo Manfredi, reveal the strong attraction of Sparta's chimeric image, which follows its own independent path indifferent to the scholars' concerns.

65. Agis, his wife and later Kleomenes' wife Agiatis, Kleomenes' mother Kratisikleia and certainly Kleomenes himself have inspired the creation of several novels and tragedies since the mid-seventeenth century (see Rawson 2002 p 205–216). In the twentieth century, Naomi Mitchinson's novel *The Corn King and the Spring Queen* describes the rise and fall of Kleomenes in a very moving way. It is significant that the chapter that refers to the end of the Spartan king in Egypt is entitled 'kings who die for the people'. Kavafy's aforementioned poems describe the scenes of Kratisikleia's dramatic parting from Kleomenes in view of her departure for Egypt. Among the many historical novels there are *King Kleomenes* (1979) by Tasos Zervos and '*Agis*'(1988) and *Kleomenes*(1986) by Lili Mavrokefalou, the theatre plays '*Agis and Kleomenes*' (1983) by John Goudelis and '*Agis*' by Michael Peristerakis (1976) to name a few. Apart from literature, the romantic side of Spartan movement had a strong impact also on historical researchers. Some people viewed Kleomenes exclusively through Phylarchos' distorting lens and went so far as to describe him as the last champion of the Classical world and as a great social revolutionary and visionary influenced by Stoic philosophy (Rodakis 1974).

Appendix C

1. Kahrstedt 1913 p. 291.

2. When Jochmus did his research (1830 and 1834) he was originally captain of staff/ headquarters of General Sir Richard Church in Greece and later in the Greek-Bavarian war school. (JRGS 1857 p. 1). In his book, he notes that the search for the identification of the battlefield had begun much earlier by the French M. De Beaujour and also the English archaeologist WM Leake.

3. JRGS 1857 p. 36

4. The earlier researchers were Ludwig Ross, an archaeologist who served as the first Curator of Antiquities of the newly established Greek State, and the English archaeologist Loring (1895).

5. Kromayer (1903 p.199–277 and 1924–1931 p.597–599)

6. Soteriades 1910 p. 5–57.
7. Soteriades 1910 p 27.
8. Walbank (1957 p 276–278) who initially accepted (albeit with some reservations) Kromayer's theory, recognizes at this point the correctness of Soteriades' assertion (Walbank 1957 p 277).
9. Pol. 2.68.3–8.
10. Attempting to explain this contradiction, Walbank argues that Polybios misrepresented the actual events in order to create narrative balance: the defenders of Evas were forced to retreat along a steep slope and thereby suffered what they had planned for their opponents (Walbank 1957 p 284).
11. Kromayer 1910 p. 508–537
12. In contrast, another German historian, Kahrstedt, who visited the battlefield in June 1912, claimed that he did not find traces of an ancient road in Kourmeki (as affirmed by Soteriades) and that, even if there had been an ancient road there, the presence of a Spartan force on Palaiogoulas (i.e. Evas Hill according to Kromayer) ensured absolute control of the road. Thus Evas retained its strategic importance on the battlefield. According to Kahrstedt. (1913 p.286–291), the problems in the identification of the battlefield were not caused by Kromayer's misperception but by Polybios' inaccurate description of the battlefield. Kahrstedt asked Soteriades to present the *ostraca* he claimed to have excavated on Palaiogoulas. Because Soteriades did not present anything, Kahrstedt stated that until all evidence is published, Kromayer's theory should be considered correct. Soteriades' views were also challenged by another German historian, Ernst Honnigman, who toured the battlefield in 1923.
13. According to Pritchett, the stone wall on the Dagla Ridge is consistent with the 'fortifications' which Jochmus had noted on the relevant map of his essay. Pritchett recognizes, however, that it is impossible to date the construction of these two fortifications, and that Polybios (2.65.9) does not mention the existence of walls but of 'ditch and palisades'. Nevertheless he insists on the obvious, in his opinion, strategic importance of the stone wall (which he presumes to reinforce the ditches and palisades) and he connects it to the only known battle in the area (Pritchett 1965 p.62). Pritchett visited the battlefield once more, in 1982. In a paper he published a little later he commented that 'it seems safe to infer that the left wing of the Spartan army, arrayed on the right side of the river, fortified the ridge which rises south of the Gorgylos , marked on Kromayer's map as carrying the khan of Dagla [Dagla's Inn]' (Pritchett 1984 p253).
14. Pritchett 1965 p 64. At least at this point Soteriades (1911) is vindicated, as he was the first who had noticed a large number of *ostraca* on Palaiogoulas and, despite the fact that he attributed the findings to a Spartan fortress rather than to a village, had expressed the belief that this hill was a 'place that, by its suitability, invited people to settle on it'.
15. The remains that were found on Agios Konstantinos Hill, which were believed to belong to the city or the acropolis of Sellasia, according to Pritchett belong to an ancient fortress comparable to that of Athenaion on Mount Chelmos. These fortifications were apparently associated with Kleomenes' fortifications.

16. Pritchett 1965 p. 69.
17. For example, Green (1993 p. 799 note 119) argues that the certainty with which Pritchett expressed the identification of the battlefield vouches for the accuracy of his claims (!).
18. Walbank 1995 p 369–70 and map 402. It should be noted that Walbank, faithfully following Kromayer, had initially cited a layout of the battlefield with Eukleidas' forces placed on top of Palaiogoulas. But then, after a relevant suggestion by Errington (1969 p.21 note1) he entirely revised his earlier views (Walbank 1957 p 276) citing a new map based on Pritchett's remarks.
19. As Pritchett himself acknowledges, the only reason that justifies deploying forces on the top of the mountain is to prevent outflanking from the west side (where the current highway passes), which is relatively smooth and accessible (Pritchett 1965 p.68). But a small surveillance force would suffice for this purpose.
20. Morgan 1981.
21. Pritchett 1984 p 254.
22. As Soteriades (1910) observes vitriolically, in this case 'the real traitor, intentionally or unintentionally, was Eukleidas who stupidly abandoned his position to the enemy without a fight'.
23. Note that Kleomenes had even prepared a backup plan in case of his defeat by Antigonos, having 'quite in advance of this event' arranged for ships waiting ready to sail at Gytheion.
24. Perhaps this is why Phylarchos' version is extremely popular and accepted in part or entirely by most modern historians. Some historians don't hesitate to declare that 'the Illyrians surprised and completely defeated Eukleidas who fell in the battle' (Piper 1986 p.71).
25. On the contrary, Polybios states clearly that Antigonos lost some days trying unsuccessfully to outflank Kleomenes' positions before attacking him frontally (Pol.2.66.2–3).
26. The deployment of almost the entire right wing of the Macedonians on Eukleidas' extreme left would put them in rugged terrain and lead them to the inaccessible and steep peaks of Tourles. On the other hand, the Spartans' counterattack from the center against 'the entire right wing of the Macedonians' would mean that in moving to the left they passed across the front of their own deployment.
27. Plut. *Philop.* 6.2. Indeed George Soteriades points out that the flanking of the attackers by Eukelidas' undermines Polybios' argument, according to which Eukleidas is presented as a bad general 'who witlessly abandoned his positions to the enemy'. Polybios certainly does not attribute the flanking of the attackers explicitly to Eukleidas' initiative. But it is very clear from his description of the battle that the defenders of Evas Hill cooperated actively with the flanking troops. Therefore, even Polybios recognizes indirectly that Eukleidas was not idle and 'stupefied', as Soteriades' floridly phrases it.
28. Philopoimen's role in the outcome of the battle is evidenced by the fact that when Antigonos praised him publicly, comparing him with the Macedonian commander of his center in a manner unfavourable to the latter (Pol. 2.68.1–2). It is quite impressive to observe the effort of some historians, and especially Errington (1969 p. 21–23), to

downplay this event, as well as the importance of the initiative of Philopoimen, who developed into the most capable general of the Achaean League, in order to support their hypothetical theories about the development of the battle.

29. This tactic was also successfully implemented at Menelaion by Philip V against Lykourgos.

Appendix D

1. Toynbee's theories about the birth and decline of civilizations, as well as other scholars' criticisms of them, will not concern us here. For reasons of limited space, this chapter is confined exclusively to Toynbee's comparison of the two Spartan kings and Jesus, omitting his discussion of the correlations between the two Spartans and the other 'archaists' (for example the Gracchi) or 'futurists' (like Euenos and Aristonikos).
2. However, Jesus died on the cross, while Kleomenes' body was crucified *after* his suicide.
3. Toynbee 1939b p.429.
4. The old legends of Greek history contributed decisively in the creation of this myth; one such was the legend of Herakles, shaped by integrating elements of Eastern legends as it was journeying through the channels of folklore tradition from Greece to Tyre. (Toynbee 1939b. p. 465)
5. Plut. *Kleom.* 39.1–2.
6. Toynbee 1939b p. 497–98.
7. Pol 5.86–87, Toynbee 1939b p. 498.
8. Toynbee 1939b p. 516.
9. According to Toynbee, the poor quality of construction materials was the reason why they haven't been preserved to present day (Toynbee 1939b p 517).
10. Toynbee 1939b p.504.
11. Obviously, some characteristic phrases and life events of the aforementioned aspiring 'saviours' like the Gracchi, Euenos, Catiline, and Aristonikos etc were incorporated in the gospels in a similar way.
12. Toynbee 1939b p. 527.
13. According to Toynbee, Panteus was an entirely fictional character that Phylarchos was inspired to create from Xenophon's *Pantheia* (Cyropaedia 4.6.11, 5.1.1–18, 6.1.31–49, 6.4.2–11, and 7.3.2–16). 'The scene in which the Friend leans on the Chest of the Hero looks like a scene from the romance between Pantheia and Abradas, who in turn could be a variant of the myth of Ishtar and Tammuz' (Toynbee 1939b p 525).
14. Bux E. *Zwei Sozialistiche Novellen bei Plutarch* (= Toynbee 1939b p. 459).
15. Toynbee 1939b p. 459
16. See p. 32 of this study
17. Africa 1961 p 58. Oliva concurs with Africa's criticism of Toynbee's views (1971 p 268 note 3)

Bibliography

Ancient Sources

Aeneas Tacticus, *Poliorcetica:.* Trnsl.Illinois Greek club.

Aristophanes, *Birds*: Translation by Eugene O'Neill, The Complete Greek Drama, vol. 2. Jr. New York, Random House. 1938.

Aristotle, *Politics*: Translation by H. Rackham, Aristotle in 23 Volumes, Vol. 21, Cambridge, MA, Harvard University Press; London, William Heinemann Ltd. 1944.

Arrian, *Anabasis* Translated by P.A. Brunt.

Athenaios, *The Deipnosophists*. Translator: Charles Burton Gulick. London, William Heinemann Ltd 1927.

Cicero *de officiis* Translation by Walter Miller. Cambridge. Harvard University Press; Cambridge, Mass, London, England.1913.

Diog. Laertios, *Lives of Eminent Philosophers* Translation by R.D.Hicks. Cambridge. Harvard University Press.1972 (first published 1925).

Diodoros Siculus *Library*. Translated by C.H. Oldfather

Herodotos *The Histories* Translation By A.D.Godley, Cambridge. Harvard University Press. 1920.

Livy *Ab Urbe Condita* Translation by Evan T. Sage, Cambridge, Mass,Harvard Univ. Press, London Will. Heinemann Ltd 1928.

Pausanias, *Description of Greece* 2, 3, 4, 7, 8: Translation by W.H.S. Jones, Litt.D., and H.A. Ormerod, M.A., in 4 Volumes. Cambridge, MA, Harvard University Press; London, William Heinemann Ltd. 1918.

Plato *Alcibiades* Translation by WRM Lamb Cambridge MA, Harvard University Press, London W. Heinemann Ltd. 1955.

Plutarch, *Agesilaos, Agis & Kleomenes, Comparison of Agis Kleomenes and the Gracchoi, Aratos, Flamininus, Lykourgos, Lysandros, Pelopidas, Pyrrhos, Philopoimen*, Translation by Bernadotte Perrin. Plutarch's Lives Cambridge, MA. Harvard University Press, London. William Heinemann Ltd. 1914–1921.

Plutarch, *Moralia*: Translation by Frank Cole Babbitt. Cambridge, MA. Harvard University Press. London. William Heinemann Ltd. 1931.

Polybios *Histories*. Translation by Evelyn S. Shuckburgh. London, New York. Macmillan. 1889. Reprint Bloomington 1962

Strabo *Geography* Translated by H. Hamilton, Esq. & W. Falconer, M.A. London, George Bell & Sons.1903

Thucidides *History of the Peloponnesian War* transl. by Thomas Hobbes, London. Bohn.1843.

Xenophon, *Hellenika*, Translated by Carleton L. Brawson, Harvard University Press, Cambridge, MA; William Heinemann Ltd London v.t.1918, v2 1921.

Xenophon, *Lakedaimonian Polity* (Constitution of the Lakedaimonians) Translated by E.C. Marchant, G.W. Bowersock, Harvard University Press, Cambridge, MA; William Heinemann Ltd 1925.

Modern Books and Articles

Africa, T.W. (1961). *Phylarchos and the Spartan Revolution*. Berkeley.

Africa, T.W. (1968). *Cleomenes III and the Helots. California Studies in Classical Antiquity* 1: 1–11.

Andrewes, A. (1992). *He tyrannia sten archaia Ellada* Greek translation of: *The Greek Tyrants* (London: Hutchinson, 1956). Athens: Kardamitsas.

Andrewes, A. (2002). 'The Government of Classical Sparta', in Whitby, M., edit. 2002, p. 49–68. (Originally in E. Badian, edited *Ancient Society and Institutions: Studies Presented to Victor Ehrenberg on his 75th birthday*. Oxford: Blackwell, 1966: 120).

Andreades, A. (1915). *He demosia oikonomia ton Spartiaton* ('The public finance of the Spartans'), *Parnassos* 11, 101–164. In Greek.

Aymard, A. (1938). *Les prémiers rapports de Rome et de la confederation achaienne* (198–189 avant J.C.) Bordeaux.

Baloglou, C. (2003). 'To metarrythmistiko programma tou Kleomenous III (235–222 BC): mia oikonomikokoinoniki analysi' ('The reform programme of Kleomenes III (235–222 BC): a socioeconomic analysis) *Parnassos* 45, p 483512. In Greek.

Baloglou, C. (2006). 'He kritike ton politeiakon thesmon tes Spartes apo ton Aristotele' (The critique of political and socioeconomic institutions of Sparta by Aristotle), Proceedings of second local congress on Lakonic Studies v.II, Athens 2006, pp 291–328). In Greek.

Baloglou, C. (2011). 'Aristoteles kai Krete. He kritike ton politeiakon thesmon tes Kretes apo ton Aristotele' (Aristotle and Crete. The critique of the political and socioeconomic institutions of Crete by Aristotle). *PLATO 57* (2010–2011) 166–194. In Greek.

Baltrusch, E. (2003). *Sparti: he historia, he koinonia kai ho politismos tes archaias lakonikis polis*. ('Sparta: the history, the society, and the civilization of the ancient lakonic city'). Greek translation of *Sparta: Geschichte Gesellschaft Kultur*, (Munchen, 1998). Athens Papademas.

Bearzot, C., Landucci Gattinoni, F. (2004). *Contro le 'leggi immutabili': Gli spartani fra tradizione e innovazione. Contributi di Storia Antica 2*. Milano: Vita & Pensiero Università.

Beloch, K.J. (1927). *Griechische Geschichte* v.IV2. Berlin-Leipzig: De Gruyter, 1927.

Bikerman, E. (1943). 'Notes sur Polybe'. *Revue des études grecques* 56: 287–304.

Birgalias, N. (1999). *L' odysée de l' education Spartiate*. Athens Vasilopoulos.

Birgalias, N., Buraselis K., and Cartledge P.A., edit. (2007). *The Contribution of Ancient Sparta to Political Thought and Practice*. Athens: Alexandria publications.

Bradford, A.S. (1977). *A prosopography of Lakedaimonians from the death of Alexander the Great 323 B.C. to the Sack of Sparta by Alaric, A.D. 396*. Munich.

Briscoe, J. (1967). 'Rome and the class struggle in the Greek States 200–146 BC', *Past and Present* 36 (April 1967): p 3–20.

Breschi D. (2012) 'Fascism, liberalism and revolution'. *European Journal of Political Theory* 11 (Oct. 2012): 410–425.

Browning, R. (1978). *The Emperor Julian*, University of California press, Berkeley and Los Angeles.

Buck, C.D. (1955). *The Greek dialects: grammar, selected inscriptions, glossary*. Chicago University Press.

Bury, J.B. edit. (1923). *The Hellenistic Age*, Cambridge.

Carlier, P. (2007). 'A propos de la double royauté *Spartiate*', in Birgalias N., Buraselis K., and Cartledge P.A., edit. 2007, p 49–60.

Cartledge, P.A. (1987). *Agesilaos and the Crisis of Sparta*. London and Baltimore.

Cartledge, P.A. (1997): Review of Kennell (1995). *Classical Review* 47/1, p 98–100.

Cartledge, P.A. (2002a). *Sparta and Lakonia. A regional History 1300–362 BC*. London and New York: Routledge (first publ. 1979).

Cartledge, P.A. (2002b). 'Hellenistic Sparta', in: Cartledge P.A, and A.Spawforth, (2002c), p 3–90.

Cartledge, P.A., και A. Spawforth (2002c). *Hellenistic and Roman Sparta: a Tale of Two Cities*. London and New York: Routledge (first publ. 1989).

Cartledge, P.A. (2004). *Hoi Spartiates* Greek translation of The *Spartans*, (publ. in 2002). Athens: Livanis.

Cartledge, P.A. (2004a). '*He idiomorphi thesi tes Spartis sten anaptyxi tes hellenikis polis-kratous*', ('The peculiar position of Sparta in the Development of the Greek City State') in: Cartledge, P.A. 2004c, p 51–83.

Cartledge, P.A. (2004b): '*He gennesi tou hopliti: he syneisphora tes Spartes sten proime hellenike stratiotike organose*' ('The birth of the hoplite: Sparta's contribution to early Greek military organization') in: Cartledge, P.A. 2004c, p 292318.

Cartledge, P.A. (2004c). *To megaleio tis Spartes, spartiatikoi stochasmoi*. Greek translation of *Spartan Reflections*, (publ. in 2001). Athens: Enalios.

Cartledge, P.A. (2009). *Ancient Greek Political Thought*. Cambridge University Press.

Cavaignac, E. (1948). *Sparte*. Paris.

Cawckwell, G.L. (2002). 'The decline of Sparta', in Whitby, M. edit. 2002, p 236–257.

Chaniotis, A. (2005). *War in the Hellenistic World*. Oxford: Blackwell.

Chrimes, K.M.T. (1999). *Ancient Sparta: a Re-examination of the Evidence*, Manchester, (first publ. 1949).

Christien, J. (2002). 'Iron money in Sparta: myth and history' in Powell A. & Hodkinson S., edit. 2002, p 171–190.

Cook, R.M. (1962). 'Spartan History and Archaeology' *Classical Quarterly* n.s. 12: 156–158.

Daubies, M. (1971). 'Cléomène III, les hilotes et Sellasie', *Historia* 20, p 665–695.

Daubies, M. (1975). 'Les combattants laconiens de Sellasie: périèques ou hilotes?' *Le monde grec: pensée, littérature, histoire, documents. Hommage à Claire Préaux*. Bruxelles: Université de Bruxelles: 383–392.

David, E. (1979). 'The Conspiracy of Cinadon', *ATHENAEUM* 57 p 239–259.

David, E. (1981). *Sparta between Empire and Revolution, 404–243 B.C.: Internal Problems and Their Impact On Contemporary Greek Consciousness*. New York.

Davies, J.K. (1984). 'Cultural, Social and Economic Features of the Hellenistic World' *CAH²* VII, part 1, P 257–320.

Dodds, E.R. (1996). *Hoi Hellenes kai to paralogo*. Greek translation of *The Greeks and the Irrational* (1962) Athens, Kardamitsas.

Ducat, J. (2002). 'The obligations of Helots', in Whitby 2002 p 196–214.

Ducat, J. (2006). *Spartan education*, The Classical Press of Wales.

Errington, R.M. (1969). *Philopoemen*, Oxford.

Erskine, A. (1990) *The Hellenistic Stoa: Political Thought and Action*. Ithaca.

Ferguson, J. (1973). *The Heritage of Hellenism*, London: Thames and Hudson.

Ferguson, J. (1975). *Utopias of the Classical World*, London: Thames and Hudson.

Figueira, T. (2002). 'Iron money and the ideology of consumption in Lakonia', in: Powell A. and Hodkinson S., edit. 2002, p 137–70.

Figueira, T. (2004a). 'The Nature of Spartan *kleros*' in: Figueira T., edit. 2004b, p 47–76.

Figueira, T. edit. (2004b). *Sparta: Studies Ideologies and Personae*. London.

Figueira, T. (2007). 'Spartan Constitutions and the Enduring Image of the Spartan Ethos', in: Birgalias N., Buraselis K., and Cartledge P.A., edit. 2007 p 143–158.

Finley, M.I. (1981). 'Sparti', (Sparta) in J.P. Vernant, edit. 1981, p. 147–166.

Fitzhardinge, L.F. (1980). *The Spartans*. London.

Flower, M.A. (2002). 'The Invention of Tradition in Classical and Hellenistic Sparta' in: Powell A. & Hodkinson S., edit. 2002, p 191–217.

Forrest, W.G. (1980). *A History of Sparta c.950–192 BC*, London, Duckworth, (first publ. 1968, London.)

Fuks, A. (1962a). '*Agis* Cleomenes and Equality', *CPh* 57, 161–6 (= Fuks 1984, p. 250–5).

Fuks, A. (1962b). 'Non Phylarchean Tradition of the Programme of *Agis* IV', *CQ* n.s.12,118–21(= Fuks1984, 256–9).

Fuks, A. (1962c). 'The Spartan Citizen Body in the Mid-Third Century B.C. and Its Proposed Enlargement by *Agis* IV'. *Athenaeum* n.s. 40, 244–63 (= Fuks 1984, 230–49).

Fuks, A. (1966). 'Social Revolution in Greece in the Hellenistic Age', *La Parola del Passato*, CXI,437–448(= Fuks 1984, σ. 40–51).

Fuks, A. (1984). *Social Conflict in Ancient Greece* edit. M. Stern, and M. Amit, (photostat reproduction of the articles edited between 1951–1980), Jerusalem and Leiden.

Green, P. (1993). *Alexander to Actium: The Hellenistic Age*. London: Thames and Hudson.

Griffin, Roger (2004). 'Withstanding the Rush of Time: The Prescience of Mosse's Anthoropological View of Fascism'. In Stanley G. Payne, David J. Sorkin, John S. Tortorice, eds. *What History Tells: George L. Mosse and the Culture of Modern Europe*. Madison, Wisc.: University of Wisconsin Press: 110–134.

Griffith,G.T. (1984). *The Mercenaries of the Hellenistic World*, Ares publishers, Chicago.

Grote, G. (2000). *A History of Greece*. Vol.2. Thoemmes Press, England (reproduction from the original: London: John Murray, 1872).

Gruen, E.S. (1972). 'Aratus and the Achaean Alliance with Macedon'. *Historia* 21/14 (October–December 1972): 609–625.

Hadas, M. (1932). 'The Social Revolution in Third-Century Sparta', *CW* 26.9–10, 65–68, 73–76.

Hamilton, C.D. (1991). *Agesilaus and the Failure of Spartan Hegemony*. Ithaca and London.

Hammond, N.G.L. and Walbaknk F.W. (1995). *Historia tes Makedonias* τ.3 (Greek translation of *A History of Macedonia* v. III.1988). Malliares-Paideia.

Hanson, V.D. (2003). *Ho Dytikos Tropos Polemou* (Greek translation of: *The Western Way of War)*. Athens: Tourikis.

Head, D. (1982). *Armies of the Macedonian and Punic Wars, 359 B.C. to 146 B.C.* WRG Publications

Herf, Jeffrey. (1984). *Reactionary Modernism: Technology, Culture Politics in Weimar and the Third Reich*. Cambridge: Cambridge University Press.

Hodkinson, S.J. (1989). 'Marriage Inheritance and Demography: Perspectives Upon the Success and Decline of Classical Sparta', in: Powell A., edit. 1989a, p 79–121.

Hodkinson, S.J. (1994). 'Blind Plutos?: Contemporary Images of the Role of Wealth in Classical Sparta', in: Hodkinson S.J. and Powell A., edit. 1994, p 183–222.

Hodkinson, S.J. and Powell A., edit. (1994). *The Shadow of Sparta*. London and New York: Routledge.

Hodkinson, S.J. (2000). *Property and Wealth in Classical Sparta*, London: Duckworth &The Classical press of Wales.

Hodkinson, S.J. (2007). 'Five Words That Shook the World: Plutarch, *Lykourgos* 16 and Appropriations of Spartan Communal Property Ownership in Eighteenth-Century France' in Birgalias N., a.o., edit. (2007), p 417–433.

Holladay, A.J. (1977). 'Spartan Austerity', *Classical Quarterly* n.s. 27 (1977): 119–124.

Holleaux, M. (1930) 'Rome and Macedon: Philip against the Romans' *CAH*¹ VIII p 116–240.

Jones, A.H.M. (1967). *Sparta*. Oxford.

[Jochmus, A.] (1857). Commentaries. Journal of the Royal Geographical Society 27: p 1–53.

Kahrstedt, U. (1913). Nachlese auf griechische Schlachtfeldern, Hermes 48 p 286–91.

Kanellopoulos, P. (1982). *Historia tes Archaias Hellados 490–146 BC*. (History of Ancient Greece, 490–146 BC). 3 vol. Athens: Gialleles. In Greek.

Keen, A. (1996). Review of Kennell (1995), *Bryn Mawr Classical Review* 96.9.28.

Kennell, N. (1995). *The Gymnasium of Virtue*. University of North Carolina Press.

Kennell, N. (2003). 'Agreste genus: Helots in Hellenistic Lakonia' in: Luraghi N. and Alcock S.E., edit. 2003, p. 81–105.

Kennell, N. (2010). *Spartans. A New History*. Wiley-Blackwell.

Koliopoulos, K. (2001). *He hypsili strategiki tes archaias Spartis*. ('The grand strategy of ancient Sparta'). Athens: Poiotita. In Greek.

Kourinou, E. (2000). *Sparti: symbole ste mnemeiake topographia tes* ('Sparta: contribution in her monumental topography'). Athens: Horos. In Greek.

Kromayer, J. (1903 & 1924–1931). *Antike Schlachtfelder in Griechenland*, volume 1 and volume 4. Berlin.

Kromayer J. (1910). Sellasia BCH 34 p508–537.

Larsen, J.A.O. (1935) 'Was Greece free between 196 and 146 B.C.?' Classical Philology XXX, July, 1935.

Larsen, J.A.O. (1966). 'The Aetolians and the Cleomenic War', in *The Classical Tradition: Literary and Historical Studies in Honour of Harry Caplan*. Ithaca, N.Y.: Cornell University Press, p 43–57.

Larsen, J.A.O. (1975). 'The Aetolian–Achaean Alliance of CA. 238–220'.*Classical Philology* 70/3.

Lazenby, J.F. (2012). *The Spartan Army*, Pen & Sword Military. (first publ. 1985).

Levy, E.(1988). 'La Kryptie et ses contradictions', *Ktema* 13, p 245–252.

Loring, W. (1895). 'Some Ancient Routes in the Peloponnese', *Journal of Hellenic Studies* 15 (1895): p. 25–89.

Luraghi, N., & Alcock S.E., edit. (2003). *Helots and Their Masters in Lakonia and Messenia: Histories, Ideologies, Structures*. (Hellenic studies 4). Washington D.C.: Center for Hellenic Studies.

MacDowell, D.M. (1988). *Spartiatiko dikaio* (Greek translation of *Spartan Law*, Edinburgh 1986), Athens: Papademas.

Mandel, J. (1979). 'A propos d' une dynastie de tyrans à Argos (IIIe siècle avant J.C.)'. *Athenaeum* 57: 293–307.

Marasco, G. (1979). 'Cleomene III, i mercenari e gli iloti', *Prometheus* 5, p 45–62.

Marasco, G. (2004). 'Cleomene III fra rivoluzione e reazione' in: Bearzot C., Landucci Gattinoni F., 2004, p 191–207.

Martinez-Lacy, R. (1977): 'The application of the concept of revolution to the reforms of *Agis*, Cleomenes and Nabis at Sparta' Quaderni di storia 46, p 95–106.

Mendels, D. (1979): 'Polybius, Nabis and equality' *Athenaeum* 57 Zs.311–333

Michell, H. (1964). *Sparta*, τό κρυπτόν της πολιτείας των Λακεδαιμονίων. Cambridge.

Michinson, N. (1990). *The Corn King and the Spring Queen* (Edinburgh. Canongate books, first publ. 1931)

Mitropoulou, E. (1977). *Deities and heroes in the form of snakes*. Pyli editions, Athens.

Morgan, J.D. (1981). 'Sellasia revisited'. *American Journal of Archaeology*. 85/3: 328–330.

Mossé, C. (1989). *Hoi tyrannoi sten Archaia Ellada*, ('The tyrants in ancient Greece') Greek translation of *La tyrannie dans la Grece antique* (Paris, 1969) Athens: To Asty.

Mündt, J. (1903) *Nabis, Konig von Sparta* (206–192 v.Chr.), Koln, Diss. Munster i.W.

Neocleous, Mark (1998). 'Revolution? Reaction? Revolutionary Reaction?' In Mark Cowling, ed. *The Communist Manifesto: New Interpretations*. New York: New York University Press: 106–118.

Oliva, P. (1971). *Sparta and her social problems*, Amsterdam and Prague.

Ollier, F. (1933). *Le mirage Spartiate:étude sur l'idéalisation de Sparte dans l'antiquité Grecque de l'origine jusqu' aux cyniques*, Paris: De Boccard.

Ollier, F. (1936). 'Le philosophe stoicien Sphairos et l'œuvre réformatrice des rois de Sparte *Agis* IV et Cléomene III' REG 49 p 536–570.

Ollier, F. (1943). *Le mirage Spartiate:étude sur l'idéalisation de Sparte dans l'antiquité Grecque, du début de l'école cynicque jusqu'à la fin de la cité*, Societe d'édition de belles lettres, Paris.

Palagia, O. (2006). 'Art and Royalty in Sparta of the third century BC'. *Hesperia* 75/2 (April-June): p 205–217.

Papachatzis, N. (1971): 'Ta hellenika hemerologia', (The Greek calendars) *Historia tou Hellenikou Ethnous*, vol.II p 10–11 Ekdotiki Athenon. In Greek.

Parker, R. (1989) 'Spartan Religion' in: Powell A., edit. 1989a p 142–172.

Petronotis Argyris P. (2001). 'Archaiai odoi kai palaioi dromoi: diachronikes diabaseis (paradeigmata apo ten Arcadia)'. ('Ancient routes and old streets: all times passages (examples from Arcadia)'. In *Epikoinonies kai metafores sten probiomehchanike period* (XI Symposium of History and Art Kastro Monembasias, 23–26 July 1998). Athens: Politistiko Technologiko Idryma ETBA, p 49–50. In Greek.

Pikoulas, Y.A. (1987). 'Symbole sten topographia tes Skiritidos'. (Contribution to the topography of Skiritis) HOROS 5 p 121–148. In Greek.

Pikoulas, Y.A. (1988a). 'The Spartan defence network of Hellenistic times', in *Acts of XIIIth International Congress of Classical Archaeology* (Berlin, 24–30.7.1988) p 478.

Pikoulas, Y.A. (1988b). *He notia megalopolitiki chora apo ton 8ᵒ P. Ch. eos ton 4ᵒ M.Ch. aiona (symboli sten topographia tes)* (the southern Megalopolitan territory from the eighth BC to the fourth AD century, contribution to its topography). Athens: Horos. In Greek.

Pikoulas, Y.A. (1990a). 'To hodiko diktyo tes kentrikes Arcadias'. ('The road network of central Arcadia') Peloponnesiaka, Appendix 19 p 201–206. In Greek.

Pikoulas, Y.A. (1990b). 'Symbole sten topographia tes notiodytikes Argolidos: hodiko diktyo kai amyna'. ('Contribution in the topography of southwest Argolid: road network and defence') *Peloponnesiaka*, appendix 19, p 226–236. In Greek.

Piper L.J (1986). *Spartan Twilight*, New York: Caratzas.

Pomeroy, S. (2002). *Spartan Women.* Oxford.

Powell, A., edit. (1989a). *Classical Sparta: techniques behind her success.* London: Routledge.

Powell, A. (1989b). 'Mendacity and Sparta's Use of the Visual' in Powell A., επιμ. 1989a, p 173–192.

Powell, A. (2002) *Athens and Sparta: Constructing Greek political and social History from 478 BC* London: Routledge.

Powell A. & Hodkinson S., edit. (1994). *The Shadow of Sparta*, Routledge, London & New York.

Powell A. & Hodkinson S., edit. (2002). *Sparta Beyond the Mirage.* The Classical Press of Wales and Duckworth.

Pritchett, W.K. (1965). *Studies on Ancient Greek Topography III.* Berkeley, p 59–70.

Pritchett W.K. (1984). 'Sellasia revisited'. Studies presented to Sterling Dow on his eightieth birthday. Eited by Alan L. Boegehold, et al. Durham, N.C: Duke UP, 1984 (Greek, Roman and Byzantine Studies monographs10): 251–266.

Ranovic, A. (2001). *O Hellenismos kai o istorikos tou rolos.* ('Hellenism and its historic role') Greek translation of *Helenizam i njegova istorijska ulog (first publ. 1962)*, Athens: Synchroni Skepsi.

Rawson, E. (2002). *The Spartan tradition in European thought*, Oxford.

Rodakis, P. (1974). *Kleomenes III tis Spartis: he megali koinoniki epanastasi (Kleomenes III of Sparta: the great social revolution).* Athens: Atermon. In Greek.

Rostovtzeff, M.I. (1941). *The Social and economic history of the Hellenistic World*, 3 volumes. Oxford: Oxford University Press.

Roussel, P. (1922). 'Boulletin epigraphique', Revue des études grecques 35 (Oct.-Dec.1922).

Ste Croix, G.E.M. de (2005). *Ta aitia tou Peloponnesiakou polemou*, Greek translation of *The origins of the Peloponnesian War*. (first publ.1972, Duckworth.) Athens. Odysseus publications.

Sakellariou, M. (1973). 'Politeia, oikonomia, koinonia, 336–200 BC'. (Polity economy, society, 336–200 BC) *Historia tou Hellenikou Ethnous* vol. IV, p 464–516. Athens: Ekdotiki Athinon. In Greek.

Sanders, J.M., edit. (1992). ΦΙΛΟΛΑΚΩΝ: *Lakonian Studies in Honour of Hector Catling*, London.

Schütrumpf, E. (1994). 'Aristotle and Sparta' in: Powell A., and Hodkinson S., edit. 1994, p 323–345.

Schütrumpf, E. (1997). 'The rhetra of Epitadeus: a Platonist's fiction', Greek, Roman and Byzantine Studies 28, p441–457.

Sekunda, N.V. (1998). *The Spartan Army*. London: Osprey.

Shimron, B. (1964a). 'Polybius and the Reforms of Cleomenes III'. *Historia* 13, p 147155.

Shimron, B. (1964b). 'The Spartan Polity after the defeat of Cleomenes III'. *Classical Quarterly* n.s.14, p 232–39.

Shimron, B. (1972). *Late Sparta: the Spartan Revolution, 243–146 BC* Buffalo: Arethusa.

Shipley, G. (2000). *The Greek World after Alexander, 323–30 BC* London: Routledge.

Snodgrass, A.M. (1999). *Arms and armour of the Greeks*. Baltimore, Maryland: The Johns Hopkins University Press (first publ. London: Thames and Hudson, 1967).

Soteriades, G. (1910). 'To pedion tes en Sellasia maches (222 BC)', (The battlefield of the battle of Sellasia (222 B.C.), BCH 34 (1910) p 5–57. In Greek.

Soteriades, G. (1911). 'Anti-Sellasia' Bulletin de Correspondance Hellenique 35, p 87–107, 241–242. In Greek.

Spawforth, A. (2002). 'Roman Sparta', in Cartledge P.A. and Spawforth A. 2002c, p 91–215.

Starr, C.G. (2002). 'The Credibility of Early Spartan History', in: M. Whitby, edit. 2002, p 26–42 (first publ. *Historia* 14 (1965), p 257–72).

Steinhauer, G. (1992). 'An Illyrian Mercenary in Sparta under Nabis', in Sanders J.M., edit. 1992, p 239–245.

Steinhauer, G. (2000). *Ho polemos sten Archaia Ellada* ('The war in Ancient Greece'), Athens: Papademas. In Greek.

Sternhell, Zeev (1994). *The Birth of Fascist Ideology: From Cultural Rebellion to Political Revolution*. Princeton: Princeton University Press.

Taiphakos, I.G. (1974). *Romaike politike stin Lakonia*. ('Roman policy in Lakonia') Athens. In Greek.

Taiphakos, I.G. (1984): 'Enas tyrannos ston Tito Livio'. ('A tyrant in Livy') A' *Panellenio Symposio Latinikon Spoudon: Literature and politics in the years of Augustus. 5–6.11.1982. Ioannina*, p. 125–136 [= Taiphakos (1995), p. 111–124]. In Greek.

Taiphakos, I.G. (1995): *Fantasia politeias isonomou* (re-edition of essays that were published during 1975–1984) Athens: Papademas. In Greek.

Tarn, W.W. (1923): 'The social question in third century', in J.B. Bury edited 1923, p 108–140.

Tarn, W.W. (1928). 'Macedonia and Greece', 'The Greek Leagues and Macedonia', in *CAH*[1] *VII*, p 197–223, 732763.

Tarn, W.W. (1930). *Hellenistic Military and Naval developments.* Cambridge University Press.

Tausend, K. (1998). Der Arkadienfeldzug Kleomenes' III im Jahre 225. *Rivista storica del antichità* 28 (1998): 51–57.

Texier, J. G. (1975). *Nabis,* Centre de recherches d histoire ancienne, vol.14 Paris.

Texier, J. G.(1977). 'Un aspect de l'antagonisme de Rome et de Sparte à l' époque Hellénistique: l' entrevue de 195 avant J.C. entre Titus Quinctius Flamininus et Nabis', Revue des etudes anciennes 78–79 (1976–77):145–154.

Tigerstedt, E.N (1965, 1974, 1978). *The legend of Sparta in Classical Antiquity.* Stockholm, Goteborg and Upsala.

Todd, S.C. (2003). *Athens & Sparta,* Bristol Classical Press.

Tomlinson, R.A. (1972). *Argos and the Argolid,* Ithaca, New York.

Toynbee A.J. (1969). *Some Problems of Greek History,* Oxford.

Toynbee A.J. (1939a, b). *A Study of History,* vol. 5 and vol. 6. Oxford.

Urban, R. (1973). Das Heer des Kleomenes bei Sellasia, *Chiron* 3, p 95–102.

Urban, R. (1979). *Wachstum und Krise des Achaischen Bundes. Quellenstudien zur Entwicklung des Bundes von 280 bis 222 v.Chr.* (Historia, einzelschriften 35.) Wiesbaden: Steiner.

Vernant, J.P. edit. (1981). *Problemata polemou sten Archaia Hellada* Greek translation of *Problemes de la guerre en Grece ancienne,* Athens: G.A.H.

Voutiras, E. (2000). Le cadavre et le serpent, ou l' héroisation manqué de Cléoméne de Sparte *Héros et heroines. Kernos,* suppl. 10 (2000) p 377–394.

Walbank, F.W. (1933). *Aratos of Sikyon,* Cambridge.

Walbank, F.W. (1951). Review of Chrimes 1999, Classical Review n.s. 1/2 (June 1951) p 98–100.

Walbank, F.W. (19571967–1979). *A Historical Commentary on Polybius,* 3 vols. Oxford.

Walbank, F.W. (1967a). *Philip V of Macedon,* Cambridge (first publ. 1940).

Walbank, F.W. (1984). 'Sources of the period', 'Monarchies and monarchic ideas', 'Macedonia and Greece', 'Macedonia and the Greek Leagues' in CAH2, *VII.1,* 1–22, 62–100, 221–56, 446480.

Walbank, F.W. (1990). *Polybios.* Berkeley, Los Angeles and London.

Walbank, F.W. (1995). Apo ti machi tis Ipsou eos to thanato tou Antigonou Dosona. Greek translation of 'From the battle of Ipsus to the end of Antigonos Doson' in Hammond N.G.L. & Walbank F.W., 1995 p 221–374.

Walbank, F.W. (1999). *Ho hellenistikos kosmos.* Greek translation of *The hellenistic world* (Hassocs and Glascow, 1981). Salonica: Vanias.

Warry, J. (1980). *Warfare in the Classical World.* London, Salamander.

Whitby, M. (1994). 'Two shadows: Images of Spartans and the Helots' in Powell A., and Hodkinson S., edit. 1994, p 87–126.

Whitby, M., edit. (2002). *Sparta.* Edinburgh University Press.

Wilcken, U. (1976). *Archaia helleniki historia* (Ancient Greek History). Greek translation of *Griechische Geschichte.* Athens: Papazeses.

Wood, F.J.R. (1939). The tradition of Flamininus 'Selfish Ambition' in Polybios and Later Historians, Transactions and Proceedings of the American Philological Association, 70 p 93–103.

Glossary

agoge: the Spartan training system to which the youth were subjected

agora: the civic centre of the Greek city-state

apophora: the dues the helots paid to the Spartans

Assembly: the gathering of the adult male citizens in most city-states

chalkaspides: the Bronze Shields, a crack unit of the Macedonian phalanx

Damos, demos: the 'people'

decarchy (-ies): an office of ten pro Spartan officials imposed by Spartan authorities on a city to make sure that it would remain loyal to Sparta

diarchy: dual kingship, the two royal houses of Sparta

ekklesia: the Assembly

elders: members of the Spartan *Gerousia*

endogamy: intermarriage

ephor(s): the five Spartan high officials, elected annually by the Spartan assembly

eunomia: state of law and good order

euzons: light armed troops

Gerousia: the chief deliberative and judicial council of Sparta, consisted of twenty-eight members plus the two kings

harmosts: governors representing the Spartan government.

hegemony: supremacy, the domination of one power or state over the others

helots: the state-serfs who farmed the Spartan estates in Lakonia and Messenia

hippeis: the Spartan Royal Guard

homoioi: the 'equals' or 'peers', the full Spartan citizens

hoplites: the heavy armed infantry of the phalanx

hetairoi: the Companions

hypomeiones: the 'inferiors'. Spartans without political rights; second rate citizens

Isonomia: equality before the law.

Isopoliteia: a treaty of equal citizenship rights between the Greek city-states.

klaros, kleros: 'land-lot' the minimum estate that every Spartan possessed after the Lykourgan reforms

klaria: the mortgaged klaroi

Kleomenistai: Kleomenists, Kleomenes' supporters

Koinon (-a): federation (s) of *komai* or cities

kome (-ai): village (s)

lakonomania: the tendency (of many Spartan admirers) to imitate the Spartan style and manners

lakonizers: Spartan sympathizers

Mirage (Spartan): the idealized image of Sparta

mora (-ai): the largest unit(s) in the Spartan army

mothax (-akes): 'inferiors', possibly sons of Spartans with helot women, brought up with the sons of wealthy Spartans, who became Spartans after completing the *agoge*

neodamodeis: helots freed for service in the army

Oliganthropia: dearth of manpower

ostraca: pottery fragments, shards

Paians: hymns

perioikoi: the inhabitants of the communities in Lakonia and Messenia

patronomoi: six officials created by Kleomenes, replacing the *ephors*

phalangites: the heavy infantry of the Macedonian phalanx.

Phiditia: syssitia, public messes

polis: the city-state.

sarissa: the long pike used by the Macedonian infantry phalanx.

stasis: civil strife, revolt.

Strategeia: generalship, the annual office of *strategos*, the supreme army commander and leader of the Achaean League.

strategos: the general, the supreme army commander and the annually elected leader of the Acahean League.

Synodos [Achaean League]: the regular meeting of the assembly of the Achaean League.

Synkletos [Achaean League]: a special meeting of the assembly of the Achaean League, summoned in urgent cases.

syssitia: the public messes in Sparta. Also known as *phiditia*.

tyranny: a government in which a single ruler (*tyrannos*) is vested with absolute power.

xenelasia: expulsion of foreigners [from Sparta].

xenoi: a term used for foreigners and also for mercenaries

Index